lonely planet

Buenos Aires

"All you've got to do is decide to go
and the hardest part is over.

So go!"

TONY WHEELER, COFOUNDER – LONELY PLANET

THIS EDITION WRITTEN AND RESEARCHED BY
Sandra Bao

Contents

Plan Your Trip   4

Explore Buenos Aires   52

Understand Buenos Aires   175

Survival Guide   201

Buenos Aires Maps   234

(left) Obelisco, Plaza de la República (p79)

(above) Puente de la Mujer, Puerto Madero (p74)

(right) *Floralis Genérica* sculpture by Eduardo Catalano, Recoleta (p119)

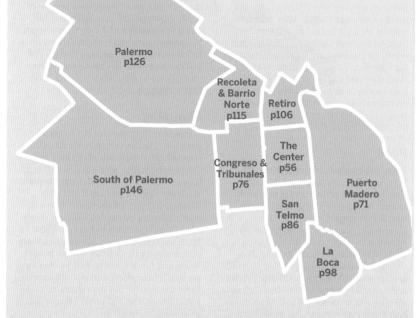

Palermo
p126

Recoleta & Barrio Norte
p115

Retiro
p106

The Center
p56

Congreso & Tribunales
p76

San Telmo
p86

Puerto Madero
p71

South of Palermo
p146

La Boca
p98

Welcome to Buenos Aires

Sexy, alive and supremely confident, this beautiful city gets under your skin. Like Europe with a melancholic twist, Buenos Aires is unforgettable.

Tango

Argentina's famous dance is possibly the country's greatest contribution to the outside world, a steamy strut that's been described as 'making love in the vertical position'. Folklore says it began in the bordellos of long-ago Buenos Aires, when men waiting for their 'ladies' passed time by dancing amongst themselves. Today, glamorized tango shows are supremely entertaining with their grand feats of athleticism. You'll also find endless venues for perfecting your moves, from salons to *milongas* (dance events) to cafes. Just realize that some people become addicted – and can spend a lifetime perfecting this sensual dance.

Food

Fancy some Indian, French, Vietnamese, Lebanese, Thai, Scandinavian, Mexican, Brazilian, Peruvian, Armenian or American cuisine during your stay in BA? No problem. But for many travelers, it's the city's carnivorous pleasures that shine. Satisfying a craving for juicy steak isn't hard to do in the land that has perfected grilling those wonderfully flavorful sides of beef. *Parrillas* (steakhouses) sit on practically every corner and will offer up myriad cuts, from *bife de chorizo* (sirloin) to *vacio* (flank steak) to *ojo de bife* (rib eye). Vegetarians, you've been warned!

Nightlife

Take a cat nap, down your coffee and be prepared to stay up all night – this is a city that never sleeps! Restaurants open at 9pm, bars at midnight and clubs at 2am – at the very earliest. If you're cool, of course, you'll show up after 4am and dance till dawn. International DJs are the rage, spinning electronica and house to legions of hip, trendy and well-dressed crowds. But you can also enjoy live music such as rock, blues, jazz and even folk – just remember that you'll be doing it all very late!

Shopping

It's no joke: Buenos Aires is a shopper's paradise. The city is laced with shopping streets lined with heaps of clothing and shoe stores, leather shops and nearly everything else you can think of. Large shopping malls are modern and family-friendly, offering designer goods, food courts and even children's play areas. But perhaps the city's best shopping is in Palermo Viejo, home to countless upscale boutiques; these offer avant-garde clothing, unique housewares and fun souvenirs. And let's not forget San Telmo, where antiques aficionados flock; the Sunday fair here is famous and entertaining, and will easily fill up a long afternoon.

Why I Love Buenos Aires

By Sandra Bao, Author

BA is an amazing city, and I'm proud to call it my birthplace. It's an astonishing metropolis that looks a bit like Europe, but with an edgy Latin American twist. *Porteños* (the city's residents) are passionate, opinionated and – once you get past their hard-city facade – very friendly. I love walking among them along the busy avenues, taking in the street life and often the craziness that goes along with it. This is a very special place, beautiful in its own unique way, resilient and creative. It's the kind of city travelers fall in love with, dream about and then move to!

For more about our authors, see p256.

Above: Galerías Pacífico (p61), Microcentro

Buenos Aires'
Top 10

Cementerio de la Recoleta (p117)

1 Meander through the maze of narrow lanes lined with elaborate mausoleums in what must be the world's most ostentatious necropolis. This 'city of the dead' was BA's first public cemetery, though it quickly became exclusive; Argentina's most illustrious historical figures are buried here, including Eva Perón ('Evita'). Myriad styles decorate the crumbling tombs, from art nouveau and art deco to neoclassical and neo-Gothic. There are also wonderfully flamboyant statues to discover, so pay your respects to Evita before getting lost among the marble angels.

◉ *Recoleta & Barrio Norte*

Tango Show (p39)

2 Nothing captures the essence of Buenos Aires like the sensual and melancholy tango, and no visit to the city is complete without experiencing tango in some form. Watch it in a San Telmo or La Boca street fair, see a slick show at a theater or join a *milonga* (dance event) at dozens of venues. Tango classes are often held before *milongas*, so take part – or just watch, but don't look too long at that handsome stranger across the room; a stare is an invitation to dance, and you could be breaking some hearts.

☆ *Tango*

JUPITERIMAGES / GETTY IMAGES ©

Football Game (p48)

3 In Buenos Aires, *fútbol* isn't just a game. The national pastime inspires near-religious passion in *porteños*, clearing the streets and sending spectators into fits of ecstasy and anguish as they huddle around TV screens or brave the explosive stadium crowds. The atmosphere is particularly boisterous (read: out of control) when River Plate and arch-rivals Boca Juniors face off during the much-anticipated *superclásico* games. The tension is palpable, and for two hours on a Sunday afternoon here, nothing else really matters. CROWD AT A MATCH BETWEEN BOCA JUNIORS AND RIVER PLATE AT LA BOMBONERA STADIUM

☆ *Sports & Activities*

Steak Dinner (p25)

4 Believe the hype: Argentine beef is some of the best in the world. Eat, drink and be merry at one of BA's hundreds of *parrillas* (steakhouses), where a leisurely meal begins with waiters pouring Malbec and carving generous slabs of prime beef. *Parrillas* run the gamut from neighborhood joints to classic establishments to upscale restaurants, so there's a price for every pocket. One thing is certain: expect some of the best meat you've ever eaten.

✖ *Eating*

Plaza de Mayo (p58)

5 Founded in 1580, Plaza de Mayo is the stage on which many of the dramatic events in Argentina's history were played out, from military bombings in 1955 to Evita's emotional speeches to massive union demonstrations (still going today). Most of the time, however, it's a peaceful place where families feed pigeons and the odd pickpocket makes off with a tourist's camera (stay sharp and you'll be OK!). If you're here on a Thursday afternoon, you might witness Las Madres de Plaza de Mayo: mothers peacefully marching for social-justice causes.

◉ *The Center*

San Telmo Stroll *(p86)*

6 The neighborhood of San Telmo is a beguiling mix of faded grandeur and bohemian spirit. The elegant belle-epoque architecture and crumbling villas are throwbacks to the district's 19th-century heyday, before yellow fever and cholera sent the aristocratic masses to higher ground. Today, you can wander along Defensa or Balcarce streets toward leafy Parque Lezama, taking in picturesque vistas of romantic facades and drooping balconies as you window-shop for antiques. There's definitely been gentrification (Starbucks has discovered San Telmo!), but much of the old-world atmosphere remains.

🏃 *San Telmo*

Cycling in Palermo's Parks *(p203)*

7 Buenos Aires could hardly be called bike-friendly, but things are slowly changing. Bike lanes now exist on some avenues, there's a bike-sharing program and Critical Mass (where cyclists take over certain streets in a semi-organized ride) happens every month. For the traveler, a bike ride around Buenos Aires – especially in Palermo's green parks – is a great way to experience cycling in this big, vehicle-dominated city. Here, miles of safe bike lanes exist, and you can enjoy the green grass instead of the gray concrete. PARQUE 3 DE FEBRERO (BOSQUES DE PALERMO)

🏃 *Palermo*

El Caminito *(p100)*

8 Rough-and-tumble La Boca, with its brightly painted metal houses, was the city's principal port until Puerto Madero was created at the close of the 19th century. El Caminito ('the little walk-way') is a curved pedestrian street lined with artists selling paintings and other creations. It has the air of a tourist trap, especially with the numerous souvenir shops nearby, but it's fun nevertheless. For something more upscale, head to Fundación Proa (p101), one of BA's fanciest art galleries, across from the (rather strongly scented) Riachuelo River.

⊙ *La Boca*

Museo de Arte Latinoamericano de Buenos Aires (Malba) *(p128)*

9 The vibrant Malba is a must, both for its brilliant modern Latin American and Argentine art, and for the stunning contemporary building that houses it. This significant collection of Argentine real-estate tycoon Eduardo Costantini spans the modernist, avant-garde, surrealist and abstract movements and includes work by Frida Kahlo and Diego Rivera. There are also temporary international art exhibits and a very fine restaurant-cafe with a lovely patio.

⊙ *Palermo*

Feria de Mataderos *(p149)*

10 Folk music emanates from the outdoor stage, local couples take to the streets to perform traditional *chacarera* and *chamamé* (folk dances and music), food stalls dish out hearty country dishes such as *locro* (a meaty stew), deep-friend *empanadas* and *humitas* (a kind of tamale) – this is Feria de Mataderos, an authentic celebration of Argentine country traditions. You might also see gauchos demonstrating their horse-riding skills by playing *sortija*, a game where they stand in their saddles and ride at full speed to spear a tiny dangling ring. Catch it on weekends during the summer.

🌿 *South of Palermo*

What's New

Pop-Up Restaurants

These one-time eating events are ideal for experimental chefs. Among others, look for GAJO (www.facebook.com/gajococina).

Metrobus & Bike Lanes

A new bus rapid transit system has improved traffic flow and provided faster service. Meanwhile, expanded bike lanes and a free bike-share program have encouraged two-wheeled recreation and commuting.

Faena Arts Center

Puerto Madero's newest darling is this art space – housed in an old flour mill – that's meant to highlight gigantic, larger-than-life installations. (p74)

Food Festivals

Popular new food fairs include Feria Masticar (www.feriamasticar.com.ar), put on by some of BA's most famous chefs, and Feria Raíz (www.facebook.com/Raiz FestivalGastronomico), an Argentine-food celebration.

New Concert Space

The Centro Cultural del Bicentenario, located in the beaux arts post office building, wasn't open at research time, but when it is it'll seat 2000 spectators. (p61)

Mercado Azul

Buenos Aires' *mercado azul* (literally 'blue market') for US dollars offers nearly twice the number of pesos over the official rate. The downsides are scams, fake bills and fly-by-night *cambios* (unofficial exchange houses). Some hotels, restaurants and shops will give discounts for US-dollar transactions and sometimes change the dollars themselves. (p213)

Molecular Gastronomy

In this interesting style of cuisine, multiple courses of just a few bites each are served to diners who want a unique food experience that encompasses taste combinations, textures and unforgettable visual appeal.

Usina del Arte

La Boca isn't known for upscale buildings, but this gorgeous new music venue, located in a remodeled electricity factory, is meant to start a gentrifying process in one of BA's shadiest hoods. (p103)

Villa Crespo

This neighborhood just south of Palermo has gained popularity as an affordable home for creative new restaurants, hotels and shops. (p147)

For more recommendations and reviews, see **lonelyplanet. com/buenos-aires**

Need to Know

For more information, see Survival Guide (p201)

Currency
Peso (AR$), though some upscale hotels quote in US dollars (US$).

Language
Spanish

Visas
Generally not required for US, Canadian, Australian, New Zealand and most Western European citizens. However, Americans, Canadians and Australians must pay a significant 'reciprocity fee' to enter Argentina.

Money
ATMs and exchange houses are common downtown. Major credit cards are generally accepted, though travelers checks are not.

Mobile Phones
Nearly everyone in Buenos Aires uses a mobile phone. Local SIM chips can be bought for unlocked international phones, and credit added as needed.

Time
Argentina is three hours behind GMT and generally does not observe daylight-saving time, but this situation may change.

Tourist Information
Tourist information offices and kiosks are dotted across the city, especially in neighborhoods popular with tourists.

Daily Costs

Budget: Less than US$60
➡ Dorm bed: US$15
➡ Double room in budget hotel: US$80
➡ Cheap main dish: US$8

Midrange: US$60-$120
➡ Three-star hotel room: US$100-175
➡ Average main dish: US$10-15
➡ Museum admission: US$1-5

Top End: US$120 and up
➡ Five-star hotel room: US$200
➡ Fine main dish: US$15-20
➡ Taxi trip across town: US$15

Advance Planning

Two months before Book accommodations if traveling during busy times and if your hotel is popular.

One month before Check reviews for tours or activities and decide on a schedule; make reservations if necessary.

One week before Pack smart, comfortable clothing. *Porteños* are a well-dressed lot, and you'll stick out as a tourist in loud shirt, shorts and flip-flops.

Useful Websites

Argentina Independent (www.argentinaindependent.com) Current affairs and culture, plus events listing and musings about expat life.

Argentine Post (www.argentinepost.com) Useful wide-ranging articles on BA and Argentina.

Pick up the Fork (www.pickupthefork.com) Restaurant and bar reviews, plus where to shop for ingredients.

Lonely Planet (www.lonelyplanet.com) Forums, travel news, updates and more.

WHEN TO GO
. . . .

Spring (September to November) and fall (March to May) are the best temperature-wise; winter (June to August) is cold but not freezing.

Buenos Aires

°C/°F **Temp**

Rainfall inches/mm

Arriving in Buenos Aires

Ezeiza airport (EZE; officially Aeropuerto Internacional Ministro Pistarini) Shuttle services are a good way to get downtown (AR$80); the transport booth area is beyond customs and has a couple of companies with frequent shuttles. Penny pinchers can take a local bus (AR$6), which takes two hours to get downtown.

For taxis, go outside the transport booth area (taxis are overpriced here) to the reception area. Avoid taxi touts like the plague; a few steps beyond, find the city's official taxi stand (a blue sign says 'Taxi Ezeiza'). In late 2013 it charged AR$270 to the center, including tolls.

Aeroparque airport (officially Aeroparque Jorge Newbery) Close to downtown and easily accessible by local bus or taxi.

For much more on **arrival** see p202

Getting Around

Despite Buenos Aires' heavy traffic, the city's public-transportation system is efficient and usually a better way to get around than driving.

➡ **Bus** The city has hundreds of bus lines that can take you within a few blocks of any destination. Sorting it all out is another matter; buy a pocket bus guide or use the 'city buses' link at www.omnilineas.com.

➡ **Subte** BA's underground, or subway, is not difficult to figure out and a quick way to get around – though it gets hot and very crowded during rush hour.

➡ **Taxi** Black and yellow street taxis are ubiquitous and generally fine, though some people prefer *remises* (radio taxis) for more safety.

For much more on **getting around** see p203

Sleeping

Buenos Aires has a very wide range of accommodations, including hostels, guesthouses, B&Bs, homestays, apartments and hotels of all stripes and budgets. Services range widely; some hostels' private rooms are nicer than many budget hotels', and can cost more. Boutique hotels are a dime a dozen in Palermo, while five-star luxury is easily found in the Retiro and Recoleta neighborhoods.

November through February are busy times, so book ahead if your hotel is a popular one.

Useful Websites

➡ **Oasis Collections** (www.oasisba.com) The cream of the crop for luxury stays.

➡ **Spare Rooms Buenos Aires** (www.spareroomsba.com) When you need just a room.

➡ **San Telmo Loft** (www.santelmoloft.com) A handful of artsy vacation rentals in San Telmo.

➡ **Craigslist** (http://buenosaires.en.craigslist.org) Endless listings for rooms, sublets, apartments, houses.

For much more on **sleeping** see p162

Top Itineraries

Day One

The Center (p56)

From leafy Plaza San Martín, walk south on pedestrian Florida and experience masses of people shopping, busking, selling or just power-walking to their next destination. You'll eventually come within a block of **Plaza de Mayo**, the heart of Buenos Aires. This historic plaza is surrounded by **Casa Rosada**, **Catedral Metropolitana** and **Museo del Cabildo**.

Lunch Outside seating and fresh offerings at the Central Market (p75).

Puerto Madero (p71)

Lined with renovated old brick warehouses, Puerto Madero is replete with fancy lofts and apartment towers, plus some of the city's most expensive (and some say overpriced) restaurants. It's a very scenic and pleasantly vehicle-free place to stroll the cobbled paths along the dikes. Art lovers shouldn't miss **Colección de Arte Amalia Lacroze de Fortabat**, highlighting the collection of Argentina's wealthiest woman. For a shot of nature, visit **Reserva Ecológica Costanera Sur**, a land-filled wetlands.

Dinner Casual and excellent Peruvian can be had at Chan Chan (p81).

Congreso & Tribunales (p76)

Take in an opera, ballet or classical-music show at **Teatro Colón**, Buenos Aires' premier theater. The traditional entertainment district of **Av Corrientes** still hops these days, showcasing many films, art events and plays.

Day Two

San Telmo (p86)

 Stroll through this colonial neighborhood's cobbled streets and window-shop for antiques. Come on a Sunday, when the famous **Feria de San Telmo** street market takes over the neighborhood. Book a tour to the stunning **El Zanjón de Granados** for a peek into the city's origins.

Lunch A sidewalk table at Bar Plaza Dorrego (p92) for great people-watching.

La Boca (p98)

The colorful corrugated houses along **El Caminito** are indeed photogenic, though this area is a bit of a tourist trap. It's still fun, however; check out the souvenir shops and artists' paintings and perhaps catch a street-tango show. Art lovers shouldn't miss **Fundación Proa**, a cutting-edge gallery, while soccer fans can head to La Bombonera stadium and visit the Boca team's **Museo de la Pasión Boquense**. But whatever you do, don't stray too far from the tourist hordes; La Boca is at times a rough neighborhood.

 Dinner Try exceptional international cuisine at Café San Juan (p91).

San Telmo (p86)

Catch a tango show at **El Viejo Almacén**, a long-running venue. Or go drinking at one of the many great watering holes in the area, from **Gibraltar** (an English pub) to **Doppelgänger** (an upscale cocktail bar).

Day Three

Recoleta & Barrio Norte (p115)

Explore Recoleta's famous **cemetery**; you can wander for hours among the crumbling sacrophagi and marble angels. It's a veritable city of the dead, fascinating and mysterious; to seek out Evita's tomb, just follow everyone else.

> **Lunch** *Empanadas* at El Sanjuanino (p120), one of the few cheap eateries.

Recoleta & Barrio Norte (p115)

Check out the **Museo Nacional de Bellas Artes**, Argentina's top classic arts museum. Just north is the cool sculpture *Floralis Genérica*, a giant metal flower whose petals open during the day and close at night (when the gears are working!). And if you've got the bucks, the city's most expensive boutiques are along **Av Alvear**, worth a stroll to also eyeball some huge old mansions. Visit **Museo de Arte Hispanoamericano Isaac Fernández Blanco** and **Palacio Paz**, in nearby Retiro, if you like gorgeous palaces filled with antiques.

> **Dinner** Looking for the locals? Then head to classic Rodi Bar (p119).

Recoleta & Barrio Norte (p115)

Time to drink up: **Milión** is a bar-restaurant in a beautiful old mansion, **Casa Bar** is a sports pub popular with expats, and **La Biela** is a traditional cafe-restaurant where the upper classes loiter over lattes.

Day Four

Palermo (p126)

Walk (or take a bike ride) along Palermo's **Parque 3 de Febrero**, where you can also visit a zoo, botanical garden and Japanese garden. Bike paths are laced throughout, and on Sunday the ring road around the Rose Garden is closed to vehicles.

> **Lunch** Malba's (p128) cafe-restaurant has a great patio for sunny days.

Palermo (p126)

Visit **Malba**, a beautiful and contemporary art museum showcasing the collection of art patron Eduardo F Costantini. The **Museo Nacional de Arte Decorativo** is another must-see; it's a beaux arts mansion that once belonged to a Chilean aristocrat, and is full of his posh belongings. Finally, Evita fans can't miss **Museo Evita**, which chronicles the life of Argentina's most internationally famous woman.

> **Dinner** For an excellent steakhouse, get a table at Don Julio (p132).

Palermo (p126)

Palermo is nightlife central. There are dozens of bars to check out, and people come from all over to dance at the famous clubs here. For outdoor action, head to **Plaza Serrano**, which is surrounded by restaurants and bars, along with dozens of their outdoor tables; it's *the* place to see and be seen.

If You Like...

Museums

Museo de Arte Latinoamericano de Buenos Aires Gorgeous, glassy art museum showcasing the private collection of art patron Eduardo F Costantini. (p128)

Museo Nacional de Bellas Artes From European impressionists to Latin American maestros, this national art museum covers them all. (p118)

Museo Nacional de Arte Decorativo Beautiful beaux arts mansion strewn with the posh belongings of a Chilean aristocrat. (p130)

Colección de Arte Amalia Lacroze de Fortabat See what the collection of Argentina's wealthiest woman has to offer. (p74)

Fundación Proa Cutting-edge gallery-museum with contemporary art exhibits, plus a rooftop cafe with a view of La Boca. (p101)

Palacio Paz Gorgeous European palace with ornate rooms, salons and guilded details. (p108)

Historic Places

Plaza de Mayo Buenos Aires' original main square, dating to the 1580s and surrounded by significant buildings. (p58)

El Zanjón de Granados Beautifully renovated, underground architectural site of the city's first settlements. (p89)

Plaza San Martín Pleasant leafy park that was once home to Spanish governors, slave quarters, a bullring and a battlefield. (p109)

Elephants at the Jardín Zoológico, Palermo (p130)

KRZYSZTOF DYDYNSKI / GETTY IMAGES ©

Parque Lezama Considered to be the very spot where Buenos Aires was founded, back in 1536. (p89)

Manzana de las Luces Taking up a whole city block, this was BA's most important center of culture and learning during colonial times. (p62)

Green Spaces

Reserva Ecológica Costanera Sur Low-lying, 350-hectare landfill site that's become a haven for wildlife and nature-seekers. (p73)

Parque 3 de Febrero Laced with miles of bike trails, this large green park also has a rose garden, planetarium and small lakes. (p129)

Jardín Japonés Tidy green oasis of tranquility in Palermo, complete with sushi restaurant and cultural offerings. (p130)

Jardín Zoológico A decent big-city zoo with lawns, lakes, trees and many natural enclosures for the critters. (p130)

Jardín Botánico Carlos Thays Surrounded by busy avenues, this modest botanical garden offers a peaceful break from the city. (p129)

Free Stuff

Cementerio de la Recoleta Buenos Aires' most popular tourist attraction and a must-visit for its amazing tombs and statues. (p117)

Museo Nacional de Bellas Artes Spend an afternoon at this large and excellent national art museum. (p118)

Street Fairs BA has several; be sure to hit **San Telmo's** Sunday fair (p95), and the one in **Mataderos** if you can get out there. (p149)

Street Tango See these (donation) tango shows at the San Telmo **Sunday fair** (p95) and on **El Caminito** in La Boca. (p100)

Reserva Ecológica Costanera Sur Marshy lands located in Puerto Madero near the city center, but miles away in atmosphere. (p73)

Cementerio de la Chacarita A larger, less flashy, less accessible and less touristed version of Recoleta's cemetery. (p118)

Free City Tour Locals who love their city offer free walking tours in English (tips appreciated but not mandatory; www.bafreetour.com).

Unusual Tours

Biking Buenos Aires Pedal around Palermo's parks and on bike lanes; a fun and easy way to tour the city (www.bikingbuenosaires.com).

Graffitimundo See Buenos Aires through its colorful and dynamic street-art scene (www.graffitimundo.com).

Foto Ruta Unique and self-guided tour via photographing clues around BA's neighborhoods (www.foto-ruta.com).

The Man Tour Smoke a cigar, get a straight razor shave and shop for a handmade hat (www.landingpadba.com/the-man-tour-buenos-aires).

Parilla Tour Explore the city's off-the-beaten-track *parrillas* (steakhouses) and learn about Argentina's food and culture (www.parrillatour.com).

Narrative Tango Tour Get the scoop on tango via classes, *milongas* and shows (www.narrativetangotours.com).

Urban Running Tour Run around BA (literally) with a guide; they'll adapt to your

For more top Buenos Aires spots, see the following:

➡ Eating (p24)

➡ Drinking & Nightlife (p32)

➡ Entertainment (p36)

➡ Shopping (p45)

➡ Sports & Activities (p48)

pace (www.urbanrunningtours.com.ar).

The Offbeat

Tierra Santa Visit this kitschy 'world's first religious theme park' and witness the resurrection every half-hour. (p23)

Museo del Patrimonio Aguas Argentinas Pretty tiles, ceramic pipes and old bidets and toilets are highlighted at this small, quirky museum. (p79)

Learn Polo Not many travelers can say they've hopped on a horse and learned to play polo while on vacation. (p50)

Closed-Door Restaurants The menu is fixed, as is the dinner time, and you won't get the address until you book – so why are they so popular? (p133)

Museo de la Policía Federal Exhibits on cockfighting, drug paraphernalia and hacked-up murder victims – only at the Police Museum. (p61)

Pato Match Like weird sports? Then try watching this one (in December's Palermo championship), originally played on horseback by gauchos. (p50)

Month by Month

February

It's still summer, but vacationing *porteños* start their return home. There are plenty of tourists in the city, some passing through on their way to or from Patagonia.

✪ Carnaval

Usually occurring in late February, BA's Carnaval is a small affair compared to Rio's or Bahia's, but it's still lots of fun. Catch some Brazilian-flavored *murga* groups (traditional Carnaval ensembles), with dancing and drumming in different neighborhoods around the city.

✪ Chinese New Year

Yes, Buenos Aires has a Chinatown, but it's only about four blocks long – on Arribeños street in Belgrano. During Chinese New Year, expect plenty of food, firecrackers and festivities. Dates vary depending on the lunar calendar.

✪ Buenos Aires Fashion Week

Four days of clothing stalls and catwalk action show off the city's latest threads and their makers. It takes place at Palermo's La Rural in February (fall/winter collections) and August (spring/summer collections). Expect plenty of beautiful people – including models, of course. (www. bafweek.com.ar)

April

It's fall in BA, and one of the best times to visit – but always be prepared for a downpour. There are still plenty of activities as the city heads into low season.

✪ Feria Internacional del Libro

BA's annual book fair attracts tens of thousands of book lovers for three weeks in April and May. Famous authors do readings and sign books, while publishers hawk their wares. Look for it at the La Rural building in Palermo. (www. el-libro.org.ar)

✪ Festival Internacional de Cine Independiente

This independent film festival highlights national and international films, with awards given out in separate categories. Over 100 films are screened, with a main venue being the Abasto shopping mall. (www.bafici.gov.ar)

May

Late autumn has hit and it's pleasantly cool as the rains die back a bit. Look for travel deals as low season starts in earnest.

✪ Arte Ba

Arte Ba features exhibitions from hundreds of art galleries, dealers and organizations, with both national and international contemporary art on display. Conferences, presentations and discussions make the rounds, while young new artists get exposure. It's at Palermo's La Rural building. (www.arteba.com)

July

It's high winter, so be prepared with warm layers. Locals who can afford it head to the ski slopes down south.

✨ Exposición de Ganadería, Agricultura e Industria Internacional (La Rural)

The mother of all livestock fairs, where prize cows, sheep, goats, horses and – especially – bulls, all strut their stuff. Gaucho shows provide entertainment. It takes place for two weeks in late July at Palermo's La Rural building. (www.exposicionrural.com.ar)

August

It's still cold, so keep those layers on, but it's also a great time to explore the city's theaters, museums and art galleries.

✨ Festival y Mundial de Tango

Taking place in mid-August, this two-week-long tango festival offers a great way to see some of the country's best tango dancers and musicians do their thing. Plenty of competitions, classes and workshops take place. (www.tangobuenosaires.gob.ar)

September

Spring has sprung and it's a lovely time to be in BA. Polo season begins and the tourists start returning.

✨ Vinos y Bodegas

A can't-miss event for wine aficionados, with vintages from dozens of Argentine *bodegas* (wineries). Mix with thousands of sommeliers, restaurateurs, journalists and general wine-lovers at Palermo's La Rural building. Expect cooking demonstrations and live music too. (www.expovinosybodegas.com.ar)

November

It's pretty darn near perfect weather in BA, and the jacaranda trees are showing off their gorgeous purple blooms. High season has arrived, so reserve your accommodation ahead.

✨ Marcha del Orgullo Gay

It's nothing like San Francisco's or Sydney's, but BA has its own gay pride march. Each year on the first Saturday in November, thousands of BA's gays, lesbians, transgenders and more strut their way through the city's center. (www.marchadelorgullo.org.ar)

✨ Creamfields

Buenos Aires' premier electronic-music festival happens in early November. Tens of thousands of ravers party non-stop for hours on end, with famous local and international DJs spinning their best. (www.creamfieldsba.com)

✨ Día de la Tradición

The closest thing to authentic gaucho culture you'll probably ever witness, with traditional foods, feats of horsemanship, and folk music and dancing. It happens in San Antonio de Areco, a day trip from BA; call the Areco tourist office (www.arecoturismo.com.ar) for exact dates, which vary yearly. If you miss it, head to Feria de Mataderos, a weekly street fair outside BA's center.

December

Summer in BA means hot and humid temperatures, and many *porteños* head to the coast. There's still plenty going on in the city, however.

☆ Campeonato Abierto Argentino de Polo

Argentina boasts the world's best polo, and the Abierto is the world's premier polo event. It takes place at Palermo's Campo Argentino de Polo. For exact dates and details, contact the Asociación Argentina de Polo (www.aapolo.com).

✨ Buenos Aires Jazz Festival Internacional

This jazz festival takes place over five days in venues all over the city. Jazz musicians of all kinds are featured – emerging and established, avant-garde and traditional, national and international. Concerts and films also take place. (www.buenosairesjazz.gob.ar)

With Kids

Although it's a megalopolis, BA is remarkably child-friendly. On sunny weekends Palermo's parks bustle with families taking walks and picnicking, while shopping malls fill with strollers. Zoos, museums and theme parks are also popular destinations – and don't forget those fun street fairs!

El Caminito, La Boca (p100)

Eating & Sleeping

Many restaurants welcome kids, but if a place looks a bit too fancy, ask if they take children. And most offer a wide selection of food suitable for kids (like pizza, pasta, meats and vegetables); a few even have children's menus. Waiters are accustomed to providing extra plates and cutlery for little tykes, though you may not always find booster seats or high chairs.

Note that Buenos Aires is a very late-night city; most restaurants don't open until 9pm, so you'll likely have to adjust your timetable during your travels here.

Don't forget to take the kids out for ice cream – it's a real Argentine treat (p119). Other local sweets to try include *alfajores* (sandwich cookies usually covered in chocolate, available at corner stores) and *dulce de leche* (a milk caramel often used in desserts).

Small boutique hotels, hostels or guesthouses are sometimes not the best places for rambunctious kids, but most hotels accept them. Some hotel rooms come with kitchenettes; apartment rentals are another good option (p166).

In Public

Once children are old enough to cross the street safely and find their way back home, *porteño* parents will often send unaccompanied pre-adolescents on errands or on visits to friends or neighbors. This is also a country where people frequently touch each other, so your children may be patted on the head by friendly strangers. In general, you can count on your children's safety in public places, though it's always a good idea to keep an eye on them.

Porteños can be helpful on public transportation. Often someone will give up a seat for a parent and young child. Baby strollers on the crowded and uneven sidewalks of BA's downtown center are a liability, however; consider a baby carrier instead.

Poorly maintained public bathrooms lacking baby-changing facilities or counter-top space are common. Always carry toilet paper and wet wipes.

Green Spaces

Buenos Aires has numerous plazas and public parks, many with playgrounds, and these are always popular gathering spots for families. If you're downtown and need a nature break, try the Reserva Ecológica Costanera Sur (p73), a large nature preserve with good birdwatching, pleasant dirt paths and no vehicles; bike rentals are sometimes available on summer weekends.

Up north, the most attractive green spots are the wide open spaces of Palermo, especially Parque 3 de Febrero (p129). This huge park has a planetarium, a Japanese Garden and a nearby zoo. And on Sunday vehicular traffic isn't allowed on the ring road around the rose garden; you can rent bikes, boats and inline skates and range freely without worrying about cars!

Fun Museums

Make sure to visit the Museo Participativo de Ciencias (p118) in the Centro Cultural Recoleta. This science museum has interactive displays that focus on fun learning – signs say *'prohibido no tocar'* (not touching is forbidden). And in San Telmo, the **Museo Argentino del Títere** (Map p242; ☑4307-6917; www.museoargdeltitere.com.ar; Estados Unidos 802; admission free; ☺9:30am-12:30pm & 3-6pm Tue, Wed & Fri, 3-6pm Thu, Sat & Sun) is a small puppet museum with a fascinating collection of international and Argentine puppets, but it's the inexpensive shows that will amuse the little ones. Call beforehand to get hours and show times, as they vary widely.

Outside the center in Caballito is the Museo Argentino de Ciencias Naturales (p148), with myriad rooms containing giant dinosaur bones, dainty seashells, scary insects and amusing stuffed animals and birds.

Animals

About a 45-minute drive outside the city, in Escobar, is the exceptional zoo **Parque Temaikén** (☑034-8843-6900; www.temaiken.com.ar; RP 25, Km 1, Escobar; adult/child 3-10 AR$82/64; ☺10am-7pm Tue-Sun Dec-Feb, to 6pm Mar-Nov). Only the most charming animal species (like meerkats and tigers) are on display here, roaming freely around spacious natural enclosures. The beautiful grounds are tidy and park-like, and exceptional exhibits include a butterfly house, a fine aquarium and a large aviary (with parrots and toucans galore). Interactive areas provide mental stimulation, and services include stroller rentals, gift stores and restaurants. Just outside Temaikén is a large playground run by Heladería Munchi. Tuesday admission is half-off (unless it's a holiday).

For something much closer in, head to Palermo's Jardín Zoológico (p130). It's a fairly pleasant zoo for Latin America, and on sunny weekends it fills with families.

Playgrounds

Some of BA's outdoor parks have playgrounds, always popular with families. However, many large modern shopping malls have indoor playgrounds (often on the top floor), along with video arcades, multiplexes and toy shops. Paseo Alcorta (p142) has plenty of mechanical rides next to the large food court, while Mercado de Abasto (p148) boasts a full-blown 'Museo de los Niños' (more like a playground than a museum) where kids enter a miniature city complete with post office, hospital and even TV station. Abasto also has a mini-amusement park. On rainy days, these are great places to be with little ones.

Amusement Parks

Heading to Tigre (p153), just north of the center, makes a great day excursion. Hop on the fun Tren de la Costa to get there; it ends at Parque de la Costa (p154), a typical amusement park with rides and activities.

Christian parents might want to take the kids to **Tierra Santa** (☑4784-9551; www.tierrasanta-bsas.com.ar; Av Costanera R Obligado 5790; admission AR$40; ☺call for hours), a religious theme park unlike anywhere you've ever been. Not far away is **Parque Norte** (☑4787-1382; www.parquenorte.com; Avs Cantilo & Guiraldes; admission AR$70 Mon-Fri, AR$90 Sat, AR$100 Sun; ☺9am-8pm Mon-Fri, 8am-10pm Sat & Sun), a large water park that's perfect on a hot day.

MICHAEL TAYLOR / GETTY IMAGES ©

Street *asado* (Argentine barbecue) seller

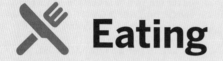 # Eating

Argentines take barbecuing to heights you cannot imagine. Their best pizzas and pastas vie with those of New York and Naples. They make fabulously tasty wines and impossibly delectable ice cream. And ethnic cuisine is rampant in Buenos Aires. In fact, you'll eat so well here that you'll need to power-walk between lunch and dinner to work off the excess calories.

MARYELLEN BAKER / GETTY IMAGES ©

Chimichurri sauce

Staples & Specialties
BEEF

Argentines have perfected the art of grilling beef on the *asado* (barbecue). This involves cooking with coals and using only salt to prepare the meat. On the grill itself, slanted runners funnel the excess fat to the sides, and an adjustable height system directs the perfect amount of heat to the meat. The *asado* is a family institution, often taking place on Sunday in the backyards of houses all over the country.

A traditional *parrillada* (mixed grill) is a common preparation at *parrillas* (steakhouses) and offers a little bit of everything. Expect *choripán* (a sausage appetizer), *pollo* (chicken), *costillas* (ribs) and *carne* (beef). It can also come with more exotic items such as *chinchulines* (small intestines), *mojellas* (sweetbreads) and *morcilla* (blood sausage).

Common steak cuts:

➡ **Bife de chorizo** Sirloin; a popular thick and juicy cut.

➡ **Bife de costilla** T-bone or Porterhouse steak.

➡ **Bife de lomo** Tenderloin; a tender though less flavorful piece.

➡ **Cuadril** Rump steak; often a thin cut.

➡ **Ojo de bife** Ribeye; a choice smaller morsel.

➡ **Tira de asado** Short ribs; thin, crispy strips of ribs.

➡ **Vacío** Flank steak; textured, chewy and flavorful.

If you don't specify how you want your steak cooked, it will come *a punto* (medium to well done). Getting a steak medium rare

NEED TO KNOW

PLAN YOUR TRIP EATING

Price Ranges

$ mains under AR$80

$$ mains AR$80-130

$$$ mains over AR$130

Look for the *menu ejecutivo* (set lunch menu); this usually includes dessert and a drink and is a good deal.

Opening Hours

➡ Restaurants are generally open daily from noon to 3:30pm for lunch and 8pm to midnight or 1am for dinner.

➡ A sure bet for that morning *medialuna* (croissant) and *cortado* (coffee with milk) are the city's many cafes, which often stay open from morning to late at night without a break.

Tipping

Tip 10% for standard service; make it 15% for exceptional service. Tips usually cannot be added to credit-card purchases. The word for tip in Spanish is *propina*.

Reservations

Reserve at popular restaurants, especially on weekends. If you don't speak Spanish, ask a staff member at your hotel to make the call for you. Or check out www.restorando.com.ar.

Etiquette

➡ Most *porteños* eat no earlier than 9pm (later on weekends).

➡ Ask for your bill by saying, '*la cuenta, por favor*' ('the bill, please') or making the 'writing in air' gesture. Be aware that not all restaurants accept credit cards – always ask first.

➡ At upscale restaurants, a per-person *cubierto* (cover charge), usually AR$10 to AR$30, is tacked on to the bill. This covers the use of utensils and bread – it does not relate in any way to the tip.

or rare is harder than you'd imagine. If you want some pink in the center, order it *jugoso;* if you like it truly rare, try *vuelta y vuelta.*

Don't miss *chimichurri,* a tasty sauce made with olive oil, garlic and parsley – it adds a tantalizing spiciness. Occasionally

Above: Ñoquis with tomato sauce
Left: Pizza Margherita

you can also get *salsa criolla,* a condiment made of diced tomatoes, onion and parsley.

ITALIAN

Thanks to Argentina's Italian heritage, the national cuisine has been highly influenced by Italian immigrants who entered the country during the late 19th century. Along with an animated set of speaking gestures, they brought their love of pasta, pizza, gelato and more.

Many restaurants make their own pasta – look for *pasta casera* (handmade pasta). Some of the varieties of pasta you'll encounter are ravioles, *sorrentinos* (large, round pasta parcels similar to ravioli), *ñoquis* (gnocchi) and *tallerines* (fettuccine). Standard sauces include *tuco* (tomato sauce, sometimes with meat), *estofado* (beef stew, popular with ravioli) and *salsa blanca* (béchamel). Occasionally the sauce is not included in the price of the pasta – you choose and pay for it separately.

Pizza is sold at *pizzerías* throughout the country, though many regular restaurants offer it as well. It's generally very cheesy and excellent, so go ahead and order a slice or three! Other common Italian-based treats include *fugazzeta* (similar to focaccia) and *fainá* (garbanzo flatbread).

OTHER ETHNIC

Spanish cooking is less popular than Italian but is another cornerstone of Argentine food. In BA's Spanish restaurants, many of them found in the Congreso neighborhood, you'll find *paella,* as well as other typically Spanish seafood dishes.

The Palermo Viejo neighborhood offers a wide range of Armenian, Brazilian, Mexican, French, Indian, Japanese, Southeast Asian and Middle Eastern cuisines (among many others). If you're craving spicy food (anathema to most Argentines), this is the place to come.

Vegetarians & Vegans

Most restaurants, including *parrillas,* serve a few items acceptable to most vegetarians, such as green salads, omelets, mashed potatoes, pizza and pasta. Words to look out for include *carne* (beef), *pollo* (chicken), *cerdo* (pork) and *cordero* (lamb), though all meat cuts are described in different words. *Sin carne* means 'without meat', and the phrase *soy vegetariano/a* ('I'm a vegetarian') comes in handy. *Pescado* (fish) and *mariscos* (seafood) are sometimes available for pescatarians.

Vegetarian restaurants have become trendy in recent years, along with health-food shops with bulk grains, wholewheat pasta, dried fruit, nuts and bakery goods.

Vegans will have a much harder time; there isn't a Spanish word for 'vegan'. Make sure homemade pasta doesn't include egg, and that fried vegetables aren't cooked in lard (*grasa; manteca* means butter). You'll need to be creative to survive here. One tip: look for accommodations with a kitchen, so you can shop for and cook your own food.

The Sweet Stuff

One of Argentina's most definitive treats is *dulce de leche,* a milk-caramel sauce that is dripped on everything from flan to cake to ice cream. *Alfajores* (round, cookie-type sandwiches) are also delicious – Argentina's version of the candy bar. The most upscale and popular brand is Havanna (also a

---

STEAK – OUTSIDE THE BOX

Going to a *parrilla* is probably on every BA visitor's to-do list, but if you want to eat meat in a different way, try these options:

Adentro (www.adentrodinnerclub.com) At this *puerta cerrada* (closed-door restaurant) it's like being at a good friend's *asado.* You'll get stuffed on juicy *empanadas,* delicious grilled shrimp and veggies, and then some amazing meat.

Argentine Experience (www.theargentineexperience.com) Learn the meaning of local hand gestures, the story of Argentina's beef and how to make *empanadas* and *alfajores.* Plus you'll eat a supremely tender steak.

Steaks by Luis (www.steakbuenosaires.net) An upscale *asado* experience where you'll nibble on cheese and sip boutique wine while watching large hunks of meat being grilled.

Parrilla Tour (www.parrillatour.com) Meet your knowledgeable guide at a restaurant for a *choripan* (traditional sausage sandwich), then an *empanada.* You'll finish at a local *parrilla.*

coffee-shop chain), but kiosks carry many other kinds.

Because of Argentina's Italian heritage, Argentine *helado* is comparable to the best ice cream anywhere in the world. Amble into a *heladería* (ice-cream shop), order up a cone (usually you pay first) and the creamy concoction will be artistically swept up into a mountainous peak and handed over with a small plastic spoon tucked in the side. Important: *granizado* means with chocolate flakes.

Some of the best *heladería* chains – with branches all over the city – are Persicco, Freddo and Una Altra Volta, but many smaller independent shops are excellent too.

Drinks
WINE

By now you've probably heard: Argentine wines are world-class. Most famous is malbec, that dark, robust plum-flavored wine that has solidly stomped the region of Mendoza on every oenophile's map (the Mendoza region produces 60% of the country's wine). But Argentina has other fine varietals that are very worthy of a sip or three – fresh *torrontés*, fruity bonarda and earthy pinot noir.

So how to know which to try? They say there's a perfect Argentine wine for every occasion and a good *vinoteca* (wine boutique) will help you find it. In Palermo, try Lo de Joaquin Alberdi (p140), in San Telmo there's **Vinotango** (Map p242; ☑4361-1101; Estados Unidos 488; ☺10:30am-9pm). Aldo's Vinoteca (p66) is a restaurant that sells wines at retail prices – even when you eat there.

Supermarket selections are usually adequate, though you miss out on the tailored advice. Among the mainstay brands are Norton, Trapiche, Zuccardi and Santa Julia, with different lines that cater to every price range. Spend a bit more to try the elegant Rutini (from Bodega La Rural) or Luigi Bosca.

For private wine tastings, your best bet is with **Anuva Wines** (Map p250; ☑15-5768-8589; www.anuvawines.com). Try five boutique vintages with food pairings; they'll also ship your wine purchases to the USA. For informal tastings, inquire at **Pain et Vin** (Map p250; ☑4832-5654; Gorriti 5132), a casual wine and bread shop. **Bar du Marche** (Map p250; ☑4778-1050; www.bardumarchepalermo.com; Nicaragua 5946; ☺9:30am-midnight Mon-

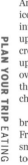

Young man drinking *mate*

Sat) is a low-key bistro offering 50 wines by the glass, while Gran Bar Danzón (p111) is an upscale lounge-restaurant that also has a good selection of wines by the glass.

Many *puertas cerradas* (closed-door) restaurants offer fine wines with their meals; **Casa Coupage** (Map p250; ☑4833-6354; www.casacoupage.com.ar), run by an Argentine sommelier couple, is especially wine-oriented. Finally, if you're really into wines consider staying at Miravida Soho (p172) in Palermo; it has a wine bar, cellar and tastings for their guests.

MATE

Mate (mah-teh) is Argentina's unofficial national beverage. More than a simple drink like tea or coffee, *mate* is more like an elaborate ritual shared among family and friends.

There's an informal etiquette to preparing and drinking *mate*. The *cebador* (server) fills the gourd with *yerba,* then pours in very hot water. Each participant drinks the gourd dry, then the *cebador* refills it and hands it to the next person. Germaphobes beware: the *bombilla* (a silvery straw with built-in filter), used to sip the *mate,* is shared by everyone.

An invitation to drink *mate* is a cultural treat you shouldn't turn down, though it's definitely an acquired taste. The tea is grassy, bitter and very hot; adding sugar can help. Saying *'gracias'* is a sign you want to stop drinking. And remember not to hold the *mate* too long before passing it on!

Because it is such a personal ritual, not many restaurants offer *mate* on the menu – but a few do, so try it if you can.

BEER, COFFEE & WATER

If Argentina has a national beer, it's Quilmes. Order a *porrón* and you'll get a half-liter bottle, or a *chopp* and you'll get a frosty mug of draft.

Argentines love their *café con leche* (coffee with milk). An espresso with a drop of milk is a *café cortado*. Black and herbal teas are also commonly available.

In Buenos Aires, the *agua de canilla* (tap water) is drinkable. In restaurants, however, most people order bottled mineral water – ask for *agua con gas* (with bubbles) or *agua sin gas* (without). In older, more traditional restaurants, carbonated water in a spritzer bottle (*un sifón de soda*) is great for drinking, though Argentines often mix it with cheap wine.

Eat Like a Local

Argentines eat little for breakfast – usually just coffee with *medialunas*, either *de manteca* (sweet) or *de grasa* (plain). *Tostadas* (toast) with *manteca* (butter) or *mermelada* (jam) is an alternative, as are *facturas* (pastries). Most hotels offer this basic breakfast, but some higher-end hotels have breakfast buffets.

Argentines make up for breakfast at lunch and dinner, and they love to dine out. Every neighborhood has basic restaurants serving the staples of pasta, pizza and steak (though for the best meats, head to a *parrilla*).

Cafes (which serve snacks, light meals and sometimes more) and *confiterías* (restaurant-cafes) are open all day and into the night. Bars or pubs usually have a more limited range of snacks and meals, though some offer full meals. A *tenedor libre* (literally, 'free fork') is an all-you-can-eat restaurant; quality is usually decent, but drinks are often mandatory and cost extra.

Heladería (ice-cream shop), Microcentro

Large, modern, chain supermarkets are common, and they'll have whatever you need for self-catering, including (usually) a takeout counter with a decent range of offerings. Smaller, local grocery stores – usually family-run – are also ubiquitous, though they won't have takeout.

The most thorough online guide to BA restaurants is www.guiaoleo.com (in Spanish); for listings in English, try www.pick upthefork.com

Eating by Neighborhood

➡ **The Center** (p63) Many restaurants here cater to the business crowd, with quick takeout and power lunches.

➡ **Puerto Madero** (p75) Upscale – and some say overpriced – restaurants here offer great dockside atmosphere and traditional cuisine.

➡ **Congreso & Tribunales** (p80) BA's political center, come here for Spanish cuisine, along with the odd Chinese, Korean or Peruvian gem.

➡ **San Telmo** (p91) Traditionally has supported many *parrillas*, though gentrification over the years translates to wider horizons.

➡ **Recoleta & Barrio Norte** (p119) BA's most exclusive neighborhood means expensive restaurants; those near the cemetery cater to tourists.

➡ **Palermo** (p132) Ground zero for the city's most creative and ethnically diverse dining scene.

COOKING COURSES

Taking a small-group cooking class or private class is probably the best option for short-term visitors who don't speak Spanish.

➡ **Norma Soued** (www.argentinecook-ingclasses.com) Cook Argentine cuisine like *empanadas*, traditional stews and *alfajores*.

➡ **Cooking with Teresita** (www.try-2cook.com) Partake of *asados* (barbecues) and *empanadas*; she'll also take you to local markets.

If you have time, speak Spanish and are considering making cooking a profession, try the highly regarded **Instituto Argentino de Gastronomía** (IAG; www.iag.com.ar) or **Mausi Sebess** (www.mausisebess.com), located in BA's suburb of Vicente López.

Top: Malbec wine

Middle: Medialunas (croissants)

Bottom: Alfajores de Maicena pastries filled with dulce de leche at Las Violetas Cafe (p149)

Lonely Planet's Top Choices

Hernán Gipponi Restaurant (p135) Beautifully prepared cuisine and memorable brunch.

Café San Juan (p91) Tattooed celebrity chef serves up fabulously tasty dishes.

Sarkis (p148) Everything is excellent at this famous Armenian restaurant.

Le Sud (p112) Exquisite French cuisine in one of BA's best hotels.

Aramburu (p81) Molecular gastronomy – not for everyone, but for some it's a peak experience.

Best by Budget

$

Chan Chan (p81) Colorful, casual Peruvian eatery with great seviche (seafood cured in citrus).

Rodi Bar (p119) Recoleta institution serving something for everyone.

Cumaná (p120) Upscale rustic joint specializing in northern Argentine cuisine.

$$

Las Pizarras (p132) Delicious, very creative dishes that can change daily.

Astor (p133) Multicultural celebrity chef starts his own excellent restaurant.

Malvón (p148) Excellent breakfast and brunches, but you'll have to wait.

$$$

Elena (p111) Probably one of the best meals you'll have in BA.

Unik (p135) Contemporary, highly sophisticated dishes in an upscale atmosphere.

Tomo 1 (p66) Five-star restaurant, five-star food, five-star prices.

Best by Cuisine

Steak

Don Julio (p132) Great traditional steakhouse with classy service.

La Cabrera (p135) Overly popular and touristy – but worth the wait.

Miranda (p134) Modern atmosphere and pleasant sidewalk seating.

Parrilla Peña (p81) No-nonsense, well priced and excellent meats.

El Desnivel (p91) Long-running, touristy and still reasonably priced.

Seafood

Oviedo (p132) Upscale dining room, fine service and amazing cuisine.

Crizia (p133) One of BA's best for fresh oysters and fish.

Casal de Catalunya (p91) Spanish restaurant with old-time atmosphere.

La Rosa Náutica (p75) Peruvian specialties like marinated octopus and seviche.

Italian

Siamo nel Forno (p133) Awesome Naples-style, thin-crust pizza.

La Parolaccia Trattoria (p75) Tasty homemade pastas with a water view.

Il Matterello (p102) Famous for its exceptional pastas and sauces.

Filo (p111) Trendy restaurant with a variety of Italian specialities.

Asian

Sudestada (p133) Consistently good, Asian-fusion cuisine that can be spicy.

Green Bamboo (p135) Vietnamese-style foods in BA-trendy dining room.

Furai-Bo (p66) Japanese ramen and other delicacies, in authentic surroundings.

Bi Won (p149) Good, long-running and no-nonsense Korean restaurant.

Comedor Nikkai (p92) A good place for sushi, tempura and teriyaki.

Vegetarian

Bio (p134) Sophisticated and very tasty vegetarian dishes.

Arevalito (p132) Tiny hippy-ish joint with great salads, sandwiches and tarts.

Granix (p66) Modern cafeteria catering to meat-weary office workers.

Vita (p66) Colorful, healthy and organic cafe, and they're friendly too.

Abuela Pan (p91) Small, very casual eatery serving daily vegetarian specials.

Drinking & Nightlife

Buenos Aires' nightlife is legendary around the world. What else could you expect from a country where dinner rarely starts before 10pm? In some neighborhoods, finding a good sports bar, trendy cocktail lounge, atmospheric old cafe or upscale wine bar is as easy as walking down the street. And dancers will be in heaven, as BA boasts spectacular nightclubs showcasing top-drawer DJs.

The Local Scene

Porteños hardly ever imbibe to the point of drunkenness – it's just not cool – but they do like to go out drinking, especially in groups, and always stay up late. Walk into any corner bar or cafe in the city and you'll see groups of friends or family sitting around a table, sipping tiny white cups of espresso or splitting a bottle of Quilmes (a popular local beer). More fashionable bars, pubs and breweries draw more of a mixed crowd of party-going tourists, with style-conscious men trying to impress their dates or girlfriends celebrating a special occasion.

How to handle the late-night scene like a *porteño?* If you're going out clubbing (some clubs open at 2am), take a nap after dinner and go easy on the booze – it will help you avoid conking out too early.

Gay & Lesbian Buenos Aires

In July 2010 Argentina became the first Latin American country to legalize same-sex marriage. Since then, Buenos Aires has become a huge gay destination, lending momentum to local events such as the **Marcha del Orgullo Gay** (Gay Pride Parade; www.marchadelorgullo.org. ar; ☉Nov) and the **Queer Tango Festival** (www. festivaltangoqueer.com.ar).

An especially gay-friendly accommodation is **Lugar Gay** (Map p242; ☎4300-4747; www. lugargay.com.ar; Defensa 1120; dm US$25, s US$50-70, d US$80-95), a casual guesthouse that also acts as an information center. Good general

websites are www.thegayguide.com.ar and www.nighttours.com/buenosaires.

Current hot gay parties include **Fiesta Plop** (www.plop-web.com.ar; ☉Fri), the monthly **Fiesta Dorothy** (www.fiestadorothy.com) and **Rheo** (www.rheo.com.ar).

Casa Brandon (Map p254; www.brandongay day.com.ar; Luis María Drago 236) is an art gallery-cultural center. And for a fun night of guided drinking and partying, there's **Out & About Pub Crawl** (www.outandaboutpubcrawl.com).

Finally, gay classes and *milongas* are given at **La Marshall** (Map p236; ☎4300-3487; www. lamarshall.com.ar; Av Independencia 572) and **Tango Queer** (Map p242; www.tangoqueer.com).

Bars

Bars abound in every neighborhood of Buenos Aires, and they come in all shapes, sizes and styles. You can choose from sports bars, cocktail lounges, Irish pubs, microbreweries, local holes-in-the-wall and more. Many of the city's upscale restaurants and hotels also have lively bars worth a visit.

Most bars serve beer, hard alcohol and wine, plus coffee and juice. Some make cocktails, and many offer a fair range of finger foods or even main dishes. Microbreweries and beer bars are catching on, offering decent selections of the hoppy stuff – but Argentina has a ways to go before competing globally, so don't expect anything mind-blowing.

Younger travelers and backpackers looking to bar-hop in a group should check out

Buenos Aires Pub Crawl (☑15-5464-1886; www.pubcrawlba.com).

Cafes

Cafes are an integral part of porteño life, and you shouldn't miss popping into one of these beloved hangouts for an afternoon break. Many cafes are old classics that have been around for more than a hundred years, and undoubtedly will take you back in time. Others are contemporary or bohemian joints with sidewalk tables – perfect spots to take a load off while sightseeing or to delve into Borges' short stories at a corner table.

Most cafes serve all meals and everything in between (including a late-night snack). For more on the classic places see p64.

Clubbing

Buenos Aires is famous for its *boliches* (nightclubs). Every weekend – and even on some weeknights – the city's clubs come alive with beautiful people moving to electronic and house music. Some of the most impressive nightlife hot spots are located in grandiose restored theaters, warehouses or factories – or perched on the banks of the Rio de la Plata where party-goers can watch the sun rise over the water as the festivities wind down. Clubs are spread out over the city, with main clusters in Palermo and on the Costanera Norte.

Electronica in Buenos Aires

Buenos Aires might be known for its tango, but there is something else to keep you dancing until dawn in this late-night city that generally looks to Europe for its trends. Since 1990 the electronic-music scene of BA has grown to become a major force in the music world. Touting some of the world's best venues and biggest crowds, Buenos Aires is listed by many DJs as a favorite place to play.

One of the most internationally acclaimed homegrown DJs is Hernán Cattaneo, who began his professional career in the early '90s playing commercial clubs of the time, such as El Cielo and Cinema. Several years later he secured a residency for the Clubland night at Pachá, where legend has it he was discovered and whisked off to international stardom by UK legend Paul Oakenfold. The success of Cattaneo and Pachá marked the beginning of a new era,

---

NEED TO KNOW

Opening Hours

➡ **Bars** Vary widely depending on location and clientele, but most are usually open in the evening into the early-morning hours.

➡ **Cafes** Usually from around 6am or 7am to 2am or 3am.

➡ **Clubs** From 2am to dawn.

Costs

'After office' is often a term for happy hour.

➡ *Chopp* (draft beer): AR$25

➡ Pint of craft beer: AR$40

➡ Cocktail: AR$60

➡ Cup of coffee: AR$15

➡ Club cover charge: varies widely depending on the club, your gender, the day of the week, the time of night and the DJ's fame. Bring cash, as credit cards aren't often accepted.

Club Door Policies

All clubs have bouncers. Dress well – smart casual is good enough at most clubs. To get in more easily, try playing up your foreign accent – *porteños* love the exotic (though foreigners are now common in BA). You can also sign up in advance via online-reservation forms that some clubs keep; this sometimes gets you in more easily and/or offers discounts.

Resources

Many newspapers have entertainment supplements published on Friday; the *Buenos Aires Herald* (an English-language publication) is particularly handy. Also check www.vuenosairez.com (in Spanish) and www.argentinaindependent.com (in English) for current happenings.

---

when electronica emerged into mainstream pop culture.

Nowadays, when the weather warms up in spring, enormous events with up to 50,000 people take place, such as **Creamfields** (www.creamfieldsba.com) and the **South American Music Conference**, while newer, smaller-scale festivals like **Festival Ciudad Emergente** (www.ciudademergente.gob.ar) pack venues with thousands of young people and feature electronica performances. In addition to these annual events, the club and underground scene is alive and well, although somewhat less kicking (and with good reason) due to stricter rules since the 2004 Cromagnon club tragedy in which almost 200 people lost their lives in a fire.

House music (referred to as '*punchi, punchi*' because of the relentless kick drum) is no longer the only option. You'll find a variety of sounds thanks to early diversification within Argentina's veteran underground DJ collective, DJ UNION, composed of **Carla Tintore** (www.carlatintore. com), **Dr Trincado** (www.drtrincado.com) and Diego Ro-k. Notoriously wild parties such as the Age of Communication and Ave Porco helped pave the way to a diverse underground tradition, which you can experience at clubs like Cocoliche (p68).

The original DJ collectives and electronica parties have paved the way for another generation of musical stylings: whether it's progressive house, breakbeat, techno, IDM, deep house, drum and bass or even experimental *cumbia* (Colombian music), Buenos Aires has it. Some of the DJs who experiment with styles are DJ Joven (http://djoven.blogspot.com) and Djs Pareja (www.djspareja.com.ar), the famous electronica twosome who spin a fusion of retro acid house techno and pop at clubs and parties around town; DJ Daleduro and his partner DJ Gone, who form the duo Groovedealers and do two-step garage and

dubstep; Franco Cinelli, who plays minimal sounds and clicks; and Chancha Via Circuito, an experimental cumbia artist who got his start at Zizek (www.zzkrecords.com).

Drinking & Nightlife by Neighborhood

➡ **The Center** (p67) Irish pub knock-offs cater to the business crowd, though there are several good cafes and clubs.

➡ **Congreso & Tribunales** (p81) This neighborhood, the political center of BA, has a few interesting bars and cafes.

➡ **San Telmo** (p92) Gentrified San Telmo is host to many fancy modern spots mixing it up with a few old classics.

➡ **Retiro** (p106) A wide choice of drinking holes attract business people during the day and into the evening, and the traveler-expat crowd at night.

➡ **Recoleta** (p115) Across from the cemetery is a two-block strip of restaurants, cafes and bars with great patios.

➡ **Palermo** (p135) BA's hippest nightlife lives here, especially near Plaza Serrano. Las Cañitas, a sub-neighborhood, is also very lively.

➡ **South of Palermo** (p149) As Palermo becomes more expensive, these blue-collar neighborhoods are gentrifying and attracting their own attention.

Lonely Planet's Top Choices

Florería Atlántico (p112) Currently BA's hottest bar, and possibly its most oddly located.

Las Violetas (p149) Gorgeous, traditional cafe full of *porteños* sipping tea and nibbling house-made pastries.

Niceto Club (p137) Famous for Club 69, its Thursday-night show highlighting drag queens, strippers and breakdancers.

Antares (p136) Atmospheric chain restaurant-bar with good food and craft beer.

Museo Evita Restaurante (p134) Upscale restaurant-cafe with a patio that's perfect on a warm day.

Best Bars

Florería Atlántico (p112) 'Secret' basement bar located inside a flower shop!

Verne (p135) Fancy drinking hole with awesome cocktails and smoking patio.

Frank's Bar (p135) Elegant speakeasy with classic cocktails; enter via the telephone booth.

Magdalena's Party (p136) Casual corner bar serving American comfort food.

Milión (p112) Glamorous setting in a lovely mansion with an elegant garden.

Best Traditional Cafes

Las Violetas (p149) BA's most beautiful cafe, with stained-glass awnings and afternoon tea.

Café de los Angelitos (p81) Ironically named for the mobsters that used to hang out here.

Esquina Homero Manzi (p151) Traditional cafe off the tourist track, with a lovely atmosphere.

La Biela (p120) Best for its excellent people-watching front patio on a warm sunny day.

Café Tortoni (p67) Very historic, very scenic and very touristy – but a classic that can't be ignored.

Best Clubs

Niceto Club (p137) Best for its raucous, Thursday-night, over-the-top burlesque show.

Pachá (p137) The temple of electronica, with pretty people and international DJs.

Boutique (p93) Famous 'after-office' party on Wednesday eves, in a building designed by Eiffel.

Crobar (p137) Electronica, Latin beats and more at this perennially popular Palermo club.

Kika (p137) Draws Tuesday-night crowds with its well-known 'Hype' party.

Best Beer Bars

Antares (p136) Popular restaurant-bar serving tasty beers from Mar del Plata.

Buller Brewing Company (p121) Recoleta microbrewery with six kinds of beer.

Cervecería Cossab (p149) Dedicated beer bar that boasts over 50 beers.

Cruzat Beer House (p82) Has a nice patio to enjoy craft beer from all around Argentina.

Broeders Not actually a beer bar, Broeders is an excellent craft beer only available at **Fukuro Noodle Bar** (www.fukuronoodlebar.com) or NOLA (www.nolabuenosaires.com).

Best Museum Cafes

Museo Evita Restaurante (p134) Excellent patio cafe-restaurant with sophisticated cuisine.

Museo Nacional de Arte Decorativo (p130) Upscale French bistro with pleasant outdoor tables.

Fundación Proa (p101) Fancy cafe with awesome rooftop terrace offering La Boca views.

Malba (p128) Not cheap, but a nice atmosphere and good people-watching.

Museo del Bicentenario (p60) Great for an indoor cafe break near Plaza de Mayo.

Best Gay Hot Spots

Alsina (p67) Monthly Fiesta Dorothy packs in the cute guys.

Glam (p137) Casual yet very sexy club in an old mansion.

Crobar (p137) Saturday night's Rheo is the place to be.

Amerika (p150) Rough and tumble, with all-you-can-drink nights.

Pride Cafe (p93) Casual San Telmo coffee shop.

⭐ Entertainment

The entertainment scene in Buenos Aires has always been lively, but there was an outburst of creative energy in the decade following the economic crisis of 2001. Filmmakers began producing quality works on shoestring budgets, troupes performed in new avant-garde theaters and live-music groups played in more mainstream venues. Today nearly every neighborhood offers great entertainment options.

Live Music

There are some fine venues that only feature live music, but many theaters, cultural centers, bars and cafes also put on shows. **Centro Cultural Torquato Tasso** (Map p242; ✆4307-6506; www.torquatotasso.com.ar; Defensa 1575) is an especially good choice for tango-music performances. For more on tango shows see p39.

CLASSICAL

Several venues offer classical-music concerts. Teatro Colón (p82) is the grandest and most famous; everyone who's anyone has played, acted, sung or danced here. It often features guest conductors from throughout Latin America. The classical-music scene takes a break from December to February, and is best from June to August.

ROCK, BLUES & JAZZ

Buenos Aires boasts a thriving rock-music scene. Smaller venues, like La Trastienda (p95), showcase mostly local groups; when huge international stars come to town they tend to play soccer stadiums or Luna Park (p63).

Blues and jazz aren't as popular as rock but still have their own loyal following. Thelonious Bar (p138) and Notorious (p121) are top-notch venues for jazz concerts.

FOLK

Música folklórica definitely has its place in Buenos Aires. There are several *peñas* (traditional music clubs) in the city, including Los Cardones (p138) and Peña del Colorado (p138), but other venues – such as Clásica y Moderna (p121) – occasionally host folk performances.

Cinema

BA's traditional cinema districts are along pedestrian Lavalle (west of Florida) and on Av Corrientes. Newer cinemas are in shopping malls throughout the city. Most cinemas offer big discounts for matinees, midweek shows or first screenings of the day. There is usually a *trasnoche* (midnight or later showing) scheduled for Friday and Saturday night.

Check the English-language *Buenos Aires Herald* for the original titles of English-language films. The entertainment sections of all the major newspapers will have movie listings as well, but be aware that Spanish translations of English-language film titles often don't translate directly. Except for children's films and cartoon features, which are dubbed, foreign films usually appear in their original language with Spanish subtitles. **Cosmos-UBA** (Map p240; ✆4953-5405; www.cosmosuba.wordpress.com; Av Corrientes 2046) and **Sala Leopoldo Lugones** (Map p240; ✆0800-333-5254; www.teatrosanmartin.com.ar/cine; Av Corrientes 1530) – in Teatro General San Martín – often show retrospectives, documentaries, foreign film cycles and art-house movies. **Espacio INCAA** (Map p240; ✆4371-3050; www.incaa.gov.ar; Av Rivadavia 1635) screens Ibero-American films only (essentially from Spanish- or Portuguese-speaking countries).

Some cultural centers have their own small cinemas, while places such as Alianza Francesa and the British Arts Centre showcase movies in their respective languages.

Theater

Theater is big in Buenos Aires. There are more than 100 venues and annual attendance is in the hundreds of thousands. Productions range from classic plays to multimedia performances to lavish cabarets, and the acting is of a professional level across the board. Note that, unsurprisingly, performances tend to be in Spanish.

Traditionally, the center for theater has been Av Corrientes between Av 9 de Julio and Callao, but there are now dozens of venues all over the city. The *Buenos Aires Herald* and other local newspapers have good listings of major productions.

Many alternative (or 'off-Corrientes') theater companies and independent troupes receive relatively little attention from the mainstream media, but they're worth seeking out if you're looking for something different. If you read Spanish, www.alternativateatral.com is a good source for current non-mainstream performances.

Tickets are generally affordable, but check *carteleras* for bargain seats. The season is liveliest in winter (June through August), when upwards of 100 events may take place, but you can find a good variety of shows any time. Many of the most popular shows move to the provincial beach resort of Mar del Plata for the summer.

Circo Moderno

A popular movement in Argentina that found international fame through the Broadway performance of the De la Guarda troupe is *circo moderno* (contemporary circus). This combination of traditional circus and contemporary dance and theater features a lot of aerial action, acrobatics and no words – great for those who don't speak Spanish. Cirque du Soleil is a well-known example of this modern gymnastic theater.

In 2005, Diqui James, one of the creators of De la Guarda, launched his solo act **Fuerzabruta** (www.fuerzabruta.net). It's a jaw-dropping, mind-blowing show of lights, electronic music, aerial dancing and water – and often the performance is above you. If you go to a show, you could get wet. The troupe is often on tour around the world, so check its website for listings.

NEED TO KNOW

Opening Hours

Show times can vary widely, but this is a city that stays up all night, so expect to be out late. Restaurants usually open around 9pm – and 10pm is a more common dinner time – so many shows start around midnight.

Resources

Many newspapers publish entertainment supplements on Friday; the *Buenos Aires Herald* has a particularly handy one. Also check www.vuenosairez.com (in Spanish) and www.argentinaindependent.com (in English).

Discount Tickets & Booking

Major entertainment venues often require booking through **Ticketek** (📞5237-7200; www.ticketek.com.ar). The service charge is about 10% of the ticket price.

Carteleras (discount-ticket offices) sell a limited number of discounted tickets for many events, such as movies, theater and tango shows, with savings of 20% to 50%. Try **Cartelera Baires** (Map p240; www.carterlerabaires.com; Av Corrientes 1382, Inside Galería Apolo), **Cartelera Vea Más** (📞6320-5319; www.veamasdigital.com.ar; Av Corrientes 1660, Local 2) or **Cartelera Espectáculos** (📞4322-1559; www.123info. com.ar; Lavalle 742). Buy tickets as far in advance as possible, but if you want to see a show or movie at short notice – especially midweek – you can also drop by to check what's available.

Entertainment by Neighborhood

➡ **The Center** (p68) Has a little of everything – theater, live music, cinemas and tango shows.

➡ **Congreso & Tribunales** (p82) Home to Av Corrientes, BA's traditional theater district; also has several cinemas and flamenco venues.

➡ **San Telmo** (p93) Some live music and tango spots.

➡ **Palermo** (p138) A few tango *milongas* and live-music venues.

➡ **South of Palermo** (p150) Ground zero for BA's avant-garde theater.

Lonely Planet's Top Choices

Teatro Colón (p78) Landmark, seven-story theater seating 2500 and boasting renowned acoustics.

Usina del Arte (p103) Old electricity factory remodeled into a premier symphony hall.

Centro Cultural Borges (p61) One of BA's top cultural centers, with countless offerings.

Best Theaters

Teatro Colón (p82) Buenos Aires' grandest entertainment concert hall and a gorgeous building.

Teatro San Martín (p82) Large venue that's great for classic theater and much more.

Teatro Nacional Cervantes (p110) Traditional old venue showing contemporary productions.

Best Live Music

Usina del Arte (p103) Amazing and beautiful new performance venue in La Boca seating 1200.

Ciudad Cultural Konex (p150) Famous for its one-of-a-kind, Monday-night percussion parties.

Centro Cultural Torquato Tasso (p36) Excellent venue for concerts, including tango music.

Best Cultural Centers

Centro Cultural Borges (p61) Quality art galleries, cinema, workshops, music and shows.

Centro Cultural Recoleta (p118) Many free or inexpensive events, plus a science museum for kids.

Centro Cultural San Martín (p80) Large cultural center with galleries, concerts, exhibitions and shows.

Best Flamenco

Ávila Bar (p83) Small stage inside a traditional Spanish restaurant.

Cantares (p83) Basement venue that once hosted the poet Federico García Lorca.

Tiempo de Gitanos (p138) Palermo restaurant offering classic Spanish food and an intimate stage.

Tango dancers

 # Tango

Once a furtive dance relegated to the red-light brothels of early-1900s Buenos Aires, tango has experienced great highs and lows throughout its volatile lifespan. These days, however, the sensual dance is back with a vengeance. Everyone from Seattle to Shanghai is slinking their way down the parquet floor, trying to master those elusive dance steps and rhythm that make it so damn hard to perfect.

NEED TO KNOW

➡ For discount tickets, show and venue descriptions and some reviews, check out www.tangotix.com.

➡ *Milongas* either start in the afternoon and run until 11pm or start at around midnight and run until the early-morning light (arrive late for the best action). They're affordable, and classes are often offered beforehand.

➡ For a unique outdoor experience, head to the bandstand at the Barrancas de Belgrano, where the casual *milonga* **La Glorieta** (www.glorietadebelgrano.com. ar) takes place on Saturday and Sunday evenings around 7pm (and possibly other evenings). Tango classes are also given.

Tango lesson

Origins

In the words of its poet laureate Discépolo, the 'tango is a sad thought you can dance to'. Though the exact origins can't be pinpointed, the dance is thought to have started in Buenos Aires in the 1880s. Legions of European immigrants, mostly lower-class men, arrived here to seek their fortune. They settled on the capital's fringes, such as La Boca and Barracas, but missing their motherlands and the women they left behind, sought out cafes and bordellos to ease the loneliness. Here (so the myth goes), these immigrant men danced with each other while they waited for their paramours to become available – women were scarce back then!

The perceived vulgarity of the dance that mainly belonged to the poor southern barrios was deeply frowned upon by the reigning porteño elites of the plush northern suburbs, but it did manage to influence some brash young members of the upper classes. These rebel jet setters, known as *niños bien*, took the novelty to Paris and created a craze – a dance that became an acceptable outlet for human desires, expressed on the dance floors of elegant cabarets. The trend spread around Europe and even to the USA, and 1913 was considered by some as 'the year of the tango'. When the evolved dance, now refined and famous, returned to Buenos Aires, it finally earned the respectability it deserved. And so the golden years of tango began.

In 1955, however, Argentina became a military state intolerant of artistic or 'nationalistic' activities – including the tango, which had been highly popular with the people. Some tango songs were banned, and the dance was forced underground due to curfews and a limit on group meetings. The dance didn't resurface until 1983, when the junta fell – and once it was back in the open again, it underwent a renaissance. After being constrained by the rigors of military rule, Argentines suddenly wanted to experience new life, be creative and move. The tango became popular once again – and remains so to this day.

Tango for Export – the Shows

If there's one thing Buenos Aires isn't short of it's tango shows. The best known are the expensive, tourist-oriented spectacles that are very entertaining and awe-inspiring, and showcase amazing feats of grace and athleticism. However, they are highly glamorized and not what purists consider 'authentic' tango.

The theatrical shows usually include various tango couples, an orchestra, a couple of singers and possibly some folkloric musicians. They last about 1½ hours and come with a dinner option – the food is usually good. VIP options mean a much higher price tag for better views, meal choices and refreshments. Nearly all of them require reservations; some offer modest online discounts and pick-up from your hotel. (Many hotels will book shows for you – which is fine, since sometimes the price is similar to what you'd pay at the venue anyway.)

Above: Dancing the tango, San Telmo
Right: Playing the *bandoneón*

More modest shows cost far less; some are even free but require you to order a meal or drink at the restaurant. For free (or rather, donation) tango, head to San Telmo on a Sunday afternoon – or sometimes other days. Dancers do their thing in the middle of Plaza Dorrego, though you have to stake out a spot early to snag a good view. Another sure bet is weekends on El Caminito in La Boca; some restaurants have couple dancing for customers. Many *milongas* also have good, affordable shows.

One thing to note: nearly all tango shows are touristy by nature. They've been sensationalized to make them more exciting for observers. 'Authentic' tango (which happens at *milongas*) is a very subtle art, primarily done for the pleasure of the dancers. It's not something to be observed so much as experienced, and not particularly interesting for casual spectators. Going to a *milonga* just to watch isn't all that cool, either: folks are there to dance. So feel free to see a more flashy tango show and enjoy those spectacular high kicks – be wowed like the rest of the crowd.

If you like listening to live tango music, head to Centro Cultural Torquato Tasso (p36). It's one of BA's best live-music venues, so don't expect any dancing.

The Real Tango – Milongas

Tango's popularity is booming at both amateur and professional levels, and among all ages and classes. And *milongas* are the dance events where people strut their stuff. The atmosphere at these venues can be modern or historical, casual or traditional. Most have tango DJs that determine musical selections, but a few utilize live orchestras. The dance floor is surrounded by many tables and chairs, and there's often a bar to the side.

At a proper, established *milonga,* choosing an adequate partner involves many levels of hidden codes, rules and signals that dancers must follow. After all, no serious *bailarina* (female dancer; the male equivalent is a *bailarín*) wants to be caught out dancing with someone stepping on her toes (and expensive tango heels). In fact, some men considering asking an unknown woman to dance will do so only after the second song, to avoid being stuck for the three to five songs that make a session. These sessions (known as *tandas*) alternate between tango, *vals* (the Argentine version of the waltz) and *milonga*; they're followed by a *cortina* (a short break when non-tango music is played). It's considered polite to dance an entire *tanda* with any partner, so if you are given a curt *gracias* after just one song, consider that partner unavailable for the rest of the night.

Not easy to describe, tango needs to be seen and experienced for its full effect. The upper bodies are traditionally held upright and close, with faces almost touching. The man's hand is pressed against the woman's back, guiding her, with his other hand and one of hers held together and out. The lower body does most of the work. The woman swivels her hips, her legs alternating in short or wide sweeps and quick kicks, sometimes between the man's legs. The man guides, a complicated job since he must flow with the music, direct the woman, meld with her steps and avoid other dancers, all at once. He'll add his own fancy pivoting moves, and together the couple flows in communion with the music. Pauses and abrupt directional changes punctuate the dance. It's a serious business that takes a good amount of concentration, so while dancing the pair often wear hard expressions. Smiling and chatting are reserved for the breaks between songs.

Your position in the area surrounding the dance floor can be critical. At some of the older *milongas*, the more established dancers have reserved tables. Ideally, you

---

CLASSES

Tango classes are available just about everywhere, from youth hostels to general dance academies to cultural centers to nearly all *milongas*. Even a few cafes and tango shows offer them.

There are also several tango schools in town, such as **Escuela Argentina de Tango.** It has two main locations: **Talcahuano 1052** (Map p246) and **San Martín 768** (Map p236; ☎4312-4990; www.eatango.org); the latter is in Galerías Pacífico.

Private teachers are also ubiquitous; there are so many good ones that it's best to ask someone you trust for a recommendation. And with so many foreigners flooding into Buenos Aires, many teach in English or other languages.

want to sit where you have easy access to the floor and to other dancers' line of sight. You may notice couples sitting further back (they often dance just with each other), while singles sit right at the front. If a man comes into the room with a woman at his side, she is considered 'his' for the night. For couples to dance with others, they either enter the room separately, or the man signals his intent by asking another woman to the floor. Then 'his' woman becomes open for asking.

The signal to dance, known as *cabeceo,* involves a quick tilt of the head, eye contact and uplifted eyebrows. This can happen from way across the room. The woman to whom the *cabeceo* is directed either nods yes and smiles or pretends not to have noticed (a rejection). If she says yes the man gets up and escorts her to the floor. A hint: if you're at a *milonga* and don't want to dance with anyone, don't look around too much – you could be breaking some hearts.

So why is it that tango becomes so addictive for some? Experienced dancers will tell you this: the adrenaline rush you get from an excellent performance is like a successful conquest. Some days it lifts you up to exhilarating heights and other days it can bring you crashing down. You fall for the passion and beauty of the tango's movements, trying to attain a physical perfection that can never be fully realized. The best you can do is to make the journey as graceful and passionate as possible.

More Tango Info

Some of the most complete tango listings are in free tango booklets around town, including **El Tanguata** (www.eltanguata.com) and **La Milonga Argentina** (www.lamilonga argentina.com.ar). All have basic information on the city's *milongas,* classes, teachers and shows. They're often available at tango venues or tourist offices. You can also check the **Caseron Porteño** (www.caseronporteno. com) tango map for *milongas* locations.

For a very practical book on tango in BA, check out Sally Blake's *Happy Tango: Sallycat's Guide to Dancing in Buenos Aires* (2nd edition). It has great information on *milongas* – how to dress for them and act in them and who you can expect to see – plus much more.

If you don't mind hiring a dance partner for classes or *milongas,* check out www. tangotaxidancers.com. There are, of course,

EVOLVING TANGO MUSIC

Nuevo tango, born in the late 1990s, was seeded by Ástor Piazzolla in the 1950s when he incorporated jazz and classical beats into traditional tango music. Dancers improvised new moves into their traditional base steps, utilizing a more open embrace and switching leads (among other things). Neo tango, the latest musical step in tango's changing landscape, fuses the dance with electronica for some decidedly nonstodgy beats that have done a superlative job of attracting the younger generation to this astounding dance. For much more on tango music, see p188.

many tango clothing and shoe stores in BA. Several accommodations cater to tango enthusiasts, including Caserón Porteño (p172). All offer on-site classes. Finally, if you're in town in mid- to late August, don't miss the **tango festival** (www.tangobuenosaires.gov.ar).

DANITA DELIMONT / GETTY IMAGES ©

Painting of Carlos Gardel (p189) near Museo Casa Carlos Gardel

Lonely Planet's Top Choices

Café de los Angelitos (p82) Well-put-together, imaginative show with great visual appeal.

Feria de San Telmo (p95) Best for its casual ambience and price – a few coins!

Salon Canning (p138) Traditional, very popular and well-located *milonga*.

Best Fancy Shows

Café de los Angelitos (p82) Well choreographed, with impressive costumes and props.

Rojo Tango (p75) Very intimate, cabaret-style show that's supremely sexy.

El Viejo Almacén (p93) Great athleticism, small venue and great folkloric segment.

La Ventana (p95) Good overall show with comedic gaucho swinging *boleadoras* (hunting weights).

Best Less-Fancy Shows

Feria de San Telmo (p95) It's street-donation tango at San Telmo's Sunday market – hustle for a good view!

Café Tortoni (p68) Decent basement show in BA's oldest, most traditional cafe.

Los 36 Billares (p82) Another very historic cafe with tango show, but much less touristy than Tortoni.

Best Milongas

Salon Canning (p138) Famous, popular and stylish *milonga* in Palermo, with good music.

Confitería Ideal (p68) BA's most historic tango venue and the set for Sally Potter's *The Tango Lesson*.

La Catedral (p150) Casual, bohemian warehouse space that attracts hip young dancers.

La Marshall (p32) Gay-friendly *milonga* where everyone is welcome – and where role reversals are OK.

Shopping

Despite a global recession and a drop in the purchasing power of the Argentine peso, porteños *continue to shop as if there's no tomorrow. A peek into the nearest mall on a weekend will make you wonder how people who seem to be making so little can spend so much. As the saying goes, 'An Argentine will make one peso and spend two'.*

Specialties & Souvenirs

Wine is one of the more obvious gifts, though it's hard to carry. Some stores will ship outside Argentina; expect to pay a premium for this service. Food items that make nice gifts are *dulce de leche* (a delicious milk caramel that Argentines have perfected) and *alfajores,* cookie sandwiches usually bathed in chocolate (Havanna is a popular brand and available at Ezeiza Airport). *Mate* gourds are also good, and they're small and light.

Argentina is known for its leather goods. There are leather stores all over the city, but for the best prices head to Calle Murillo. Silverwork is also high quality, and many items are gaucho-inspired. Looking for a gift for that aristocratic friend? There are a few polo stores with items that might fit the bill – whether or not he or she plays polo.

Finally, soccer memorabilia always make popular souvenirs – especially from Boca, the most well-known team.

Street Markets

Wandering through a weekend *feria* (street market) is a quintessential BA experience. Artisans display their wares while buskers, mimes and tango dancers entertain. Often there are nearby restaurants with sidewalk tables for people-watching. At some of the more touristed markets, especially Feria de San Telmo, watch for pickpockets.

➡ Feria Plaza Francia (p123)
➡ Feria de Mataderos (p149)
➡ Feria de San Telmo (p95)
➡ Feria Plaza Serrano (p138)

Antique Markets & Shopping Malls

A couple of antique markets might be worth your time. Try Mercado de las Pulgas (p143) or Mercado de San Telmo (p96). Don't expect dirt-cheap bargains, though you might find a cool glass soda bottle or vintage lamp. Feria de San Telmo is a fun place to look for old coins and jewelry, though there's a lot of kitsch as well. The San Telmo neighborhood has some pricey antique stores too.

Many of the bigger shopping malls in BA are slick and modern; some cater to families with children by offering special play areas and video arcades. Paseo Alcorta (p142) has an especially large kids' playground on the 3rd floor, while Mercado de Abasto (p148) sports an excellent children's museum and small amusement park complete with rides. Almost all of these malls also have multiplex cinemas and large food courts complete with fast-food outlets and ice-cream parlors. Expect all the popular chain stores; some even offer health clubs, beauty shops and internet cafes.

High Fashion

Interested in clothing design? Then make a beeline for Palermo Soho (p141), where avant-garde fashion designers' boutiques grace the pretty tree-shaded streets. After the 2001 economic crash, dozens of young designers emerged from the woodwork to set up shop

NEED TO KNOW

Opening Hours

Store hours generally run from 9am or 10am to 8pm or 9pm weekdays, with many open for a few hours on Saturday. Most stores close on Sunday.

Taxes & Refunds

Taxes are included in prices; what you see is what you pay.

If you buy more than AR$70 in merchandise from a store that displays a 'Tax Free Shopping' sticker, you're entitled to a tax refund. Just ask the merchant to make out an invoice for you (you'll need ID); upon leaving the country show the paperwork to a customs official, who'll stamp it and tell you where to obtain your refund. Give yourself some extra time at the airport for this transaction.

Bargaining

Bargaining is not acceptable in stores, except possibly for high-price items like jewelry and leather jackets (in some places). Some shops will give a *descuento* (discount) for cash payments. At street markets you can try negotiating, but keep in mind you may be talking to the artists themselves.

Be clear about whether the vendor is quoting in pesos or dollars. Always check your change before walking away with your purchase, and keep a lookout for fake bills (p212).

in this then-affordable neighborhood (rents have gone way up since then, driving some out). Some made it big, maturing into fully fledged designers with luxury sportswear lines and outposts in the US, Europe and Asia. Names you may come across include Maria Cher (known for deconstructed garments with an urban twist), Jazmín Chebar (with playful, feminine designs) and Martín

Churba (known for recycling fabrics). Cora Groppo and Jessica Trosman are other big names with chain stores in Buenos Aires malls and elsewhere.

If you're looking for leather bargains, avoid Calle Florida and head to the shops on Calle Murillo's 600 block, in the neighborhood of Villa Crespo. This is the best place in town to snag a relatively cheap but high-quality leather jacket and accessories. Bargain like mad, especially if you're paying in cash. One of the nicer (and pricier) shops is Murillo 666.

For outlet shopping there's the 800 block of Calle Aguirre, with deals on shoes and clothes. Ladies, check out the Prüne outlet for stylish leather bags. There are also lots of other outlets on nearby Av Córdoba.

The largest concentration of jewelry shops is on Libertad south of Av Corrientes.

Shopping by Neighborhood

⇒ **The Center** (p68) The area on and around Calle Florida offers modern shops selling pretty much everything.

⇒ **Congreso & Tribunales** (p83) Not known for its shopping, though there are discount bookstores along Av Corrientes.

⇒ **San Telmo** (p95) *The* place for antique stores, with clothing and other boutiques here and there.

⇒ **Retiro** (p113) Bustling Av Santa Fe starts here and heads through Palermo, lined the whole way with shops of every kind.

⇒ **Recoleta & Barrio Norte** (p123) Upscale stores selling the city's most expensive threads and leather products live on Av Alvear.

⇒ **Palermo** (p138) Best known for its locally designed clothing stores, with plenty of housewares shops and boutiques.

⇒ **South of Palermo** (p148) Av Pueyrredón near Once train station has cheap goods made in countries like China.

Lonely Planet's Top Choices

Walrus Books (p96) A terrific range of new and used books, plus Argentine classics translated into English.

Zival's (p83) Music store with a great selection of tango, jazz and classical.

Wildlife (p83) Meets all your outdoor-gear needs.

Lo de Joaquin Alberdi (p140) A wine-lover's paradise; offers tastings too.

Gil Antiguedades (p96) Gorgeous vintage clothes are the star here, though there are *objets* too.

Autoría (p113) Ingenious, edgy, high-quality art and accessories, with an emphasis on Argentine designers' work.

Best for Clothing

Rapsodia (p138) At times exotic clothing utilizing various genres and different textiles.

Juana de Arco (p140) Frilly, silky, cute, sexy and very feminine items for the girl inside every woman.

Hermanos Estebecorena (p140) Cutting-edge, creative and stylish clothes for men.

Bolivia (p138) Metrosexual designs for men who aren't afraid of patterns and pastels.

Punto Sur (p96) Dozens of designers stock the racks here with awesome, creative clothing.

Best for Wacky Gifts

Materia Urbana (p95) Funky things like leather animal desk accessories and wood jewelry.

Autoría (p113) Creative, high-quality and well-priced contemporary items made by local designers.

Cualquier Verdura (p96) Expect the unexpected at this fun shop with eclectic and novelty gifts.

L'Ago (p96) Kitschy home decor like colorful metal *mate* sets,

paper lamps and vintage-look pillows.

Calma Chicha (p140) Cow- and sheepskin rugs, fun tablecloths, leather bags and more.

Best for Argentine Souvenirs

Feria de San Telmo (p95) Everything-goes, multi-block street fair selling anything you can think of.

Arte y Esperanza (p70) Fair-trade Argentine souvenirs handmade by Argentina's indigenous peoples.

Feria Plaza Serrano (p138) Fun hippie products created by local craftspeople.

Harapos Patagonia (p140) Woollen goods, alpaca jewelry, wood and ceramics from Patagonia.

Nobrand (p140) T-shirts, mugs and notebooks stamped with iconic Argentine symbols.

Sports & Activities

When it comes to spectator sports, only one thing really matters to most porteños – *fútbol (soccer). If you go to a game – or even watch one on TV – you'll witness human passion to the core. But other spectator sports also exist in Buenos Aires. And for those who'd rather play than watch, you'll have opportunities to run, bike, swim and even rock climb – though some activities will be harder to seek out than others.*

Spectator Sports

FÚTBOL

Fútbol is a national obsession, and witnessing a live game is an integral part of the BA experience. This is no amateur league – Argentina's national team won the World Cup in both 1978 and 1986 (one of only eight nations to have ever won the cup). The men's team also walked away with gold at the 2004 and 2008 summer Olympics. And Lionel Messi (p102), currently Argentina's most famous player, has won FIFA's World Player of the Year (or Ballon d'Or) award *four* times – from 2009 to 2012.

Argentines are avid fans of the sport, and on game day (and there are many) you'll see TVs everywhere tuned to the soccer channels. Cheers erupt when goals are scored, and after a big win, cars sporting team flags go honking by – especially around the Obelisco.

For more information on Argentine *fútbol*, see www.futbolargentino.com and www.afa.org.ar. Or check Daniel Schweimler's musings (via the team Argentina Juniors) at www.handofdan.com.

GOING TO A GAME

In a land where Maradona (p102) is God, going to see a *fútbol* game can be a religious experience. The *superclásico* match between the Boca Juniors and River Plate has been called the number-one sporting event to see before you die, but even the less-celebrated games will give you insight into Argentina's national passion.

Attending a regular match isn't too difficult. Keep an eye on the clubs' websites, which inform when and where tickets will be sold; often they're sold at the stadium before the game. You'll get a choice between *populares* (bleachers) and *plateas* (seats). Avoid the *populares*, as these can get far too rowdy and sometimes dangerous.

If you want to see a *clásico* – a match between two major teams – getting a ticket will be much harder. Plus Boca doesn't even put tickets for its key matches on sale; all tickets go to *socios* (members). Instead, you're better off going with an agency such as Tangol (p207) or via organizations like www.fcbafa.com or www.landingpad.com. It won't be cheap, but it's much easier (and safer) getting a ticket this way; fake tickets do exist.

DON'T JUST WATCH – PLAY FÚTBOL!

Inspired by watching professional *fútbol* teams play the game? Well, you can partake yourself – just contact FC **Buenos Aires Fútbol Amigos** (www.fcbafa.com) to join fellow travelers, expats and locals for fun on the pitch. There's a modest charge for the experience, but *asados* (barbecues) often lie at the end of the *fútbol* rainbow – and the sporty memories can be priceless.

If you want to chance getting your own *clásico* or *superclásico* ticket, however, you can always look online at www.buenosaires.craigslist.org or www.mercadolibre.com.ar. And if you're confident in your bargaining skills, scalpers will always exist.

Dress down, and try to look inconspicuous when you go. Take only minimum cash and keep your camera close. You probably won't get in with water bottles, and food and drink in the stadium is meager and expensive. Arrive early to get a good seat and enjoy the insane build-up to the game. And most importantly: don't wear the opposing team's colors.

The following are some of the clubs based in Buenos Aires:

➡ **Estadio Argentinos Juniors** (☎4551-6887; www.argentinosjuniors.com.ar; Gavilán 2151)

➡ **Boca Juniors** Map (p244; ☎4309-4700; www.bocajuniors.com.ar; Brandsen 805) A popular club in Buenos Aires.

➡ **Club Atlético Vélez Sársfield** (☎4641-5663; www.velezsarsfield.com.ar; Juan B Justo 9200)

➡ **Club Deportivo Españo** (☎4619-1516; www.cde.com.ar; Santiago de Compostela 3801)

➡ **Club Ferro Carril Oeste** (☎4431-8282; www.ferrocarriloeste.org.ar; Federico G Lorca 350)

➡ **Club Huracán** (☎4911-0757; www.clubahuracan.com.ar; Av Caseros 3159)

➡ **River Plate** (☎4789-1200; www.cariverplate.com; Alcorta 7597)

➡ **San Lorenzo de Almagro** (☎4918-4237; www.sanlorenzo.com.ar; Varela 2680)

BASKETBALL

The basketball scene in Buenos Aires has been picking up significantly since 2002, when Argentina's men's team played in the World Basketball Championship in Indianapolis. They only won silver but made history by beating the US 'Dream Team' in international competition. Then, with a similar roster, they defeated the US squad again (along with Italy in the finals) to win gold in the 2004 summer Olympics – their first Olympic medal in basketball ever. No team had beaten the Americans in the Olympics since 1992, when pro basketball players were allowed to play. They also won the FIBA Americas Championship in 2011.

NEED TO KNOW

➡ **Bike rentals** are available at Palermo's Parque 3 de Febrero (where you can also rent inline skates, quadricycles and pedal boats), Reserva Ecológica Costanera Sur and via some bike-tour companies (p207).

➡ Speaking of bikes, **Masa Critica** (Critical Mass; a semi-organized bike ride for thousands) is alive and well here – and a heap of fun to partake in (p204).

➡ In November, Buenos Aires' **Marathon** (www.maratondebuenosaires.org) is the southern hemisphere's biggest, attracting nearly 27,000 runners annually.

➡ Feel the need for **yoga**? There are many places that offer it, including some with instructors that speak English. Try **Buena Onda Yoga** (www.buenaondayoga.com), started by expats; it offers classes in Palermo and San Telmo.

➡ Rock climbers should head to **Punto Cumbre** (www.puntocumbre.com), a small climbing wall located inside a Megatlon gym. You'll be provided with belays if you need them. There's a small bouldering cave, too, along with classes and excursions.

Argentina's best players include Emanuel 'Manu' Ginobili, Fabricio Oberto, Andrés Nocioni, Luis Scola, Pablo Prigioni, Walter Herrmann and Carlos Delfino, all of whom have played for or currently play in the NBA.

Today BA has several major squads, the most popular being Boca Juniors. You can watch them play in La Boca at **Estadio Luis Conde** (La Bombonerita; Map p244; www.bocabasket.com.ar; Arzobispo Espinosa 600). Other popular basketball teams include Obras Sanitarias and Ferro Carril Oeste.

RUGBY

Rugby is getting more popular by the year in Argentina, in part because the country's national team – Los Pumas – has done well in past years. After placing third at the Rugby World Cup in 2007 (no mean feat), Los Pumas was rated the best rugby team in the Americas. And at the 2011 Rugby World Cup it put in a pretty decent showing.

In Buenos Aires, the long-running **Club Atlético de San Isidro** (www.casi.org.ar) is the capital's best rugby team; in 1935 it gave birth to its own biggest rival, the **San Isidro Club** (www.sanisidroclub.com.ar).

Rugby season runs from April to October; contact the **Unión de Rugby de Buenos Aires** (www.urba.org.ar) for current happenings. Fanatics can visit the **Museo de Rugby** (☑4732-2547; www.museodelrugby.com; Juan Bautista de Lasalle 653) in San Isidro.

HORSE RACING

Races in BA are held at the Hipódromo Argentino, a grand building designed by French architect Louis Fauré-Dujarric that dates from 1908 and holds up to 100,000 spectators. Race times vary, so check the schedule for details. The most important races take place in November, both here and at San Isidro's famous grass racetrack.

POLO

Add Argentina's history of gauchos and horses to its past British influence, and you'll understand why the best polo in the world is played right here. The country has dominated the sport for over 70 years, boasting most of polo's top players. Forget those British princes: the world's best player is considered to be the handsome Adolfo Cambiaso.

Matches take place in Buenos Aires from September to mid-November. They culminate in the annual Campeonato Argentino Abierto de Polo (Argentine Open Polo Championship) – the world's most prestigious polo tournament – in Palermo's Campo Argentina de Polo. For current information, contact the **Asociación Argentina de Polo** (Map p236; ☑4777-6444; www.aapolo.com), which keeps a schedule of polo-related activities throughout the country.

For polo camps (all outside BA) where you can learn to play yourself, check out www.argentinapoloday.com.ar, www.poloelite.com and www.lasofiapolo.info.

PATO

Of gaucho origins, the polo-like game of *pato* (literally 'duck') takes its name from the original game ball – a live duck encased in a leather bag. The unfortunate fowl has since been replaced by a ball with leather handles, and players no longer face serious injury in what was once a very violent sport.

For information on *pato* matches and tournaments (which usually take place 30km outside the city in the Campo Argentino de Pato), contact the **Federación Argentina de Pato** (Map p242; ☑4342-5271; www.pato.org.ar). The national championships occur in December, and are more centrally located in Palermo's polo grounds.

Activities

Buenos Aires is a big concrete city, so you'll have to seek out the outdoor spots in which to work out. Extensive greenery in Palermo provides good areas for recreation, especially on weekends when the ring road around the rose garden is closed to motor vehicles. Recoleta also has grassy parks, but not as extensive. Best of all is the Reserva Ecológica Costanera Sur (p73), an ecological paradise just east of Puerto Madero that might just make you forget you're in a big city; it's excellent for walks, runs, leisurely bike rides and even a bit of wildlife viewing.

CYCLING

The city's new bike lanes are making cycling in the center a safer proposition, but there are better places in which to spin your wheels. Bike paths run along many roads in Parque 3 de Febrero (p129) – here, bicycle rentals are available in good weather on weekends, when the ring road is closed to motor vehicles. Look for rental companies along Av de la Infanta Isabel; four-wheeled pedal carts and inline skates can also be rented.

For safe family cycling, head to Nuevo Circuito KDT in Palermo's Parque General

---

PERÚ BEACH

An interesting sports complex for those seeking outdoor activities is **Perú Beach** (☑4793-5986; www.peru-beach.com.ar; Elcano 794; ☺8am-midnight). Short soccer fields, a covered roller rink, a freestanding climbing wall and water sports such as kayaking all bring in the crowds. In addition there's also a grassy lawn and outdoor tables for refreshments – great on a sunny day. It's more of a social scene than anything else, and families are welcome. Perú Beach is located in Acassuso, a suburb way north of Buenos Aires' center, just across from the Tren de la Costa's Barrancas station.

PARQUE NORTE

When the temperatures and humidity skyrocket, head north to this large water park. Parque Norte (p23) is great for families, with huge shallow pools (perhaps 4ft at their deepest), plus a large water slide and lots of umbrellas and lounge chairs (both cost extra). There are plenty of grassy areas in which to enjoy a picnic or *mate*. Bring your own towels.

Belgrano. Here, **Sprint Haupt** (☑4804-2870; www.sprinthaupt.com.ar; Salguero 3450; ☺9am-8:30pm Tue & Thu, to 7pm Wed, Fri, Sat & Sun) rents bicycles for use around a plain, 1250m-long concrete bike path (bring your passport). Helmets available. Look for the overpass parking lot, then go past the pedestrian bridge.

The Reserva Ecológica Costanera Sur on the eastern side of Puerto Madero along the coast, is green and tranquil and has some flat dirt roads that are great to bike on. Cheap bicycle rentals are available in good weather on weekends, just outside either entrance.

GOLF

BA's most convenient course is the 18-hole **Campo Municipal de Golf** (☑4772-7261; Tornquist 6397; ☺7:30am-5pm Tue-Sun); be sure to reserve your spot in advance. Practice your long shots at the **Costa Salguero Driving Range** (☑4805-4732; www.costasalguerogolf.com.ar; Avs Costanera R Obligado & Salguero), which also has a golf store, a cafe and a nine-hole, family-friendly course.

SWIMMING

Some upscale hotels have decent-size pools, but they charge hefty prices for nonguests (so hefty you might as well stay there). The fee generally includes gym use, at least. Try the **Panamericano Hotel** (www.panamericano.us), whose pool has the best view in BA.

A more economical option is to find a health club with an indoor pool; **Megatlon** (www.megatlon.com) is a popular gym with many branches. You can also try the pool at **Parque General Belgrano** (Map p250; ☑4807-7918; Salguero 3450; park AR$8, pool

AR$20; ☺10am-7pm Sat & Sun Jan, daily Feb), in Palermo. For a more casual environment, especially with kids, head to Parque Norte.

TENNIS

A few places in BA offer courts, such as **Parque General Belgrano** (☑4807-7879; Salguero 3450; park entry AR$8, court hire per hr AR$50-60; ☺8:30am-midnight Mon-Fri, to 8pm Sat & Sun), in Palermo. Bring your own racquet from home if you're serious about getting in touch with the Nalbandian or del Potro inside you.

HORSEBACK RIDING

If you want to get out of town for a few hours and hop on a horse, forget those touristy estancias (ranches) and check out **Caballos a la Par** (☑15-5248-3592, 4384-7013; www.caballos-alapar.com). Guided, private rides are given in a provincial park about an hour's drive from central Buenos Aires, and it's not just one of those 'follow-the-horse-in-front' deals. They'll take you around woodsy lanes and fields, and you'll have fun learning how to ride and even gallop on the fine horses.

Sports & Activities by Neighborhood

➡ **Puerto Madero** Reserva Ecológica Costanera Sur is great for running, bicycling or walking. These activities are also possible along the dikes' cobbled lanes.

➡ **Palermo** Provides most of central BA's green spaces, along with tennis and golf courses, running paths and bicycling lanes.

Explore Buenos Aires

Neighborhoods at a Glance

❶ The Center p56

Buenos Aires' Center is where bustle meets hustle and endless lines of business suits move hastily along the narrow streets in the shadow of skyscrapers and old European buildings. Stretching from Retiro to San Telmo, this downtown area is the heart and brains of the city, and made up of the sub-neighborhoods of the Microcentro and Montserrat.

❷ Puerto Madero p71

BA's youngest and least conventional barrio, Puerto Madero is home to old brick warehouses that have been converted into some of the city's trendiest lofts, offices, hotels and restaurants. Cobbled promenades make walking a pleasure for pedestrians, and there are plenty of upscale restaurants and cafes to check out.

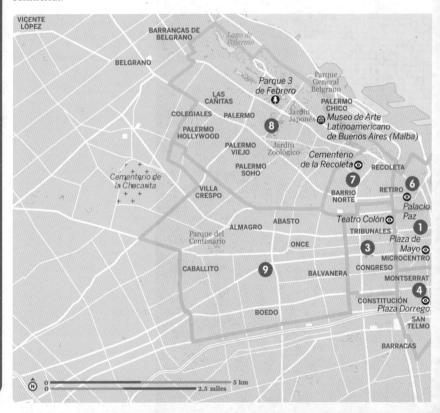

③ Congreso & Tribunales p76

Congreso is an interesting neighborhood full of old-time cinemas, theaters and bustling commerce tinged with a hard-core political flavor. The buildings still hold a European aura, but there's more local feel, faded-glory atmosphere and grittiness than in the Center. It's a great place to wander around and explore.

④ San Telmo p86

San Telmo is a lovely neighborhood full of cobbled streets, colonial mansions and rich history. Only a quick walk south of Plaza de Mayo, it's like stepping 100 years into the past. As a popular tourist destination it's been gentrifying fast, and some wonder if it might become the next Palermo.

⑤ La Boca p98

Blue-collar and raffish to the core, La Boca is very much a locals' neighborhood. Its colorful shanties are often portrayed as a symbol of Buenos Aires, while El Caminito is the barrio's most famous street, full of art vendors, buskers and tango dancers twirling for your spare change.

⑥ Retiro p106

Well located right between the Center and Recoleta, exclusive Retiro is one of the ritziest neighborhoods in Buenos Aires. Giant mansions, art deco apartments and other landmark buildings characterize this area, along with Plaza San Martín – a pleasant grassy park on a hill overlooking the Retiro train and bus stations.

⑦ Recoleta & Barrio Norte p115

Recoleta is where the rich live in luxury apartments and mansions while spending their free time sipping coffee at elegant cafes and shopping in expensive boutiques. Full of lush parks, grand monuments, French architecture and wide avenues, Recoleta is also famous for its cemetery.

⑧ Palermo p126

Palermo's large, grassy parks – regally punctuated with grand monuments – are popular destinations on weekends, when families fill the shady lanes, cycle the bike paths and paddle on the peaceful lakes. The sub-neighborhood of Palermo Viejo is home to dozens of ethnic restaurants, bars, nightclubs and shops, along with the city's largest selection of boutique hotels.

⑨ South of Palermo p146

The neighborhoods south of Palermo are part of the 'real' Buenos Aires largely unaffected by the tourist trade. Villa Crespo is up and coming, benefiting from its proximity to Palermo; Abasto and Once are cultural melting pots and busy commercial districts; and Boedo has bohemian flavor and some very traditional cafes.

NEIGHBORHOODS AT A GLANCE

The Center

MICROCENTRO | MONTSERRAT

Neighborhood Top Five

1 Hanging out at **Plaza de Mayo** (p58), steeped in history and surrounded by some of Buenos Aires' most important buildings, including the main cathedral, the Cabildo, the Museo del Bicentenario and – last but not least – Casa Rosada, where Argentina's president's office is located.

2 Strolling down **Calle Florida** (p69) to see BA's hustle and bustle at its most intense.

3 Shopping at **Galerías Pacífico** (p61), a beautiful shopping mall with an amazing painted ceiling.

4 Visiting historic **Manzana de las Luces** (p62), a symbol of the city's culture and higher learning.

5 Taking a break at **Café Tortoni** (p67), one of BA's most traditional – and touristy – cafes.

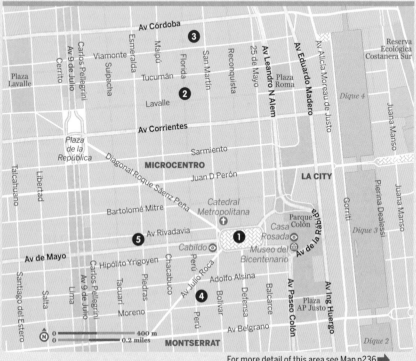

For more detail of this area see Map p236

Explore: the Center

During the day, the Center is a heaving mass of humanity moving hastily along narrow streets in the shadow of skyscrapers and old European buildings – but in the evening, it's practically deserted. Stretching from Retiro to San Telmo (and flanked by Congreso and Puerto Madero), this area is the heart and brain of the city. It's made up of the Microcentro and Montserrat neighborhoods.

Plaza de Mayo is a good place to start. Here you'll see the Casa Rosada presidential palace, with the Museo del Bicentenario right behind it; plan ahead if you want to visit, as it's closed Monday and Tuesday. The Cathedral Metropolitana is nearby – stop by for a Pope Francis souvenir – and the Cabildo has a nice back patio that's good for a break. If you want to see the Madres de la Plaza de Mayo, time your visit for Thursday afternoon (p70).

From here you can head south just one block, crossing over into Montserrat, and visit the Manzana de las Luces, a city block full of historic buildings. There are also a couple of small but interesting museums to visit around here. Further south a few more blocks is San Telmo (p86).

If you're going north, walk on Calle Florida. This very busy pedestrian street is packed during the day with business men and women, street vendors, tourists, beggars, buskers and hustlers. Every few feet you'll hear *arbolitos* (street money changers, called 'little trees' because they stand in place) chanting '*cambio, cambio, cambio*'. Use their services at your own risk! If you prefer more peace, Reconquista and Suipacha are also pedestrian.

Local Life

➡**Shopping** Pedestrian streets Florida and Lavalle are lined with shops and services, and there's great people-watching too.

➡**Hanging out** Stop for a cup of coffee or – if it's later – a stiff drink at one of the many downtown cafes and bars, alongside locals who're taking a break.

➡**Tango** True aficionados head to historic Confitería Ideal (p68) for classes, shows and *milongas* (dance events).

Getting There & Away

➡**Bus** Take bus 29 from San Telmo; 29, 64 and 152 from La Boca; 59 from Recoleta; 29, 59, 64 and 152 from Palermo's Plaza Italia.

➡**Subte** Nearly all Subte lines radiate from the Center, going either north–south from Retiro to San Telmo, or towards Palermo and other points west.

Lonely Planet's Top Tip

Because there are so many business people in the Center, many restaurants offer *menu ejecutivos* – or lunch specials – to attract this valuable clientele. These set lunches are offered weekdays and usually consist of a main course with dessert and drink, all for a reasonable fixed price. Sometimes an appetizer is included as well. It's a good way to try out otherwise pricey restaurants.

Parts of downtown can be a bit sketchy at night, so tread carefully.

✕ Best Places to Eat

➡ Tomo 1 (p66)
➡ Aldo's Vinoteca (p66)
➡ Granix (p66)

For reviews, see p63 ➡

☕ Best Places to Drink

➡ Café Tortoni (p67)
➡ La Cigale (p67)
➡ London City (p67)

For reviews, see p67 ➡

◉ Best Museums

➡ Museo del Bicentenario (p60)
➡ Museo de la Ciudad (p63)
➡ Museo Etnográfico Juan B Ambrosetti (p63)

For reviews, see p61 ➡

TOP SIGHT
PLAZA DE MAYO

Plaza de Mayo is the political, social and symbolic center of Buenos Aires. Surrounded by the Casa Rosada, the Cabildo and the city's main cathedral, this plaza is ground zero for the city's political rallies and protests – both peaceful and vehement. When the plaza isn't full of activists, however, it attracts camera-toting tourists enjoying the sights – along with the occasional camera thief.

When Juan de Garay refounded Buenos Aires in 1580, he laid out the large Plaza del Fuerte (Fortress Plaza) in accordance with Spanish law. Later called the Plaza del Mercado (Market Plaza), then the Plaza de la Victoria (after victories over British invaders in 1806 and 1807), the plaza acquired its present name of Plaza de Mayo after the date Buenos Aires declared independence from Spain: May 25, 1810.

At the center of the plaza is the **Pirámide de Mayo**, a white obelisk built to mark the first anniversary of BA's independence from Spain. Looming on the plaza's northern side is the headquarters of **Banco de la Nación** (1939), the work of famed architect Alejandro Bustillo. Most other public buildings in this area belong to the late 19th century, when the Av de Mayo first connected the Casa Rosada with the Plaza del Congreso, obliterating most of the historic and dignified Cabildo in the process.

Plaza de Mayo is famously known as being the preferred site of many civil protests; note the unsightly barricades separating the plaza in two, meant to discourage large numbers of *piqueteros* (picketers) from congregating. But these barricades haven't prevented the Madres de la Plaza de Mayo – the mothers of the 'disappeared children' during the the Dirty War military dictatorship between 1976 and 1983 – from marching around the

DON'T MISS...

➡ The bullet holes left on the side of the Ministerio de Economía as a symbolic reminder of past intolerance.

➡ The balconies where Juan and Evita Perón preached to their loving masses.

➡ The interior of the Banco de la Nación building – but only if you're an architecture fan!

PRACTICALITIES

➡ Map p236

➡ cnr Av de Mayo & San Martín

plaza every Thursday afternoon at 3:30pm since 1977. Originally they demanded a full account of the atrocities that occurred during this war, but in 2006 they declared a truce with Néstor Kirchner's presidency, as he was sympathetic to their requests. To this day they march on, but as a reminder of the past – and for other social-justice causes.

Casa Rosada

Taking up the whole eastern side of the Plaza de Mayo is the unmistakeable pink facade of the **Casa Rosada** (Pink House; Map p236), the presidential palace that was begun during the presidency of Domingo F Sarmiento. It occupies a site where colonial riverbank fortifications once stood; today, however, after repeated landfills, the palace stands more than 1km inland. The offices of 'La Presidenta' Cristina Kirchner are here (a small raised pennant, under Argentina's national flag, notes her presence in the building), but the presidential residence is in the calm suburb of Olivos, north of the center.

The side of the palace that faces Plaza de Mayo is actually the back of the building. It's from these balconies that Juan and Eva Perón, General Leopoldo Galtieri, Raúl Alfonsín and other politicians have preached to throngs of impassioned Argentines when they felt it necessary to demonstrate public support. Madonna also crooned from here for her movie *Evita*.

The salmon-pink color of the palace, which positively glows at sunset, could have come from President Sarmiento's attempt at making peace during his 1868–74 term (by blending the red of the Federalists with the white of the Unitarists). Another theory, however, is that the color comes from painting the palace with bovine blood, which was a common practice back in the late 19th century.

Off-limits during the military dictatorship of 1976–83, the Casa Rosada is now reasonably accessible to the public. Free half-hour **tours** (☎4344-3600; ☺10am-6pm Sat & Sun) are given.

Underneath the Casa Rosada, excavations have unearthed remains of the **Fuerte Viejo**, a ruin dating from the 18th century. These are accessible via entry to the Museo del Bicentenario.

In 1955 naval aircraft strafed the Casa Rosada and other nearby buildings during the Revolución Libertadora, which toppled Juan Perón's regime. On the northern side of the appropriately bureaucratic **Ministerio de Economía**, an inconspicuous plaque commemorates the attacks (look for the bullet holes to the left of the doors). The inscription translates as, 'The scars on this marble were the harvest of

THE OLD MUSTARD TRICK

It's one of the oldest tricks in the book. You're in a tourist hot spot like Plaza de Mayo, minding your own business, and suddenly someone tells you that there are 'bird droppings' (or another substance) on your clothing. While this kind stranger takes out their surprisingly handy tissues to clean you up, their friend is cleaning out your pockets or stealing your bag.

Madonna sang 'Don't Cry for Me Argentina' from the Casa Rosada's balconies for her movie *Evita*. It was a controversial film as many Argentines were not happy that the actress – associated with skimpy outfits and sex – was chosen to represent their beloved heroine. Also from the Casa Rosada's balconies, a triumphant Diego Maradona hoisted the 1986 World Cup, to the delight of thousands of soccer fans below. And on December 20, 2001, President Fernando de La Rua fled the Casa Rosada's roof by helicopter as the economic crash climaxed.

confrontation and intolerance. Their imprint on our memory will help the nation achieve a future of greatness'.

Towering above the Casa Rosada, just south of Parque Colón on Av Colón, is the army headquarters at the **Edificio Libertador**, the real locus of Argentine political power for many decades. It was built by military engineers inspired by the beaux arts Correo Central. A twin building planned for the navy never got off the ground.

Museo del Bicentenario

Behind the Casa Rosada you'll notice a glassy wedge marking this airy and sparkling – and free! – underground **museum** (Map p236; ☑4344-3802; www.museo bicentenario.gob.ar; cnr Avs Paseo Colón & Hipólito Yrigoyen; ☺10am-6pm Wed-Sun Apr-Nov, 11am-7pm Wed-Sun Dec-Mar) housed within the brick vaults of the old *aduana* (customs house). Head down into the open space, which has over a dozen side rooms – each dedicated to a different era of Argentina's tumultuous political history. There are mostly videos (in Spanish) and a few artifacts to see, along with temporary art exhibitions and an impressive restored mural by Mexican artist David Alfaro Siqueiros. A pleasant cafe-restaurant provides nourishment and rest.

Catedral Metropolitana

This solemn **cathedral** (Map p236; ☺7:30am-6:30pm Mon-Fri, 9am-7pm Sat & Sun) was built on the site of the original colonial church and not finished until 1827. It's a significant religious and architectural landmark, and carved above its triangular facade and neoclassical columns are bas-reliefs of Jacob and Joseph. The spacious interior is equally impressive, with baroque details and an elegant rococo altar.

More importantly, however, the cathedral is a national historical site that contains the tomb of General José de San Martín, Argentina's most revered hero. In the chaos following independence, San Martín chose exile in France, never returning alive to Argentina (although in 1829 a boat on which he traveled sighted Buenos Aires on its way to Montevideo). Outside the cathedral you'll see a flame keeping his spirit alive.

Tours of the church and crypt (in Spanish) were suspended at research time, but check during your tenure to see if they're being offered again. If you want a Pope Francis souvenir (he's Argentine, after all), explore the tiny gift shop inside. Occasional free choir concerts are also on the docket.

Cabildo

This mid-18th-century town hall building is now a **museum** (Map p236; ☑4342-6729; www.cabildonacional.com.ar; Bolívar 65; admission AR$10; ☺10:30am-5pm Wed-Fri, to 6pm Sat & Sun). It used to have colonnades that spanned Plaza de Mayo, but, unfortunately, the building of surrounding avenues destroyed them. Inside you'll find a few mementos of early-19th-century British invasions, some paintings in colonial and early independence style, and the occasional temporary exhibit. On Thursday and Friday a lively crafts market sets up in the patio – and the cafe here is a great place to relax. Tours in Spanish offered.

⊙ SIGHTS

⊙ Microcentro

PLAZA DE MAYO PLAZA
See p58.

GALERÍAS PACÍFICO LANDMARK
Map p236 (🖉5555-5110; cnr Avs Florida & Córdoba; ☺10am-9pm) Covering an entire city block, this beautiful French-style building has fulfilled the commercial purpose that its designers envisioned when they constructed it in 1889. Galerías Pacífico is now a shopping center – dotted with lovely fairy lights at night – and boasts upscale stores along with a large food court (which has longer hours than the stores). The excellent Centro Cultural Borges takes up the top floor. Tours are offered at 11:30am from Monday to Friday, in English and Spanish.

When you step inside, check out the ceiling. In 1945 the completion of a central cupola made space for a dozen paintings by muralists Antonio Berni, Juan Carlos Castagnino, Manuel Colmeiro, Lino Spilimbergo and Demetrio Urruchúa. All were adherents of the *nuevo realismo* (new realism) school, heirs of an earlier social-activist tendency in Argentine art. For many years the building went semi-abandoned, but a joint Argentine-Mexican team repaired and restored the murals in 1992.

**CENTRO CULTURAL
BORGES** CULTURAL CENTER
Map p236 (🖉5555-5359; www.ccborges.org.ar; cnr Viamonte & San Martín) One of the best cultural centers in BA, with inexpensive but high-quality art exhibitions and galleries, cinema, music, lectures, classes and workshops. Tango lessons are also available.

IGLESIA SANTA CATALINA CHURCH
Map p236 (🖉5238-6040; www.santacatalina.org.ar; Plaza San Martín 705; ⑤Línea B Florida, Línea C Lavalle) Santa Catalina was founded in 1745, when it became Buenos Aires' first convent. In 1806 British troops invaded the city, and in July 1807 they took shelter in the convent. The soldiers holed up here for two days, and despite damaging the property did not hurt the nuns. Today Santa Catalina is a church, and a peek inside reveals beautiful gilded works and a baroque altarpiece created by Isidro Lorea, a Spanish carver.

**CENTRO CULTURAL DEL
BICENTENARIO** NOTABLE BUILDING
Map p236 (Ex-Correo Central; www.ccb.gov.ar; Sarmiento 151) It took 20 years to complete the massive Correo Central (main post office; 1928), which fills an entire city block. This beaux arts structure was originally modeled on New York City's main post office; the mansard roof was a later addition. The building is now being turned into a cultural center with concert space for the national philharmonic orchestra (and holding nearly 2000 spectators), but no one knows when it will open; check it out during your tenure and cross your fingers.

MUSEO MUNDIAL DEL TANGO MUSEUM
Map p236 (🖉4345-6967; Av de Mayo 833, 1st fl; admission AR$20; ☺2:30-7:30pm Mon-Fri) Located below the **Academia Nacional del Tango** is this tango museum – for fans of the dance only. Just a couple of large rooms are filled with tango memorabilia, from old records and photos to historic literature and posters. Tango shoes are also featured, but the highlight has to be one of Carlos Gardel's famous fedora hats.

MUSEO MITRE MUSEUM
Map p236 (🖉4394-8240; San Martín 336; admission AR$15; ☺1-5pm Mon-Fri) This museum is located in the colonial house where Bartolomé Mitre – Argentina's first legitimate president elected under the constitution of 1853 – resided with his family. Mitre's term ran from 1862 to 1868, and he spent much of it leading the country's armies against Paraguay. Two courtyards, salons, an office, a billiards room and Mitre's old bedroom are part of this complex. Since part of the museum is open air, you may find it closed during heavy rain.

MUSEO DE LA POLICÍA FEDERAL MUSEUM
Map p236 (🖉4394-6857; San Martín 353, 7th fl; ☺2-7pm Tue-Fri) **FREE** This quirky police museum displays a whole slew of uniforms and medals, along with 'illegal activities' exhibits (cockfighting and gambling), drug paraphernalia (including a fake arm stuck with a needle!) and even a stuffed police dog. The forensic room way in the back was being remodeled at research time – it may or may not keep its grisly photos and dummies of hacked-up murder victims; something to keep in mind if you bring the kids.

POPE FRANCIS

After Cardinal Jorge Mario Bergoglio, the archbishop of Buenos Aires, was named successor to Pope Benedict XVI in March 2013, he took the name Francis I. Not only was he the first pontiff to bear that moniker (adopted to honor St Francis of Assisi), he was also the first to hail from the Americas and the first to belong to the Jesuit order, which incidentally was expelled from most of South America for 47 years (1767–1814). It's a fair bet that he's also the first pope to have grown up drinking *mate*, tangoing at *milongas* and ardently supporting the San Lorenzo *fútbol* club.

Francis has taken charge at a particularly low point in the church's modern history. It has been rocked by a seemingly endless series of sexual-abuse scandals, and subjected to investigations into charges of high-level corruption and financial malfeasance. These events and widening parishioner dissatisfaction with the Vatican's stance on homosexuality, divorce, abortion and the role of women in the church have caused congregations to shrink, a problem compounded in the Americas by the increasing popularity of various Pentecostal, evangelical and other denominations.

While it remains to be seen what direction Francis will take on various aspects of Catholic doctrine, he has roundly criticized the structure and workings of the church at its highest levels, and vowed to make them more transparent and outward-looking, and less closed and hierarchical.

Francis appointed a special commission to delve into the workings of the Vatican bank, which has been under pressure from the Council of Europe's anti-money laundering committee to submit to independent supervision. In October 2013, the bank published an annual report for the first time in its history.

In a more headline-worthy move, Francis summoned Limburg's 'Bishop of Bling', free-spending prelate Franz-Peter Tebartz-van Elst, to Rome to explain how he managed to spend tens·of millions of euros renovating his official residence. After eight days of cooling his heels, the bishop was granted a 20-minute audience with Francis, who ended up suspending him from his duties for an 'indefinite period'.

This pope doesn't just talk the talk, he walks the walk. After arriving in Rome for his 2001 anointment as cardinal by John Paul II, Archbishop Bergoglio left the modest priests' quarters on foot the morning of his ceremony, arriving at the Vatican accompanied only by his assistant and a couple of relatives. No surprise, as he had already eschewed the archbishop's palace in Olivos, remaining in his modest apartment and getting around Buenos Aires by bus and the Subte rather than with a car and driver.

He has continued these habits as Francis I, emulating his namesake and personal hero, the saint from Assisi who once renounced all worldly possessions including his clothing. These humble aspects, coupled with the very personable humanity Francis displays, have made him an extremely popular pontiff. Many Catholics speak of feeling 'understood' by him, and his popularity extends beyond the faithful. The church has a new face, just when it needed it the most.

⊙ Montserrat

MANZANA DE LAS LUCES　　NOTABLE BUILDING
Map p236 (Block of Enlightenment; ☎4342-3964; www.manazadelasluces.org; Perú 272; tours AR$15; ⊗tours 3pm Mon-Fri, 3pm, 4:30pm & 6pm Sat & Sun) In colonial times, the Manzana de las Luces was Buenos Aires' most important center of culture and learning. Even today, this collection of buildings still symbolizes high culture in the capital. On the northern side of the block are two of the five original buildings; Jesuit defensive

tunnels were discovered in 1912. Tours (in Spanish) are available, and a cultural center on the premises offers classes, workshops and theater.

The first people to occupy the Manzana de las Luces were the Jesuits, who built several structures including the Procuraduría (1730; administrative headquarters), part of which still survives today. (Unfortunately for the Jesuits, they were eventually expelled from the premises – and Argentina – in 1767 by the Spanish, who felt politically threatened by them.) Along with housing offices, these buildings hosted converted

LUNA PARK

If unique large-scale spectacles such as the Beijing Circus, the New York Ballet, the Philadelphia Philharmonic, Julio Iglesias or Tom Jones come to town, the dressing rooms of **Luna Park** (Map p236; ☎5279-5279; www.lunapark.com.ar; cnr Bouchard & Av Corrientes) are probably their destination. Bordered by the thoroughfares of Lavalle, Bouchard, Av Corrientes and Madero, Luna Park was originally a boxing stadium built on the old grounds of the Pacific Railway. Finished in 1931, the venue gradually became a mecca for public events needing large spaces. When Carlos Gardel died in a plane crash in 1935, his wake was held here for the thousands of grieving fans. In 1944, a relatively unknown actress named Eva Duarte first met general Juan Perón here during a benefit for victims of an earthquake in San Juan province. And on November 7, 1989, Diego Maradona was married here before 11,000 fans.

But Luna Park never forgot its roots; throughout its history 25 boxing titles have been decided within its walls. Many other sports, including volleyball, basketball and tennis, are also occasionally highlighted at this stadium, and productions such as fashion shows, ice-skating spectacles and mass religious baptisms have found their way here as well. With a capacity of 15,000 (it's Argentina's largest enclosed stadium), Luna Park can easily handle these crowds, which also come to see recent big-time performers such as Liza Minnelli, Luciano Pavarotti, Norah Jones, Ricky Martin, David Byrne and Chrissie Hynde.

indigenous people from the provinces. Later, during the 19th century, they were home to various museums, legislative offices, schools and universities.

The city's oldest church, the **Iglesia San Ignacio** (1734), is also located here, originally built in adobe in 1661 and rebuilt or remodelled several times since. Today there remains only a single original cloister; it shares a wall with the **Colegio Nacional de Buenos Aires** (1863), a prep school where generations of the Argentine elite still send their children to receive secondary schooling. The city's oldest bookstore, **La Librería de Avila**, is also nearby at Alsina and Bolívar.

MUSEO DE LA CIUDAD — MUSEUM

Map p236 (☎4343-2123; Defensa 219; admission AR$1; ⏱11am-7pm Mon-Fri, 10am-8pm Sat & Sun) This upstairs museum was closed at research time due to major restoration, but in the future you should expect both permanent and temporary exhibitions on porteño life and history here. Downstairs is a large hall showcasing salvaged doors and ancient hardware. Nearby, at the corner of Alsina and Defensa, is the **Farmacia de la Estrella** (1835), a functioning homeopathic pharmacy with gorgeous woodwork and elaborate late-19th-century ceiling murals depicting health-oriented themes. Occasionally the museum opens via its Alsina 412 door.

MUSEO ETNOGRÁFICO JUAN B AMBROSETTI — MUSEUM

Map p236 (☎4331-7788; www.museoetnografico.filo.uba.ar; Moreno 350; admission AR$4; ⏱1-7pm Tue-Fri, 3-7pm Sat & Sun) This small but attractive anthropological museum was created by Juan B Ambrosetti not only as an institute for research and university training but also as an educational center for the public. On display are archaeological and anthropological collections from the Andean Northwest and Patagonia. Beautiful indigenous artifacts are also featured, while an African and Asian room showcases some priceless pieces.

EATING

You won't find Buenos Aires' best cuisine in the Center, as most restaurants here cater to business power-lunches or quick takeout. Some eateries don't even open for dinner since the working masses beeline home after the day is done. Even bars tend to open and close relatively early here. All this doesn't mean you won't find a decent bite to eat, however, and vegetarians especially might find some good choices. Also, five-star hotels often house top-notch restaurants that are worth a visit – and are definitely open for dinner. Nearby options include Le Sud (p112)

1. Café cortado 2. Bar El Federal, San Telmo (p91)
3. Café Tortoni, The Center (p67) 4. La Poesia, San Telmo (p91)

Cafes of Buenos Aires

Thanks to its European heritage, Buenos Aires has a serious cafe culture. *Porteños* will spend hours dawdling over a single *café cortado* (coffee with milk) and a couple of *medialunas* (croissants), discussing the economy, politics and that latest soccer play. Indeed, everything from marriage proposals to revolutions has originated at the local corner cafe.

Some of BA's cafes have been around for over 100 years, and many retain much of their original furniture, architectural details and rich atmosphere. They've always been the haunts of Argentina's politicians, activists, intellectuals, artists and literary greats, including Jorge Luis Borges and Julio Cortázar.

Most cafes have adapted to modern times by serving alcohol as well as coffee, and many offer a surprisingly wide range of food and snacks; you can often order a steak as easily as a *cortado*. A few even double as bookstores or host live music, poetry readings and other cultural events. And, as a sign of the times, Starbucks has finally infiltrated BA's cafe life, and its franchises have become very popular as *porteños* embrace the modern frappuccino world.

Cafes have long hours and are usually open from early morning to late at night, making them easy places to visit. And visit you should; sipping coffee and hanging out at an atmospheric cafe, perhaps on some lazy afternoon, is part of the Buenos Aires experience. At the very least, they're great for a late tea or a welcome break from all that walking you'll be doing.

in the Sofitel, Elena (p111) at the Four Seasons, La Bourgogne in the Alvear Palace (p171) and El Mercado and El Bistró in the Faena (p166).

GRANIX   VEGETARIAN $

Map p236 (☑4343-4020; Florida 165, 1st fl; all-you-can-eat AR$85; ☺11am-3:30pm Mon-Fri; ☑) Stepping into this large, modern lacto-ovo-vegetarian eatery will make you wonder if *porteños* have had enough steak already. Pick from the many hot appetizers and mains; there's also a great salad bar and plenty of desserts. It's only open for weekday lunches, and located in a shopping mall (look for the stairs on the right). Takeout is available.

VITA   HEALTH FOOD $

Map p236 (☑4342-0788; www.vitamarket.com.ar; Hipólito Yrigoyen 583; mains AR$34-36; ☺8am-8pm Mon-Fri, 10am-8pm Sat, noon-7pm Sun; ☑) Here's a hippie-ish, casual and health-oriented eatery offering tasty vegetarian dishes like organic soy *milanesas*, zucchini and eggplant lasagne and tofu in mustard sauce with mashed potatoes. Various freshly mixed juices and *licuados* are available (with the option of adding a wheatgrass shot) and there are plenty of gourmet salads. Organic coffee is also served.

A few shelves are lined with health-oriented products for sale.

CALIFORNIA BURRITO
COMPANY (CBC)   MEXICAN $

Map p236 (☑4328-3057; www.cbcburrito.com; Lavalle 441; mains AR$60-100; ☺11am-3pm Mon-Fri) This convenient burrito joint is popular with the business crowd at lunchtime and is passable if you don't expect authentic Mexican. Flour tortillas are loaded up with your choice of meat, rice, beans and salsa, and rolled into large burritos that will sustain you well into the evening. Tacos, fajitas and margaritas available.

Branches in Palermo and Recoleta (see the website for addresses).

ALDO'S VINOTECA   ARGENTINE $$

Map p236 (☑4334-2380; Moreno 372; mains AR$70-100; ☺11am-midnight Sun-Thu, to 1am Fri & Sat) Located under the Moreno Hotel, this restaurant–wine shop is an upscale eatery serving a small but tasty menu of meat, seafood and pasta dishes, all amidst walls lined with wine. What makes this place unique, however, is that the wine is sold at *retail* prices – thus making it easier to sample (and buy) the nearly 500 labels available.

FURAI-BO   JAPANESE $$

Map p236 (☑4334-3440; Adolfo Alsina 429; mains AR$80-120; ☺noon-11pm Sun-Thu, to midnight Fri & Sat) Walk up the staircase of this old building into a calm space meant to resemble a Buddhist temple; on weekend evenings, live instrumentalists set the mood with ambient ceremonial music. The house specialty is homemade ramen noodles with pork. The menu also includes excellent sushi and *katsu* (a type of cutlet), plus unusual sweet treats like ginger ice cream.

D'ORO   ITALIAN $$

Map p236 (☑4342-6959; Perú 159; mains AR$90-150; ☺noon-7pm Mon-Thu, to midnight Fri) Despite its downtown location, D'Oro is a serious Italian wine bar and restaurant to rival others in more gastronomically famous neighborhoods. Come for thin, crispy oven-baked pizzas, mushroom risotto, fettucine with shellfish, garlic-topped focaccia and capellini tossed with fresh basil and tomatoes. To go with it all, there's also a short but well-chosen selection of wines by the glass.

BROCCOLINO   ITALIAN $$

Map p236 (☑4322-7754; www.broccolino.com; Esmeralda 776; mains AR$50-120; ☺noon-11:30pm) Pick from over 20 sauces (including squid ink!) for your pasta, with a choice of rigatoni, fusilli, pappardelle and all sorts of stuffed varieties. If you can't decide on your topper, try the delicious Sicilian sauce (spicy red peppers, tomato and garlic) or the pesto with mushrooms and garlic. Portions are large and the bread homemade.

★TOMO 1   MODERN ARGENTINE $$$

Map p236 (☑4326-6695; Carlos Pellegrini 521; mains AR$190-320; ☺noon-3pm & 5:30pm-midnight Mon-Fri, 5:30pm-midnight Sat) At renowned Tomo 1, European-influenced Chef Federico Fialayre promotes a blend of Italian and Spanish cooking methods in dishes featuring seasonal produce, homemade pasta and fresh fish. For a splash-out, sample his famed cuisine with a three-course *prix fixe* menu (AR$370 lunch, AR$430 dinner); it comes with amuse-bouches, two glasses of wine, mineral water, coffee and petits fours.

① KEEPING YOUR PEÑAS & MAYOS STRAIGHT

Some first-time (or maybe second-time) visitors may get confused with certain similar-sounding street and attraction names. Keep them straight:

25 de Mayo Street that goes north–south from Retiro to Plaza de Mayo (Mayo is Spanish for the month of May).

Av de Mayo Large avenue that goes east–west from Plaza del Congreso to Plaza de Mayo.

Plaza de Mayo BA's most important plaza.

Diagonal Roque Sáenz Peña Diagonal street that stretches from Plaza de Mayo to the Obelisco.

Luis Sáenz Peña Street that goes from Plaza del Congreso through Constitución.

Rodriguez Peña Street that goes from Recoleta to Plaza del Congreso.

⊗ DRINKING & NIGHTLIFE

Many watering holes in the Center are Irish-pub knock-offs that cater to the business crowd on weekdays. Because of this, some might close a bit earlier than in other neighborhoods, but the most popular ones stay packed all night long. The Center also has some of the oldest cafes in town, delightfully atmospheric venues that offer a welcome break while you're wandering around.

CAFÉ TORTONI   CAFE

Map p236 (☑4342-4328; www.cafetortoni.com. ar; Av de Mayo 829; ◎8am-2am Mon-Fri, 9am-2am Sat & Sun) BA's oldest and most famous cafe, the classic Tortoni has become so popular with foreigners that it's turned into a tourist trap. Still, it's practically an obligatory stop for any visitor to town: order a couple of *churros* (fried pastry dough) with your hot chocolate and forget about the inflated prices. There are also tango shows nightly (AR$150) – reserve ahead.

LA CIGALE   BAR

Map p236 (☑4893-2332; 25 de Mayo 597; ◎noon-4pm & 6pm-close) This upstairs bar-restaurant is very popular with both office workers (during the day) and music-industry folks (later in the evening). There's either live music or DJs most nights, but it's best known for its 'French Tuesday', when electronica and exotic cocktails draw heavy crowds. Fusion foods are served for both lunch and dinner.

LONDON CITY   CAFE

Map p236 (☑4343-0328; Av de Mayo 599) This classy and historic cafe (being remodelled at research time) has been serving java enthusiasts for over 50 years, and claims to have been the spot where Julio Cortázar wrote his first novel. Your hardest work here, however, will most likely be choosing which pastry to try with your fresh cup of coffee.

NEW BRIGHTON   BAR

Map p236 (☑4322-1515; Sarmiento 645; ◎8am-close Mon-Sat) This beautifully restored landmark and historic gem feels like the well-kept secret of refined local gentlemen who gather here after work. A doorman welcomes guests in while bartenders stir and shake drinks behind a polished-wood bar; during mealtimes, a pianist entertains on the baby grand. Order a classic cocktail and enjoy the tray of elegant finger food that comes with it.

LA PUERTO RICO   CAFE

Map p236 (☑4331-2215; www.lapuertoricocafe. com.ar; Adolfo Alsina 416; ◎7am-8pm Mon-Fri, 8am-7pm Sat, noon-7pm Sun) One of the city's most historic cafes, La Puerto Rico has been going strong since 1887 but remains miraculously un-touristy. Located a block south of Plaza de Mayo, the place serves great coffee and pastries, the latter baked on the premises. Old photos on the walls hint at a rich past and the Spanish movies that have been filmed here.

ALSINA   CLUB

Map p236 (☑4331-3231; www.palacioalsina.net; Adolfo Alsina 940; ◎Sun, plus 1 Fri per month) One of BA's biggest gay parties is Alsina's **Fiesta Dorothy**, on just one Friday a month. Expect the city's majority population of cute gay guys in attendance as DJs crank up the house – a beautiful building with three floors of open balconies, chandeliers and thick drapes – with dance, hip-hop and techno riffs. Sunday's Club One is more hetero-friendly.

BAHREIN
CLUB

Map p236 (☎6225-2731; www.bahreinba.com; Lavalle 345; ☻Wed, Fri & Sat) Attracting a good share of BA's tattooed youth, Bahrein is a hugely popular downtown club housed in an old bank (check out the 'vault' in the basement). On the ground floor is the lounge-like Funky Room where resident DJs spin house music and electronica. Downstairs is the happening Xss discotheque, an impressive sound system and a dance floor for hundreds.

COCOLICHE
CLUB

Map p236 (☎4342-9485; Av Rivadavia 878; ☻Fri & Sat) An effortlessly cool DJ club in BA is this electronic-music paradise, based in a slightly run-down old mansion. It's the downstairs basement, gritty and nearly always packed, that holds the main stage, a fantastic sound system and a state-of-the-art light show. Breakbeat, drum and bass, reggaeton and electronic *cumbia* (Colombian music) entertain; when you need a break, head to the 2nd-floor chill-out room.

☆ ENTERTAINMENT

CAFÉ TORTONI
TANGO SHOW

Map p236 (☎4342-4328; www.cafetortoni.com.ar; Av de Mayo 829; show AR$150-200) Nightly tango shows (reserve ahead) take place at this historic yet very touristy place, and they're fine if you don't expect too much. The overpriced food isn't included. If you come earlier for the cafe, you may have to line up outside beforehand. Despite these downfalls, the Tortoni is BA's most famous cafe and still offers a beautiful atmosphere.

Get your ticket the day of or one day beforehand at the cafe between 11am and 5pm (cash only).

CONFITERÍA IDEAL
TANGO SHOW

Map p236 (☎4328-7750; www.confiteria ideal.com; Suipacha 384, 1st fl) This institution (since 1912) is the mother of all historic tango halls, with classes and *milongas* offered daily. Live orchestras occasionally accompany dancers, and there are dinner-tango shows on Friday and Saturday. The actual cafe section could use a facelift, as it's a bit dim, stodgy and impersonal, but it remains a classic. Featured in the film *The Tango Lesson*.

EL QUERANDÍ
TANGO SHOW

Map p236 (☎5199-1770; www.querandi.com.ar; Perú 322; show from US$60, dinner & show from US$130) This large corner venue is also an elegant restaurant boasting an upscale atmosphere. This show follows tango's evolution from its bordello origins to cabaret influences to *milongas* and modernism. There's more low-key dancing than at other shows – and also more singing and musical interludes – so don't expect overly athletic moves. One minus: columns can block some views.

TEATRO OPERA
THEATER

Map p236 (☎4326-1335; www.operaciti-teatro.com.ar; Av Corrientes 860) This classic theater, which boasts an art-deco exterior, offers nearly 2000 seats and has performances that range from piano recitals to rock concerts to tango and ballet. It served many years as a cinema, later becoming a live-theater venue.

TEATRO GRAN REX
THEATER

Map p236 (☎4322-8000; www.teatro-granrex.com.ar; Av Corrientes 857) A huge theater seating 3300, this place hosts myriad national and international musical productions, from Cyndi Lauper to Kenny G to Björk.

🔒 SHOPPING

The main shopping street in the Center is Florida. Most travelers to Buenos Aires take the obligatory stroll down this heaving pedestrian street, lined with shops and vendors selling clothes, shoes, jewelry, housewares and cheesy souvenirs. Touts zero in on tourists, offering currency exchange and leather jackets. We'll tell you now: you won't find the cheapest prices on leather jackets here (try Calle Murillo or Calle Aguirre instead) and you should definitely avoid changing money on the streets – fake bills and other scams are an occasional problem here.

EL ATENEO
BOOKS, MUSIC

Map p236 (☎4325-6801; Florida 340 & 629; ☻9am-8pm Mon-Fri, to 5pm Sat) Buenos Aires' landmark bookseller stocks a few books in English (including some Lonely Planet guidebooks) and also has a decent selection of CDs. There are several branches within the city, including the gorgeous

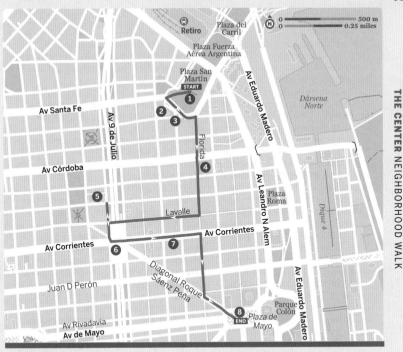

🏃 Neighborhood Walk
Through the Heart of BA

START PLAZA SAN MARTÍN
END PLAZA DE MAYO
LENGTH 3KM; THREE HOURS

Start at the leafy **①Plaza San Martín**, the green heart of Retiro and a haven for loungers on a sunny day. At the bottom of the hill there's a monument to the fallen from the Falklands War.

Now cross Av Santa Fe to the striking **②Palacio Paz** (p108). Time it right so you can catch a tour and take in the grandeur of a long-ago era. On the same block is the **③Museo de Armas** (p109), an astounding collection of guns, swords and cannon.

Find your way to pedestrian Calle Florida and walk south to the elegant **④Galerías Pacífico** (p61) shopping mall, one of the capital's most beautiful. Even if you don't like to shop, you should take a peek inside at the gorgeously painted ceiling murals.

Now head west a few blocks on pedestrian Lavalle and cross Av 9 de Julio, considered by many the world's widest street.

Your destination is the impressive **⑤Teatro Colón** (p78), BA's opera house and a major source of pride for *porteños*.

The **⑥Obelisco** is the city's premier landmark. Not only is it used as ground zero for measuring distances from the city center, it's the place to honk your car's horn when your soccer team wins a major victory.

Back in the day **⑦Av Corrientes** was BA's main theater district, and some of the city's largest theaters are still found here. It's also known for its many bookstores.

Hit Florida again and make your way south to Diagonal Roque Sáenz Peña. You'll end up at historic **⑧Plaza de Mayo** (p58), where you'll want to linger and take in the historic atmosphere. Behind the Cabildo is a cafe where you can sit and relax after your long walk.

TAKING IT TO THE STREETS

Just like the tango and *dulce de leche,* street protests are a well-known pastime for *porteños.* Whether the city is booming or in the midst of a depression, unless there's martial law, someone is out on the street demonstrating against something. Plaza de Mayo has long been the focal point of protests.

The best-known voices of dissent are the famed Madres de la Plaza de Mayo (the Mothers of Plaza de Mayo). On April 30, 1977, 14 mothers whose children had disappeared in the Dirty War marched on the Plaza de Mayo. They demanded to know what had happened to their missing children. The military government dismissed them, claiming that their children had simply moved abroad, but the women continued to march in their iconic white handkerchiefs every Thursday. They played an essential historical role as the first group to openly oppose the military junta and they opened the doors for later protests. In 1986 the Madres split into two groups. Asociación Madres de Plaza de Mayo announced that the group would stop participating in *la marcha de la resistencia* around Plaza de Mayo. The other group, Madres de Plaza de Mayo Línea Fundadora, still marches every Thursday.

Even in 1996, when the economy was good and the country was under civilian control, a number of protests broke out against corruption and the reform of pensions. Senior citizens hurled eggs at government buildings and were chased by trucks mounted with water cannon. The protests after the economic collapse in 2001 were particularly large and vociferous. Thousands of people – in the poorer areas as well as middle-class neighborhoods – spontaneously gathered in public parks in Buenos Aires. To the shouts of *'¡Que se vayan todos!'* (get rid of them all), they banged pots and pans – an act known as a *cacerolazo.* Both the economic minister and the president eventually stepped down, and some of the politicians who hadn't fled the country were beaten in the streets.

There are still occasional grievances on Plaza de Mayo, whether it's a protest against the price of beef and tomatoes, or against the closure of a hospital. You can always count on protests being loud, but these days they're usually peaceful.

Grand Splendid (Map p246; Av Santa Fe 1860; ⊗9am-10pm Mon-Thu, to midnight Fri & Sat, noon-10pm Sun), a renovated cinema where Carlos Gardel got his career started; soak up the glamour at the cafe, located on the old stage.

ARTE Y ESPERANZA   CRAFTS & TEXTILES

Map p236 (☑4343-1455; www.arteyesperanza. com.ar; Balcarce 234; ⊗9am-6pm Mon-Fri) This store sells fair-trade, handmade products that include many from Argentina's indigenous craftspeople. Shop for silver jewelry, pottery, textiles, *mate* gourds, baskets,

woven bags and animal masks. Also in **Retiro** (Map p248; Suipacha 892).

EL COLECCIONISTA   MUSIC

Map p236 (☑4322-0359; www.elcoleccionistacd. com.ar; Esmeralda 562; ⊗noon-7:30pm Mon-Fri) This music store has an eclectic selection of jazz, blues, salsa, Celtic and symphonic rock CDs. It will buy used musical instruments, so trade in that guitar or drum you're tired of lugging around for a cool *bandoneón* (the accordion-esque instrument you'll hear in every tango band). Staff members are knowledgeable.

Puerto Madero

Neighborhood Top Five

1 Escaping the city's hustle and bustle with a walk or bike ride through the unique **Reserva Ecológica Costanera Sur** (p73), wild wetlands where you can spot birds or perhaps a nutria or iguana.

2 Strolling down the scenic and vehicle-free **cobbled lanes** next to Puerto Madero's dikes.

3 Visiting the **Colección de Arte Amalia Lacroze de Fortabat** (p74), the contemporary museum showing the collection of Argentina's richest woman.

4 Eating lunch or dinner at an upscale **restaurant** with a water view – it'll be pricey but good.

5 Seeing what's being exhibited at the slick new **Faena Arts Center** (p74).

For more detail of this area see Map p238 ➡

Lonely Planet's Top Tip

If you want to explore every corner of the Reserva Ecológica Costanera Sur, it's much easier on a bike. On weekends in good weather there are rentals outside the north and south entrances, but if you want to make sure you get a bike you might want to rent one beforehand at one of several bike tour companies in BA (or via the city's free bike share program, p207).

✖ Best Places to Eat

➡ i Central Market (p75)

➡ La Rosa Náutica (p75)

For reviews, see p75

⊙ Best Museums

➡ Colección de Arte Amalia Lacroze de Fortabat (p74)

➡ Fragata Sarmiento (p75)

For reviews, see p74 ➡

Explore: Puerto Madero

Put on your most comfortable walking shoes, because you'll be on your feet all day here. You can start walking pretty much anywhere and make a big loop around the dikes, though if you start at the tourist office (under an old cargo crane at Dique 4), you can pick up some practical information and a map.

There are a few interesting museums around the dikes, including the Colección de Arte Amalia Lacroze de Fortabat (also called Museo Fortabat). This shiny, glassy museum is in a cutting-edge building and art lovers shouldn't miss it. Another quirky place is the Museo Fragata Sarmiento. Walk the plank, pay your ticket and explore all the fascinating holds of this naval vessel. The Corbeta Uruguay, a couple blocks away, is another similar 'ship' museum. In between these two is the Puente de la Mujer – a pedestrian bridge that you'll be tempted to cross.

When you get towards the south, cut east on R Vera Peñaloza and look for the elegant fountain called La Fuente de las Nereidas. Just beyond is the southern entrance to the marshy Reserva Ecológica Costanera Sur, which offers the only real nature walk (or bike ride) in central BA. It's a peaceful place full of reedy lagoons, wildlife and dirt paths, and you can get a close-up look at the muddy waters of the Río de la Plata. The reserve is a sharp contrast to the upscale lofts, restaurants and hotels nearby, and thankfully it's available to everyone for no cost at all – just be sure you're not there on a Monday, when it's closed.

Local Life

➡**Food stands** The road lining the Reserva Ecológica Costanera Sur is dotted with several barbecue stands selling cheap *choripán* (spicy sausage sandwiches) or *bondiolas* (pork sandwiches). You'll be mingling with the locals at sidewalk tables, and the view of the reserve is pleasant enough.

Getting There & Away

➡**Bus** Buses 64, 126 and 152 run along LN Alem/Paseo Colón, which gets you within three blocks of Puerto Madero.

➡**Subte** The closest Subte stops are LN Alem (Línea B) and the end lines of Líneas A, D and E, which terminate at Plaza de Mayo.

➡**Tram** BA's short light-rail system parallels Puerto Madero's docks, and may someday extend to La Boca.

TOP SIGHT
RESERVA ECOLÓGICA COSTANERA SUR

The beautiful marshy land of this nature preserve makes it a popular site for sunny weekend outings, when hundreds of picnickers, cyclists and families come for fresh air and natural views. If you're lucky, you may spot a river turtle, iguana or nutria (semi-aquatic rodent); bird-watchers will adore the 250-plus bird species that pause to rest here.

During the military Proceso of 1976–83, access to the Buenos Aires waterfront was limited, as the area was diked and filled with sediments dredged from the Río de la Plata. While plans for a new satellite city across from the port stalled, trees, grasses, birds and rodents took advantage and colonized this low-lying, 350-hectare area that mimics the ecology of the Delta del Paraná.

In 1986 the area was declared an ecological reserve. Mysterious arson fires, thought to have been started by those with financial interests in the prime real estate, have occasionally been set. But permanent scars haven't remained – this beautifully lush marshy land survives hardily, and the reserve has become a popular site for outings and walks. Bring binoculars if you're a birder – ducks, swans, woodpeckers, parakeets, hawks, flycatchers and cardinals are just a few kinds of the feathered critters that can be spotted. Further in at the eastern shoreline of the reserve you can get a close-up view of the Río de la Plata's muddy waters – a rare sight in Buenos Aires.

Tours are available on weekends; monthly Friday night full-moon tours are also available (call for schedules). On warm weekends and holidays you can rent bikes just outside either the northern or southern entrances.

DON'T MISS...

➡ Walking the trails.
➡ Birdwatching and bike riding.
➡ Views of the Río de la Plata.

PRACTICALITIES

➡ Map p238
➡ 4893-1588
➡ Av Rodríguez 1550
➡ 8am-7pm Tue-Sun Nov-Mar, to 6pm Apr-Oct

◉ SIGHTS

RESERVA ECOLÓGICA
COSTANERA SUR   NATURE RESERVE
See p73.

COLECCIÓN DE ARTE AMALIA
LACROZE DE FORTABAT   MUSEUM
Map p238 (Museo Fortabat; ☑4310-6600; www.
coleccionfortabat.org.ar; Olga Cossettini 141; admission AR$35; ☉noon-8pm Tue-Sun) Rivaling
Palermo's Malba for cutting-edge looks is
this stunning art museum, prominently
located at the northern end of Puerto Madero. It shows off the collection of billion-
airess, philanthropist and socialite Amalia
Lacroze de Fortabat, Argentina's wealthiest woman. There are galleries devoted
to Antonio Berni and Raúl Soldi (both
famous Argentine painters) and works by
international stars like Dalí, Klimt, Rodin
and Chagall; look for Warhol's colorful take
on Fortabat herself in the family portrait
gallery.

The building was designed by renowned
Uruguayan architect Rafael Viñoly, and is
a creation of steel, glass and concrete – the
last a most appropriate material considering its patroness (Fortabat is the major
stockholder of Argentina's largest cement
company). Finished in 2008, it encompasses
over 6000 sq meters, with several airy
floors showcasing works by famous Argentine and international artists. The most
interesting thing about the museum itself,
however, might be the movable aluminum
panels above the glassy ceiling. They tilt
open and shut, keeping sun off the delicate
artworks. Lacroze requested this feature
so that she could see her collection and the
stars at the same time.

Spanish tours are given Tuesday to Sunday at 3pm and 5pm; call ahead for group
tours in English.

FAENA ARTS CENTER   ARTS CENTER
Map p238 (☑4010-9233; www.faenaartscenter.
org; Aime Paine 1169; admission AR$40, Mon
free; ☉varies depending on exhibition) This very
large, airy art space – in a beautifully renovated flour mill – highlights the contemporary dreams of local and international
artists and designers. You should expect
the most cutting-edge exhibits that utilize
these spaces to the maximum – think rope
nets hanging from the ceiling or light pyra-
mids reaching for the sky. Check the website for upcoming shows.

PUENTE DE LA MUJER   BRIDGE
Map p238 (Dique 3) The striking Puente de la
Mujer (Bridge of the Woman) is the barrio's
signature monument. Unveiled in 2001,
this gleaming, white structure spans Dique
3 and resembles a sharp fishhook or even a
harp – but is supposed to represent a couple
dancing the tango. Designed by acclaimed
Spanish architect Santiago Calatrava and
mostly built in Spain, this 160m-long pedestrian bridge cost AR$6 million and rotates
90 degrees to allow water traffic to pass.

A FAILED PORT

Buenos Aires' waterfront was an object of controversy in the mid-19th century, when
competing commercial interests began to fight over the location of a modernized
port for Argentina's burgeoning international commerce. Two ideas came to light.
One was to widen and deepen the channel of the Riachuelo to port facilities at La
Boca, which indeed happened as planned. The other was proposed by Eduardo Madero, a wealthy exporter with strong political ties and solid financial backing. Madero
proposed transforming the city's mudflats into a series of modern basins and harbors consistent with the aspirations and ambitions of a cosmopolitan elite. This also
occurred, but not quite as he had planned.

By the time of its completion in 1898 (four years after Madero's death), Puerto Madero had exceeded its budget and Madero himself had come under scrutiny. Suspi-
cions arose from Madero's attempts to buy up all the landfill in the area and from his
links to politicians who had acquired nearby lands likely to increase in value. And the
practical side of the scheme didn't go so well either. By 1910 the amount of cargo was
already too great for the new port, and poor access to the rail terminus at Plaza Once
made things even worse. New facilities in a rejuvenated La Boca partly assuaged
these problems, but congressional actions failed to solve the major issues – until the
1926 completion of Retiro's Puerto Nuevo.

FRAGATA SARMIENTO   MUSEUM

Map p238 (☑4334-9386; Dique 3; admission AR$2; ☺10am-7pm) Over 23,000 Argentine naval cadets and officers have trained aboard this 85m sailing vessel, which traveled around the world 37 times between 1899 and 1938. On board are detailed records of its lengthy voyages, plenty of nautical items including old uniforms, and even the stuffed remains of Lampazo (the ship's pet dog). Peek into the ship's holds, galley and engine room and note the hooks where sleeping hammocks were strung up.

Built in Birkenhead, England, in 1897 at a cost of £125,000, this impeccably maintained ship never participated in combat. US president Theodore Roosevelt (look for his photo) was a distinguished guest on board, but perhaps the greatest test of the ship's seaworthiness was the visit of Roosevelt's successor, William Howard Taft, who weighed more than 140kg.

CORBETA URUGUAY   MUSEUM

Map p238 (☑4314-1090; Dique 4; admission AR$2; ☺10am-7pm) This 46-meter-long military ship did surveys along Argentina's coast and supplied bases in Antarctica until it was decommissioned in 1926, after 52 years of service. Displayed below the main deck are interesting relics from Antarctica expeditions, such as crampons and snowshoes, along with historical photos and nautical items. Check out the tiny kitchen, complete with *mate* supplies (of course).

EATING

Nearly all of Puerto Madero's restaurants are upscale and expensive, and many sport covered outdoor terraces with views of the nearby *diques* (dikes). You won't get the best bang for your buck in this elegant strip and the cuisine is more traditional than inspired, but it's the location that counts. Cabaña Las Lilas is the most famous *parrilla* restaurant here, but many consider it a tourist trap – a bit overrated and way overpriced. We don't review it here, but if you have money to burn, by all means try it.

I CENTRAL MARKET   MODERN ARGENTINE $$

Map p238 (☑5775-0330; Macacha Güemes 302; mains AR$80-135; ☺8am-midnight) In the morning, this pleasant airy restaurant has a coffee counter for espresso and scones; in the afternoon there are paninis, a gourmet deli and a kitchenwares shop to poke around; and by night, the fancy dining room serves contemporary Argentinian dishes. Great waterfront seating for people-watching. Also in Dique 3 at **Villaflor 300** (Map p238; ☑5775-0330; www.icentralmarket. com.ar; Villaflor 300; ☺8am-midnight).

LA PAROLACCIA TRATTORIA   ITALIAN $$

Map p238 (☑4343-1679; www.laparolaccia.com; Av Alicia Moreau de Justo 1052; mains AR$80-140; ☺noon-midnight Sun-Thu, to 2am Fri & Sat) This popular Italian eatery specializes in delicious homemade pastas. Reserve one of the few tables with a water view, then enjoy sweet potato gnocchi, gorgonzola ravioli or *cappelletti* (a small stuffed pasta) in four cheeses. If you're here at midday, the lunch menu is a great deal (available Monday to Saturday). A nearby branch, **La Parolaccia del Mare** (Map p238; Av Alicia Moreau de Justo 1170), specializes in seafood.

LA ROSA NÁUTICA   PERUVIAN $$$

(☑4311-5560; Av Alicia Moreau de Justo 246; mains AR$80-160; ☺noon-1am) This branch of the Lima (Peru) restaurant is worth a shot if you like seafood and fusion foods. Start with the house specialty – the marinated octopus *carpaccio* (in looks only – it's not raw) with Parmesan and olive oil. Then move on to the seviche, grilled fish or perhaps a Japanese sushi roll. It's not cheap, but it'll be tasty.

ENTERTAINMENT

ROJO TANGO   TANGO SHOW

Map p238 (☑4952-4111; www.rojotango.com; Faena Hotel & Universe, Martha Salotti 445; show AR$210, dinner & show AR$290) This sexy performance is the tango show to top all others – especially with its hefty price tag. Offering only 100 seats, the Faena's cabaret room is swathed in blood-red curtains and gilded furniture. The show itself loosely follows the history of tango, starting from its cabaret roots to the modern fusions of Ástor Piazzolla. The orchestra is first-rate, there are plenty of sexy period costumes and even a brief (shock!) nude scene. This is tango foreplay at its best.

Congreso & Tribunales

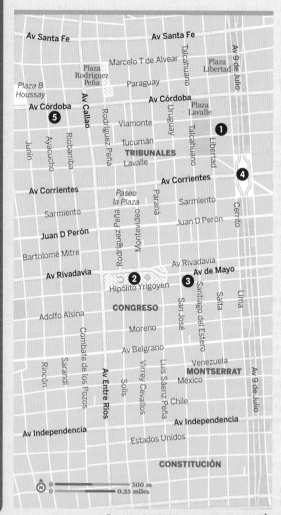

Neighborhood Top Five

1 Touring the backstage corners of the gorgeous **Teatro Colón** (p78), or perhaps taking in a play or concert there later in the evening.

2 Strolling down Av de Mayo to the stately buildings around **Plaza del Congreso** (p79).

3 Getting the history of the unique and stunning, Dante-inspired building that is **Palacio Barolo** (p79).

4 Standing at the base of Buenos Aires' iconic symbol, the **Obelisco** (p79).

5 Visiting the toilets and bidets at the bizarre little museum in **Palacio de las Aguas Corrientes** (p79).

For more detail of this area see Map p240 ➡

Explore: Congreso & Tribunales

Plaza del Congreso is at the heart of this neighborhood and an easy walk from Plaza de Mayo (in the Center) along the important thoroughfare Av de Mayo. This avenue connects the city's two most significant political centers and is itself lined with beautiful buildings, so be sure to take a stroll along it.

To do this, however, you'll have to experience crossing Av 9 de Julio (p110), which is 'the widest street in the world!' as proud *porteños* love to boast. This may be true, as it's 16 lanes at its widest; nearby side streets Cerrito and Pellegrini make it look even broader. Fortunately, traffic islands provide raised breaks for the thousands of pedestrians who cross this monstrosity every day, but it's still an intimidating barrier (and can't be done in one green light without breaking into a run – trust us).

Once you've explored the Plaza de Congreso area, head up to Av Corrientes and have a look around – it's the city's traditional old theater district, but there's still plenty of action going around. Further north is Plaza Lavalle, home to its own important cluster of buildings, including one of the principal gems of the city, Teatro Colón. Just a couple blocks from here is the Obelisco, Buenos Aires' key landmark, with a small plaza near the base.

Local Life

→**Hangouts** Break for afternoon teatime at the classic institutions of Café de los Angelitos (p81) or El Gato Negro (p81).
→**Culture** Av Corrientes is lined with theaters and cultural centers where locals catch inexpensive art exhibitions and plays.

Getting There & Away

→**Bus** Take bus 29 from Palermo or San Telmo, bus 64 from the Microcentro.
→**Subte** Líneas A and B from the Microcentro.

Lonely Planet's Top Tip

Check the big theaters like Teatro San Martín or Teatro Colón for inexpensive or even free events that are occasionally put on. Cultural centers like Centro Cultural San Martín are also good sources of free or affordable entertainment.

Congreso is busy during the day, but certain smaller streets feel desolate at night when all the stores close and businesspeople go home. Take a taxi if you feel uncomfortable.

CONGRESO & TRIBUNALES

✕ Best Places to Eat

→ Aramburu (p81)
→ Chan Chan (p81)
→ Parrilla Peña (p81)

For reviews, see p80 →

🍷 Best Places to Drink

→ Café de los Angelitos (p81)
→ El Gato Negro (p81)
→ Cruzat Beer House (p82)

For reviews, see p81 →

☆ Best Entertainment

→ Teatro Colón (p82)
→ Tango Porteño (p83)
→ Ávila Bar (p83)

For reviews, see p82 →

TOP SIGHT
TEATRO COLÓN

Sinking into a red velvet seat for a performance at Teatro Colón is a magical experience. This is one of the world's greatest opera houses: Mikhail Baryshnikov once called it 'the most beautiful of the theaters I know'. And you can experience it yourself, by attending a concert here or taking a behind-the-scenes tour.

The gorgeous and impressive seven-story building is one of Buenos Aires' biggest landmarks (and sources of pride). It's the city's main performing-arts venue and the only facility of its kind in the country, a world-class forum for opera, ballet and classical music. The theater's opening night was a presentation of Verdi's *Aïda*, and visitors have been wowed ever since. After all, the acoustics are considered among the top five of the world's concert venues.

Occupying an entire city block, the Teatro Colón can seat 2500 spectators and provide standing room for another 500. Started in 1880 and finished in 1908, it was the southern hemisphere's largest theater until the Sydney Opera House was built in 1973. Even at times of economic hardship, the elaborate Colón remains a high national priority. Italian Francesco Tamburini was the main architect, but after his death in 1891 his partner Vittorio Meano – who designed the Palacio del Congreso – was put in charge. After Meano was murdered (possibly due to a love triangle!), Belgian Jules Dormal took over and added some French elements to the theater. Over the years, the Colón has hosted some very prominent figures, such as Enrico Caruso, Plácido Domingo, Luciano Pavarotti, Maria Callas and Arturo Toscanini.

DON'T MISS...

➡ For theater aficionados, the backstage tour is a must.

➡ The occasional free concerts – check the website and click on 'Intérpretes Argentinos'.

PRACTICALITIES

➡ Map p240

➡ ☎4378-7127

➡ www.teatrocolon. org.ar

➡ Tucumán 1171

➡ tours residents/ non-residents AR$30/110

➡ ⊙tours 9am-5pm

⊙ SIGHTS

TEATRO COLÓN   NOTABLE BUILDING
See p78.

PLAZA DEL CONGRESO   SQUARE
Map p240 (☎4010-3000, ext 2410; ☻tours 12:30pm & 5pm Mon, Tue, Thu & Fri; ⑤Línea A Congreso, Sáenz Peña) At the western end of Av de Mayo lies Plaza del Congreso, often dotted with cooing pigeons and families feeding them. The **Monumento a los Dos Congresos** honors the congresses of 1810 in Buenos Aires and 1816 in Tucumán, both of which led to Argentine independence. The enormous granite steps symbolize the high Andes, and the fountain at its base represents the Atlantic Ocean. West of the plaza is the colossal green-domed **Palacio del Congreso** (Congress building).

Costing more than twice its projected budget, the Palacio del Congreso set a precedent for contemporary Argentine public-works projects. Modeled on the Capitol in Washington, DC, and topped by an 85m dome, the palace was completed in 1906. Inside the Congreso, there are free guided tours in English and Spanish. Go to the entrance at Hipólito Yrigoyen 1849; bring photo ID.

PALACIO BAROLO   NOTABLE BUILDING
Map p240 (☎4381-1885; www.palaciobarolo. com; Av de Mayo 1370; standard tours AR$80, longer tours incl glass of wine AR$150; ☻standard tours 4-7pm Mon-Thu, longer tours 8pm Wed & Fri & 8:30pm Thu) One of the Congreso area's most striking buildings is this 22-story concrete edifice. The building's unique design was inspired by Dante's *Divine Comedy*; its height (100m) is a reference to each canto (or song), the number of its floors (22) to verses per song and its divided structure represents hell, purgatory and heaven.

Palacio Barolo was commissioned by cotton tycoon Luis Barolo and designed by Italian architect Mario Palanti. Finished in 1923, it was Buenos Aires' highest skyscraper (until construction of Edificio Kavanagh, in Retiro). At the top is a lighthouse with an amazing 360-degree view of the city.

PALACIO DE LAS AGUAS
CORRIENTES   NOTABLE BUILDING, MUSEUM
Map p240 (cnr Córdoba & Riobamba) FREE Swedish engineer Karl Nyströmer and Norwegian architect Olaf Boye helped create this gorgeous and eclectic waterworks building. On the 2nd floor is the small and quirky **Museo del Patrimonio** (Map p240; ☎6319-1104; ☻9am-1pm Mon-Fri; tours in Spanish 11am Mon, Wed & Fri) FREE. The collection of pretty tiles, faucets, handles, ceramic pipe joints and plenty of old toilets and bidets is well lit and displayed. Guided visits offer a backstage glimpse of the building's inner workings and huge water tanks. Bring photo ID and enter via Riobamba.

Also known as Obras Sanitarias, Palacio de las Aguas Corrientes dates from 1894 and occupies an entire city block. Topped by French-style mansard roofs, the building's facade consists of 170,000 glazed tiles and 130,000 enameled bricks, all shipped from England and assembled here.

OBELISCO   LANDMARK
Map p240 (cnr Av 9 de Julio & Corrientes) The city's unmistakable landmark is the famous Obelisco, which soars 67m above the oval Plaza de la República. Dedicated in 1936, on the 400th anniversary of the first Spanish settlement on the Río de la Plata, this stately spire symbolizes Buenos Aires much as the Eiffel Tower represents Paris or the Washington Monument does Washington, DC. Following major soccer victories, boisterous fans circle the Obelisco in jubilant, honking celebration; it's also often used as the zero point for measuring distances from the city center. Unfortunately, you can't enter the structure – you'll have to admire it from outside.

PLAZA LAVALLE   PLAZA
Map p240 (Libertad btwn Córdoba & Lavalle) A couple of blocks northwest of the Obelisco is Plaza Lavalle, three blocks of parks surrounded by some important buildings. Two big landmarks here are the Teatro Colón and the Teatro Nacional Cervantes (p110). But there's also the austere neoclassical **Escuela Presidente Roca** (1902), an educational facility that's often mistaken for Teatro Colón. Across from it lies the French-style **Palacio de Justicia** (1904) and its Tribunales (federal courts).

MUSEO JUDIO DR SALVADOR
KIBRICK   MUSEUM
Map p240 (☎4123-0832; www.museojudio.org. ar; Libertad 769; admission AR$50; ☻11am-5pm Tue-Thu, to 4pm Fri) At the northeastern end of Plaza Lavalle, Jewish symbols adorn the facade of the **Templo de la Congregación Israelita**, Argentina's oldest and largest

BUENOS AIRES' CARTONEROS

You'll see them mostly at night, hunched over at the curb, picking through the garbage and pushing loaded-down carts. These are not the homeless, or the crazy, or the drug-addicted, or even the city's petty thieves. These are regular people, but some of Buenos Aires' poorest citizens – they're *cartoneros* (cardboard collectors). Many used to have regular jobs as skilled laborers or even businesspeople but have been laid off with the 2001 crisis. With unemployment still substantial and no social security to cover them, collecting recyclables is one way they can make a living.

It's estimated that around 20,000 *cartoneros* rummage through Buenos Aires' trash heaps; some are even accredited by the city and wear uniforms. They sort through the city's 5000 daily tons of waste, collecting cardboard, paper, metal, plastic, glass – anything they can sell by the kilo to the *depositos* (recycling companies). They stake out their territory, perhaps about 15 city blocks, and are occasionally forced to pay police bribes. Many have been pricked by syringes or cut by broken glass. This isn't an easy job, but it's decent work – once established, the daily take-home pay for a *cartonero* can be AR$100 or more.

While most *cartoneros* work independently, some work for neighborhood cooperatives that pay them a regular wage and organize vaccinations. Some cooperatives even provide child care for parents who go off on their nightly rounds. In the poorest families, however, even the young children have to work all night long. And some *cartoneros* are in their 50s and 60s.

It's not surprising that Argentina's economic crash has inflamed this side-business in recyclables, and that those less fortunate had to use their ingenuity to organize for themselves what their government could not. The *cartoneros* are a reminder to us that there is another side to the glittering richness of Buenos Aires' center, and that there is another part of this city where the poor people live.

synagogue. Concrete sidewalk planters, constructed after recent attacks against Jewish targets, discourage potential car bombs; police stand guard nearby. The Museo Judio Dr Salvador Kibrick is in the synagogue and contains many items and exhibits related to Jewish history. Bring photo ID for admission.

MUSEO BEATLE MUSEUM

Map p240 (☑6320-5362; www.thecavern.com.ar; Av Corrientes 1660; locals/foreigners AR$30/60; ☺10am-midnight Mon-Sat, 2pm-midnight Sun) Located in the Paseo La Plaza complex, this museum claims to be the only Beatles museum in South America. It showcases the Beatles memorabilia collection of owner Rodolfo R Veasquez – expect plenty of records, collector plates, toys, figurines, eight-track tapes, games and a couple of guitars from musicians related to the group. There's even a brick from the Cavern Club, a music club (now demolished) where the Beatles got their start. To find the museum, follow 'The Cavern' signs.

CENTRO CULTURAL RICARDO ROJAS CULTURAL CENTER

Map p240 (☑4954-5523; www.rojas.uba.ar; Av Corrientes 2038) This exceptional cultural center has a wide range of affordable classes, including dance, music, photography, theater, film and language studies.

CENTRO CULTURAL SAN MARTÍN CULTURAL CENTER

Map p240 (☑4374-1251; www.elculturalsanmartin.org; Sarmiento 1551) One of Buenos Aires' best resources, this large cultural center has free or inexpensive galleries, music, films, lectures, art exhibitions, classes and workshops.

✗ EATING

Hardly inspiring in terms of contemporary cuisine, the Congreso area caters mostly for business with cheap *parrillas* (steakhouses) and quick takeout. Walk around the side streets, though, and you're bound to stumble across some Chinese, Korean and Peruvian gems. The biggest cultural

footprint in this area, however, is **Buenos Aires' Little Spain neighborhood (in the blocks around Avs de Mayo and Salta); here you'll find a few good traditional Spanish and Basque eateries.**

★CHAN CHAN   PERUVIAN $

Map p240 (☑4382-8492; Hipólito Yrigoyen 1390; mains AR$35-65; ☺noon-4pm & 8pm-midnight Tue-Sun) Thanks to fair prices and relatively quick service, this colorful Peruvian eatery is jam-packed at lunchtime with office workers devouring plates of seviche (seafood cured in citrus) and *ajiaco de conejo* (rabbit and potato stew). There are also plenty of *arroz chaufa* (Peruvian-style fried rice) dishes, easily downed with a tangy pisco sour or a pitcher of *chicha morada* (a sweet fruity drink).

PARRILLA PEÑA   PARRILLA $

Map p240 (☑4371-5643; Rodríguez Peña 682; mains AR$50-90; ☺noon-4pm & 8pm-midnight Mon-Sat, noon-4pm Sun) This simple, traditional and long-running *parrilla* is well known for its excellent-quality meats and generous portions. The service is fast and efficient and it's great value. Don't expect many tourists – this is a locals' sort of place. Also on offer are homemade pastas, salads and *milanesas* (breaded steaks), along with several tasty desserts and a good wine list.

PIZZERÍA GÜERRÍN   PIZZERIA $

Map p240 (☑4371-8141; Av Corrientes 1368; slices AR$8; ☺11am-1am Sun-Thu, to 2am Fri & Sat) A quick pit-stop on Av Corrientes is this cheap but classic old pizza joint. Just point at a pre-baked slice behind the glass counter and eat standing up with the rest of the crowd. Or sit down and order one freshly baked – this way you can also choose from a greater variety of toppings for your pizza.

Empanadas (meat or vegetable pies) and plenty of desserts are also available.

CHIQUILÍN   PARRILLA $$

Map p240 (☑4373-5163; Sarmiento 1599; mains AR$60-100; ☺noon-2am Sun-Thu, to 3am Fri & Sat) A local mainstay for 80 years, Chiquilín is an excellent place to safely take, say, your parents. It's a large, comfortable restaurant with a cozy and classic atmosphere (including hanging hams). Dressed-up staff are efficient, which is great because this place can bustle – even at 1am on a Saturday night. The best choices here are steak and pasta.

PLAZA ASTURIAS   SPANISH $$

Map p240 (☑4382-7334; Av de Mayo 1199; mains AR$80-140; ☺11:30am-5pm & 7pm-1am Sun-Thu, to 2:30am Fri & Sat) This old-fashioned Spanish restaurant draws in a regular midday crowd with its set lunch (AR$90), which includes a main dish plus coffee, dessert and a glass of wine. Otherwise, the regular menu features staples like chorizo, ham and potato casserole, and pasta, as well as more adventurous dishes like *cazuela de mariscos,* a powerful seafood stew rich with mussels, garlic and herbs.

★ARAMBURU   GOURMET $$$

(☑4305-0439; www.arambururesto.com.ar; Salta 1050; prix-fixe AR$390; ☺8:30-11pm Tue-Sat) 'Molecular' dining has taken Buenos Aires by storm, and Chef Gonzalo Aramburu is leading the pack. The set 12-course meal might take you up to three hours to enjoy, each artistically created plate just a few bites of gastronomic delight. Expect enlightening tastes, textures, smells, plus unique presentations and a highly memorable meal. Located in the edgy but upcoming neighborhood of Montserrat.

🍷 DRINKING & NIGHTLIFE

This neighborhood is not known for its drinking holes, but there are at least a few atmospheric spots where you can toast the town while the politicos scurry past on the sidewalks.

CAFÉ DE LOS ANGELITOS   CAFE

Map p240 (☑4314-1121; Av Rivadavia 2100; ☺8am-midnight) Originally called Bar Rivadavia, this cafe was once the haunt of poets, musicians, even criminals, which is why a police commissioner jokingly called it *'los angelitos'* (the angels) in the early 1900s. Recently restored to its former glory, this historic cafe is now an elegant hangout for coffee or tea; it also puts on tango shows in the evening.

EL GATO NEGRO   TEAHOUSE, CAFE

Map p240 (☑4374-1730; Av Corrientes 1669; ☺9am-10pm Mon, to 11pm Tue, to midnight Wed & Thu, to 2am Fri & Sat, 3-11pm Sun) Tea-lined wooden cabinets and a spicy aroma welcome you to this pleasant little sipping paradise. Enjoy imported cups of coffee or tea, along with breakfast and dainty *sandwiches de miga* (thin, crustless sandwiches, traditionally eaten at tea time). Imported teas and coffees are sold in bulk, and a range of exotic herbs and spices are also on offer.

CRUZAT BEER HOUSE
BAR

Map p240 (☏6320-5344; www.cruzatba.com; Sarmiento 1617; ⏰10am-2am Mon-Fri, 7pm-3am Sat) In wine-soaked Buenos Aires, Cruzat is as close as you can get to a German beer garden. Kick back on the shaded terrace and choose craft beers from all over Argentina – look for El Bolsón (from Río Negro), Antares (from Mar del Plata) and Gulmen (from Viedma). There are also imports from Belgium, Chile, Spain and Italy.

LOS 36 BILLARES
CAFE, BAR

Map p240 (☏4381-5696; www.los36billares.com.ar; Av de Mayo 1265; shows from AR$50; ⏰8am-2am Mon-Sat) Dating from 1894, this is one of the city's most historic cafe-bars. As its name implies, it's big on pool and billiard tables (check out the basement); the back room is full of men shuffling cards for a poker game. Tango shows, highlighting different singers and dancers every night, happen at 9pm from Monday to Wednesday; tango classes also available.

MALUCO BELEZA
CLUB

Map p240 (☏4372-1737; www.malucobeleza.com.ar; Sarmiento 1728; ⏰Wed & Fri-Sun) Located in an old mansion is this popular Brazilian *boliche* (nightclub). It gets packed with up-beat revellers moving to samba fusion and others watching half-naked dancers writhing on the stage. For a more sedate atmosphere, climb the stairs, where it's more laid-back. If you're craving Brazilian cuisine, get here at 8:30pm on Wednesday, when dinner and a show are on tap.

EL BESO
MILONGA

Map p240 (☏4953-2794; Riobamba 416, 1st fl) Another traditional and popular place, El Beso attracts some very good dancers – you should be very confident of your dancing skills if you come here. Located upstairs, it has good music and a cozy feel.

On Friday night, El Beso hosts the far less traditional but still well-known **La Marshall Milonga** (http://lamarshallmilonga.com.ar), a gay *milonga*, for all who want to try a change of roles in their tango. There's a class at 10:30pm before the *milonga* (tango session) at 11:30pm.

⭐ ENTERTAINMENT

TEATRO COLÓN
CLASSICAL MUSIC

Map p240 (☏4378-7100; www.teatrocolon.org.ar; Cerrito 628) BA's premier venue for the arts, with ballet and opera as well as classical music. For more on Teatro Colón, see p78.

TEATRO SAN MARTÍN
CLASSICAL MUSIC

Map p240 (☏0800-333-5254; www.complejoteatral.gob.ar; Av Corrientes 1530) This major venue has several auditoriums (the largest seats over 1000 people) and showcases international cinema, theater, dance and classical music, covering conventional and more unusual events. It also has art galleries and often hosts impressive photography exhibitions.

TEATRO PASEO LA PLAZA
THEATER

Map p240 (☏6320-5300; www.paseolaplaza.com.ar; Av Corrientes 1660) Located in a small and pleasant outdoor shopping mall, this complex features several theater halls that run both classic and contemporary productions, including tango, theater and comedy.

TEATRO PRESIDENTE ALVEAR
THEATER

Map p240 (☏4373-4245; www.complejoteatral.gob.ar; Av Corrientes 1659) Inaugurated in 1942 and named after an Argentine president whose wife sang opera, this theater holds over 700 and shows many musical productions, including ballet. Occasional free shows are on offer.

TEATRO AVENIDA
CLASSICAL MUSIC

Map p240 (☏4812-6369; www.balirica.org.ar; Av de Mayo 1222) In 1979 a fire closed down this beautiful 1906 theater for 15 years, but it was later restored to its former glory. Today the Avenida highlights Argentine productions, mostly classical music, ballet and flamenco. But its biggest strength is opera.

CAFÉ DE LOS ANGELITOS
TANGO SHOW

Map p240 (☏4952-2320; www.cafedelosangelitos.com; Av Rivadavia 2100; show from US$90, show & dinner from US$130) Angelitos puts on one of the best shows in Buenos Aires. It's tango – but also a bit more. The performers dress in top-notch costumes and use interesting props, like drapes and moving walls. They also dance to modern tunes such as those by local band Bajofondo, and despite a nightclub feel at times – especially due to the lighting – it's all very tastefully and creatively done.

The stage is well set up (the musicians are on a different level, out of the way but well in sight) and everyone gets a good view. If you can't afford Rojo Tango (p75), come here; it's choreographed by the same folks and offers some sexy elements.

TANGO PORTEÑO
TANGO SHOW

Map p240 (☑4124-9400; www.tangoporteno. com.ar; Cerrito 570; show US$80, show & dinner from US$127) One of the city's best shows takes place in this renovated art deco theater. Snippets of old footage are interspersed with plenty of athletic (and at times sensual) dancing. There's an interesting blindfold number, the orchestra is excellent and Juan Carlos Copes – a famous Argentine dancer in his time – makes a rug-cutting cameo if he's in good health.

It's right in the center near Teatro Colón. Complimentary tango class offered beforehand.

ÁVILA BAR
FLAMENCO

Map p240 (☑4383-6974; Av de Mayo 1384; ☉Thu-Sat) Offering flamenco for many years now is this cozy little Spanish restaurant with good traditional food. Main dishes can include rabbit, paella and seafood stews. Shows have older, experienced dancers and cost AR$220 (drinks not included). They start around 10:30pm and reservations are a must on weekends.

CANTARES
FLAMENCO

Map p240 (☑4381-6965; www.cantarestablao. com.ar; Av Rivadavia 1180; show $AR90; ☉shows 9pm Fri & Sat) This flamenco venue, in the old Taberna Español, once hosted the Spanish poet Federico García Lorca. It's a small basement space with only 85 seats, providing a wonderfully intimate place for the highly authentic dances. An à la carte dinner is on offer; reserve in advance. Flamenco classes also available.

🛍 SHOPPING

Congreso is where the city's politicos hang out and it's not really known as a shopping destination. That said, Av Corrientes has many of the city's discount bookstores, and despite most books being in Spanish, it's fun to wander through them. And if you're looking for jewelry or electronics like used cameras, check out Calle Libertad between Lavalle and Rivadavia.

ZIVAL'S
MUSIC

Map p240 (www.zivals.com; Av Callao 395; ☉9:30am-9:30pm Mon-Sat) This is one of the better music stores in town, especially when it comes to tango, jazz and classical music. Listening stations are a big plus, and many books are also for sale. There's also a branch in **Palermo Viejo** (Map p250; Serrano 1445).

WILDLIFE
CAMPING & OUTDOOR EQUIPMENT

Map p240 (☑4381-1040; Hipólito Yrigoyen 1133; ☉10am-8pm Mon-Fri, to 1pm Sat) If you're looking to buy (or sell) all manner of outdoor and camping equipment before traveling on from Buenos Aires, this is the place to do it. Crampons, knives, tents, backpacks, climbing ropes, foul-weather clothing, military gear and even the occasional mule saddle can be found at this somewhat offbeat and musty shop.

1. Palacio Barolo (p79)
Inspired by Dante's *Divine Comedy* the palace's structure represents hell, purgatory and heaven.

2. Puerto Madero (p71)
Residential buildings line the waterfront of Buenos Aires' newest barrio.

3. Museo Fortabat (p74)
Architect Rafael Viñoly devised roof panels that tilt with the sun for this modernist gallery.

4. Basílica Nuestra Señora del Pilar (p118)
A Peruvian altar adorned with silver is the highlight of the basilica, built by Jesuits in 1716.

San Telmo

Neighborhood Top Five

1 Jostling with fellow shoppers at the Sunday **Feria de San Telmo** (p95), where vendors sell all manner of goods, and buskers and tango dancers compete for your spare change.

2 Taking a break in peaceful **Plaza Dorrego** (p88) – when it's *not* a Sunday.

3 Exploring the reconstructed tunnels at **El Zanjón de Granados** (p89).

4 Visiting the **Museo Histórico Nacional** (p89) at historic Parque Lezama.

5 Strolling cobbled streets and taking in old-time atmosphere at places like **Pasaje de la Defensa** (p89).

For more detail of this area see Map p242 ➡

Explore: San Telmo

Two central thoroughfares in this barrio are Balcarce and Defensa; they're where you'll find most things of interest to travelers.

Everyone is drawn to Plaza Dorrego, the heart and soul of San Telmo. It's a nice leafy place to snag an outdoor table under an umbrella and have a coffee or full meal (though on Sundays the *feria* takes over and tables disappear). Sometimes tango dancers provide entertainment for a few pesos, though you can also be hassled for spare change by beggars or asked to buy items by roving vendors. Keep a good hold of your bag, just in case.

Generally everything of interest is reachable by walking in this neighborhood. From Plaza Dorrego you can stroll up or down the main drag of Defensa, window-shopping for pricey antiques or trendy new trinkets along the way. Several museums are also on or just off this street. If you head south, you'll hit Parque Lezama, a local park where families hang out at the playground and lovers smooch on benches. Heading north, you can be in the Plaza de Mayo area in 15 minutes.

The adventurous can walk further south down busy Av Almirante Brown to La Boca (note: this will take you along the gritty edges of this blue-collar neighborhood).

Local Life

→**Markets** Explore the Mercado de San Telmo (p96) to get a dose of history and a feel for how the locals buy their meats and vegetables.

→**Hangouts** Classic cafes like Bar Plaza Dorrego (p92), Bar El Federal (p91) and La Poesia (p92) drip with traditional atmosphere and old-time locals taking in their morning *medialunas* (croissants) or afternoon coffee breaks.

→**Games** Like chess? Then head to Parque Lezama (p89) and find the cluster of chess tables there – and, if you dare, make a challenge.

Getting There & Away

→**Bus** Take bus 59 from Recoleta and Palermo, bus 29 from La Boca, Plaza de Mayo and Palermo.

→**Subte** Línea C connects the western edge of San Telmo with the Center, Congreso and Retiro.

Lonely Planet's Top Tip

On Sundays the *feria* (street market) is full-on, which means tons of people are visiting and you'll need to watch for pickpockets and over-charging more carefully. On the other hand, it's a fun time to be in the neighborhood and the museums and most stores are all open. For more peace, visit San Telmo from Monday to Saturday, especially to sit at one of Plaza Dorrego's outdoor tables.

East of Balcarce the streets become industrial and, along with the more southern edges toward La Boca, should probably be avoided at night. During the day they're fine, however, and provide access to Puerto Madero.

SAN TELMO

✖ Best Places to Eat

→ Café San Juan (p91)
→ Casal de Catalunya (p91)
→ Origen Café (p91)

For reviews, see p91

🍷 Best Places to Drink

→ Bar Plaza Dorrego (p92)
→ Doppelgänger (p92)
→ Gibraltar (p92)

For reviews, see p92

⊙ Best Shopping

→ Feria de San Telmo (p95)
→ Materia Urbana (p95)
→ Puntos en el Espacio (p95)

For reviews, see p95

TOP SIGHT
PLAZA DORREGO

At the heart of San Telmo is Plaza Dorrego, normally a peaceful little plaza strewn with locals and tourists sitting at tables under their umbrellas. A few hippie street vendors hawk their wares on the sidewalks while tango dancers occasionally perform for a few pesos. Come Sundays, however, the plaza and Calle Defensa become packed with craft stalls selling everything from antiques to knick-knacks to creative homemade souvenirs. It's a bit of a crazy scene, but worth experiencing nonetheless.

After Plaza de Mayo, Plaza Dorrego is the city's oldest plaza. It dates to the 18th century and was originally a pit stop for caravans bringing supplies into Buenos Aires from around Argentina. At the turn of the 19th century it became a public square surrounded by colonial buildings that survive to this day. There's still a wonderful old-time atmosphere here and cafe-restaurants like Bar Plaza Dorrego (p92) will definitely take you back in time. However, things are changing; across from this traditional cafe, a branch of Starbucks recently opened and prominently announced the arrival of the 21st century.

Plaza Dorrego's biggest claim to fame is likely now its extremely popular Sunday *feria*. Tourists and locals alike flock to this fun event, which brings together hundreds of street vendors, buskers and shoppers. Originally started in 1970 as an antiques fair, the *feria* has now become a craft market offering all manner of items – jewelry, souvenirs, knick-knacks, quality artwork, vintage clothing, old collectibles, hand-made crafts, leather jackets and much, much more. Defensa is closed to traffic from Plaza de Mayo to Parque Lezama (which has its own little craft market) and lined with hundreds of stalls. Street performers from metallic human statues to *candombe* drumming groups to professional tango dancers entertain the crowds, while sidewalk tables provide welcome breaks. It's a tight and crowded scene, so be prepared to bump into people – and watch your bag carefully.

DON'T MISS...

➡ Relaxing at a table on the plaza while tango dancers perform nearby.

➡ Sunday's bustling street *feria*.

PRACTICALITIES

➡ Map p242

⊙ SIGHTS

PLAZA DORREGO PLAZA
See p88.

**EL ZANJÓN DE
GRANADOS** ARCHAEOLOGICAL SITE
Map p242 (☑4361-3002; www.elzanjon.com.ar;
Defensa 755; 1 hr tour Mon-Fri AR$90, 30 min
tour Sun AR$60; ⊙tours 11am, noon, 2pm & 3pm
Mon-Fri, every 30min 1-6pm Sun) One of the
more unique places in BA is this amazing
urban architectural site. A series of old
tunnels, sewers and cisterns (built from
1730 onwards) were constructed above a
river tributary and provided the base for
one of BA's oldest settlements, which later
became a family mansion and then tenement housing and some shops. It's best to
reserve ahead for tours.

The Zanjón is the realized dream of
Jorge Eckstein, who found these ruins in
1986 after purchasing land for a business
project and then spent years renovating
them into what you see today. It offers a
fascinating glimpse into the city's history;
meticulously reconstructed brick by brick
and very attractively lit, this site also
contains several courtyards and even a
watchtower. There are a few relics on display in the various halls and rooms, but
the highlights are the spaces themselves.

**MUSEO DE ARTE MODERNO DE
BUENOS AIRES (MAMBA)** MUSEUM
Map p242 (☑4342-3001; www.museode
artemoderno.buenosaires.gob.ar; Av San Juan
350; admission AR$5, Tue free; ⊙11am-7pm
Tue-Fri, to 8pm Sat & Sun) Housed in a recycled tobacco warehouse, this spacious and
newly remodeled museum shows off the
works of both national and international
contemporary artists. Expect temporary
exhibitions showcasing everything from
photography to industrial design, and
from figurative to conceptual art. There's
also an auditorium, and there are plans
to integrate the old cinema museum next
door, too – and add a cafe and gift shop.

**MUSEO DE ARTE
CONTEMPORÁNEO BUENOS AIRES** MUSEUM
Map p242 (MACBA; ☑5299-2010; www.macba.
com.ar; Av San Juan 328; admission AR$25;
⊙noon-7pm Mon & Wed-Fri, 11am-7:30pm Sat
& Sun) Art lovers shouldn't miss this fine
museum, which specializes in geometric
abstraction drawn from the technology-
driven world that surrounds us today
(think architecture, maps and computers).
So rather than traditional paintings, you'll
see large, colorful and minimalist pieces
meant to inspire reflection. It mostly
shows off the works of young Argentine
artists, though occasional international
guests' work appears. There are four
floors; the first two hold rotating, permanent exhibits. Guided visits in Spanish are
available at 5pm daily.

PASAJE DE LA DEFENSA NOTABLE BUILDING
Map p242 (Defensa 1179; ⊙10am-6pm Tue-Fri,
to 8pm Sun) Originally built for the Ezeiza
family in 1880, this building later became
a *conventillo* (tenement house) and was
home to 32 families. These days, it's a
charmingly worn building with antique
shops clustered around atmospheric leafy
patios.

PARQUE LEZAMA PARK
Map p242 (Defensa & Av Brasil) Scruffy
Parque Lezama was once thought to be
the site of Buenos Aires' founding in 1536,
but archaeological teams have refuted
the hypothesis. Today's green park hosts
old chess-playing gentlemen, bookworms
toting *mate* (traditional Argentine tea)
gourds and teenagers kissing on park
benches. Don't miss the striking late-19th-
century **Iglesia Ortodoxa Rusa** (Russian
Orthodox Church) on the north side of the
park; it's the work of architect Alejandro
Christopherson and was built from materials shipped over from St Petersburg.

MUSEO HISTÓRICO NACIONAL MUSEUM
Map p242 (☑4307-1182; Defensa 1600; ⊙11am-
6pm Wed-Sun) `FREE` Located in Parque
Lezama is the city's national historical
museum. It's dedicated to exhibiting
items related to Argentina's revolution
on May 25, 1810. Argentine hero Manuel
Belgrano's watch was stolen from this
museum in 2007, and things have never
been the same since. Bags and backpacks
have to be checked in, and guards are
everywhere.

Inside, exhibits are a bit sparse, but at
least they're neatly displayed. There are
several portraits of presidents and other
major figures of the time, and you can
peek into a recreated version of José de
San Martín's bedroom – he was a military
hero and liberator of Argentina (along
with other South American countries).

SAN TELMO: A BRIEF HISTORY

San Telmo is known for the violent street fighting that took place when British troops, at war with Spain, invaded the city in 1806. They occupied it until the following year, when covert porteño resistance became open counterattack. British forces advanced up narrow Defensa, but the impromptu militia drove the British back to their ships. Victory gave *porteños* confidence in their ability to stand apart from Spain, even though the city's independence had to wait another three years.

After this San Telmo became a fashionable, classy neighborhood, but in the late 19th century a yellow-fever epidemic hit and drove the rich onto higher ground, west and north of the present-day Microcentro. As European immigrants began to pour into the city, many older mansions in San Telmo became *conventillos* (tenements) to house poor families. Today you can see one such *conventillo* at Pasaje de la Defensa (p89), originally built for the Ezeiza family; later it housed 32 families.

Old documents are also on display, and there's a video room as well.

Perhaps the most interesting exhibit, however, is of a few paintings depicting Africans in Argentina celebrating Carnaval and playing *candombe* (a drum-based musical genre invented in the early 18th century by slaves brought to the Rio de la Plata region). Argentina's black history is limited and mysterious – the country did have a slave trade, but today there are very few people of African descent here.

MUSEO PENITENCIARIO
MUSEUM

Map p242 (✒4361-0917; museopenitenciario argentino.blogspot.com.ar; Humberto Primo 378; ☺2-6pm Thu, Fri & Sun) **FREE** Dating from 1760, this building was a convent and later a women's prison before it became a penal museum in 1980; reconstructed old jail cells give an idea of the prisoners' conditions. Don't miss the homemade playing cards and shivs, plus the tennis balls used to hide drugs. A prison infirmary is also exhibited. Next door, the neocolonial and baroque **Iglesia Nuestra Señora de Belén** (Map p242; Humberto Primo 340) was a Jesuit school until 1767, when the Bethlemite order took it over.

CONVENTO DE SANTO DOMINGO
CHURCH

Map p242 (✒4331-1668 ext 201; cnr Defensa & Belgrano; ☺basílica tours by appointment only; ⑤Línea E Bolívar, Línea A Plaza de Mayo) Marking the approach into San Telmo, this 18th-century Dominican building has a long and colorful history. On its left tower you'll see the replicated scars of shrapnel launched against British troops who holed up here during the invasion of 1806. The **basílica** displays the flags that were captured from the British. Secularized during the presidency of Bernardino Rivadavia (1826–27), the building became a natural history museum, its original single tower serving as an astronomical observatory, until Governor Juan Manuel de Rosas restored it to the Dominican order. For (free) basilica tours, call between 3:30pm and 6:30pm; most tours run on Sundays.

MUSEO DEL TRAJE
MUSEUM

Map p242 (✒4343-8427; www.funmuseodel traje.com.ar; Chile 832; ☺3-7pm Tue-Sun; ⑤Línea C Independencia) **FREE** Near the Montserrat border, this small clothing museum is always changing its wardrobe. You can hit upon wedding outfits from the late 1800s, popular fashions from the early 1900s or even clothing worn by travelers on the Silk Rd. If you're lucky, accessories such as hair combs, top hats, antique eyeglasses and elegant canes might be on display.

FACULTAD DE INGENIERIA
NOTABLE BUILDING

Map p242 (Av Paseo Colón 850) This neoclassical and monstrous building is the engineering school for the Universidad de Buenos Aires. It was originally built for the Fundación Eva Perón and is an oddball landmark once described by Gerald Durrell as 'a cross between the Parthenon and the Reichstag.'

In front of the building and in the middle of Av Paseo Colón is **Plazoleta Olazábal**, a tiny park that features Rogelio Yrurtia's masterful sculpture **Canto al Trabajo**. It was moved here from its original site on Plaza Dorrego.

EATING

The heart of San Telmo, Plaza Dorrego is surrounded by several cafe-restaurants that pop open their umbrellas from Monday to Saturday. On Sunday, however, the plaza (and a few surrounding streets) is taken over by vendors and tourists jamming the ever-popular antiques market. San Telmo has traditionally supported a large cluster of *parrillas*, but as the neighborhood inexorably gentrifies, more innovative, upscale and pricier restaurants and bars are moving in.

ORIGEN CAFÉ
INTERNATIONAL $

Map p242 (☎4362-7979; Primo 599; mains AR$50-70; ⊙8am-10pm Tue-Fri & Sun, to 9:30pm Mon & Sat) Modern but unpretentious, this stylish corner bistro spills out onto the wide sidewalks; snag an outdoor table on a sunny afternoon. The creative menu features health-conscious dishes from stir-fries and whole-wheat pizzas to homemade soups and green salads. There's an emphasis on vegetarian food, and the cappuccinos are served in delightfully oversized mugs.

EL DESNIVEL
PARRILLA $

Map p242 (☎4300-9081; Defensa 855; mains AR$45-80; ⊙noon-4:30pm & 7pm-1am Mon-Fri, noon-1am Sat & Sun) This famous and long-running *parrilla* joint packs in both locals and tourists, serving them treats like chorizo sandwiches and *bife de lomo* (tenderloin steak). The sizzling grill out front is torturous while you wait for a table (which could be in the large back room) – get here early, especially on weekends.

BAR EL FEDERAL
ARGENTINE $

Map p242 (☎4300-4313; cnr Perú & Carlos Calvo; mains AR$35-110; ⊙8am-2am Sun-Thu, to 4am Fri & Sat) Dating from 1864, this historic bar has a classic, somewhat rustic atmosphere accented with original wood, tile, and an eye-catching antique bar. The specialties here are sandwiches (especially turkey) and *picadas* (shared appetizer plates), but there are also lots of pastas, salads, desserts and tall mugs of icy beer.

LA POESIA
ARGENTINE $

Map p242 (☎4300-7340; www.cafelapoesia. com.ar; Chile 502; mains AR$40-110; ⊙8am-2am) Step back in time at this historic, traditional cafe. Originally a gathering place for artists and poets, this small corner spot still retains its bohemian atmosphere with live music recitals on Thursdays and Fridays. Snack on a turkey sandwich, *milanesa* (beef cutlet) or some pasta, and try to relive the past.

ABUELA PAN
VEGETARIAN $

Map p242 (☎4361-4936; Chile 518; daily menu AR$43; ⊙8am-7pm Mon-Fri, 9am-4pm Sun; ☑) Tiny but atmospheric spot with just a handful of tables. The vegetarian special changes daily – expect things like spinach omelets, stuffed cannelloni and burghul hamburgers.

CASAL DE CATALUNYA
SPANISH $$

Map p242 (☎4361-0191; Chacabuco 863; mains AR$60-100; ⊙8pm-midnight Mon, noon-4pm & 8pm-midnight Tue-Sat, noon-4pm Sun) Located in BA's Catalan cultural center is this excellent Catalan restaurant. Big on seafood, its specialties run from garlic shrimp to fresh mussels and clams in tomato sauce to fish of the day with aioli. Other typical dishes include *jamón serrano* (prosciutto-like ham), seafood paella and suckling pig. Don't miss the luscious *crema Catalana* for dessert.

LA PANADERÍA
DE PABLO
MODERN ARGENTINE $$

Map p236 (☎4331-4683; Defensa 269; mains AR$70-110; ⊙9:30am-6pm Mon-Wed, 9:30am-midnight Thu & Fri, 8pm-midnight Sat, 10am-7pm Sun) Enter this modern restaurant and be comforted by the awesome design, airy spaces and cozy booths. Try the smoked salmon salad with avocado, rib-eye marinated in rosemary and thyme or Yamani rice stir fries. There are a few elegant pizzas and pastas too, along with over a dozen cocktails to accompany. You'll also find a great patio in back for warm days, plus breakfast offerings.

GRAN PARRILLA DEL PLATA
PARRILLA $$

Map p242 (☎4300-8858; www.parrilladelplata. com; Chile 594; mains AR$65-100; ⊙noon-4pm & 8pm-1am) There's nothing too fancy at this traditional corner *parrilla* – just old-time atmosphere and generous portions of good grilled meats at decent prices. There are also pastas for that vegetarian who gets dragged along. Divided into two sections but they're right next to each other.

★CAFÉ SAN JUAN   INTERNATIONAL $$$

Map p242 (☑4300-1112; Av San Juan 452; mains AR$125-150; ☺12:30-4pm & 8pm-1am) Having studied in Milan, Paris and Barcelona, celebrity TV-chef Leandro Cristóbal now runs the kitchen at this renowned San Telmo bistro. Start with fabulous tapas, then delve into the grilled Spanish octopus, *molleja* (sweetbreads) cannelloni and the amazing pork *bondiola* (deliciously tender after nine hours' roasting). Most of the seafood is flown in daily from Patagonia. Reserve for lunch and dinner.

If you can't get a table here, try the **Café San Juan La Cantina** (Map p242; ☑4300-9344; Chile 474; ☺noon-3:30pm & 8:30pm-midnight Tue-Sun). It's located a few blocks away and has a different menu.

COMEDOR NIKKAI   JAPANESE $$$

Map p242 (☑4300-5848; Av Independencia 732; mains AR$80-250; ☺noon-3pm & 7:30-11pm Mon-Thu, noon-3pm & 8pm-midnight Fri, 8pm-midnight Sat) Housed in the Asociación Japonesa building, this restaurant has some of BA's most authentic Japanese food, and the locals know it – come early if you don't want to wait. All your favorites are here, including tempura, teriyaki, ramen or udon noodles and – of course – lots of sushi and sashimi choices. Imported sake is available too.

🍷⚓ DRINKING & NIGHTLIFE

San Telmo keeps gentrifying. Fancy restaurants and bars continue to pop up with regularity, mixing it up with a few old classics like historic cafes that have hardly changed over the years. Here older gentlemen still show up for their morning coffee and *medialunas*, but there's space for everyone – and this neighborhood has become very popular with locals, travelers and expats.

★BAR PLAZA DORREGO   CAFE

Map p242 (☑4361-0141; Defensa 1098; ☺8am-2am Sun-Thu, to 3am Fri & Sat) You can't beat the atmosphere at this traditional joint; sip your *submarino* (hot milk with chocolate) by a picturesque window and watch the world pass by, or grab a table on the busy plaza. Meanwhile, traditionally suited waiters, piped-in tango music, antique bottles and scribbled graffiti on walls and counters might take you back in time.

DOPPELGÄNGER   COCKTAIL BAR

Map p242 (☑4300-0201; Av Juan de Garay 500) This cool, emerald-hued corner bar is one of the only places in BA where you can count on a perfectly mixed martini. That's because Doppelgänger specializes in vermouth cocktails. The atmosphere is calm and the lengthy menu is fascinating: start with the journalist, a martini with a bitter orange twist, or channel Don Draper and go for the bar's bestseller – an old-fashioned.

GIBRALTAR   PUB

Map p242 (☑4362-5310; Perú 895; ☺noon-4am) One of BA's classic pubs, the Gibraltar has a cozy atmosphere and good bar counter for those traveling alone. It's also a great place for fairly authentic foreign cuisine – try the Thai, Indian or English dishes (full English breakfast offered from noon to 5pm). For a little friendly competition, head to the pool table in the back.

COFFEE TOWN   COFFEE

Map p242 (☑4361-0019; www.coffeetown argentina.com; Bolívar 976, inside Mercado de San Telmo; ☺10am-8pm) For some of BA's best coffee, drop into this very casual kiosk inside the Mercado de San Telmo (enter via Carlos Calvo). Experienced baristas serve up organic, fair-trade coffee derived from beans from all over the world – think Colombia, Kenya, Sumatra and Yemen. A few pastries help the java go down easy.

BAR BRITÁNICO   CAFÉ

Map p242 (☑4361-2107; Av Brasil 399; ☺24hr Tue-Sun, 8am-midnight Mon) A classic corner cafe on the edge of Parque Lezama, Bar Británico has an evocative old wooden interior and big glass windows that open to the street. Drop in for a *café cortado* (small espresso with milk) in the morning or a beer on a sunny afternoon.

LA PUERTA ROJA   BAR

Map p242 (☑4362-5649; Chacabuco 733; ☺5pm-late) There's no sign at this upstairs bar – just look for the red door. It has a cool, relaxed atmosphere with low lounge furniture in the main room and a pool table tucked behind. This is a traditional place, so you won't find fruity cocktails on

AN EXPAT'S SAN TELMO

New Jersey native Jessica Pollack, a cultural historian and expert city tour guide with Buenos Tours (p208), tells us what she loves about San Telmo, one of Buenos Aires' most historic 'hoods and the barrio that she's chosen to call home.

San Telmo's Got Character

I am always impressed by the palpable history on the cobbled streets: on Pasaje San Lorenzo you see layers of time. The once-grand Spanish mansions, later occupied by immigrant families, are now covered in street art and graffiti and house anything from music venues to pilates studios. If you peek into the courtyard at San Lorenzo 317, there's an artisan workshop called El Moro, a family operation that makes traditional *mates* and *bombillas* – it's full of the history, personality and artistry typical of an old neighborhood.

The Old & the New

Despite gentrification, the traditional is not sacrificed for the trendy; they coexist wonderfully. I love that on any night I can get a craft beer at historic Bar El Federal (p91) or contemporary cocktails at dimly lit Doppelgänger (p92). Even inside the century-old indoor Mercado de San Telmo (p96) you'll find delicious preserves homemade by a woman named Margarita just a few stalls down from Coffee Town, serving specialty blends and imported coffees at its fashionable new stand.

Sunday Suggestions

We all know Sunday is San Telmo's big day: the area comes to life with the hugely popular and highly enjoyable street fair (p95). But for most of the city, Sunday means relaxation and quiet time. To me, Sunday means waking up late for a slice of ricotta cake from **Confitería Europa** (Carlos Calvo 678), where Argentine men watch *fútbol* and sip *cafe con leche*. The service is terribly slow, but it's Sunday after all, and the leisurely pace is a welcome escape from the street-fair bustle.

SAN TELMO ENTERTAINMENT

the menu – but there's good international food like curries, tacos and chicken wings.

BAR SEDDÓN   BAR RESTAURANT
Map p242 (☑4342-3700; Defensa 695; ⊙10am-4am Mon-Thu, to 6am Fri-Sun) This long-running corner bar-restaurant, outfitted with black and white tiles and rustic wood tables, is housed in an old restored pharmacy. Drop in for an icy *chopp* (mug of draught beer) or a late-night glass of red – there are also sandwiches, pizzas and daily specials if you're hungry.

PRIDE CAFE   CAFE
Map p242 (☑4300-6435; Balcarce 869; ⊙9am-8pm Mon-Fri, 11am-8pm Sat & Sun; ☎) This small, gay-friendly and contemporary cafe is especially swamped by cute men on Sunday during San Telmo's antiques fair, attracted by the homemade pastries, healthy snacks and flavored coffees. Peruse the foreign mags or utilize the free wi-fi, and maybe pick up a hot date.

BOUTIQUE   CLUB
Map p242 (☑4543-3894; www.museumclub.com.ar; Perú 535; ⊙Wed, Fri & Sat) This cavernous disco is best known for its Wednesday-night 'after-office' party (read: meat market), which starts at the normally ungodly-early hour of 7pm and runs to the ungodly-early finishing hour of 2am. It's a huge space with multiple balconies and a great sound system highlighting '80s and '90s pop music. Note the amazing building, an old factory designed by Eiffel – who also did that particular Parisian landmark.

☆ ENTERTAINMENT

EL VIEJO ALMACÉN   TANGO SHOW
Map p242 (☑4307-7388; www.viejoalmacen.com; cnr Balcarce & Av Independencia; show from US$90, show & dinner from US$140) One of Buenos Aires' longest-running shows (since 1969), this venue is a charming old

🏃 Neighborhood Walk
Historical Saunter

START EL ZANJÓN DE GRANADOS
END BAR BRITÁNICO
LENGTH 1.5KM; 2½ HOURS

Time your walk to tour the amazing series of tunnels and brick archways of **1 El Zanjón de Granados** (p89), which formed the foundations of BA's oldest homes.

The decaying white-stucco-and-brick **2 Casa Mínima** at San Lorenzo 380 is a good example of the narrow-lot style known as *casa chorizo* (sausage house). Barely 2m wide, the lot was reportedly an emancipation gift from slave owners to their former bondsmen.

Stop at the lively **3 El Desnivel** (p92) for a good steak experience. And don't miss strolling through the covered **4 Mercado de San Telmo** (p96), which has been running since 1897.

Back on Defensa you'll soon reach the heart of the barrio, **5 Plaza Dorrego** (p88). From Monday to Saturday it's a relatively peaceful place, but come Sunday the lively **6 Feria de San Telmo** (p95) sets up in the plaza and surrounding streets.

For funky prison paraphernalia, check out the **7 Museo Penitenciario** (p90); note the **8 Iglesia Nuestra Señora de Belén** (p90), an old Jesuit school, next door.

A block south, the **9 Museo de Arte Moderno de Buenos Aires** (p89) offers cutting-edge exhibitions, along with works by classic Argentine artists. Next door is the **10 Museo de Arte Contemporáneo Buenos Aires** (p89), great for abstract art.

The freeway location of the **11 Club Atlético Memorial** is simply awful – but so is its history. This is one of the secret detention centers where thousands of people were tortured and killed during Argentina's Dirty War (1976–83). There isn't much left beyond an excavated basement where a three-story building used to be.

Stroll through the large **12 Parque Lezama** (p89) to the **13 Museo Histórico Nacional** (p89) for a bit of insight into Argentina's history. And finally, rest your tired feet at the atmospheric corner **14 Bar Británico** (p92), snag a prized window seat and order a drink – you deserve it.

SAN TELMO NEIGHBORHOOD WALK

building from the 1800s. A good dinner is served at a multi-story restaurant in the main building, then everyone heads across the street to the small theater with intimate stage. The show starts with a quick movie about the tango show's history, then moves on to the highly athletic dancers with plenty of glitz. One highlight is the exceptionally good folklore segment.

LA VENTANA TANGO SHOW

Map p242 (☑4334-1314; www.laventanaweb.com; Balcarce 431; show from US$90, dinner & show from US$140) This long-running basement venue is located in an old converted building with rustic brick walls. The tango show is excellent and includes a folkloric segment with Andean musicians and a display of *boleadores* (balls on cords that gauchos used to tangle up prey). There's also a patriotic tribute to Evita as a singer belts out 'Don't Cry for Me, Argentina.' The dinner offers a wide variety of tasty main dishes – unusual for tango shows. Gala Tango is a more upscale experience and happens upstairs.

LA TRASTIENDA ROCK, REGGAE

Map p242 (☑5533-5533; www.latrastienda.com; Balcarce 460) This large, atmospheric theater welcomes over 700, features a well-stocked bar, and showcases national and international live-music acts almost nightly. Look for headers such as Charlie Garcia, Divididos, José Gonzalez, Damien Rice and Conor Oberst. Get tickets at the office here or check www.tuentrada.com.ar.

TODO MUNDO TANGO, FLAMENCO

Map p242 (☑4362-2354; Pasaje Anselmo Aieta 1095) This restaurant puts on free tango, flamenco and other types of shows, but you do have to order at least AR$100 worth of food – basic Argentine fare like *empanadas*, pasta and *parrilla*. Tango shows happen on Monday and Thursday nights, while flamenco flutters on Friday and Saturday nights. Expect rock, salsa, folk and jazz on other nights; all shows start around 10:30pm.

LA SCALA DE SAN TELMO CLASSICAL MUSIC

Map p242 (☑4362-1187; www.lascala.org.ar; Pasaje Giuffra 371) This small San Telmo venue, located in a refurbished colonial building, puts on classical and contemporary concerts that highlight piano, tango, musical comedies and other musical-related

shows and workshops. Affordable or free admission.

🔒 SHOPPING

San Telmo has traditionally been Buenos Aires' antiques neighborhood. In recent years, however, San Telmo's popularity with tourists has attracted other kinds of stores. Fashion boutiques and housewares shops are moving in, changing the general feel on the streets. Locals fear that their beloved neighborhood might become another Palermo, but even with rising real-estate prices, San Telmo is not likely to lose its gritty authenticity or charm.

FERIA DE SAN TELMO MARKET

Map p242 (Defensa; ⊙10am-6pm Sun; 🚌10, 22, 29, 45, 86) On Sundays, San Telmo's main drag is closed to traffic and the street is a sea of both locals and tourists browsing craft stalls, waiting at vendors' carts for freshly squeezed orange juice, poking through the antique glass ornaments on display on Plaza Dorrego, and listening to street performances by myriad music groups. Runs from Av San Juan to Plaza de Mayo.

MATERIA URBANA HOUSEWARES, ART

Map p242 (☑4361-5265; www.materiaurbana.com; Defensa 702; ⊙11am-7pm Wed-Fri, 2-7pm Sat, 10:30am-7pm Sun) This innovative design shop shows the work of over 100 local artists; one-of-a-kind finds include offbeat line drawings, abstract photography, carved wood statuettes, leather animal organizers, clothes, and jewelry made from silver, wood and coral. There's nearly constant foot traffic at Materia Urbana, especially during the street fair on Sunday.

PUNTOS EN EL ESPACIO FASHION

Map p242 (☑4307-7906; www.puntosenelespacio.com.ar; Carlos Calvo 450; ⊙11am-8pm) With over 40 designers represented, this store is a good place to check out edgy women's collections by rising stars in the local fashion world. There are also kids' and mens' clothes, handbags, jewelry and a few shoes. A second location, focused on accessories and home decor, is on the corner of Defensa and Independencia, a few blocks away.

IMHOTEP
ANTIQUES

Map p242 (☑4862-9298; Defensa 916; ⊙11am-6pm Sun-Fri) Come find the funkiest old knickknacks at this eccentric shop. Small oddities such as Indian statuettes, Chinese snuff boxes, precious stone figurines and gargoyles make up some of the bizarre trinkets here. Also look for fantastical and mythological creatures; there are also plenty of skulls.

GIL ANTIGUEDADES
ANTIQUES

Map p242 (Humberto Primo 412; ⊙11am-1pm & 3-7pm Tue-Sun) A window display of Great Gatsby–style flapper dresses and vintage nightgowns pulls the passerby into San Telmo's finest antiques emporium. Decorative objects like china teapots and leather hatboxes are overshadowed by the stunning array of silk slips and lacy Victorian gowns – John Galliano, Catherine Deneuve and Salvatore Ferragamo are among the famous people who've stopped by for inspiration on visits to Buenos Aires.

MERCADO DE SAN TELMO
MARKET

Map p242 (Defensa, Bolívar, Carlos Calvo & Estados Unidos block; ⊙9am-8pm) This market was built in 1897 by Juan Antonio Buschiazzo, the same Italian-born Argentine architect who designed Recoleta Cemetery. It occupies the inside of an entire city block, though you wouldn't be able to tell just by looking at the modest sidewalk entrances. The wrought-iron interior (note the amazing original ceiling) makes it one of BA's most atmospheric markets; locals shop here for fresh produce and meat. Peripheral antique stalls offer luggage, wine decanters and other treasures. More stalls are open on weekends.

WALRUS BOOKS
BOOKS

Map p242 (☑4300-7135; Estados Unidos 617; ⊙noon-8pm Tue-Sun) Run by an American photographer, this tiny shop is probably the best English-language bookstore in BA. Thousands of new and used literature and nonfiction books line the shelves here, and there's a selection of Latin American classics translated into English. Bring your quality books (including Lonely Planet guides!) to trade; literary workshops offered too.

CUALQUIER VERDURA
CLOTHING HOUSEWARES

Map p242 (☑4300-2474; Humberto Primo 517; ⊙noon-8pm Thu-Sun) Located in a lovely, refurbished old house, this fun store sells eclectic items from vintage clothing to funny soaps (look for these in the 'bathroom') to recycled floppy-disc lamps to contemporary knickknacks and novelty toys. Wander through the outdoor patio and note the stained-glass windows on the wall and *mate*-drinking Buddha above the fountain.

MOEBIUS
CLOTHING

Map p242 (☑4361-2893; Defensa 1356; ⊙3-8pm Mon, noon-8pm Tue-Sat) This funky little shop's racks are crowded with owner-designer Lilliana Zauberman's kaleidoscopic products: 1970s-style jersey dresses, whimsical ruffled bikinis, skirts printed with koi fish and frog patterns, cherry-red trench coats and handbags made from recycled materials. Around 60 designers sell their work here, so there's always something different, fun and new to keep an eye out for.

PUNTO SUR
CLOTHING

Map p242 (☑4300-9320; www.feriapuntosur.com.ar; Defensa 1135; ⊙11am-7:30pm) This is a great clothing store highlighting the works of over 60 Argentine designers. Creativity is rampant and it's a fun walk-through for one-of-a-kind funky threads, including interesting knitwear, colorful skirts, printed T-shirts, jewelry and accessories, cool handbags and even a few shoes. These are definitely clothes that make a statement.

SIGNOS
JEWELRY

Map p242 (☑15-5949-9193; www.signosac.blogspot.com.ar; Carlos Calvo 428; ⊙11am-7pm Mon-Fri, to 5pm Sun) This is the tiny silversmithing shop of Alberto Codiani and Laura Romero, both artists who create beautiful jewelry. Amber, ammonites and precious stones are incorporated into unique pieces that are sure to attract attention. Custom work available; silversmithing classes also on offer.

L'AGO
HOUSEWARES, ACCESSORIES

Map p242 (☑4362-4702; Defensa 970; ⊙11am-8pm) Kitschy-cool home decor – from fluorescent *mate* sets and funky pillows to Frida Kahlo kitchen magnets, eclectic lighting, recycled Elvis wallets and Marilyn Monroe handbags – attracts hipsters and travelers to cute-as-a-button L'Ago. Also at Thames 1247 in Palermo.

EN BUEN ORDEN   ANTIQUES

Map p242 (☑15-5936-2820; Carlos Calvo 431; ☺2-6pm Tue-Sat, 10am-7pm Sun) If you fancy an old-fashioned little shop where you can sort through shelves full of knickknacks, old jewelry, Jackie O–style sunglasses, old lace, musty shoes, opera gloves, pillbox hats and antique figurines, then this place is for you. Despite the name, there's no real order to the place.

La Boca

Neighbourhood Top Five

1 Strolling the cobblestones of **El Caminito** (p100), lined with colorful shanties, art vendors and buskers performing for your spare change.

2 Seeing the modern exhibits at **Fundación Proa** (p101), the neighborhood's cutting-edge art museum.

3 Watching tango dancers strut their stuff while shopping nearby at the **Feria de Artesanos Caminito** (p103).

4 Analyzing the powerful artwork at **Museo de Bellas Artes de La Boca Benito Quinquela Martín** (p101).

5 Going to a *fútbol* game at **La Bombonera Stadium** (p103), home to the scrappy Boca Juniors team.

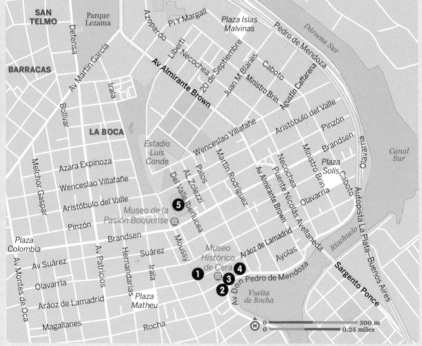

For more detail of this area see Map p244

Explore: La Boca

On your way into La Boca, note the Casa Amarilla, in the 400s block along the main drag Av Almirante Brown. This is a replica of the country house belonging to Almirante Brown, the Irish founder of the Argentine navy. Three blocks further on (look to your left at the kink in the road), you'll notice the curious Gothic structure called Torre Fantasma (Ghost Tower). As you reach the Riachuelo, you can alight from your bus or taxi and walk the last few hundred meters. Get a good look at the Puente Nicolás Avellaneda, which spans the Riachuelo, linking La Boca to the industrial suburb of Avellaneda; before the bridge's completion in 1940, floods had washed away several others. From here follow the riverside walkway all the way to El Caminito.

Boca's main attractions – museums, shops, eateries, Bombonera stadium – are all within a few blocks of El Caminito. There's no reason to venture beyond the touristy streets in this neighborhood, whose bullies have a reputation for occasionally mugging careless tourists for their cameras. Be discreet, stick close to the busier streets and you should be fine. Buenos Aires' mayor, Mauricio Macri, is from La Boca and has been trying to improve the neighborhood by developing destinations such as the Usina del Arte; eventually he wants to gentrify the thoroughfare of Pedro de Mendoza, linking Puerto Madero with La Boca.

The symbol of the community's solidarity is the Boca Juniors soccer team, the former club of disgraced superstar Diego Maradona. The team plays at La Bombonera Stadium, which is just four blocks inland from the Riachuelo and contains a museum detailing the team's players and successes; you can take a peek at the stadium from this museum.

Local Life

➡ **Stick to El Caminito** La Boca's local life is pretty local, and should stay that way. Visitors should stay around the El Caminito area: muggings of obvious tourists (ie those carrying large cameras) have occurred.

Getting There & Away

➡ **Bus** Take buses 29, 64 and 152 from Palermo and the center; they all end up at El Caminito.

Lonely Planet's Top Tip

La Boca is not the kind of neighborhood for casual strolls – it can be downright rough in spots. Don't stray far from the riverside walk, El Caminito (and its nearby tourist streets) or the Bombonera Stadium, especially while toting expensive cameras. And certainly don't cross the bridge over the Riachuelo; there's nothing to see there anyway. Anda Responsible Travel (p207) and Graffitimundo (p208) have good walking-tour options for this area.

✖ Best Places to Eat & Drink

➡ Il Matterello (p102)
➡ El Obrero (p103)
➡ Proa Cafe (p102)

For reviews, see p102 ➡

⊙ Best Museums

➡ Fundación Proa (p101)
➡ Museo de Bellas Artes de La Boca Benito Quinquela Martín (p101)

For reviews, see p101 ➡

TOP SIGHT
EL CAMINITO

La Boca's most famous street – Argentina's only 'open air' museum – is a magnet for visitors, who come to witness its brightly painted houses. Meanwhile, artists sell their colorful paintings while tango dancers ask you to pose with them or behind cardboard cut-outs and nearby weekend craft stalls offer handmade goods. Everywhere there are groups of tourists taking photos – can you say 'tourist trap'?

This block-long cobbled walk does have its unique charms, though, like the various bas-reliefs and sculptures dotted about. And there are the super-colorful tenement shacks, covered in corrugated zinc and originally brushed with leftover paint that Genoese immigrants begged off ships. Surrounding streets also offer souvenirs, and restaurants with pleasant sidewalk tables.

Caminito (or 'little path') was named after a 1926 tango song by composer Juan de Dios Filiberto and lyricist Gabino Coria Peñaloza (hunt for the lyrics on a wall plaque), which tells of a love lost. This song inspired Benito Quinquela Martín, La Boca's most famous artist, to help create Caminito as the neighborhood's main landmark in 1955.

Quinquela Martín mostly painted dark scenes of the barrio's port on the Riachuelo and its workers. His house and workshop have been turned into a museum and are worth a visit, but you can get an idea of his style on Caminito. Look for a small tiled reproduction of his *Día de Trabajo* (Day of Work) on a green wall and a much bigger one of his *Regreso de la Pesca* (Return from Fishing) at the end of the street, both by Ricardo Sánchez.

At the end of Caminito is a small plaza with a mural depicting past struggles of the neighborhood, such as the dangerous task of volunteer firemen and the faces of La Boca's 'disappeared' during the military regime. There are also other themes, such as Aztec figures and local *fútbol* heroes.

DON'T MISS...

➡ The tiled reproductions of Benito Quinquela Martín's artwork on El Caminito's walls.

➡ Exploring the inside of some *conventillos* (tenements) – such as the one at Magallanes 861.

PRACTICALITIES

➡ Map p244

➡ Av Don Pedro de Mendoza, near Del Valle Iberlucea

◉ SIGHTS

EL CAMINITO   STREET
See p100.

FUNDACIÓN PROA   MUSEUM
Map p244 (☑4104-1001; www.proa.org; Av
Don Pedro de Mendoza 1929; admission AR$15;
⊘11am-7pm Tue-Sun) Only the most cutting-
edge national and international artists
are invited to show at this elegant art museum, which features high ceilings, white
walls and large display halls. Stunning
contemporary installations utilize a wide
variety of media and themes, while the
rooftop terrace is *the* stylish place in La
Boca for relaxing with a drink or snack –
it boasts a view of the Riachuelo. Plenty of
cultural offerings include talks, lectures,
workshops, music concerts and cinema
screenings.

Proa also boasts video rooms, an auditorium and an impressive library.

**MUSEO DE BELLAS ARTES
DE LA BOCA BENITO
QUINQUELA MARTÍN**   MUSEUM
Map p244 (☑4301-1080; Av Don Pedro de Mendoza 1835; suggested donation AR$10; ⊘10am-
6pm Tue-Fri, 11am-6pm Sat & Sun) Once the
home and studio of Benito Quinquela
Martín (1890–1977), this fine-arts museum exhibits his works and those of more
contemporary Argentine artists. The top
floor displays Martín's surrealist paintings, whose broad, rough brush-strokes

and dark colors use the port, silhouettes
of laboring men, smokestacks and water
reflections as recurring themes. There
are outdoor sculptures on the rooftop terraces, and the top tier has awesome views
of the port.

In keeping with the museum's maritime
theme there is also a small but excellent
permanent collection of painted wooden
bowsprits, which are the carved statues
projecting forward at the front of ships.

MUSEO DE LA PASIÓN BOQUENSE   MUSEUM
Map   p244   (☑4362-1100;   www.museo
boquense.com; Brandsen 805; admission from
AR$60; ⊘10am-6pm) High-tech and spiffy,
this *fútbol* (soccer) museum chronicles
the rough-and-tumble neighborhood of
La Boca, La Bombonera Stadium (p103),
soccer idols' histories, the championships,
the trophies and, of course, the gooooals.
There's a 360° theater in a giant soccer-
ball auditorium, an old jersey collection
and a gift shop. The museum is right under the stadium, a couple of blocks from
the tourist part of El Caminito; get a tour
of the pitch for a few extra pesos.

MUSEO HISTÓRICO DE CERA   MUSEUM
Map p244 (☑4301-1497; www.museodecera.
com.ar; Del Valle Iberlucea 1261; admission
AR$20; ⊘11:30am-7pm Mon-Fri, 11am-8pm Sat
& Sun; ◻29, 64, 152) Wax reconstructions
of historical figureheads (literally) and
dioramas of scenes in Argentine history

LA BOCA'S COLORS & THE RIACHUELO

In the mid-19th century, La Boca became home to poor Spanish and Italian immigrants who settled along the Riachuelo – the sinuous river that divides the city from
the surrounding province of Buenos Aires. Many of them came during the booming
1880s and ended up working in the numerous meat-packing plants and warehouses
here, processing and shipping out much of Argentina's vital beef. After sprucing up
the barges, the port dwellers splashed leftover paint on the corrugated-metal siding
of their houses, unwittingly giving the neighborhood what would become one of its
main claims to fame.

However, La Boca's other leftover industrial materials have also eventually found
their way into the river. Decades of untreated sewage, garbage dumping and industrial wastes have taken their toll, and today the abandoned port's waters are trapped
under a thick layer of incredibly smelly rainbow sludge. For years politicians have
vowed to clean up the river, but funds have been misappropriated by the corrupt and
very little money has actually gone into improving the river's situation. Rusting boat
hulks have been removed and other efforts have taken place, but the Riachuelo's
health does not look to be improving in the near future. If you can stand the smell,
take a walk along the riverfront path to get a close-up look at the poor Riachuelo –
and hope that some day, someone in power will actually do something to clean it up.

MARADONA & MESSI

Born in 1960 in abject poverty in a Buenos Aires shantytown, Diego Armando Maradona played his first professional game before his 16th birthday. Transferring to his beloved Boca Juniors, he continued to prosper. After a good showing at the 1982 World Cup, he moved to Europe. Here, his genius inspired unfashionable Napoli to two league titles, and in 1986 he single-handedly won the World Cup for a very average Argentina side. In the quarter-final against England, he scored a goal first with his hand – later saying the goal was scored partly by the hand of God – and then a second one with his feet, after a mesmerizing run through the flummoxed defense that led to its being named the Goal of the Century by FIFA.

But the big time also ruined Diego. Earning huge sums of money, Maradona became addicted to cocaine and the high life. A succession of drug-related bans, lawsuits and weight issues meant that by his retirement in 1997 he had been a shadow of his former self for some years.

Since his retirement, overdoses, heart attacks, detoxes, his own TV program and offbeat friendships have all been par for the course in the Maradona circus. Most unbelievably of all, he was chosen to manage the national team: the highlight in a colorful spell – after qualifying for the 2010 World Cup in South Africa – was his triumphant suggestion that his critics could pleasure him orally. Nevertheless, those numerous touches of magic in the number 10 shirt have sealed his immortality. To many Argentines, the hand of God and the hand of Maradona are one and the same.

Every talented Argentine since has been dogged with the label 'the new Maradona', but these days there's one who's the real deal. Rosario-bred Lionel Messi, a little genius who runs at defenses with the ball seemingly glued to his feet, has been captivating the world with his prodigious talents and record-breaking goal-scoring feats for Barcelona and, increasingly, for the national team. Many shrewd judges consider him better even than the great Diego, and his humble off-field demeanor is certainly an improvement. If he manages to inspire the *albiceleste* (Argentina's national football team) to win the World Cup again, it will truly be the Second Coming.

Andy Symington

are the specialty of this small and tacky private institution. Among the historical Argentine personages depicted are no less than Juan de Solís, Guillermo Brown, Mendoza, Garay and Rosas. In addition, there are also stuffed snakes and creepy wax limbs depicting bite wounds – all barely worth the price of admission.

✕ EATING

Though limited to just a handful of streets, the tourist area of La Boca does contain a number of traditional Argentine eateries – mostly offering classic steaks and pastas. As long as you don't expect fine cuisine, you shouldn't be disappointed.

★ PROA CAFE   CAFE $
Map p244 (☑4104-1003; www.proa.org/eng/cafe.php; Av Don Pedro de Mendoza 1929; mains AR$45-80; ⊙11am-7pm Tue-Sun) Chef Lucas

Angelillo presides over this airy eatery on the top floor of Fundación Proa. Stop in briefly for a fresh juice and gourmet sandwich, or stay longer and order a meat, seafood or pasta dish. Don't miss the rooftop terrace on a warm, sunny day – you'll get good views of the Riachuelo, hopefully without its corresponding scents.

IL MATTERELLO   ITALIAN $$
Map p244 (☑4307-0529; Martín Rodríguez 517; mains AR$80-120; ⊙noon-midnight Tue-Sat) This Genovese trattoria serves up awesome lasagne bolognese and *tagliatelle alla rucola* (tagliatelle with arugula). For a special treat, however, try the *tortelli bianchi con burro foso al aglio* (pasta pillows stuffed with chard and Parmesan in a burned garlic sauce). For dessert there's a great tiramisu and seasonal *crostate* (cream-filled pastry). Also in **Palermo** (Map p250; ☑4831-8493; cnr Thames & Gorriti).

EL OBRERO
PARRILLA **$$**

Map p244 (☎4362-9912; Agustín R Caffarena 64; mains AR$60-100; ◷noon-4pm & 8pm-midnight Mon-Sat) The same family has been running El Obrero since 1954, and a number of famous people have passed through over the years, including Bono and Robert Duvall (check out the photos on the walls). You'll also see old Boca Juniors jerseys, antique furniture, old tile floors and chalkboards showing the day's specials and standard *parrilla* fare. Take a taxi.

⭐ ENTERTAINMENT

USINA DEL ARTE
THEATER

(http://agendacultural.buenosaires.gob.ar; Agustín Caffarena 1) This restored old electricity factory is a valiant attempt to breathe new life into an edgy section of La Boca. It's a gorgeous red-brick building complete with scenic clock tower, and its concert hall is now the home to Buenos Aires' philharmonic and national symphony orchestras.

The Usina can hold up to 1200 spectators and also hosts dance, theater and art exhibitions – the acoustics are top-notch. It's open only during concerts and guided tours; check the city's website for current happenings.

LA BOMBONERA STADIUM
STADIUM

Map p244 (Brandsen) The La Bombonera Stadium is home of the Boca Juniors football team – the former club of disgraced superstar Diego Armando Maradona. You can take a peek at it via the Museo de la Pasión Boquense (p101). Game tickets are hard to come by – it's best to go via travel or tour agencies like Tangol (p207).

TEATRO DE LA RIBERA
THEATER

Map p244 (☎4302-1536; Av Don Pedro de Mendoza 1821) This small, colorful theater, funded by famous Argentine painter Benito Quinquela Martín, was built in 1971 and holds nearly 650 seats. Check out the upright piano in the lobby; it was painted by Quinquela Martín.

🛍 SHOPPING

FERIA DE ARTESANOS CAMINITO
STREET MARKET

Map p244 (cnr Caminito & Mendoza; ◷noon-6pm Thu-Sun & holidays) Homemade crafts and tango-themed goods are for sale at this small and lively crafts fair, giving La Boca even more color than usual. Tango dancers and buskers compete for your attention, and along Caminito itself are many drawings, paintings and pictures to buy.

1. Painted facade near Museo Casa Carlos Gardel 2. Colorful houses on Jean Jaurés Street, Abasto 3. Rear of a bus decorated in *fileteado* style 4. Sign at the Caminitos Regalos store in La Boca

Fileteado Porteño

Walk around Buenos Aires enough and you can't help noticing the colorful painted swirls of *fileteado* (also known as *filete*) decorating some public signs and buildings. Thought to have been inspired by intricate Italian metal designs, this beautiful stylistic artwork originally appeared on early-20th-century horse carts.

As time progressed, *fileteado* migrated to trucks and buses, softening these hulking vehicles with gaudy colors and symbols such as flowers, vines, birds, dragons and – of course – the Argentine flag. Today, *fileteado* on plaques serves to communicate proverbs and poetry.

Interestingly, this art form was once in danger of extinction. During the Proceso (Dirty War; 1976–83) *fileteado* was banned from public-transportation systems. *Fileteadores* (*fileteado* artists) had to think of other creative places for their works. They started decorating signs, posters, newsstands and buildings, eventually evolving their labors from simple decorative touches into independent works of art. *Fileteado* has since become an integral part of Buenos Aires' artistic culture.

You can buy plaques at *ferias* (street fairs), especially in San Telmo, where Carlos Gardel is a popular subject. The San Telmo workshop of **Martiniano Arce** (☏4362-2739; www.martinianoarce. com) is another good place to explore. To see buildings covered in *fileteado*, keep your eyes peeled in San Telmo, La Boca and Abasto (especially near **Museo Casa Carlos Gardel** (p148)). You can also visit the **Bar de Filete** (at Defensa 217), a restaurant with an informal *filete* museum next door.

And to create this lovely artwork yourself, check out the classes given by **Alfredo Genovese** (www.fileteado. com.ar) or **Lucero Maturano** (www. fileteadoslucerom.com.ar).

Retiro

Neighborhood Top Five

① Wandering around **Plaza San Martín** (p109) and getting an eyeful of the impressive surrounding buildings.

② Touring the opulent mansion **Palacio Paz** (p108), once Argentina's largest private residence at 12,000 sq meters.

③ Splurging on dinner at one of Retiro's five-star hotel restaurants like **Elena** (p111) and **Le Sud** (p112).

④ Checking out the amazing silverwork at **Museo de Arte Hispanoamericano Isaac Fernández Blanco** (p110).

⑤ Being astounded by the quantity of lethal weapons at **Museo de Armas** (p109).

For more detail of this area see Map p248 ➡

Explore: Retiro

Retiro is a small, compact neighborhood most easily seen on foot. Wander around the Plaza San Martín area, perhaps touring a mansion or two – just double-check the visiting times as they're very limited. The museums around here also tend to be open just in the afternoon and closed on Mondays, so plan ahead if you want to visit them. Join the crowds on pedestrian Calle Florida and follow it down into the Center; Reconquista is another pedestrian street that isn't quite as crowded and better for taking a lunch or coffee break, as there are many restaurants with sidewalk tables there.

For any tips on Buenos Aires or Argentina, stop by the Secretaría de Turismo de la Nación, at Av Santa Fe 883 – it's located at the end of a hallway entrance and has good information and plenty of pamphlets. If you're heading north, walk on Esmeralda or Suipacha to Arroyo. The Museo de Arte Hispanoamericano Isaac Fernández Blanco is not far from here and has a leafy garden if you need a green break. Continue west, crossing Av 9 de Julio into Recoleta; you're now on upscale Av Alvear. As you follow this route you'll see plenty of gorgeous art deco buildings built by European immigrants decades ago.

Local Life

→**Hanging Out** Sip a coffee or down a drink at one of the neighborhood's many cafes or bars catering to thirsty businesspeople.

→**Picnic** On a sunny day, grab a to-go lunch and head to Plaza San Martín's grassy lawns to join the locals out for some fresh air.

→**Shopping** Feel the bustle (and hustle!) of porteño crowds on Calle Florida, which starts near Plaza San Martín and heads south.

Getting There & Away

→**Bus** Take bus 59 from Recoleta and Palermo, buses 22, 45 and 126 from San Telmo, bus 150 from Congreso.

→**Subte** Línea C connects Retiro with the Congreso and western edge of San Telmo.

Lonely Planet's Top Tip

Calle Florida heaves with people of all kinds doing all sorts of things – businesspeople power-walking, tourists shopping, vendors selling, buskers busking. It's also dotted every few meters with *arbolitos* – 'little trees,' or street money changers. With the US dollar being in such high demand, these shady figures are trying to bring in as much revenue as possible. While some have used them successfully, be aware that fake bills and scams do exist.

✕ Best Places to Eat

→ Elena (p111)

→ Le Sud (p112)

→ Dill & Drinks (p111)

For reviews, see p111 ➡

⊜ Best Places to Drink

→ Florería Atlántico (p112)

→ Milión (p112)

→ Florida Garden (p112)

For reviews, see p112 ➡

◉ Best Buildings

→ Palacio Paz (p108)

→ Edificio Kavanagh (p109)

→ Palacio San Martín (p109)

For reviews, see p109 ➡

TOP SIGHT
PALACIO PAZ

Once a private residence, this opulent, French-style palace (1909; also called Palacio Retiro) is the grandest in BA. Inside its 12,000 sq meters are three wings, four floors and 140 rooms decorated with marble columns and gilded accents, while halls boast beautiful wood-carved details and velvet-covered walls. It's worth visiting to get an idea of the richness that Argentina once represented.

José Camilo Paz, founder of the still-running newspaper *La Prensa*, originally commissioned French architect Louis-Marie Henri Sortais to design and build his personal mansion in 1902. Construction took 12 years and finished in 1914; unfortunately, Paz couldn't see his completed masterpiece as he had passed away two years earlier (check out his family's elaborate tomb in Recoleta cemetery). He also couldn't realize his aspiration to become Argentina's president and make Palacio Paz his presidential residence.

Nearly all of the palace's materials – including the marble – were shipped from France. There's a definite resemblance to the Palace of Versailles, especially in the ballroom, but other rooms show more of a Louis XVI, Renaissance or Tudor style. With seven elevators and 40 bathrooms, it remains Argentina's largest single-family home ever built.

One section of the palace has been a military officer's club since 1938, and the Museo de Armas (p109) takes up another wing. The palace can only be visited via guided tours on certain days, so plan ahead.

DON'T MISS...

➡ The circular Hall of Honor, decorated with mosaic floors, marble details and a stained-glass cupola.

➡ The Presidential Room, where hermaphroditic figures look uneasy as they are stabbed in their genitals.

PRACTICALITIES

➡ Círculo Militar

➡ Map p248

➡ ☏4311-1071 ext 147

➡ www.palaciopaz.com.ar

➡ Av Santa Fe 750

➡ tours in English/Spanish AR$55/45

➡ ⏱English tours 3:30pm Wed & Thu, Spanish tours 11am & 3pm Wed-Fri, 11am Sat

◉ SIGHTS

PALACIO PAZ   NOTABLE BUILDING
See p108.

PLAZA SAN MARTÍN   PLAZA
Map p248 French landscape architect Carlos Thays designed the leafy Plaza San Martín, which is surrounded by some of Buenos Aires' most impressive public buildings. The park's most prominent monument is the obligatory equestrian **statue of José de San Martín**; important visiting dignitaries often come to honor the country's liberator by leaving wreaths at its base. On the downhill side of the park you'll see the **Monumento a los Caídos de Malvinas** (Map p248), a memorial to the young men who died in the Falklands War.

Retiro was the site of a monastery during the 17th century, and later became the country *retiro* (retreat) of Agustín de Robles, a Spanish governor. Since then, Plaza San Martín – which sits on a bluff – has played host to a slave market, a military fort and even a bullring. Things are much quieter and more exclusive these days.

At the south end of the plaza is Estación Retiro (Retiro train station), which was built in 1915 when the British controlled the country's railroads.

MUSEO DE ARMAS   MUSEUM
Map p248 (Weapons Museum; ☏4311-1071 ext 179; www.museodearmas.com.ar; Santa Fe 702; admission AR$10; ☉1-7pm Tue-Fri, 2-7pm Sat) Even if you've spent time in the armed forces, you probably have never seen so many weapons of destruction. This maze-like museum exhibits a frighteningly large but excellent collection of over 3000 bazookas, grenade launchers, cannons, machine guns, muskets, pistols, armor, lances and swords; even the gas mask for a combat horse is on display. The evolution of rifles and handguns is especially thoroughly documented, and there's a small but impressive Japanese weapons room.

The whole collection is very extensive, impressive, clean and well labeled.

PALACIO HAEDO   NOTABLE BUILDING
Map p248 (Av Santa Fe 690) On an odd triangular block at the corner of Florida and Santa Fe, the neo-Gothic Palacio Haedo was the mansion of the Haedo family at the turn of the 19th century; it now houses the country's national park service.

PALACIO SAN MARTÍN   NOTABLE BUILDING
Map p248 (☏4819-7000 ext 8092; Arenales 761; ⓢLínea C San Martín) This impressive art nouveau mansion (1912) is actually three independent buildings around a stone courtyard. It was designed by architect Alejandro Christophersen and boasts marble staircases, grandiose dining rooms and a garden containing a chunk of the Berlin Wall. A small but good **museum** displays pre-Columbian artifacts from the northwest, along with some paintings by Latin American artists. Free tours happen at 3pm on Thursdays (bring ID), but can be suspended at any time. Enter via Esmeralda 1231.

Originally built for the powerful Anchorena family, Palacio San Martín later became the headquarters of the Foreign Ministry; today it's used mostly for official purposes.

EDIFICIO KAVANAGH   NOTABLE BUILDING
Map p248 (Florida 1035) A feisty Irishwoman funded the construction of this handsome 120m art-deco apartment building, which was the tallest skyscraper in Latin America at the time of its construction in 1935. A local rumor claims that the heiress, vengeful towards another aristocratic family for scorning her daughter, built the structure that high to block light from entering the basilica where her rivals attended Mass every Sunday.

BASÍLICA DE SANTÍSIMO SACRAMENTO   CHURCH
Map p248 (Plaza San Martín 1039) In the shadow of the Kavanagh building is this French-style church built by the Anchorena family in 1916. Inside, check out the original tiled floor, stained-glass windows, stone columns and wedding-cake-like altar.

TORRE DE LOS INGLESES   LANDMARK
Map p248 (Torre Monumental; ☏4311-0186; Plaza Fuerza Aérea Argentina; ☉10am-6pm Mon-Fri, 10am-6:30pm Sat & Sun; ⓢLínea C Retiro) **FREE** Standing prominently across from Plaza San Martín, this 76m-high miniature version of London's Big Ben was a donation from the city's British community in 1916. During the Falklands War of 1982 the tower was the target of bombs, and the government officially renamed it Torre Monumental – but the name never really stuck. You can enter inside the base of the tower,

AVENIDA 9 DE JULIO

It's one Buenos Aires landmark that all visitors to the city will have to cross, in one way or another – Avenida 9 de Julio, hailed as the world's widest avenue and named after Argentina's independence day. It's only one kilometer long but 16 lanes wide (140 m) – and takes a walking pedestrian at least two traffic-light cycles to cross, via raised islands. *If* they don't dillydally.

When the widening construction started in 1935, the avenue was considered a patriotic symbol of the city's modern aspirations. Designers modelled it on Paris' Champs-Élysées, but made it twice as wide as a way to one-up its predecessor. For the construction, dozens of blocks of traditionally-styled European buildings had to be demolished through the city's center, and thousands of residents displaced. It was an epic destruction of glorious architecture – all in the name of progress. But one significant building refused to be touched; the original French Embassy. It still stands today, as the lanes of 9 de Julio forcefully curve around it.

It took until 1980 to fully complete the widening of Avenida 9 de Julio. Today, several landmark buildings and monuments dot the thoroughfare. At its southern end lies Plaza de la Constitución, home to a Beaux-arts train station (but not a safe place to hang out, day or night). At Av de Mayo is a statue of Don Quixote astride his horse. A bit further north, the 67m-high white Obelisco punctuates the sky, while nearby is the beautiful neoclassical facade of the Teatro Colón opera house. And finally, at the northern end of the avenue, you'll find the French Embassy – which stuck to its guns and won the right to remain.

where there are a few historical photos, but folks aren't allowed up the elevator.

The plaza in which it stands used to be called Plaza Británica, but is now the Plaza Fuerza Aérea Argentina (Argentine Air Force Plaza).

MUSEO DE ARTE HISPANOAMERICANO ISAAC FERNÁNDEZ BLANCO   MUSEUM

Map p248 (Palacio Noel; ☑4327-0228; www. museofernandezblanco.buenosaires.gob.ar; Suipacha 1422; admission AR$5; ⊙2-7pm Tue-Fri, 11am-7pm Sat & Sun) Dating from 1921, this museum is in an old mansion of the neocolonial Peruvian style that developed as a reaction against French influences in turn-of-the-19th-century Argentine architecture. Its exceptional collection of colonial art includes silverwork from Alto Perú (present-day Bolivia), religious paintings and baroque instruments. There's little effort to place items in any historical context, but everything is in great condition and well lit, and the curved ceiling in the main salon is beautifully painted. There's also a peaceful garden.

Also known as the Palacio Noel, after the designing architect, the museum building and its collections suffered damage (since repaired) from the 1992 bombing of the Israeli embassy, which at the time was located at Arroyo and Suipacha. The space where the embassy was located has since become a small memorial park; you can still see the outline of the building on a neighboring wall.

The museum has an **annex** in the Congreso neighborhood at Hipólito Yirogoyen 1420 (open noon to 6pm Tuesday to Friday and 11am to 5pm Saturday and Sunday) whose main strength is an antique doll collection.

TEATRO NACIONAL CERVANTES   NOTABLE BUILDING

Map p240 (☑4815-8883; www.teatrocervantes. gov.ar; Libertad 815) Six blocks southwest of Plaza San Martín, you can't help but notice the lavishly ornamented Cervantes theater. From the grand tiled lobby to the main theater, with its plush red-velvet chairs, you can smell the long history of this place (somewhat musty). The Cervantes is definitely showing its age, with worn carpeting and rough edges, but improvement projects are planned. Until then, enjoy the elegance – however faded – with a tour (call for current schedules). It presents theater, comedy, musicals and dance at affordable prices.

The landmark building dates from 1921 and was built with private funds, but was acquired by the state in 1926. Its facade was designed as a replica of Spain's Universidad de Alcalá de Henares. The building underwent remodeling after a fire in 1961.

MUSEO NACIONAL DEL TEATRO   MUSEUM
Map p240 (☑4815-8883 ext 156; cnr Av Córdoba & Libertad; ⏱10am-6pm Mon-Fri) FREE This small museum traces Argentine theater from its colonial beginnings, stressing the 19th-century contributions of the Podestá family – Italian immigrants who popularized the *gauchesca* (gaucho literature) drama *Juan Moreira*. Items include a gaucho suit worn by Gardel in his Hollywood film *El día que me quieras* and the *bandoneón* belonging to Paquita Bernardo, the first Argentine woman to play the accordionlike instrument (she died of tuberculosis in 1925 at the age of 25).

There's also a photo gallery of famous Argentine stage actors.

✖ EATING

Restaurants in Retiro tend to cater to the business crowds, offering good-value midday specials and food to go – so all you have to do is find yourself a nice, grassy spot or shady bench in nearby Plaza San Martín where you can enjoy your impromptu picnic. Don't ignore the area's bars and cafes, which also serve meals and are sometimes more casual and interesting than traditional restaurants, and of course also offer a wider range of drinking options.

EL CUARTITO   PIZZA $
Map p240 (☑4816-1758; Talcahuano 937; slices AR$10-14, pizzas AR$75-150; ⏱12:30pm-1am Sun & Tue-Thu, to 2am Fri & Sat) In a hurry? Think fast, order and pay for your piece of pie, then eat at the counters standing up. Not only is it cheaper and faster this way, but you can enjoy the old sports posters without turning around. You can't get more local or traditional, and while it's mostly full of businessmen and male waiters, the gals are equally welcome. Sit down for more menu choices.

DILL & DRINKS   INTERNATIONAL $$
Map p248 (☑4515-0675; www.dillanddrinks.com; San Martiín 986; mains AR$70-140; ⏱noon-6pm Mon, to 2am Tue-Fri, 2pm-2am Sat) Here's an intimate bar-restaurant with contemporary and trendy design. Order the daily lunch special, which includes a principal plate and two cocktails (!), the latter made with fresh juices and fruits. Bring your own Negroni recipe; it'll be filed away in their collection. Dishes are made with quality ingredients and can be things such as shrimp risotto or pork medallions in honey mustard.

GRAN BAR DANZÓN   INTERNATIONAL $$
Map p246 (☑4811-1108; Libertad 1161; mains AR$90-150; ⏱7pm-2am Mon, to 2:30am Tue, to 3am Wed, to 3:30am Thu, to 4am Fri, 8pm-4am Sat, 8am-2am Sun) It's hard to be hipper than this popular lounge-bar-restaurant. A cool-looking wine-conservation system makes it possible to order several wines by the glass, easily paired with the duck confit, grilled salmon or mushroom risotto. The food is fine, if not fabulous, but make no mistake – you're here for the scene, the beautiful people and, of course, the Bonarda and Torrontés.

FILO   ITALIAN $$
Map p248 (☑4311-0312; www.filo-ristorante.com; San Martín 975; mains AR$75-110; ⏱noon-1am) Popular with the business lunch crowd, this large, pop-art-style Italian pizzeria tosses great thin-crust pies with fresh toppings – try a pie piled high with prosciutto and arugula. Other tasty choices include panini, gourmet salads, various pastas and a whirlwind of desserts. The menu is extensive – there's something to please just about everyone here.

DADÁ   INTERNATIONAL $$
Map p248 (☑4814-4787; San Martín 941; mains AR$75-130; ⏱noon-2am Mon-Thu, to 5am Fri & Sat) The tiny bohemian Dadá, with walls painted red and a bar cluttered with wine bottles, feels like an unassuming neighborhood bar in Paris. Order something savory off the bistro menu – the fresh guacamole and homemade potato chips are perfect for sharing. At night you can dine on grilled salmon and down an expertly mixed cocktail.

★ELENA   MODERN ARGENTINE $$$
Map p246 (☑4321-1728; www.elenaponyline.com; Four Seasons Hotel, Posadas 1086; mains AR$200-250; ⏱6:30-11am, 12:30-3:30pm & 7:30pm-1am) If you're looking for a splurge night out, Elena should be your destination. Located in the Four Seasons Hotel, this highly-rated restaurant uses the best ingredients and cooking methods to create

superb dishes. Order the dry-aged rib-eye steak or seared prawns with charred baby fennel for something really special. Expect the cocktails, desserts and service to be five-star as well.

★ LE SUD
FRENCH $$$

Map p248 (☑4131-0131; Hotel Sofitel, Arroyo 841; mains AR$150-235; ☺6:30-11am, 12:30-3pm & 7:30pm-midnight) For a taste of Europe, dress up and head on over to Le Sud, one of the city's finest French restaurants, elegantly ensconced in a posh hotel. Chef Olivier Falchi whips out simple yet authentic French fusion dishes like brie and squash ravioli, seafood paella with smoked paprika and grilled lamb chops with goat cheese. The five-course tasting menu is AR$780.

SIPAN
PERUVIAN $$$

Map p248 (☑4315-0763; www.sipanrestaurants.com; Paraguay 624; mains AR$100-200; ☺noon-4pm & 8pm-1am Mon-Fri, 8pm-1am Sat) Japanese-Peruvian food is all the rage in BA, and Sipan is at the head of it. Tucked away in a shopping gallery, this sleek, low-lit restaurant turns out imaginative sushi and seviche, along with fancier dishes like seafood appetizers heaped high on ceramic spoons, and stir-fried tamarind pork. Try the passion-fruit pisco sour – it's delicious. Also in Palermo at the Hotel Palermitano.

EL FEDERAL
ARGENTINE $$$

Map p248 (☑4313-1324; www.elfederalrestaurante.com; San Martin 1015; mains AR$110-170; ☺10am-midnight Mon-Sat) This traditional corner eatery is something of a neighborhood institution. You'll find Argentinian comfort food – simple pastas, steaks and *empanadas* – as well as higher-end specialties like Patagonian lamb, *ñandu milanesas* (cutlets of the emu-like, flightless *ñandu*) and northern river fish. Elaborate desserts top things off, and a rustic wooden bar adds charm. The lunchtime *menu ejecutivo* is only AR$70 to AR$90.

🍷 DRINKING & NIGHTLIFE

Retiro has a good range of bars and cafes that cater to businesspeople during the day and into the evening, and at night attract the traveler-expat crowd.

★ FLORERÍA ATLÁNTICO
COCKTAIL BAR

Map p248 (☑4313-6093; Arroyo 872) One of BA's hottest bars, this basement speakeasy is located within a flower shop, adding an air of mystery and likely a main reason for its success. Hipsters, artists, chefs, businesspeople and expats all flock here for the excellent cocktails, whether they're classic or unique – and the lack of gas lines means all of the delicious tapas and main dishes are cooked on the *parrilla* grill.

If you're a gin lover, note that the owner, Renato Giovannonni, produces and sells his own brand – called 'Príncipe de los Apóstoles' – aromatically infused with mint, grapefruit, eucalyptus and *yerba mate*. Reserve ahead for dinner.

MILIÓN
COCKTAIL BAR

Map p246 (☑4815-9925; www.milion.com.ar; Paraná 1048; ☺6pm-2am Sun-Wed, to 3am Thu, to 4am Fri & Sat) This elegant and sexy bar takes up three floors of a renovated old mansion. The garden out back is a leafy paradise, overlooked by a solid balcony that holds the best seats in the house. Nearby marble steps are also an appealing place to lounge with a frozen mojito or basil daiquiri, the tastiest cocktails on the menu. Downstairs, the restaurant serves passable international dishes.

FLORIDA GARDEN
CAFÉ

Map p248 (☑4312-7902; Florida 899; ☺6am-midnight Mon-Fri, to 11pm Sat, 8am-11pm Sun) Usually full of businesspeople drinking up a storm of coffee, this two-story cafe – now sporting modern touches such as glass walls and copper-covered columns – was historically popular with politicians, artists and writers. In fact, Jorge Luis Borges and Pérez Célis (a famous Argentine painter) used to hang out here before the era of skinny lattes. The people-watching here is excellent.

CAFÉ RETIRO
CAFÉ

Map p248 (☑4516-0902; Retiro Station Lobby, Ramos Meija 1358; ☺6:30am-9pm Mon-Fri, 8am-4pm Sat) Catching a train out of town? Allow an extra half hour for coffee at this grand cafe, which boasts soaring ceilings, polished wood and a bronze interior. One of the original fixtures of the station, built in 1915, the cafe has undergone a thorough restoration – the chandeliers twinkle beautifully at night. Look for it nearly across from the Torre de los Ingleses.

DRUID IN   IRISH PUB

Map p248 (📇4312-3688; Reconquista 1040; ⊗noon-midnight Mon-Fri, to 3am Sat) This cozy Irish pub sports an intimate and uncrowded atmosphere. A wide range of aged whiskeys, imported liquor, blended cocktails and a handful of beers temper the pizza, sandwiches and British food that is served. Live rock, jazz, Celtic or Irish music groups may occasionally play.

KILKENNY   IRISH PUB

Map p248 (📇4312-7291; Marcelo T de Alvear 399; ⊗noon-4am Mon-Thu, to 5am Fri & Sat, 7pm-1am; 🐾) Buenos Aires' most popular Irish bar has become, well, just too damn popular. Weekends are a crush and thumping music makes it hard to chat up your date, but the dark-woodsy atmosphere is congenial enough. Come early on weekdays if you want to score one of the cozy deep booths for easy conversation. There's a good whiskey and beer selection, too.

FLUX   BAR

Map p248 (📇5252-0258; Marcelo T de Alvear 980; ⊗7pm-3am Sun-Thu, to 4am Fri & Sat) Run by a friendly Englishman and his Russian partner, this gay bar is hetero-friendly – so everyone's welcome to come on down. The large basement space has a slightly artsy feel. Feeling adventurous? Try the Buenos Aires iced tea (made with Fernet, that popular Argentine mixer that's something of an acquired taste). Happy hour runs every day from 7pm till 10pm.

⭐ ENTERTAINMENT

TEATRO COLISEO   CLASSICAL MUSIC

Map p246 (📇4816-3789; www.fundacioncoliseo.com.ar; Marcelo T de Alvear 1125) Classical music, jazz, ballet, opera and symphony orchestras entertain at this theater most of the year, but a few surprises – such as Argentine-American rock star Kevin Johansen – occasionally show up.

🛍 SHOPPING

The Retiro neighborhood, is classy, expensive and home to a fair share of the city's upscale leather shops and art galleries. But it also serves the downtown business and tourism sector, with a mix of bookstores, outdoor clothing stores, and souvenir and wine shops.

AUTORÍA   ART, ACCESSORIES

Map p248 (📇5252-2474; www.autoriabsas.com.ar; Suipacha 1025; ⊗9:30am-8pm Mon-Fri, 10am-6pm Sat) This cool designer's showcase – stocked with edgy art books, sculptural fashions, whimsical leather desk sculptures and unique jewelry of all materials (silk cocoons!) – strives to promote Argentine designers. Especially interesting are the recycled materials – check out the bags made of tyvek, inner tubes, firehoses or even old sails. Products are of high quality and prices are accessible.

MEMORABILIA   CRAFTS & TEXTILES

Map p246 (📇4811-7698; www.memorabiliabazar.com; Arenales 1170; ⊗11am-7:30pm Mon-Fri, to 1:30pm Sat) For unique, fun and handmade Argentine items, explore the corners of this tiny boutique. The stock is ever-changing, but can include such things as ceramic bowls and mugs painted in animal faces, silver jewelry in super-creative shapes and a few knit tops for women. Expect cute small items easily packed into a suitcase for the flight back home.

PATIO BULLRICH   SHOPPING MALL

Map p246 (📇4814-7500; www.shoppingbullrich.com.ar; Av del Libertador 750; ⊗10am-9pm) Buenos Aires' most exclusive shopping center once hosted livestock auctions, but these days it tends toward sales of Persian rugs, double-breasted tweed suits and Dior's latest designs. Three floors hold fine boutiques such as Lacoste, Salvatore Ferragamo and Tiffany & Co, along with fancy coffee shops, a cinema complex and a food court.

CASA LÓPEZ   LEATHER GOODS

Map p248 (📇4311-3044; www.casalopez.com.ar; Marcelo T de Alvear 640/658; ⊗9am-8pm Mon-Fri, 10am-7pm Sat & Sun) Start up the limousine and make sure there's enough room for some of BA's finest selection of quality leather jackets, luggage, bags and accessories. The look is conservative, not hip; service is almost too attentive, so be prepared to chat. Other branches are located in **Galerías Pacífico** and **Patio Bullrich**.

LA MARTINA
SPORTING EQUIPMENT

Map p248 (☑4576-7999; www.lamartina.com; Paraguay 661; ☺10am-8pm Mon-Fri, 10am-2pm Sat) Polo is a high-class sport in Buenos Aires, an unmistakable symbol of wealth and refinement – but even if you've never mounted a horse, it's interesting to look around at the gorgeous leather riding boots, helmets and saddles at Argentina's premier polo shop. Street wear clothes are also available if you don't ride.

GABRIELLA CAPUCCI
FASHION

Map p246 (☑4815-3636; Av Alvear 1477; ☺10:30am-8pm Mon-Sat) While certainly not for everyone, this girly boutique is undeniably unlike other stuffy ones on this upscale avenue. Come check out the unique sequined T-shirts, creative handbags, wispy scarves, vintage tops and eclectic rhinestone accessories. Expect also a load of crocheted flowers, huge beads, satin and animal prints, wild costume jewelry and a general over-saturation of bright colors. Real men – wait for your gals outside.

GALERÍA 5TA AVENIDA
SHOPPING MALL

Map p246 (Av Santa Fe 1270; ☺noon-8pm Mon-Sat) Looking for vintage or secondhand clothing? This old shopping gallery is an obligatory stop. Used funky wearables are sold here at several shops, and prices are relatively fair for even the grungiest backpacker. Find the bargain racks for the best deals, though some selections are for the desperate only. Individual store hours vary widely, with many opening after 4pm.

Recoleta & Barrio Norte

Neighborhood Top Five

1 Wandering the elegant sarcophagi in **Cementerio de la Recoleta** (p117), an astonishing necropolis where, in death as in life, generations of the Argentine elite rest in ornate splendor.

2 Relaxing on the sunny patio of one of the many **restaurants** or **cafes** on RM Ortiz (p119).

3 Finding that perfect hand-made souvenir in one of the dozens of stalls at **Feria Plaza Francia** (p123).

4 Seeking out the beautiful European impressionistic artwork at **Museo Nacional de Bellas Artes** (p118).

5 Getting a close-up look at **_Floralis Genérica_** (p119), an interesting giant metal flower sculpture.

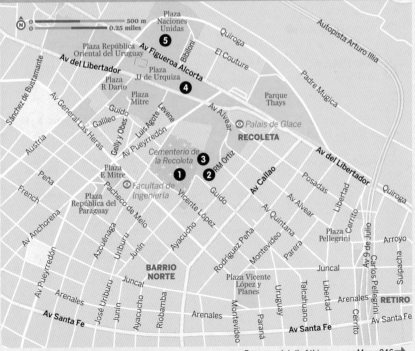

For more detail of this area see Map p246 ➡

Lonely Planet's Top Tip

Recoleta is an expensive neighborhood. For a cheap lunch, get takeout somewhere –such as **El Sanjuanino** (p120) – and find a nice park bench, such as in Plaza Intendente Alveear, where you can hang out, eat and watch the world go by.

✗ Best Places to Eat

➡ L'Orangerie (p120)
➡ Como en Casa (p119)
➡ Rodi Bar (p119)

For reviews, see p119 ➡

🍷 Best Places to Drink

➡ La Biela (p120)
➡ Buller Brewing Company (p121)
➡ Casa Bar (p121)

For reviews, see p120 ➡

🔒 Best Places to Shop

➡ Feria Plaza Francia (p123)
➡ Av Santa Fe (p123)
➡ Galería Bond Street (p123)

For reviews, see p123 ➡

Explore: Recoleta & Barrio Norte

Recoleta's main attractions are concentrated around the cemetery. This fashionable barrio was, interestingly enough, first constructed as a result of sickness. Many upper-class *porteños* in the 1870s originally lived in southerly San Telmo, but during the yellow-fever epidemic they relocated as far away as they could, which meant clear across town to Recoleta and Barrio Norte. Today you can best see much of the wealth of this sumptuous quarter on Av Alvear, where many of the old mansions (and newer boutiques) are located.

Behind the cemetery is the impressive Museo Nacional de Bellas Artes – this national art museum is free, but note that it's closed in the mornings and on Mondays. And just beyond the museum is the landmark flower sculpture *Floralis Genérica*. From here you can walk to Palermo's fancy Malba museum and green parks in about 15 to 20 minutes.

Barrio Norte is not an official neighborhood as such but rather a largely residential southern extension of Recoleta. Some people consider it a sub-neighborhood of Recoleta (and parts of it are sometimes lumped in with Retiro or Palermo, too) – it all really depends on who you talk to. However, Barrio Norte does have a more accessible feel than its ritzier sibling, especially around busy Av Santa Fe. Here you'll find hundreds of shops, all vying for shoppers' attention, and all conveniently located on bus and Subte lines – not things you'll see much of in Recoleta itself.

Local Life

➡**Hanging Out** La Biela (p120) is in a touristy location, but locals still flock here to sit at the front patio on warm sunny days.

➡**Shopping** Grab your wallet and head to Av Santa Fe, where hundreds of stores cater to *porteños'* every whim (p123).

➡**Ice Cream** Recoleta has more than its fair share of excellent ice cream shops, so find one and order up.

Getting There & Away

➡**Bus** Buses 59 heads from Palermo to San Telmo, stopping along Av Las Heras along the way.
➡**Subte** Línea D covers the southern section of Recoleta.

TOP SIGHT
CEMENTERIO DE LA RECOLETA

Recoleta cemetery is arguably Buenos Aires' number-one attraction, and a must on every tourist's list. You can wander for hours in this amazing city of the dead, where countless 'streets' are lined with impressive statues and marble sarcophagi. Peek into the crypts and check out the dusty coffins, and try to decipher the history of its inhabitants.

Originally the garden of the church next door, Recoleta cemetery was created in 1822. It covers four city blocks and contains about 4800 mausoleums decorated in many architectural styles, including art nouveau, art deco, classical, Greek, baroque and neo-Gothic. Popular motifs include crosses of all kinds, marble angels, stone wreaths, skulls and crossbones, draped urns, winged hourglasses and the occasional gargoyle. All decorate the final resting places of past presidents, military heroes, influential politicians, famous writers and other very noteworthy personages, including those of the Paz family (José C Paz founded *La Prensa*), Liliana Crociati de Szaszak (famous for dying in an avalanche in Austria), Rufina Cambaceres (the urban myth goes that she was buried alive) and boxer Luis Angel Firpo.

The most impressive tomb is not Evita's, which is rather plain. Instead, get a good map and look for other sarcophagi; interesting stories, odd facts and myths abound. Also note the cemetery's rough edges – the cobwebs and detritus inside many of the tombs, the vegetation growing out of cracks, the feral cats prowling the premises. All add to the charm.

Free **tours** are offered in English at 11am Tuesday and Thursday and in Spanish at 9:30am, 11am, 2pm and 4pm from Tuesday to Sunday (weather permitting). For a great map and information, order Robert Wright's PDF guide (www.recoletacemetery.com); touts also sell maps at the entrance.

DON'T MISS...

➡ **Evita's grave** Go to the first major intersection, turn left at the statue; continue until a mausoleum blocks your way. Go around it and turn right at the wide 'street'. After three blocks it's to your left.

PRACTICALITIES

➡ Map p246
➡ ☎0800-444-2363
➡ cnr Junín & Guido
➡ ⊙7am-5:30pm

⊙ SIGHTS

CEMENTERIO DE LA RECOLETA CEMETERY
See p117.

**BASÍLICA DE NUESTRA
SEÑORA DEL PILAR** CHURCH
Map p246 (☎4806-2209; Junín 1904; museum AR$6; ◻10, 17, 60, 92, 110) Yes, that's a pair of skulls on your right as you enter the basilica. But the centerpiece of this gleaming white colonial church, built by Jesuits in 1716, is a Peruvian altar adorned with silver from Argentina's northwest. Inside, head to the left to visit the small but historic cloisters **museum** (⊙10:30am-6:15pm Mon-Sat, 2:30-6:15pm Sun); it's home to religious vestments, paintings, writings and interesting artifacts. You can also snap a photo of the Recoleta cemetery through the window grilles.

**CENTRO CULTURAL
RECOLETA** CULTURAL CENTER
Map p246 (☎4803-1040; www.centrocultural recoleta.org; Junín 1930; ◻59) Part of the original Franciscan convent and alongside its namesake church and cemetery, this renovated cultural center houses a variety of facilities, including art galleries, exhibition halls and a cinema. Events, courses and workshops are also offered, and its **Museo Participativo de Ciencias** (Map p246; ☎4806-3456; www.mpc.org.ar; Junín 1930; admission AR$40; ⊙vary widely, see website) is a children's hands-on science museum.

**MUSEO NACIONAL DE BELLAS
ARTES** MUSEUM
(☎5288-9945; www.mnba.org.ar; Av del Libertador 1473; ⊙12:30-8:30pm Tue-Fri, 9:30am-8:30pm Sat & Sun) **FREE** This is Argentina's most important national arts museum and contains many key works by Benito Quinquela Martín, Xul Solar, Edwardo Sívori

GLORIOUS DEATH IN BUENOS AIRES

Only in Buenos Aires can the wealthy and powerful elite keep their status after death. When decades of dining on rich food and drink have taken their toll, Buenos Aires' finest move ceremoniously across the street to the **Cementerio de la Recoleta** (p117), joining their ancestors in a place they have religiously visited all their lives.

Argentines are a strange bunch who tend to celebrate their most honored national figures not on the date of their birth, but on the date of their death (after all, they're nobody when they're born). Nowhere is this obsession with mortality more evident than at Recoleta, where generations of the elite repose in the grandeur of ostentatious mausoleums. Real estate here is among Buenos Aires' priciest: there's a saying that goes, 'It is cheaper to live extravagantly all your life than to be buried in Recoleta.'

It's not just being rich that gets you a prime resting spot here: your name matters. Those lucky few with surnames like Alvear, Anchorena, Mitre or Sarmiento are pretty much guaranteed to be laid down. Evita's remains are here (in the Familia Duarte sarcophagus), but her lack of aristocracy and the fact that she dedicated her life not to BA's rich but rather to its poor infuriated the bigwigs.

A larger and much less touristy graveyard is **Cementerio de la Chacarita**, located in the neighborhood of Chacarita. The cemetery opened in the 1870s to accommodate the yellow-fever victims of San Telmo and La Boca. Although much more democratic and modest, Chacarita's most elaborate tombs match Recoleta's finest. One of the most visited belongs to Carlos Gardel, the famous tango singer. Plaques from around the world cover the base of his life-size statue, many thanking him for favors granted. Like Evita, Juan Perón and others, Gardel is a quasi saint toward whom countless Argentines feel an almost religious devotion. The anniversaries of Gardel's birth and death days see thousands of pilgrims jamming the cemetery's streets.

Another spiritual personality in Chacarita is Madre María Salomé, a disciple of the famous healer Pancho Sierra. Every day, but especially on the second day of each month (she died on October 2, 1928), adherents of her cult cover her tomb with white carnations. To visit Chacarita, take Línea B of the Subte to the end of the line at Federico Lacroze and cross the street.

and other Argentine artists of the 19th and 20th centuries. There are also impressive international works by European masters such as Cézanne, Degas, Picasso, Rembrandt, Toulouse-Lautrec and Van Gogh. Everything is well displayed, and there's also a cinema, concerts and classes. The museum's peaceful interior is a welcome respite from the busy avenue outside. Call in advance for tours in English.

The museum's building is a former pump house for the city waterworks, and was designed by architect Julio Dormala. It was later modified by Alejandro Bustillo, famous for his alpine-style civic center in the northern Patagonian city of Bariloche.

FLORALIS GENÉRICA   MONUMENT

Map p246 (cnr Av Figueroa Alcorta & Bibiloni) This gargantuan solar-powered flower sculpture, located smack in the center of Plaza Naciones Unidas is the inspired creation of architect Eduardo Catalano, who designed and funded the project in 2002. The giant aluminum and steel petals are 20m high and used to close like a real flower, from dusk until dawn – until the gears broke, that is.

PALAIS DE GLACE   NOTABLE BUILDING

Map p246 (☑4804-1163; www.palaisdeglace.gov. ar; Posadas 1725; ☺noon-8pm Tue-Fri, 10am-8pm Sat & Sun; ☐17, 62, 67) **FREE** Housed in an unusual circular building that was once an ice-skating rink and a tango hall (happily not at once, however!), the spacious Palais de Glace now offers a variety of rotating cultural, artistic and historical exhibitions. Be sure to check out the 2nd floor, worth a peep for its interesting ceiling and other architectural details. Musical concerts are also occasionally hosted here.

FACULTAD DE INGENIERÍA   NOTABLE BUILDING

Map p246 (Engineering School; cnr General Las Heras & Azcuénaga) This beautiful but decrepit neo-Gothic building (1912) was designed by Uruguayan architect Arturo Prins and never quite completed. It's currently being given a face-lift.

EATING

Recoleta is the playground for the wealthy elite, full of beautiful apartment buildings, upscale boutiques and the occasional baroque mansion. As you can imagine, the restaurants here aren't cheap, but if you want to rub shoulders with the upper classes, this is the place to be.

Practically everyone visits Recoleta's cemetery, so the two-block strip of touristy restaurants, bars and cafes lining nearby RM Ortiz is very convenient. Food here tends toward the overpriced, but many restaurants have outdoor terraces that are choice hangout spots on warm days. And the people-watching here is excellent, especially on weekends when the nearby craft market is in full swing.

There are three ice-cream shops on Av Quintana near the cemetery: **Persicco** (cnr Av Quintana & RM Ortiz), **Una Altra Volta** (Map p246; ☑4805-1818; www.unaltravolta.com.ar; cnr Av Quintana & Ayachuco) – both within one or two blocks of the cemetery – and **Arkakao** (Av Quintana 188), which is five blocks from the cemetery.

COMO EN CASA   ARGENTINE $

Map p246 (☑4816-5507; www.tortascomoen casa.com; Riobamba 1239; lunch mains AR$45-70; ☺8am-midnight Tue-Sat, 8am-8:30pm Sun & Mon) This gorgeous, upscale cafe-restaurant has a very elegant atmosphere and attracts Recoleta's wealthiest. Its best feature is the shady patio, complete with large fountain and surrounded by grand buildings, a must on a warm day. For lunch there are fancy sandwiches, salads, wraps and stir-fries, while dinner options include goulash, shrimp ragout and spinach gnocchi. Plenty of luscious desserts, plus breakfast too.

RODI BAR   ARGENTINE $

Map p246 (☑4801-5230; Vicente López 1900; mains AR$50-90; ☺7am-1am) A great option for well-priced, unpretentious food in upscale Recoleta. This traditional corner restaurant with fine old-world atmosphere and extensive menu offers something for everyone, from inexpensive combo plates to relatively unusual dishes such as marinated beef tongue.

NATURAL DELI   CAFE, DELI $

Map p250 (☑4822-1228; www.natural-deli.com; Laprida 1672; mains AR$50-72; ☺8am-midnight Mon-Sat, 9am-midnight Sun; ☑) Modern, organic cafe offering fresh dishes with a natural bent. Choose from creative gourmet sandwiches and wraps, fresh salads or stir fries. There are also fresh juices and *licuados* (blended fruit smoothies), plus many organic gourmet products are sold. Great for breakfast; muffins, scones, brownies and even key lime pie available. Also in **Las Cañitas, Palermo** (Map p250; ☑4514-1776; Gorostiaga 1776; ⊙8am-midnight Mon-Sat, 9am-midnight Sun).

TEA CONNECTION
CAFE $

Map p246 (☑4805-0616; www.teaconnection.com.ar; Uriburu 1595; mains AR$60-75; ⊙8am-midnight Mon-Sat, 9am-midnight Sun) At this sleek corner cafe, choose from over 20 types of black, red and green teas and health-conscious sandwiches, salads, vegetable tarts and pastries. Drinks include fruit juices and *licuados*. Other nearby locations include at **Arenales 2102** (Map p246) and **Montevideo 1655** (Map p246).

CUMANÁ
ARGENTINE $

Map p246 (☑4813-9207; Rodriguez Peña 1149; mains AR$40-50; ⊙noon-4pm & 8pm-1am) To sample Argentina's regional cuisine, check out this colorful, budget-friendly eatery with huge picture windows and an old-fashioned adobe oven. Cumaná specializes in delicious *cazuela*, stick-to-your-ribs stews filled with squash, corn, eggplant, potatoes and meat. Also popular are the *empanadas, locro* and *humita* (corn, cheese and onion tamales). Come early to avoid a wait.

EL SANJUANINO
ARGENTINE $

Map p246 (☑4805-2683; Posadas 1515; empanadas AR$13, mains AR$40-70; ⊙noon-4pm & 7pm-1am) This long-running, cozy little joint probably has the cheapest food in Recoleta, attracting both penny-pinching locals and thrifty tourists. Sit either upstairs or downstairs (in the basement) and order spicy *empanadas*, tamales or *locro* (corn and meat stew). The curved brick ceiling adds to the atmosphere, but many take their food to go – Recoleta's lovely parks are just a couple of blocks away.

MUNICH RECOLETA
ARGENTINE $$

Map p246 (☑4804-3981; www.munich-recoleta.com.ar; RM Ortiz 1871; mains AR$70-125; ⊙noon-3pm & 8pm-midnight Wed-Mon) This traditional restaurant hasn't changed much since Jorge Luis Borges was a regular; try the *brochettes* (shish-kebabs), grilled salmon or homemade ravioli. Service is exceptional and the white window curtains make this a semiprivate affair – perhaps a reason why more locals than tourists eat here. Warning

to animal lovers: there are trophy animal heads on the walls.

L'ORANGERIE
FRENCH $$$

Map p246 (☑4808-2100; Alvear Palace Hotel, Av Alvear 1891; full tea AR$190; ⊙breakfast 7-11am daily, lunch buffet noon-3.30pm Mon-Sat, afternoon tea 4:30-7pm Mon-Sat & 5-7pm Sun, brunch 12:30-4pm Sun) The grand tearoom at the Alvear Palace Hotel is fit for a special occasion. The formal afternoon tea, served from 4:30pm (from 5pm on Sunday), offers an endless array of exquisite cakes, sandwiches and pastries (two people can share one tea service). At breakfast and lunch, chefs in tall white hats attend lavish buffet spreads; Sunday brunch is particularly elaborate.

EL BURLADERO
SPANISH $$$

Map p246 (☑4806-9247; www.elburladero.com.ar; Uriburu 1488; mains AR$120-175; ⊙noon-4pm & 8pm-midnight) Treat yourself to an upscale meal in Recoleta at this exceptional Spanish restaurant. The menu changes seasonally, but will usually include a paella dish and perhaps the marinated rabbit, black hake fish or lamb with mushrooms. For a good deal, come at midday and get the three-course lunch menu (AR$109). Tapas are also available, and there's a long, high communal table for large groups.

🍷 DRINKING & NIGHTLIFE

RM Ortiz, across from Recoleta's famous cemetery, is a two-block strip of restaurants, cafes and bars. On warm sunny days most of them open up their fine outdoor front patios, perfect for a drink or meal and some people-watching.

LA BIELA
CAFE

Map p246 (☑4804-0449; www.labiela.com; Av Quintana 600; ⊙7am-2am Sun-Thu, to 3am Fri & Sat) A Recoleta institution, this classic landmark has been serving the porteño elite since the 1950s – when race-car champions used to frequent the place. The outdoor front terrace is unbeatable on a sunny afternoon, especially when the nearby weekend *feria* (street market) is in full swing. Just know that this privilege will cost 20% more.

NIP & TUCK

Wander around Recoleta, the ritzy neighborhood that is home to many of Buenos Aires' plastic surgery clinics, and nobody bats an eyelid at someone walking down the street with plasters on their faces – they've obviously just had a nip and tuck.

The president herself – Cristina Kirchner – is sometimes dubbed 'the queen of botox' in the local media. It comes as no surprise, then, to learn that Argentina has the highest per capita ratio of plastic surgery operations in the world. Reports suggest that one in 30 Argentines have had some sort of procedure during their lifetime.

Demand for plastic surgery has risen exponentially in the last decade, especially with the boom in 'medical tourism.' Rather than paying up to US$15,000 for a facelift in the United States, some have elected to head to the 'Paris of the South' and combine the surgery with a bit of tango, beef and sightseeing – for a third of the price.

Be aware, however, of the dangers of any medical procedure – *let alone* one on foreign turf where you may not speak the language. If you're considering such a procedure, do your homework very, very carefully and thoroughly.

BULLER BREWING COMPANY   BAR

Map p246 (☑4808-9061; www.bullerpub.com; RM Ortiz 1827; ☺noon-1am Mon-Wed, to 2am Thu & Sun, to 4am Fri & Sat) Yes, it's a microbrewery in Buenos Aires, and in Recoleta, no less. Six kinds of beer are brewed on the premises, including a stout, hefeweisen, pilsen and a honey beer. Alcohol content ranges from 4.5% to 8.5%. There's a great outdoor patio in front and an extensive menu of snacks and sandwiches. Also in **Retiro** (Map p248; Paraguay 428).

CASA BAR   SPORTS BAR

Map p246 (☑4816-2712; www.casabarbuenos aires.com; Rodríguez Peña 1150; ☺7pm-3am Wed-Fri, to 5am Sat) This recycled antique house turned sports bar offers a large selection of spirits and microbrews, along with a wine list stocked with higher-end bottles. You'll also find nachos, pizza and spicy hot wings on the menu, plus happy-hour specials from 7pm to 10pm. Casa Bar is stylish but casual – and a great spot to watch sports on TV, especially American football and baseball.

CLÁSICA Y MODERNA   CAFE

Map p246 (☑4812-8707; www.clasicaymoderna.com; Av Callao 892; ☺8am-2am Mon-Sat, 5pm-2am Sun) Catering to the literary masses since 1938, this cozy and intimate bookstore-restaurant-cafe continues to ooze history from its atmospheric brick walls. It's nicely lit, serves fine, simple meals and offers nightly live performances of folk music, jazz, bossa nova and tango. Mercedes Sosa (may she rest in peace), Susana Rinaldi and Liza Minnelli have all chirped here.

SHAMROCK   BAR

Map p246 (☑4812-3584; Rodríguez Peña 1220; ☺6pm-4am Mon-Wed, to 6am Thu & Fri, 8pm-6am Sat) Popular with both locals and tourists for its cheap happy hour, this long-running and not very traditional Irish pub in Barrio Norte is decked out in dark wood and has a dim, moody atmosphere. Women beware: this is a serious pick up joint. DJs rule from Thursday to Saturday, when the Basement Club opens up downstairs, usually around midnight.

BASEMENT CLUB   CLUB

Map p246 (☑4812-3584; Rodriguez Peña 1220; ☺Thu-Sat) This cool but unpretentious subterranean club is known for first-rate DJ lineups, pounding house music and a diverse young crowd. Thanks to the Shamrock, the ever-popular Irish pub upstairs, the place sees plenty of traffic throughout the night. Come at 3am to see the club in full swing, or just descend the stairs after enjoying a few pints at ground level.

⭐ ENTERTAINMENT

NOTORIOUS   JAZZ

Map p246 (☑4813-6888; www.notorious.com.ar; Av Callao 966) This stylish, intimate joint is one of Buenos Aires' premier jazz venues. Up front you can buy CDs of various music genres, while in the back the restaurant-cafe (overlooking a verdant garden) hosts live shows nearly every night at 9:30pm. Log on to the website for schedules; most performances are jazz, but there's also Brazilian music.

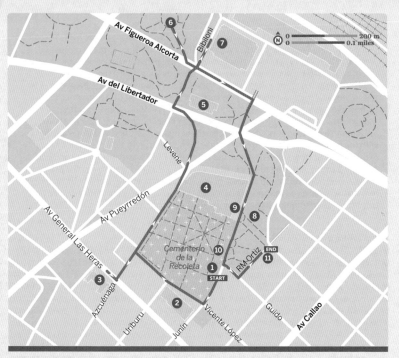

Neighborhood Walk
Death, Art & Shopping

START CEMENTERIO DE LA RECOLETA
END LA BIELA CAFE
LENGTH 2-3KM; THREE HOURS

Start with a bang and visit BA's top tourist destination: **1 Cementerio de la Recoleta** (p117). You can easily spend hours in here examining the hundreds of elaborate sarcophagi. Turn right out of the cemetery and swing past the upscale **2 Recoleta Mall**.

Head to the neo-Gothic **3 Facultad de Ingeniería** (p119), designed by Uruguayan architect Arturo Prins and never quite completed. It was being given a face-lift at research time so hopefully will look spiffy when you get there.

Need to shop for your home? Then stop in at the large **4 Buenos Aires Design mall**, worth a look for the most cutting-edge furniture and lifestyle products. Now cut across Plaza Francia and head to the excellent **5 Museo Nacional de Bellas Artes** (p118), containing classical art from all over

the world. Everything is well displayed and lit and, best of all, it's free.

Cross Av Figueroa Alcorta to reach the giant metal flower sculpture, **6 Floralis Genérica** (p119); it's cool to see your reflection in the petals. Head back down Alcorta – passing the mammoth **7 Facultad de Derecho** (School of Law) building along the way. Cross the footbridge and make your way up Plaza Intendente Alvear. If it's a weekend, browse through the craft stalls at **8 Feria Plaza Francia** (p123).

Stop by the **9 Centro Cultural Recoleta** (p118) to explore the galleries. If you have small kids, the Museo Participativo de Ciencias will grab their attention. Right next to the cultural center is the pretty **10 Basílica de Nuestra Señora del Pilar** (p118); check out the small museum upstairs.

Amble down to restaurant-filled RM Ortiz and end your walk at the fine cafe **11 La Biela** (p120). If it's sunny grab a table on the front patio – it's worth the extra pesos.

🛍 SHOPPING

Exclusivity is the key word here. If you have the bucks and are willing to pay top dollar for the best quality goods, then you'll want to shop in these neighborhoods. The city's best leather shops are based here, along with a few top fashion boutiques. Av Santa Fe is a catch-all for fashion, housewares and everything in-between.

FERIA PLAZA FRANCIA   MARKET
Map p246 (www.feriaplazafrancia.com; ⊙11am-8pm Sat, Sun & holidays) Located right in front of Recoleta's cemetery, in Plaza Intendente Alvear, this large and popular street fair features hundreds of booths selling leather accessories, bronze jewelry, fused glass, ceramic mugs, woven hats and kitschy souvenirs – essentially dozens of handmade crafts of all kinds. Hippies gather, bakers circulate their pastries and mimes perform (or just stand very still). The website gives a great overview of what's available.

BUENOS AIRES DESIGN   SHOPPING MALL
Map p246 (☎5777-6000; Av Pueyrredón 2501; ⊙10am-9pm Mon-Sat, noon-9pm Sun) The trendiest and finest home furnishings are all under one roof here. This is the ideal place to look for that snazzy light fixture, streamlined toilet or reproduction Asian chair. Also good for everyday appliances and housewares, along with cute decor and art objects.

WUSSMANN SHOP   STATIONERY
Map p246 (☎4811-2444; Rodriguez Peña 1399; ⊙10:30am-8pm Mon-Fri, 11am-2pm Sat) Writers and artists delight in the gorgeous handmade paper at this chic stationery shop. Leatherbound journals, monogrammed stationery, and oversized sketchbooks are made with recycled paper; come here for one-of-a-kind invitations and notecards or hand-painted wrapping paper to spruce up a special gift.

PORTOBELLO VINTAGE BOUTIQUE   CLOTHING
Map p240 (☎4811-2619; Paraguay 1554; ⊙noon-8pm Mon-Fri) Excellent vintage clothing boutique. Find that special jacket, dress, shirt and bottom from the 1940s on up. All clothes are in great condition and sold at affordable prices. Some jewelry and other accessories are also for sale.

GALERÍA BOND STREET   SHOPPING MALL
Map p246 (Av Santa Fe 1670; ⊙10am-9pm Mon-Sat) For the edgiest tattoos and piercings in town, you can't beat this grungy shopping center. Buenos Aires' skateboarder-wannabes, along with their punk-rock counterparts, also come here to shop for the latest styles, sounds and bongs. Expect everything from Hello Kitty to heavy metal.

1. Postcard depicting Eva Perón 2. Eva Perón's tomb in Recoleta cemetery (p117)

The Immortal Evita

From her humble origins in the pampas to her rise to power beside President Juan Perón, María Eva Duarte de Perón is one of Argentina's most revered political figures. Known affectionately to all as Evita, she is Argentina's beloved First Lady.

At the age of 15, Eva Duarte left her hometown of Junín for Buenos Aires, looking for work as an actor but eventually landing a job in radio. Her big chance came in 1944, when she attended a benefit at Buenos Aires' Luna Park. Here Duarte met Colonel Juan Perón, who fell in love with her; they were married in 1945.

Shortly after Perón won the presidency in 1946, Evita went to work in the office of the Department of Labor and Welfare. During Perón's two terms, Evita empowered her husband both through her charisma and by reaching out to the nation's poor, who came to love her dearly. She created the Fundación Eva Perón, which built housing for the poor, created programs for children, extended subsidies and distributed clothing and food to needy families. She fervently campaigned for the aged, urging her husband to add rights for the elderly to the constitution and successfully pushing through a law granting pensions to elderly people in need. She successfully advocated for a law extending suffrage to women.

Perón won his second term in 1952, but that same year Evita – aged just 33 and at the height of her popularity – died of cancer. It was a blow to Argentina and to her husband's presidency.

Although Evita is remembered for extending social justice to those she called the country's *descamisados* (shirtless ones), her rule with Perón was hardly free from controversy. Together they ruled the country with an iron fist, jailing opposition leaders and closing opposition newspapers. When *Time* magazine referred to her as an 'illegitimate child', she banned the publication, and when she traveled to Europe in 1947 she was refused entrance to Buckingham Palace. However, there is no denying the extent to which she empowered women at all levels of Argentine society and helped the country's poor.

When Evita said, 'I will come again, and I will be millions' in a speech shortly before her death, she probably had no idea of her words' prophetic truth. Today she enjoys near-saint status and has practically become a pop icon after the release of the Hollywood musical *Evita*. She was, for many, 'our Lady of Hope'.

Get to know her better at **Museo Evita** (p130) or visit her tomb in the **Recoleta cemetery** (p117). You can also read her ghostwritten autobiography *La razón de mi vida* (My Mission in Life; 1951).

Palermo

Neighborhood Top Five

❶ Checking out the contemporary artwork at **Museo de Arte Latino-americano de Buenos Aires** (p128), a modern glassy museum where you can commune with Diego Rivera and Frida Kahlo.

❷ Bicycling, jogging, rollerblading or just walking along the paths at **Parque 3 de Febrero** (p129).

❸ Eating your way through the dozens of ethnic restaurants in **Palermo Viejo** and **Las Cañitas** (p132).

❹ Visiting **Museo Evita** (p130) to get the scoop on Argentina's most famous international woman.

❺ Shopping the **designer clothing boutiques** and other fun shops in Palermo Viejo (p138).

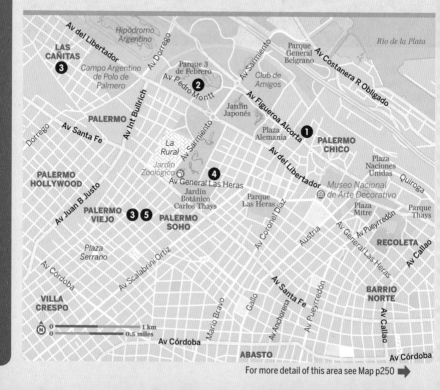

For more detail of this area see Map p250 ➡

Explore: Palermo

Most of Palermo's museums are located near its green parks. They're spread out over this large neighborhood, so give yourself plenty of time to see them. Museo Evita, Museo Nacional de Arte Decorativo and Museo de Arte Latinoamericano de Buenos Aires (Malba) all have pleasant cafe-restaurants with outdoor areas, great for taking a relaxing lunch or snack break.

Palermo Viejo, the city's most trendsetting neighborhood, is roughly bounded by Santa Fe, Scalabrini Ortiz, Córdoba and Dorrego. It's further divided into Palermo Hollywood (north of the train tracks) and Palermo Soho (south of the tracks), both full of old buildings, leafy sidewalks and cobbled streets. These areas have BA's best cutting-edge restaurants, along with trendy bars and nightclubs; Plaza Serrano has dozens of sidewalk tables and heaves with crowds on weekends.

Buenos Aires' most famous fashion designers have opened up dozens of boutiques here, and there are many fancy housewares stores and other themed shops. It's not the cheapest place to shop, but likely the most fun – wear comfortable shoes as you'll be walking a lot.

Another popular but much smaller neighborhood in Palermo is further north in Las Cañitas; it occupies a wedge of blocks close to the polo grounds. It's mostly a residential area on the border with Belgrano and named after the fields of sugar cane that used to grow here. The only sweet things here now, however, are the luscious desserts at the dozens of restaurants on Av Báez, the main business street. Just a few blocks long, it's densely packed with eateries, bars, cafes and even a club or two, and it positively buzzes at night.

Local Life

➤ **Shopping** Trendy locals dress up to be seen fashionably shopping Palermo's fancy boutiques.

➤ **Nightlife** Young, hip *porteños* wait until after midnight to congregate at bars, and after 2am head out to the clubs.

➤ **Sunny Weekends** Local families grab their strollers and head to the Jardín Zoológico (p130) for a day of animal-watching.

Getting There & Away

➤ **Bus** Take buses 29, 59, 64 and 152 from the Microcentro to Plaza Italia; bus 39 from Congreso to Palermo Viejo; bus 111 from the Microcentro to Palermo Viejo.

➤ **Subte** Línea D is the fastest way to Palermo's Plaza Italia area.

Lonely Planet's Top Tip

Grab a bike, along with a good lock and helmet, and make use of the miles of protected bike paths along Palermo's green parks. It's a great way to see the area's many spread-out sites while breathing in some fresh air and getting exercise. The bike paths also exist within Palermo Soho and Hollywood. Bike rentals are available at a few bike-touring companies and on nice weekends near Av de la Infanta Isabel and Av Pedro Montt (p207).

PALERMO

✗ Best Places to Eat

➤ Hernán Gipponi Restaurant (p135)
➤ Oviedo (p132)
➤ Don Julio (p132)
➤ Las Pizarras (p132)

For reviews, see p132➤

➊ Best Places to Drink

➤ Verne (p135)
➤ Frank's Bar (p135)
➤ Magdalena's Party (p136)
➤ Home Hotel (p136)

For reviews, see p135➤

◉ Best Museums

➤ Museo de Arte Latinoamericano de Buenos Aires (p129)
➤ Museo Nacional de Arte Decorativo (p130)
➤ Museo Evita (p130)

For reviews, see p130➤

TOP SIGHT MUSEO DE ARTE LATINOAMERICANO DE BUENOS AIRES (MALBA)

Sparkling inside its glass and cement walls is this airy modern-art museum, one of BA's finest. It contains some of the best works by classic and contemporary Argentine artists, such as Xul Solar and Antonio Berni, plus some pieces by other Latin American painters like Mexican duo Diego Rivera and Frida Kahlo.

Christened in 2001, the building is home to Eduardo F Costantini's private art collection. The millionaire and philanthropist gathered over 200 of Latin America's best artworks from the 20th century. Well-known Argentine painters represented here include Linoenea Spilimbergo, Jorge de la Vega, Emilio Pettoruti and Guillermo Kuitca. If they're on display, check out figurative artist Antonio Berni's *Nuevo Realismo* (social realism) oeuvres. Many of these artists confront social issues in their works.

Among the collection is the work of Tarsila do Amaral, one of Brazil's most famous painters; look for her *Abaporu* (1928), one of Brazil's most important paintings and for which Costantini paid US$1.4 million in 1995. Colombian Fernando Botero depicts human figures in cartoonish, overly plump sizes, as in his *Los Viudos* (1968). And Frida Kahlo's charming *Self-Portrait with Monkey and Parrot* (1942) cost Costantini nearly US$3.2 million.

Excellent temporary exhibits are shown in several halls, and there are occasional kids' programs and a cinema that screens art-house films. A terrace, bookstore, gift shop and cafe-restaurant (expensive but great for people-watching) complete the picture. Call for tours in English.

DON'T MISS...

➡ Andy Warhol's photography, especially if it includes abstract artist Marta Minujín (an Argentine conceptual artist).

➡ One of Diego Rivera's early cubist works, *Retrato de Ramón Gómez de la Serna* (Portrait of Ramón Gómez de la Serna, 1915).

PRACTICALITIES

➡ Malba

➡ Map p250

➡ ☏4808-6500

➡ www.malba.org.ar

➡ Av Figueroa Alcorta 3415

➡ admission AR$40, Wed AR$20

➡ ⏱noon-8pm Thu-Mon, to 9pm Wed

TOP SIGHT
PARQUE 3 DE FEBRERO

Also known as Bosques de Palermo, this sweeping green space abounds with small lakes and paddleboats, pretty gazebos, a monument to literary greats called El Jardín de los Poetas (the Garden of Poets) and the pleasant Rosedal (Rose Garden). On weekends it's filled with families picnicking, friends playing *fútbol*, lovers smooching and strolling, and outdoor enthusiasts jogging and bicycling.

The area around Parque 3 de Febrero was originally the private retreat of 19th-century dictator Juan Manuel de Rosas and became public parkland only after his fall from power – on February 3, 1852. Ironically for Rosas, the man who overthrew him – former ally Justo José de Urquiza – sits on his mount in a mammoth equestrian **monument** at the corner of Avs Sarmiento and Presidente Figueroa Alcorta.

In 1875, Parque 3 de Febrero was inaugurated by Argentina's president, Nicolas Avellaneda. It was designed by Charles Thays, a French botanist and landscape architect who also worked on Plaza de Mayo, Barracas de Belgrano and Parque Lezama. Thays used London's Hyde Park and Paris' Bois de Boulogne as inspiration for his work here.

The park's most interesting destinations include the Jardín Japonés (p130), the Jardín Zoológico (p130), the **Jardín Botánico Carlos Thays** (Botanical Gardens; Map p250; ⊙dawn-dusk) FREE and the **Planetario Galileo Galilei** (Map p250; ☑4771-9393; www.planetario.gov.ar; cnr Avs Sarmiento & Belisario Roldán). More exclusive are the Campo Argentino de Polo (p143) and the **Hipódromo Argentino** (the racetrack). Just south of the zoo, and a major landmark in Palermo, is Plaza Italia, a half-moon-shaped traffic island and important transport hub.

DON'T MISS...

➡ Walking, bicycling or roller-blading around the rose garden and nearby lakes on a warm sunny weekend, when the ring road is closed to vehicular traffic and outdoor rentals abound.

PRACTICALITIES

➡ Map p250
➡ cnr Avs del Libertador & de la Infanta Isabel
➡ ▣10, 34, 130

⊙ SIGHTS

MUSEO DE ARTE LATINOAMERICANO DE BUENOS AIRES (MALBA)　MUSEUM
See p128.

PARQUE 3 DE FEBRERO　PARK
See p129.

MUSEO NACIONAL DE ARTE DECORATIVO　MUSEUM
Map p250 (☑4802-6606; www.mnad.org; Av del Libertador 1902; admission AR$15, Tue free; ☉2-7pm Tue-Sat Jan, 2-7pm Tue-Sun rest of year) This museum is housed in the stunning beaux arts mansion called Residencia Errázuriz Alvear (1917), once the residence of Chilean aristocrat Matías Errázuriz and his wife, Josefina de Alvear. It now displays many of their very posh belongings, along with beautiful features such as Corinthian columns and a gorgeous marble staircase inspired by the Palace of Versailles. There's also an amazing hall which has a carved wooden ceiling, stained-glass panels and a huge stone fireplace.

Everything from renaissance religious paintings and porcelain dishes to Italian sculptures and period furniture was owned by Errázuriz, and some artwork by El Greco, Manet and Rodin can also be seen. There are guided tours in English Tuesday to Saturday at 2:30pm (AR$15 plus admission). There's also a lovely cafe outside, Croque Madame, which provides a relaxing break on a sunny day.

JARDÍN ZOOLÓGICO　ZOO
Map p250 (☑4011-9900; www.zoobuenosaires. com.ar; cnr Avs Las Heras & Sarmiento; admission AR$75, under 12yr free; ☉10am-6pm Tue-Sun Oct-Mar, to 5pm Apr-Sep) Set on 18 hectares, Buenos Aires' Jardín Zoológico is a decent zoo, offering over 350 species – many in 'natural' and good-sized animal enclosures. On sunny weekends it's packed with families enjoying the large green spaces and artificial lakes. Some of the buildings housing the animals are impressive; check out the elephant house. An aquarium, a monkey island, reptile house and large aviary are other highlights; a few special exhibits (like the sea lion show or carousel) cost extra.

The zoo is noted for having successfully bred condors and white tigers, and for having an educational farm with petting zoo for the kids. Waterfowl, Patagonian hares, nutria (semi-aquatic rodents) and feral cats roam wild.

JARDÍN JAPONÉS　GARDENS
Map p250 (☑4804-4922; www.jardinjapones. ar; cnr Avs Casares & Berro; admission AR$24, under 12yr free; ☉10am-6pm) First opened in 1967 and then donated to the city of Buenos Aires in 1979 (on the centenary of the arrival of Argentina's first Japanese immigrants), Jardín Japonés is one of the capital's best-kept gardens – and makes a wonderfully peaceful rest stop. Inside there's a Japanese **restaurant** along with lovely ponds filled with koi and spanned by pretty bridges. Japanese culture can be experienced through occasional exhibitions and workshops on ikebana, haiku, origami, *taiko* (Japanese drumming) and other events.

MUSEO DE ARTES PLÁSTICAS EDUARDO SÍVORI　MUSEUM
Map p250 (☑4774-9452; www.museosivori.org. ar; Av de la Infanta Isabel 555; admission AR$5, Wed & Sat free; ☉noon-8pm Tue-Fri, 10am-8pm Sat & Sun; ▣10, 34) Named for an Italo-Argentine painter who studied in Europe, this modern museum of Argentine art has open spaces allowing frequent and diverse exhibitions. Sívori's Parisian works reflect European themes, but later works returned to Argentine motifs, mainly associated with rural life on the Pampas. However most works on display are by other well-known Argentine artists, such as Benito Quinquela Martín, Antonio Berni and Fernando Fader. There's a sculpture garden and slick **cafe** on the premises, and occasional theater, concerts, courses and workshops are offered.

MUSEO EVITA　MUSEUM
Map p250 (☑4807-0306; www.museoevita.org; Lafinur 2988; local/foreigner AR$10/20; ☉11am-7pm Tue-Sun) Everybody who's anybody in Argentina has their own museum, and Eva Perón (1919–52) is no exception. Museo Evita immortalizes the Argentine heroine with plenty of videos, historical photos, books, old posters and newspaper headlines. However, the prize memorabilia has to be her wardrobe: dresses, shoes, handbags, hats and blouses lie proudly behind glass, forever pressed and pristine. Even Evita's old wallets and perfumes are on display. Our favorite is a picture of her kicking a soccer ball – in heels.

WALKING THE DOG

Buenos Aires supports a legion of *paseaperros* (professional dog walkers), who can be seen with up to a dozen canines on leashes. They'll stroll through areas like Palermo's parks, Recoleta and even downtown with a variety of dogs ranging from scruffy mongrels to expensive purebreds, each of their tails happily a-waggin'.

Paseaperros are employed by busy apartment dwellers who either can't or won't take the time to exercise their animals properly – and are willing to pay up to AR$200 per month for this unique walking service. Since most *paseaperros* don't pay taxes, they can really 'clean up' in the city – figuratively speaking.

Every day thousands of canines deposit tons (almost literally) of excrement in the streets and parks of the capital. You'll be aware of this fact soon after stepping onto the streets of Buenos Aires. Cleaning up after one's pooch is already a city requirement, but enforcement is nil, so be very careful where you tread – you'll see dog piles of all textures and sizes lining almost every sidewalk. One to especially step clear of is the author-named *dulce de leche* variety.

Still, the capital's leashed packs are a remarkably orderly and always entertaining sight, and make great snapshots to bring back home.

Head around to the corner if you need refreshment – attached to the museum is the pleasant Museo Evita Restaurant (p134) with wonderfully leafy patio, perfect for relaxing on a warm day.

MUSEO DE ARTE POPULAR JOSÉ HERNÁNDEZ
MUSEUM

Map p250 (✆4803-2384; www.museohernan dez.buenosaires.gob.ar; Av del Libertador 2373; admission AR$5, Sun free; ☺1-6:30pm Wed-Fri, 10am-7pm Sat & Sun) This museum is being remodelled at research time, but the emphasis here is on both traditional and contemporary arts and crafts, mostly from Argentina. Expect to see intricate gaucho-related silverwork like knives and mate sets, Mapuche textiles like ponchos and folk crafts from the country's northern regions. The back halls hold changing exhibits.

MUSEO XUL SOLAR
MUSEUM

Map p250 (✆4824-3302; www.xulsolar.org.ar; Laprida 1212; admission AR$20; ☺noon-8pm Tue-Fri, to 7pm Sat, closed Feb) Xul Solar was a painter, inventor, poet and friend of Jorge Luis Borges. This museum (located in his old mansion) showcases over 80 of his unique and colorful yet subdued paintings. Solar's Klee-esque style includes fantastically themed, almost cartoonish figures placed in surreal cubist landscapes. It's great stuff, and bizarre enough to put him in a class of his own. Tours in Spanish are available Tuesday and Thursday at 4pm and Saturday at 3:30pm.

MUSEO CASA DE RICARDO ROJAS
MUSEUM

Map p250 (✆4824-4039; Charcas 2837; ⓢLínea D Aguero, Pueyrredón) Walk under the facade, modeled after the Casa de Independencia in Tucumán, and behold a quaint courtyard surrounded by European and Incan architectural motifs. Famous Argentine educator and writer Ricardo Rojas lived here from 1929 to 1957, and in his office wrote his renowned work *El Santo de la Espada* (1933). An old dining room with period furniture also gives an idea of the past. Phone for opening hours, as the museum is closed for remodeling at research time.

BIBLIOTECA NACIONAL
LIBRARY

(✆4808-6000; www.bn.gov.ar; Agüero 2502; ☺9am-9pm Mon-Fri, noon-7pm Sat & Sun; 🚌59, 60) **FREE** Prominent Argentine and Latin American literary figures, such as Ernesto Sábato, have lectured here, and other events include workshops, concerts and cultural activities. Tours in English are offered on Monday, Tuesday and Thursday at 3pm. Bring photo ID and be ready to fill out a form to enter.

CENTRO ISLÁMICO REY FAHD
MOSQUE

Map p250 (✆4899-0201; www.ccislamico reyfahd.org.ar; Av Int Bullrich 55) This landmark mosque, built by Saudis on land donated by former president Carlos Menem, is southeast of Las Cañitas. Free tours in Spanish are offered on Tuesday, Thursday and Saturday at noon (bring your passport, dress conservatively and enter via Av Int Bullrich).

✕ EATING

Palermo Viejo is at the heart of innovative cuisine in Buenos Aires. Dozens of upmarket restaurants serve creative cuisine in a contemporary setting, but it's important to be discerning – a new eatery opens every week, and while quality is generally high, only a few places are truly special. Apart from the high-end *parrillas* where fine steaks and expensive wines rule, Palermo chefs often take inspiration from different ethnic cuisines. You'll find elements of Japanese, Indian, Vietnamese, Brazilian, Mexican, Middle Eastern, Greek and even Norwegian food throughout the neighborhood's dining scene. Just remember that most restaurants offer an Argentine approach to these international styles of cooking: don't expect spicy flavors, for example, because the locals can't stomach it.

Another sub-neighborhood of Palermo with exceptional eating is Las Cañitas, not far from Palermo Viejo. Traffic jams up here on the weekends, when hordes of diners descend on the few blocks of Av Báez where most of the area's restaurants and bars are concentrated.

OUI OUI
INTERNATIONAL **$**

Map p250 (🖉4778-9614; www.ouioui.com.ar; Nicaragua 6068; mains AR$40-70; ⏱8am-8pm Tue-Sun) *Pain au chocolat* and shabby chic? *Oui.* This charming and popular French-style cafe produces the goods – dark coffee, buttery croissants and jars of tangy lemonade – and boasts a small and cozy interior. Choose also from creative salads, gourmet sandwiches and luscious pastries. Its annex, **Almacén Oui Oui** (Map p250; cnr Dorrego & Nicaragua; ⏱8am-9pm Tue-Sun), is on the same block and stays open an hour later.

SOCIAL LA LECHUZA
ARGENTINE **$**

Map p250 (🖉4773-2781; Uriarte 1980; mains AR$40-75; ⏱8:30pm-midnight Tue, 12:30-3:30pm & 8:30pm-midnight Wed-Sat, 1-3:30pm Sun) A world away from its trendy neighbors, this classic joint holds on to tradition and offers a breath of fresh air from all those overpriced, overhip restaurants in Palermo. Funky art adorns the walls including amateur owl paintings (*lechuza* means 'owl'). Meats and pastas are served in abundant portions, but don't miss the desserts like chocolate mousse and tiramisu.

AREVALITO
VEGETARIAN **$**

Map p250 (🖉4776-4252; Arévalo 1478; mains AR$40; ⏱9am-midnight Mon-Sat; 🖉) The menu is hardly extensive at this tiny bohemian eatery, but everything is good and very healthy, and the portions are generous. There's homemade yogurt, daily sandwich specials, hearty salads, vegetable tarts and more. Exceptional coffee and lemonade too.

LAS CHOLAS
ARGENTINE **$**

Map p250 (🖉4899-0094; Arce 306; mains AR$40-75; ⏱noon-4pm & 8pm-midnight) Good food and bargain prices keep this popular corner eatery packed. Choose from typical *parrilla* cuts or traditional Argentine foods like *locro* and *cazuela* (meat and veggie stews). Negatives include uncomfortable chairs, spotty service and the owner's large dog roaming the dining room.

★OVIEDO
MEDITERRANEAN **$$**

Map p250 (🖉4822-5415; Beruti 2602; mains AR$90-140; ⏱noon-midnight Mon-Sat) Famed chef Martin Rebaudino brings a contemporary Spanish flair to seafood (the fish is shipped daily from Mar del Plata) and serves up melt-in-your-mouth *cochinillo* (suckling pig) dishes that are worth writing home about. Desserts are homemade, as are the breads. A fantastic wine list and cordial service make Oviedo a fine-dining experience you won't mind shelling out for.

★DON JULIO
PARRILLA **$$**

Map p250 (🖉4832-6058; Guatemala 4699; mains AR$80-120; ⏱noon-4pm & 7:30pm-1am) Classy service and a great wine list add an upscale bent to this traditional corner steakhouse. The *bife de chorizo* (sirloin steak) is the main attraction here, but the exposed-brick interior, original floor tiles and cowhide tablecloths enhance the sensory experience, and the gourmet salads – served with a flourish by the uber-professional wait staff – are a treat.

★LAS PIZARRAS
INTERNATIONAL **$$**

Map p250 (🖉4775-0625; Thames 2296; mains AR$80-90; ⏱8pm-midnight Tue-Sun) At this simple and unpretentious yet excellent restaurant, Chef Rodrigo Castilla cooks up a changing rainbow of eclectic dishes such as grilled venison or rabbit stuffed with cherries and pistachios. Those with meeker stomachs can choose the asparagus and mushroom risotto or any of the homemade pastas. The chalkboard menu on the wall adds to the casual atmosphere.

★ SIAMO NEL FORNO PIZZA $$

Map p250 (4775-0337; Costa Rica 5886; pizza AR$65-95; 8pm-midnight Tue-Thu & Sun, to 1am Fri & Sat) Possibly the city's best Naples-style pizzas, made with quality ingredients and finished in a hot wood-fired oven so the thin crusts char beautifully. Try the Margherita, with tomatoes, fresh mozzarella, basil and olive oil; the Champignon & Prosciutto comes with mushrooms, ham and goat cheese. Also bakes up excellent calzoni.

ASTOR MODERN ARGENTINE $$

(4554-0802; www.astorbistro.com; Ciudad de la Paz 353; mains AR$80-90; 12:30-3:30pm Mon-Wed, 12:30-3:30pm & 8:30pm-midnight Thu & Fri, 8:30pm-midnight Sat) French-trained Chef Antonio Soriano presides over the kitchen at this contemporary restaurant in a residential neighborhood. The few main dishes change weekly but are always delicious and beautifully presented, accented with edible flowers. If you order the tasting menu (AR$149), bring your appetite – it's nine courses. To watch your meals being created, sit at the bar, which offers a view of the open kitchen.

SUDESTADA ASIAN $$

Map p250 (4776-3777; Guatemala 5602; mains AR$105-135; noon-3:15pm & 8pm-midnight Mon-Thu, to 1am Fri & Sat) Sudestada's well-earned reputation comes from its beautifully prepared curries, stir-fries and noodle dishes, all inspired by the cuisines of Thailand, Vietnam, Malaysia and Singapore. Don't forgo an exotic cocktail or delicious lychee *licuado* (milkshake). Note that if you order something spicy, it's actually spicy. The popular set-lunch special is great value.

CRIZIA INTERNATIONAL $$

Map p250 (4831-4979; www.crizia.com.ar; Gorriti 5143; mains AR$90-135; 7pm-1am) One of BA's best seafood restaurants. Start with a half-dozen oysters, then follow with the grilled Camembert over porcini mushrooms and seared red tuna in lime vinaigrette. End with the semifreddo of ginger and fresh mango. Chef Gabriel Oggero will make yours a night to remember.

OLSEN SCANDINAVIAN $$

Map p250 (4776-7677; Gorriti 5870; mains AR$105-125; noon-midnight Tue-Sat, 10:30am-midnight Sun) With its hip, relaxed vibe, too-cool crowd and dramatic central fireplace, Olsen could easily be located in the frosty climes of Scandinavia. Chef German Martitegui's dishes are limited but inspired, and the vodka selection – over 60 – is superlative. Luxuriate with an exotic cocktail in the lovely front garden, or try the popular Sunday brunch. Limited menu between lunch and dinner.

PALERMO EATING

BEHIND CLOSED DOORS

A very popular Buenos Aires culinary offshoot in the last few years are 'closed-door restaurants', or *puertas cerradas*. These places are open only a few days per week, have timed seatings and are generally prix fixe (and mostly cash only). They're not marked with signs and you have to ring a bell to enter. They won't even tell you the address until you make reservations (mandatory, of course). But for that tingly feeling brought on by discovering something off the beaten path – with some of the city's best food to boot – these places are for you.

There are two kinds of *puertas cerradas*: the first is where you dine in the chef's actual home, and usually sit at a large communal table. This is a great way to meet other people, often interesting travelers or expats; it's ideal for folks traveling alone. The second kind has more of a restaurant feel and tables are for separate groups – just like a regular restaurant, but not open to walk-ins. Many *puertas cerradas* are located in Palermo.

Some of BA's best *puertas cerradas* include **iLatina** (www.ilatinabuenosaires.com/en), serving exquisite Colombian food; **Casa Saltshaker** (www.casasaltshaker.com), where you'll sample ex–New Yorker Dan Perlman's culinary creations; **NOLA** (www.nolabuenosaires.com), home to New Orleans–fusion dishes; **Casa Felix** (www.colectivofelix.com/casa-felix), a pescatarian's delight; and **Cocina Sunae** (www.cocinasunae.com), for near-authentic Asian-fusion meals.

BELGRANO

Bustling Av Cabildo, the racing heartbeat of Belgrano, is an overwhelming jumble of noise and neon. It's a two-way street of clothing, shoe and housewares shops that does its part in supporting *porteños'* mass consumerism. For a bit more peace and quiet, head to the blocks on either side of the avenue, where Belgrano becomes a leafy barrio of museums, plazas, parks and good local eateries.

A block east of Av Cabildo, the barrio's plaza is the site of the modest but fun **Feria Plaza Belgrano** (cnr Juramento & Cuba; ☉10am-8pm Sat & Sun). On a sunny weekend it's full of shoppers and families with strollers. Near the plaza stands the Italianate **Iglesia de la Inmaculada Concepción**, a church popularly known as La Redonda (The Round One) because of its impressive dome.

Just a few steps from the plaza is the **Museo Histórico Sarmiento** (☑4782-2354; www.museosarmiento.gov.ar; Juramento 2180; admission AR$15; ☉1-6pm Mon-Fri, 3-7pm Sat & Sun), which honors one of the most forward-thinking Argentines in history. Also close by is the **Museo de Arte Español Enrique Larreta** (☑4784-4040; www.museolarreta.buenosaires.gov.ar; Juramento 2291; admission AR$5; ☉1-7pm Mon -Fri, 10am-8pm Sat & Sun), a mansion with gorgeous art pieces and gardens. About five blocks north is yet another museum, the **Museo Casa de Yrurtia** (☑4781-0385; O'Higgins 2390; admission AR$10, Wed free; ☉11:30am-6pm Wed-Fri, 3-7pm Sat & Sun), honoring the well-known Argentine sculptor.

Four blocks northeast of Plaza Belgrano, French landscape architect Carlos Thays took advantage of the contours of **Barrancas de Belgrano** to create an attractive, green public space on one of the few natural hillocks in the city. Retirees spend the afternoon at the chess tables beneath its ombú tree, and on Saturday and Sunday evenings the band shell hosts a popular outdoor *milonga* (tango event).

Across Juramento from Barrancas, Belgrano's growing **Chinatown** fills three blocks on Arribeños, with more Chinese businesses spilling over into the side streets. Don't come on Mondays, however, as many places are shut; do come on Chinese New Year, when festivities abound.

You'll probably head into Belgrano via Av Cabildo, either by bus or Subte (the Subte runs right under Cabildo). Plaza Belgrano is one block east of Cabildo at Juramento; most sights are around the plaza. Barrancas de Belgrano is the location of Belgrano's bus and train stations and is located about four blocks from the plaza.

MIRANDA — PARRILLA $$

Map p250 (☑4771-4255; www.parrillamiranda.com; Costa Rica 5602; mains AR$70-125; ☉8am-1am Sun-Thu, to 2am Fri & Sat) Fashionable Miranda is the *parrilla* of choice for those looking for both style and substance. It's a pleasant modern steakhouse with concrete walls, high ceilings and rustic wooden furniture, but high-quality grilled beef is the main attraction here – try the popular *ojo de bife*. If you score a sidewalk table on a warm day, life doesn't get much better.

IL BALLO DEL MATTONE — ITALIAN $$

Map p250 (☑4776-4247; www.ilballo.tv; Gorriti 5737; mains AR$50-100; ☉noon-4pm & 8pm-midnight Mon-Sat) This artsy, eclectic trattoria attracts artists, musicians and tourists, among others, with its delicious homemade pastas. Try the popular *caramel diburata* appetizer (a soft cheese), then go

for the *fusilles escarparo* with garlic, green onion and parmesan in a tomato sauce. Cute little patio for warm days; reserve at night. Its annex is two blocks away at **Gorriti 5950** (Map p250).

MUSEO EVITA RESTAURANTE — MODERN ARGENTINE $$

Map p250 (☑4800-1599; www.museoevitaresto.com.ar; JM Gutierrez 3926; mains AR$70-100; ☉9am-midnight Mon-Sat, to 7pm Sun) This restaurant's charming tiled courtyard may be the city's prettiest spot for an alfresco lunch, and the cuisine is thoroughly sophisticated, too. Locals and visitors alike come for the gourmet sandwiches, steaks and salads; the lunch specials are good too.

BIO — VEGETARIAN $$

Map p250 (☑4774-3880; www.biorestaurant.com.ar; Humboldt 2192; mains AR$68-100;

☺11am-midnight Sun-Thu, to 1am Fri & Sat; ☑) The supremely health-conscious should make a beeline for this casual corner joint, which specializes in healthy, organic and vegetarian fare. Try the quinoa risotto, seitan stirfry, Mediterranean couscous or mushrooms a la Bahiana (Brazilian-style). Don't miss the refreshing ginger lemonade. Also caters to celiacs, vegans and raw foodists.

AZEMA   INTERNATIONAL $$

Map p250 (☑4774-4191; AJ Carranza 1875; mains AR$75-120; ☺8:30-midnight Mon-Thu, to 1am Fri & Sat) With exotic spices and foreign ingredients, Paul Jean Azema goes where few local chefs have gone before. His eclectic menu takes inspiration from his diverse travels – expect dishes like lamb cooked Mauritius-style, rabbit in chardonnay wine sauce and mango and curry duck – and Azema himself occasionally makes an appearance in the dining room.

★HERNÁN GIPPONI
RESTAURANT   MODERN ARGENTINE $$$

Map p250 (☑3220-6820; www.hgrestaurant. com.ar; Soler 5862; mains AR$120-135, set menu AR$260, wine pairings AR$160 extra; ☺7:30am-midnight Mon-Fri, 8am-midnight Sat & Sun) Located in the Fierro Hotel, this exceptional restaurant offers highly sophisticated, Spanish-influenced dishes created by chef Hernán Gipponi. Order the seven-course tasting menu for the full experience – it's pricey but worth it. Set menu on weekday lunches runs AR$150; the six-course weekend brunch costs AR$175 and is a must. On Monday nights, everyone sits at one communal table. Reserve ahead.

LA CABRERA   PARRILLA $$$

Map p250 (☑4831-7002; Cabrera 5099; mains AR$115-150; ☺12:30-4:30pm & 8:30pm-1am Mon-Thu, to 2am Fri & Sat, 12:30pm-1am Sun) Hugely popular for grilling up BA's most sublime meats. Steaks come in 200g or 400g sizes and arrives with heaps of little complimentary side dishes. Come at 7pm for 'happy hour,' when everything is 40% off – just make sure you get here early enough to score a table. There's an annex at **Cabrera 5127** (Map p250); expect a long wait at both locations.

UNIK   MODERN ARGENTINE $$$

Map p250 (☑4772-2230; www.unik.pro; Soler 5132; mains AR$135-190; ☺8:30pm-midnight Mon, 12:30-3pm & 8:30pm-midnight Tue-Sat) For a splurge night out, you can't do much better than Unik. Start with an appetizer of roasted beets with goat cheese and walnut-truffle vinaigrette (AR$90), then move on to the main courses: rabbit with eggplant purée, suckling pig with grilled apples in Dijon mustard sauce or Patagonian lamb with pickled figs and a tagine sauce. Unik indeed.

GREEN BAMBOO   VIETNAMESE $$$

Map p250 (☑4775-7050; www.green-bamboo. com.ar; Costa Rica 5802; mains AR$115-160; ☺8:30pm-1am Sun-Thu, to 2:30am Fri & Sat) This sultry Vietnamese eatery offers just a small selection of dishes, but all are well prepared and flavorful. Sample things like seafood curry, marinated sirloin in lemongrass and 'traditional' *pho* (well, Argentine-style – so don't expect much tradition). The atmosphere is dim and romantic, with a few low tables, and the tropical cocktails are excellent. Reserve on weekends.

🍷 DRINKING &
🍸 NIGHTLIFE

You'll find Buenos Aires' hippest drinking scenes in and around Palermo, especially near Plaza Serrano in Palermo Soho. Many restaurants in this neighborhood also have good bars. Las Cañitas has a lively three blocks of nonstop restaurants and bars, and is also worth a drop-in, especially later in the evening.

★VERNE   COCKTAIL BAR

Map p250 (☑4822-0980; Medrano 1475; ☺9pm-2am Sun-Wed, to 4am Thu-Sat) Upscale yet casual bar with slight Jules Verne theme. Cocktails are the specialties here, whipped up by one of BA's best bartenders, Fede Cuco. A few tables, some cushy sofas and an airy outdoor patio offer a variety of seating options, but plant yourself at the bar to see drinks being made; check out the French absinthe server.

FRANK'S BAR   COCKTAIL BAR

Map p250 (☑4777-6541; www.franks-bar.com; Arévalo 1445; ☺9pm-4am Wed-Sat) Very popular plush, elegant speakeasy bar that 'requires' a password (via telephone booth) to get in – or just sweet talk the bouncer.

Inside it's a beautiful space with crystal chandeliers, billowy ceiling drapes and exclusive feel. Classic cocktails from before the 1930s are stirred – never blended – and served to a crowd of locals and foreigners. Check out the balcony bar too.

MAGDALENA'S PARTY BAR

Map p250 (4833-9127; www.magdalenasparty. com; Thames 1795) Popular bar-restaurant with laid-back atmosphere and *buena onda* (good vibes). DJs spin from Thursday to Saturday nights, and with cheap drinks this is a good preclub spot; try the vodka lemonade by the pitcher. Happy hour runs from noon to midnight daily, and tasty expat-friendly food is served, such as freshly ground hamburgers, California-style burritos and organic coffee. It does weekend brunch too.

HOME HOTEL BAR

Map p250 (4778-1008; www.homebuenosaires. com; Honduras 5860; 8am-midnight) Some of Palermo's best cocktails can be found at Home Hotel's very intimate bar-restaurant. During the day, relax in the grassy garden next to the slick infinity pool. At night, settle down at the polished cement bar with a house cocktail, created by some of Buenos Aires' best-known bartenders. Friday evenings in summer are livened up by DJ parties. A wide variety of vodkas, along with tapas are available.

ANTARES BAR

Map p250 (4833-9611; www.cervezaantares. com; Armenia 1447; 7pm-4am) Thirsty for a decent *cerveza*? Look no further than this modern but relaxed restaurant-bar with Argentine-brewed ales, pilsners, lagers and barley wine. Order a beer flight, sample the brewmaster's special-edition selection or just enjoy the two-for-one pints during happy hour (from 7pm to 8pm). Also in Las Cañitas at **Arévalo 2876**.

CONGO BAR

Map p250 (4833-5857; www.barcongo.com.ar; Honduras 5329; 8pm-4am Mon-Thu, 9pm-5am Fri & Sat) The highlight at this trendy bar is the beautiful back patio – *the* place to be seen on hot summer nights, with its slick bar, leafy atmosphere and comfy wood booths. The music is great, too, with DJs spinning from Wednesday to Saturday, and inside there are elegant low lounges in romantic spaces. A full food menu is available, along with strong cocktails.

EL CARNAL BAR

Map p250 (4772-7582; www.carnalbar.com.ar; Niceto Vega 5511; 7pm-5am Tue-Fri, 9pm-5am Sat) See and be seen – preferably in the open air with an icy vodka tonic in hand – on the rooftop terrace at this ever-popular watering hole. With its bamboo lounges and billowy curtains, the place can't be beat for a cool chill-out on a warm summer night. Early in the week reggae rocks, while Thursdays to Saturdays means pop and '80s tunes.

SHANGHAI DRAGON PUB

Map p250 (4778-1053; Aráoz 1199; 5pm-3am Mon-Wed, to 4am Thu-Sun) Good corner pub with mellow vibe, sports on TV and slight Asian theme, attracting the 25 and over crowd. Come for dinner if you want cheap Chinese food like vegetable stir fries and Kung Pao chicken, while happy hour means cheap drinks from 5pm to 10pm. DJs spin funk and rock on Saturdays. Same owners as popular Gibraltar (p92) and Bangalore (Indian) pubs.

MUNDO BIZARRO BAR

Map p250 (4773-1967; www.mundobizarrobar. com; Serrano 1222; 8pm-late) This red-lit, futuristically retro and stylish lounge bar is open pretty much all through the night on weekends, when everything from old-time American music to hip DJs to jazz stirs up the air waves. If you're feeling peckish, check out the American-inspired bar food, which ranges from Tex-mex to burgers to hot apple pie with ice cream. Dance on the stripper pole after you've had a few drinks.

VAN KONING PUB

Map p250 (4772-9909; Av Báez 325; 7pm-3:30am Sun-Thu, to 5am Fri & Sat) Wonderfully rustic spaces make this Dutch-themed pub feel like the inside of a boat; after all, it's a 17th-century-style seafaring theme complete with dark wood beams, flickering candles and blocky furniture. Bars on two floors serve over 30 kinds of both local and imported brews, with at least three on draft. A magnet for expats; the first Wednesday of the month is Dutch night.

SUGAR
BAR

Map p250 (✆4831-3276; www.sugarbuenos aires.com; Costa Rica 4619; ⏰7pm-5:30am Mon-Fri, 11am-5:30am Sat, 11am-3am Sun) This lively expat watering hole brings in a youthful nightly crowd with well-priced drink specials and comfort food like chicken fingers and buffalo wings. Watch sports on the two huge TV screens or come on Thursdays – also known as ladies' night – when things can get a little rowdy. On weekends, you can roll out of bed and arrive in time for eggs and mimosas.

ACABAR
BAR

Map p250 (✆4772-0845; www.acabarnet.com. ar; Honduras 5733; ⏰8pm-2am Sun-Thu, to 4am Fri & Sat) One of the quirkiest restaurant-bars in town. A maze of a half-dozen rooms and spaces are decked out in mismatched chandeliers, funky furniture, clashing pastel colors and frilly wallpaper; it's a texture and pattern overload. It's also famous for board games, which Argentines love to play. Serves food earlier on.

KIKA
CLUB

Map p250 (www.kikaclub.com.ar; Honduras 5339; ⏰Tue-Sun) Being supremely well located near the heart of Palermo Viejo's bar scene makes Kika's Tuesday-night popular 'Hype' party (www.hype-ba.com) easily accessible for the trendy crowds. It's a mix of electro, rock, hip-hop, drum and bass and dubstep, all spun by both local and international DJs. Other nights see electronica, raggaeton, Latin beats and live bands ruling the roost.

PACHÁ
CLUB

(✆4788-4288; www.pachabuenosaires.com; Av Rafael Obligado 6151; ⏰Sat) Popular, long-running electronica club well-known for attracting famous international DJs who spin tunes for the sometimes spaced-out crowds. Laser light shows and a great sound system makes the chic crowds happy through the early morning light – be sure to bring your shades and watch the sun come up from the terrace.

CLUB ARÁOZ
CLUB

Map p250 (✆4832-9751; www.clubaraoz.com.ar; Aráoz 2424; ⏰Thu-Sat) Also known as 'Lost', this intimate club's finest hour is on Thursday, when hip-hop rules the roost and the regulars start break dancing around 2am (reggaeton comes on later in the evening). National and international DJs liven up the

weekends. There's no dress code – a good thing, since it tends to get hot and sweaty in here.

CROBAR
CLUB

Map p250 (✆4778-1500; www.crobar.com.ar; cnr Av de la Infanta Isabell & Freyre; ⏰Fri & Sat) Year after year, stylish Crobar remains one of BA's most popular nightlife spots. Friday usually features international DJs mashing up the latest electronic selections, while Saturday tends to feature more commercial or Latin beats. There's also a back room for those who prefer classic rock, '80s remixes and occasional live bands, while the main levels are strewn with mezzanines and catwalks that allow views from above.

GLAM
CLUB

Map p250 (✆4963-2521; José Antonio Cabrera 3046; ⏰Thu-Sat) Housed on three floors of an old mansion with tall brick hallways, this mazelike gay club still brings in a crowd of young, good-looking guys. They're here to dance and get to know each other better – there are no shows to distract, just casual lounges, pretty bars and a dark room where anything goes. Saturday is the biggest night here.

NICETO CLUB
CLUB

Map p250 (✆4779-9396; www.nicetoclub.com; Niceto Vega 5510; ⏰Thu-Sat) One of the city's biggest crowd-pullers, the can't-miss event at Niceto Club is Thursday night's Club 69, a subversive DJ extravaganza featuring gorgeously attired showgirls, dancing drag queens, futuristic video installations and off-the-wall performance art. On weekend nights, national and international spin masters take the booth to entertain lively crowds with blends of hip-hop, electronic beats, cumbia and reggae.

LA VIRUTA
MILONGA

Map p250 (✆4774-6357; www.lavirutatango. com; Armenia 1366, basement) Popular basement venue. Good beginner tango classes are available before *milongas* – translating into many inexperienced dancers on the floor earlier on – so if you're an expert get here late (after 3:30am). Music can run the gamut from tango to rock to cumbia to salsa earlier in the evening, with more traditional tunes later. Tango shows also on offer.

PALERMO DRINKING & NIGHTLIFE

SALON CANNING
MILONGA

Map p250 (☑4832-6753; www.parakultural.com.ar; Av Scalabrini Ortiz 1331) Some of BA's finest dancers (no wallflowers here) grace this traditional venue with its great dance floor. Well-known tango company **Parakultural** often stages good events here involving live music, tango DJs, singers and dancers. Expect big crowds and plenty of tourists.

ENTERTAINMENT

THELONIOUS BAR
JAZZ

Map p250 (☑4829-1562; www.theloniousclub.com.ar; Salguero 1884, 1st fl; ⊙9pm-1am Wed-Thu, to 3am Fri & Sat) Up the stairs in an old mansion lies this dimly lit jazz bar, with high brick ceilings and a good sound system. Come early to snag a seat (or reserve one ahead of time) and partake in the typically Argentine menu and good range of cocktails. Thelonious is known for its classic and contemporary Argentine jazz lineups, though international musicians sometimes entertain.

LA PEÑA DEL COLORADO
FOLK

Map p250 (☑4822-1038; www.lapeniadelcolorado.com; Güemes 3657; ⊙8pm-4am) Nightly music shows (mostly folkloric) start at 10pm and are memorable at this rustic restaurant, and after midnight audience members pick up nearby guitars to make their own entertainment. There's also tasty northern Argentine food on offer, including *locro*, *chipá* (chewy cheese balls) and *humitas de Chala* (like tamales) – the spicy *empanadas* are excellent.

LOS CARDONES
FOLK

Map p250 (☑4777-1112; www.cardones.com.ar; Borges 2180; ⊙from 9pm Wed-Sat) Come to this friendly, low-key *peña* (folk club) for audience-participatory jam sessions (and possible dancing), mellow guitar shows, hearty regional cuisine from northern Argentina and free-flowing red wine. Shows start at 10pm on weekdays and 11pm weekends. Check out the website for details on the current lineup and reserve ahead for a good table.

TIEMPO DE GITANOS
FLAMENCO

Map p250 (☑4776-6143; www.tiempodegitanos.com.ar; El Salvador 5575; ⊙Wed-Sun) This venue in Palermo Hollywood offers good flamenco shows in an intimate restaurant setting. Shows start at 11:30pm and cost AR$60 to AR$90, depending on the night. Classic Spanish foods like paella and tapas are on tap (food purchase is obligatory). Reserve in advance.

SHOPPING

Palermo Viejo, a large sub-neighborhood of Palermo, is a fashionista's shopping paradise. A few years ago, most of the storefronts were showcases for cutting-edge clothes; these days, the barrio hosts a wider range of designers selling high-end wares from home accessories and books to fancy stationery, soaps, candles, souvenirs, kids' toys and gourmet chocolate. It's easy to spend hours or even days shopping in Palermo; many design-minded travelers consider an afternoon here part of the sightseeing circuit.

FERIA PLAZA SERRANO
MARKET

Map p250 (Plaza Serrano; ⊙10am-8pm Fri-Sun) Costume jewelry, hand-knit tops, funky clothes, hippie bags, glass jewelry, leather accessories and much more fill the craft booths at this popular street fair on fashionable Plaza Serrano (also known as Plaza Cortazar). It's not huge, but the plaza is in the middle of Palermo's bustling nightlife and surrounded by trendy bars, restaurants and upscale stores.

RAPSODIA
FASHION

Map p250 (☑4831-6333; www.rapsodia.com; Honduras 4872; ⊙10am-9pm) With fabrics from linen to leather and details like fringe and sequins, this large and popular boutique is a must for fashion mavens. Old and new are blended into creative, colorful styles with exotic and bohemian accents. Locals covet its dresses and jeans; over a dozen branches in the city.

BOLIVIA
CLOTHING

Map p250 (☑4832-6284; Gurruchaga 1581; ⊙11am-8pm Mon-Sat, 3-8pm Sun) There's almost nothing here that your young, hip and possibly gay brother wouldn't love, from the stylish plaid shirts to the skin-tight jeans to the military-styled jackets. Metrosexual to the hilt, and paradise for the man who isn't afraid of patterns, plaid or pastels. Also at **Nicaragua 4906.**

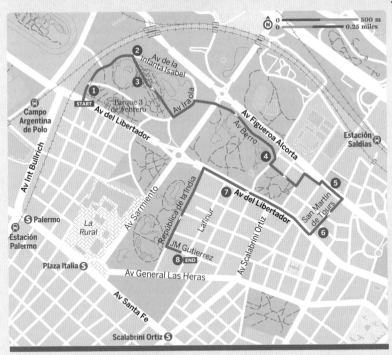

Neighborhood Walk
Walking the Green

START PARQUE 3 DE FEBRERO
END MUSEO EVITA
LENGTH 4.5KM, 3-4 HOURS

Start in **① Parque 3 de Febrero** (p129) these expansive green spaces were once the aristocracy's stomping ground. It's best on weekends, when the road around the rose garden is cut off to vehicular traffic (this is when you can rent bicycles and rollerblades).

Those interested in modern art can peek into the contemporary **② Museo de Artes Plásticas Eduardo Sívori** (p130), which showcases Argentine work. There's a relaxing cafe here as well. If you like flowers, head across the road and cross the bridge to the **③ Rosedal** (p129), where you can stop to sniff the roses. Continue across the garden until you come to Av Iraola, turn left onto it for about a block, then veer to the right to reach Av Sarmiento.

Cross Av Sarmiento (carefully!), and head along Av Berro for about 500m to

BA's **④ Jardín Japonés** (p130). This little paradise is meticulously maintained with koi ponds, pretty bridges and a tea shop, making it a welcome break from roads and traffic.

Now skim around Plaza Alemania and jog around a few residential streets to reach **⑤ Museo de Arte Latinoamericano de Buenos Aires** (p128), an airy museum that's home to some excellent paintings. For more culture, go two blocks south to the much more modest **⑥ Museo de Arte Popular José Hernàndez** (p131), which exhibits handicrafts and folkloric items.

On Av del Libertador, stop in at luscious ice-cream shop **⑦ Un Altra Volta** for a peaked cone of *dulce de leche granizado* (milk caramel with chocolate flakes). Now head down the street (alongside the odiferous zoo) to **⑧ Museo Evita** (p130), where you can check out the collected memorabilia of Argentina's most famous woman. There's a fine cafe-restaurant here where you can end your long walk.

LO DE JOAQUIN ALBERDI
FOOD & WINE

Map p250 (☑4832-5329; www.lodejoaquin
alberdi.com; JL Borges 1772; ☺11am-9:30pm
Mon-Sat, noon-9:30pm Sun) Nationally produced wines for every taste and budget
line the racks and cellar of this attractive
wine shop. Tastings happen Thursdays and
Fridays at 7:30pm (double-check ahead
of time) and include four wines and some
cheeses; the cost is AR$100.

HERMANOS ESTEBECORENA
CLOTHING

Map p250 (☑4772-2145; www.hermanoseste
becorena.com; El Salvador 5960; ☺11am-8pm
Mon-Sat) The Estebecorena brothers apply
their highly creative skills toward smartly
designed tops, jackets that fold into bags,
polo-collar work shirts and even supremely
comfortable, nearly seamless underwear.
The focus is on original, highly stylish, very
functional men's clothing that makes the
artsy types swoon. Selection is limited, but
what's there really counts.

LA MERCERÍA
FASHION & ACCESSORIES

Map p250 (☑4831-8558; Armenia 1609; ☺11am-
8pm) Attracting crowds of gossipy ladies
on a busy weekend, this boutique is stuffed
with bright and colorful accessories like
costume jewelry, pillows, scarves, belts,
perfumes, hats and lots of handbags. Frilly,
glitzy and designed for self-assured women.

CALMA CHICHA
HOUSEWARES

Map p250 (☑4831-1818; www.calmachicha.com;
Honduras 4909; ☺10am-8pm Mon-Fri, 11am-8pm
Sat, 1-7pm Sun) Calma Chicha specializes in
creative housewares and accessories that
are locally produced from leather, faux
leather, sheepskin, cowhide, and brightly
hued fabric. Look for butterfly chairs,
throw rugs, leather placemats, bright pillows and cowskin bags.

JUANA DE ARCO
FASHION & ACCESSORIES

Map p250 (☑4833-1621; www.juanadearco.net; El
Salvador 4762; ☺10am-8pm Mon-Fri, 11am-8pm
Sat, 1-8pm Sun) Mariana Cortes has designed
adorable bits of fabrics sewn into girly sets
that would be best showcased during a pil-
low fight – think brightly colored T-shirts,
flowery boxer shorts and tight leggings.
Descend the staircase to discover more
treasures.

NOBRAND
SOUVENIRS

Map p250 (☑4776-7288; www.nobrand.com.
ar; Gorriti 5876; ☺noon-8pm Tue-Sun) For that
modern, locally inspired gift, check out this
slick shop. Two designers created Argentine
logos such as the cow, *mate, asado, empanadas* and tango (along with people like
Evita and Che Guevara), and transferred
those iconic logos onto T-shirts, aprons,
mugs, notebooks, caps and even shoes. Fun
gifts for folks back home.

CAPITAL
HOUSEWARES

Map p250 (☑4834-6555; www.capitalpalermo.
com; Honduras 4958; ☺10am-8pm) There's
nothing you really *need* at this whimsical
knickknacks store, but it's a fun place to
visit anyhow. The stock is always changing,
but expect things like mugs with iconic images, funky computer accessories and car-
toonish shower curtains.

HUMAWACA
LEATHER GOODS

Map p250 (☑4832-2662; www.humawaca.com; El
Salvador 4692; ☺11am-8pm Mon-Sat, 2-7pm Sun)
Award-winning designs bring both form
and functionality to Argentine leather, producing handbags, tote bags and wallets with
clean modernist lines and colorful hues. Visit this tiny boutique and you'll always find
something different and eye-catching.

28 SPORT
SHOES

Map p250 (☑4833-4287; www.28sport.com; Gurruchaga 1481; ☺11am-1:30pm, 2:30-7pm Mon-Sat)
For the retro-sports fanatic, there's nothing
better than this unique shop with a sense
of humor and a vintage twist. Focusing on
only one product and one style – men's '50s
sport-style shoes – the cobblers here can
concentrate on quality and craftsmanship.
Inspiration comes from football, boxing
and bowling shoes, and only 12 pairs of
each design are produced.

MISHKA
SHOES

Map p250 (☑4833-5655; www.mishkashoes.com.
ar; El Salvador 4673; ☺10:30am-8:30pm Mon-Sat,
3-8pm Sun) Well-regarded designer Chelo
Cantón was once an architect but now cre-
ates wonderfully unique footwear with a
retro-hip, feminine and slightly conservative vibe. Try on a pair of patent-leather
sandals for size, or go for more traditional
ballet flats in velvet and brocade (though
styles are always changing). Check the website for other locations around the city.

HARAPOS PATAGONIA
SOUVENIRS

Map p250 (☑2058-7810; Malabia 1635; ☺11am-
7:30pm Mon-Sat, 2-7:30pm Sun) Can't make

BUENOS AIRES' EMERGING DESIGNERS

One of the most notable transitions in Buenos Aires fashion in the last few years is the growing prominence of emerging designers. Based mostly out of private homes and apartments, known locally as 'showrooms,' a young community of recent fashion school grads and 20-somethings with an entrepreneurial spirit are taking over BA's inventive design world. Recent initiatives by the Buenos Aires City government such as competitions like IncuBA and La Ciudad de Moda (which allowed several of the most promising emerging designers to stage runway shows at Buenos Aires Fashion Week), have given the industry the boost it desperately needs to make BA one of the most intriguing fashion hotspots in Latin America. Whether you're on the hunt for casual streetwear, luxurious leather or innovative jewelry design, BA's best emerging designers take pride in their originality and skilled craftsmanship.

When it comes to clothing design, rising names like **Belén Amigo** (www.belenamigo. com.ar) and **Joan Martorello** (www.facebook.com/JMARTORELLO), both present at La Ciudad de Moda's runway show, are capturing stylish locals with their alternative, street-chic designs that range from Martorello's signature knits to Amigo's tailored pants and drapey silk organza tops. For more comfy casual wear, stop in at **Deleon's** (www.deleonba.com) Palermo Hollywood showroom, a destination for young fashionable locals looking to expand their collection of urban cool garments that scream sophistication.

Yet another exciting fresh face in BA's emerging fashion scene is **Julia Schang-Viton** (www.schangviton.com.ar), a young design prodigy whose structured, architectural cuts and neutral color palette draw upon her Asian heritage.

If you're in the market for leather, you've come to the right city. The independent design team behind artsy leather jacket label **Oveja Oveja** (www.ovejaoveja.com) have created a stir with their high-quality, hand-painted jackets that fit perfectly with BA's cosmopolitan vibe.

For leather bags, don't miss the geometric gems by **Bellebas** (www.bellebas.com), whose sleek clutches and embossed satchels make for the quintessential Buenos Aires accessory.

In the world of jewelry, both **Inés Bonadeo** (www.inesbonadeo.com.ar), a metal-working craftswoman who has already shown her work in New York at the international design fair NY Now, and **Vendaval** (www.vendavalbuenosaires.com.ar), whose amulets are available at indie boutique **Monoambiente** (www.mono-ambiente.com.ar) can't be missed.

While popular among locals, shopping in showrooms can prove intimidating for visitors. To gain access to these hidden treasures, it takes some local knowledge and the right connections. Thankfully, a few ambitious expats are giving tourists the chance to discover the exciting world of BA's emerging design through personalized shopping tours that'll take you to some of the most notable showrooms in town as well as the hippest open-door boutiques. Sophie Lloyd at **ShopHopBA** (www. shop-buenosaires.com) is the perfect option for those looking to get inside the city's exclusive showrooms. Warm, welcoming and knowledgeable, Sophie's tours include champagne toasts and privately catered lunches, and she also offers personal color consultations to those in need of a wardrobe makeover. Vanessa Bell at **Creme de la Creme** (www.cremedelacreme.com.ar) is known for her extensive contacts and excellent taste.

Natalie Schreyer is a fashion writer who has been living in Buenos Aires for five years. She is the creator of www.bashopgirl.com, a fashion blog covering BA's best emerging designers. In addition to her blog, she has written for LandingPadBA.com.

it all the way down to Patagonia? Well, then just visit to this small store to grab a southern souvenir. There are woolen goods (sheep are big down there), hand-made ceramics, wooden utensils and silver and alpaca jewelry. All products are made by Patagonian craftspeople.

SUGAR & SPICE
FOOD & WINE

Map p250 (☑4777-5423; www.sugarandspice.
com.ar; Guatemala 5419; ☉10am-7pm Mon-Fri,
9am-1pm Sat) Nibble the exotic (for Argentina, at least) creations of Frank Almeida,
a long-time American expat. Herb cookies,
almond biscotti, hazelnut panettone and
peanut-butter brownies soothe homesick
taste buds, and daily-baked bagels, muffins
and scones are also available.

CENTRICO
SHOES

Map p250 (☑4865-0143; www.centrico
centrica.com.ar; Figueroa 1800; ☉10:30am-
8:30pm Mon-Sat) Leonardo Mancuso designs
these handmade leather shoes with a classic, traditional styling that emphasizes
simplicity over showiness. Both men's and
women's shoes available, and some have
unisex looks; there are also a few ankle and
knee-high boots. Prices run from AR$1000,
but check out the sale items in the back
room.

PANORAMA
CLOTHING

Map p250 (www.pnrm.com.ar; República de la India
2905; ☉11am-8pm Mon-Sat) About 20 emerging
young designers are showcased at this small,
upscale store in Palermo Chico. Peruse the
clothing racks for one-of-a-kind, eclectic tops,
pants, dresses and coats that can be definite
show-stoppers. Small sizes dominate, though
custom orders are possible. There are also a
few accessories and shoes.

ALTO PALERMO
SHOPPING MALL

Map p250 (☑5777-8000; www.altopalermo.com.
ar; Av Santa Fe 3253; ☉10am-10pm) Smack on
bustling Av Santa Fe, this popular, shiny
mall offers dozens of clothing shops, bookstores, jewelry boutiques, and electronics
and houseware stores. Look for Timber-
land, Lacoste, Hilfiger and Levi's (plus
many Argentine brands, too). Services include a food court, a cinema complex and a
good kids' area on the 3rd floor.

PASEO ALCORTA
SHOPPING MALL

Map p250 (☑5777-6500; www.paseoalcorta.com.
ar; Salguero 3172; ☉10am-10pm) One of the
largest and most upscale malls in the city.
All the popular Argentine women's clothing shops are represented, as are international boutiques such as Adidas, Nike and
Swatch. Other stores sell leather goods,
kids' clothes, men's designs, sportswear and
accessories. There's also a large food court
and a children's play area.

PATIO DEL LICEO
SHOPPING MALL

Map p250 (☑4822-9433; Santa Fe 2729; ☉2-8pm
Mon-Sat) Wonderful little shopping mall
with funky, casual and very artsy vibe. In
the past few years, young struggling artists
have taken over and created an artistic hub
here, filling it with various small stores, exhibition spaces and workshops. You'll find
a couple of book shops, a record store and
some design stores. For refreshment there's
a small cafe called Baby Snakes.

LIBROS DEL PASAJE
BOOKS

Map p250 (☑4483-6637; www.librosdelpasaje.
com.ar; Thames 1762; ☉10am-10pm Mon-Sat,
2-9pm Sun) This cool literary sanctuary offers history, culture and art books. They're
mostly in Spanish, but look for the small
English section near the front door (with

TIERRA SANTA

Tired of the same old Sunday sermons? Praying for kitsch? Then **Tierra Santa**
(☑0800-444-3467; www.tierrasanta-bsas.com.ar; Av Costanera R Obligado 5790; adult/
child 3-11yr AR$60/30; ☉9am-9pm Fri, noon-10pm Sat, Sun & holidays Apr-Nov, 4pm-
midnight Fri-Sun & holidays Dec-Mar) might be exactly what you need.

Enter this religious and wonderfully tacky theme park, roughly based on Jerusalem, and head straight to the manger scene. Here, colorful lights and minimally animatronic figures swoon over baby Jesus. Better yet is the creation of the world, which
features real rushing waters and life-size fake animals. From here it's a 30-second
walk to witness the 12m-tall animatronic Jesus rise from the Calvary mound, open his
eyes and finally turn his palms toward the emotional devoted below. Miss the show?
Don't fret: another resurrection is just around the corner.

The park isn't just for Christians – there are reproductions of the Wailing Wall,
along with a synagogue and a mosque. So regardless of religious affiliation, enjoy
nibbling on a shawarma or take in an Arabic dancing show. It's a spectacle you won't
find anyplace else on earth – especially not in Jerusalem.

some Lonely Planet books). There's a cute cafe in back, with small inside patio, for a snack or cup of coffee.

PAPELERA PALERMO   STATIONERY
Map p250 (✆4833-3081; www.papelerapalermo. com; Cabrera 5227; ⊙10am-8pm Mon-Fri, 11am-8pm Sat) Everyone emails these days, but step into this stationery store and you'll be tempted to start penning letters again. A large selection of gorgeous wrapping papers, handmade stationery and funky spiral notebooks (look for the Evita motif) all inspire.

EL CID   FASHION
Map p250 (✆4832-3339; www.elcid.us; Gurruchaga 1732; ⊙11am-8pm Tue-Sat, 3-7pm Sun) Some of the finest men's threads can be found at this Palermo Viejo boutique, which highlights Nestor Goldberg's designer shirts, pants, jackets, accessories and jeans. Materials are of the highest quality, and tailoring is classy, hip and casual.

ARTE ÉTNICO ARGENTINO   CRAFTS & TEXTILES
Map p250 (✆4832-0516; www.monteargentino. com; El Salvador 4656; ⊙11am-6pm Mon-Fri, 11am-4pm Sat) Bright and beautiful woven *mantas* (blankets) from Santiago del Estero are the main attraction at this upscale shop, located in an old house. All are made from wool and natural dyes, and can also be used as light rugs. Expect to pay from AR$2500 up.

MERCADO DE LAS PULGAS   MARKET
Map p250 (cnr Álvarez Thomas & Dorrego; ⊙11am-7pm Tue-Sun) This large, covered warehouse is full of caged booths selling antiques, vintage objects and some modern items – precious things such as wood furniture, glass soda bottles, chandeliers, old clocks, silver trays, bird cages, elegant mirrors and ironwork.

🏃 SPORTS & ACTIVITIES

CAMPO ARGENTINO DE POLO   POLO
Map p250 (cnr Av del Libertador & Av Dorrego) Just across from the Hipódromo Argentino in Palermo, this stadium holds up to 30,000 spectators and hosts polo's most important events (including the Argentine Open Polo Championship in November and December). However, the northern suburb of Pilar has the highest density of polo clubs.

Street Art

Buenos Aires' turbulent history, its passion and its creativity have driven the growth of an internationally acclaimed street-art scene.

In the years following the 2001 economic crisis a generation of artists took to the streets to reclaim public spaces. At first graffiti and stencils delivered scathing criticisms of the government, then gradually a new style began to emerge, bringing humor, color and creative experimentation. Stencil artists, graffiti writers, activists and art collectives began to work together, giving the city walls a new role: channeling artistic expression. Out of a dark period of political and social upheaval, a vibrant new art movement was born.

Graffiti in Buenos Aires incorporates a dizzying array of techniques and styles and is found everywhere from sidewalks and shutters to garbage cans and towering walls. Huge-scale murals reflect both the talents of local artists and the tolerance their work enjoys. It's not unusual to find artists creating enormous, detailed pieces in broad daylight, and they travel from across the world to experience the freedom of painting BA's streets.

To check out works from some of the scene's leading artists head to **Post Street Bar** (Thames 1885), a hip Palermo bar covered in stencils. There's a gallery at the back (www.hollywoodincambodia. com.ar) that specializes in street art.

To learn more and see some of the city's most impressive art, why not take a graffiti tour? **Graffitimundo** (p208) is an arts organization that works closely with leading local artists. Reserve a spot on its tour and venture off the beaten track to discover spectacular murals and the hidden history of this remarkable scene.

DAN HERRICK / GETTY IMAGES ©

1. Street art in San Telmo, created by Malegria and Nomada **2.** Street artist at work

South of Palermo

Neighbourhood Top Five

1 Communing with tango's most famous singer via his old recordings, news clippings and personal items at **Museo Casa Carlos Gardel** (p148), located in the very house he used to live.

2 Visiting the impressive **Mercado de Abasto** (p148), a gorgeously remodelled shopping center.

3 Wandering among old skeletons, taxidermy rooms and natural science exhibits at **Museo Argentino de Ciencias Naturales** (p148).

4 Finding that hidden Peruvian, Korean or Jewish jewel of a **restaurant** (p148).

5 Dancing it up at Monday night's drumming parties at **Ciudad Cultural Konex** (p150).

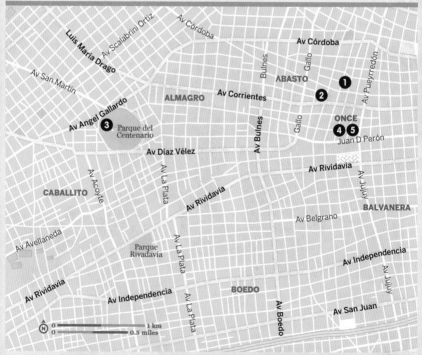

For more detail of this area see Map p254 ➡

Explore: South of Palermo

Buenos Aires' easterly regions – south of Palermo and east of Congreso – are refreshingly local, blue-collar neighborhoods with occasional surprises for the tourist, such as some artsy galleries, a few renovated cafes and a bunch of shopping outlet stores.

Villa Crespo is a good place to start. It's a good place for outlet shopping and has become home to several casual, tasty restaurants as well. A short walk to the south is Caballito, a calm and pleasant neighborhood with the large, circular Parque del Centenario. The main attraction here is the Museo Argentino de Ciencias Naturales, a good natural-science museum that's worth a peek for its musty taxidermy and cool skeleton room.

East of Villa Crespo are the Abasto and Once (pronounced 'ohn-seh') neighborhoods, both melting-pot destinations that have attracted sizable populations of Jews, Peruvians and Koreans – and their respective ethnic cuisines as well. The main attraction in Abasto is the Mercado de Abasto, one of the city's most attractive shopping malls. On a side street just east of the mall, look for a small statue of Carlos Gardel, the famous tango singer; four blocks northeast is the Museo Casa Carlos Gardel, a museum honoring him. Many alternative theaters can also be found in this area.

South of Abasto is Once and its bustling train station, surrounded by hundreds of street vendors selling garments and cheap electronic devices. There's a colorful, almost third-world feel to this neighborhood – a welcome change in BA, though you should avoid this area late at night. South of Once is the bohemian neighborhood of Boedo, which has a few atmospheric cafes such as Las Violetas and Esquina Homero Manzi.

Local Life

➡**Hanging Out** Local ladies take a break at Las Violetas (p149), quite possibly the most beautiful traditional cafe in Buenos Aires.

➡**Eating** A lack of tourists at classic eateries like Café Margot (p149) will take you back in time.

➡**Theater** Artsy *porteños* head to one of the many alternative theater productions going on in Abasto (p150).

Getting There & Away

➡**Bus** Take bus 140 from the Microcentro to Villa Crespo, bus 26 to Once, bus 105 to Caballito, bus 126 to Boedo.

➡**Subte** Líneas A, B and E are the fastest way to these neighborhoods.

Lonely Planet's Top Tip

Consider finding a place to stay in Villa Crespo, which is just south of Palermo and becoming more hip every day. New restaurants, outlet shops and guest houses continue to pop up here as rents become too expensive for many businesses in Palermo. Some accommodations might even be located just as close or even closer to Plaza Serrano – the commercial and social heart of Palermo Viejo – than many places in Palermo Soho or Hollywood.

Parts of Once can be a bit sketchy at night, so tread carefully.

✕ Best Places to Eat

➡ Sarkis (p148)
➡ Malvón (p148)
➡ Café Crespin (p148)

For reviews, see p148➡

☕ Best Places to Drink

➡ Las Violetas (p149)
➡ 878 (p149)
➡ Cervecería Cossab (p149)

For reviews, see p149➡

◉ Best Entertainment

➡ Ciudad Cultural Konex (p150)
➡ Esquina Carlos Gardel (p150)
➡ Complejo Tango (p150)

For reviews, see p150➡

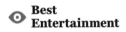

SOUTH OF PALERMO

⊙ SIGHTS

MUSEO CASA CARLOS GARDEL — MUSEUM
Map p254 (☑4964-2071; Jean Jaurés 735; admission AR$5, Wed free; ☺11am-6pm Mon & Wed-Fri, 10am-7pm Sat & Sun) Small but noteworthy is this tribute to tango's most famous voice. Located in Gardel's old house, this museum traces his partnership with José Razzano and displays old memorabilia like photos, records and news clippings. There isn't a whole lot to see, so it's best for real fans or just the curious; look for the cluster of colorfully painted buildings. Free tango classes offered Wednesday and Friday at 6pm, and Saturday at 3pm.

MERCADO DE ABASTO — NOTABLE BUILDING
Map p254 (☑4959-3400; www.abasto-shopping.com.ar; Av Corrientes 3247; ☺10am-10pm; ⓈLínea B Carlos Gardel) The historic Mercado de Abasto (1895) has been recycled by US-Hungarian financier George Soros into one of the most beautiful shopping centers in the city. The building, once a large vegetable market, received an architectural prize in 1937 for its Av Corrientes facade; at night the spotlighted and lofty arches are visible all the way from Av Pueyrredón. It holds more than 200 stores, a large cinema, a large food court and a kosher McDonald's (the one upstairs).

It's great for families, with a good children's museum, video/arcade games and even a small amusement park. The small Abasto neighborhood was once home to tango legend Carlos Gardel, and on the gentrified pedestrian street off Av Anchorena is a **statue** (Map p254) of the singer.

MUSEO ARGENTINO DE CIENCIAS NATURALES — MUSEUM
Map p254 (Natural Science Museum; ☑4982-6595; www.macn.secyt.gov.ar; Av Ángel Gallardo 490; admission AR$10; ☺2-7pm) Way over to the west, the oval Parque del Centenario is a large open space containing this excellent natural-science museum. On display are large collections of meteorites, rocks and minerals, seashells, insects and dinosaur skeleton replicas. Life-size models of a basking shark and ocean sunfish are impressive, and the taxidermy and skeleton rooms are especially good. Bring the kids; they can mingle with the hundreds of children who visit on school excursions.

Nearby is the **Observatorio Astronómico** (Map p254; ☑4863-3366; www.asaramas.com.ar; Patricias Argentinas 550). Call or check the website, as observation hours change depending on the season.

✖ EATING

These neighborhoods have yet to be discovered by the tourist masses, but things are changing. Rents in Palermo Viejo have skyrocketed over the years, driving some new businesses to nearby Villa Crespo. Meanwhile, Boedo has a few traditional places that are just starting to be visited by foreigners looking for something different. And Once is a good place to hunt for ethnic foods with Jewish, Peruvian or Korean flavors.

★SARKIS — MIDDLE EASTERN $
Map p254 (☑4772-4911; Thames 1101; mains AR$55-90; ☺noon-3pm & 8pm-1am) The food is fabulous and well-priced at this longstanding Middle Eastern restaurant – come with a group to sample many exotic dishes. Start with the hummus platter, *baquerones* (marinated sardines), *keppe crudo* (raw meat) or *parras rellenas* (stuffed grape leaves), then follow with kebabs, couscous with lentils or lamb in yogurt sauce. Less busy at lunchtime; a long wait for dinner.

CAFÉ CRESPIN — CAFE $
Map p254 (☑4855-3771; Vera 699, cnr of Acevedo; mains AR$30-60; set brunches AR$140-225; ☺8am-8pm Tue-Fri, 9am-8pm Sat, noon-7pm Sun) Cute corner cafe in Villa Crespo. Stock up on pancakes, French toast and bagel sandwiches for breakfast, or go for the quesadillas, salmon salad or ham and cheese tostadas at lunchtime. Tasty brunches, and there are also good pastries and a bakery on the premises.

PAN Y ARTE — ARGENTINE $
Map p254 (☑4957-6922; www.panyarte.com.ar; Av Boedo 878; mains AR$50-80; ☺8am-midnight Sun-Thu, to 1am Fri & Sat) There's a wonderful old-time atmosphere at this bohemian eatery, which features a hippie waitstaff and organic bakery. Food ranges from the same old boring stuff (*milanesas,* pastas and pizza) to more interesting choices like vegetarian *picadas* (a plate of appetizers), stuffed squash and goat stew. There are also organic products like cheese and *mate*

FERIA DE MATADEROS

In the working-class barrio of Mataderos is this excellent **folk market** (☑Mon-Fri 4342-9629, Sat 4687-5602; www.feriademataderos.com.ar; cnr Avs Lisandro de la Torre & de los Corrales; ⊘11am-8pm Sun Apr–mid-Dec, 6pm-midnight Sat late Jan–mid-Mar). Merchants offer handmade crafts and regional cuisine like *locro* (a corn and meat stew) and *humita* (a savory corn and cheese mixture wrapped in husks). Folk singers, dancers and gauchos on horseback entertain, and there's a nearby **gaucho museum** (☑4687-1949; Av de los Corrales 6436; admission AR$5; ⊘noon-6:30pm Sun Mar-Dec). From downtown, take bus 155 (also marked 180) or 126; the market is up to an hour's ride away, but worth it – you can also take a taxi to and from Mataderos if you're pinched for time. Call ahead in between seasons to make sure it's open.

to purchase, plus it's in a busy, interesting and nontouristy neighborhood.

CAFÉ MARGOT ARGENTINE $

Map p254 (☑4957-0001; Av Boedo 857; mains AR$40-80; ⊘8am-late) This classic cafe, one of the city's official *bares notables* (notable bars), is an off-the-beaten-path spot where you can relax with a platter of *picadas* (meat, cheese and olives) and a bottle of wine, or a frosty mug of artisan-crafted beer and a huge sandwich piled high with sliced turkey. The atmospheric main room is a bit snug; sidewalk tables are best for the claustrophobic.

★MALVÓN CAFE $$

(☑4774-2563; www.malvonba.com.ar; Serrano 789; mains AR$50-130; ⊘8am-8:30pm) Famous for its US-style weekend brunch – which features pancakes, French toast and eggs Benedict – Malvón is an eatery with a wonderfully rustic yet upscale atmosphere. The gourmet sandwiches are tasty, but there are also great bagels, burgers, tapas and baked treats like scones, muffins and pecan pie. Expect a wait on the weekend. Also in **Palermo** (Map p250; Lafinur 3275).

BI WON KOREAN $$

Map p254 (☑4372-1146; Junín 548; mains AR$90-120; ⊘noon-3pm & 7:30-11:30pm Mon-Fri, 7:30-11:30pm Sat) Korean food can't be beat at this simple restaurant. Go for the *bulgogi* (grill the meat yourself at the table), *bibimbap* (rice bowl with meat, veggies, egg and hot sauce) or *kim chee chigue* (kimchi soup with pork – for adventurous, spice-loving tongues only!). And don't forget to say *kamsamnida* (thank you) to your server at the end.

⊘ DRINKING & NIGHTLIFE

★LAS VIOLETAS CAFE

Map p254 (☑4958-7387; www.lasvioloetas.com; Av Rivadavia 3899; ⊘8am-2am) Dating back to 1884, this historic coffeehouse was renovated in 2001 into the gorgeous place it is today. Lovely stained-glass awnings, high ceilings and gilded details make this cafe possibly the most beautiful in the capital. Come for the luxurious afternoon tea and be sure to pick something up in the chocolate-pastry shop on the way out.

878 BAR

Map p254 (☑4773-1098; www.878bar.com.ar; Thames 878; ⊘8pm-2am Sun-Thu, to 4am Fri & Sat) Hidden behind an unsigned door is this 'secret' bar – you have to ring the bell to get in, but it's hardly exclusive. Enter a wonderland of elegant low lounge furniture and red brick walls; for whiskey lovers there are over 80 kinds to try, but the cocktails are tasty too. If you're hungry, tapas are available (reserve for dinners).

CERVECERÍA COSSAB BAR

Map p254 (☑2060-5023; Carlos Calvo 4199; ⊘7pm-1am Wed-Thu, to 4am Fri, 9pm-4am Sat) Beer lovers unite and head down to bohemian Boedo and this dedicated beer bar – a unique find for BA. Over 50 tasty suds are served, including seven on tap. Delicious pizzas, cheese plates and sandwiches help you make a night of it – but for something out of the ordinary, try the *picada Patagonica* with smoked wild boar and venison.

AVANT-GARDE THEATER

Get off the beaten play path and go for something out of the ordinary – there's plenty of choice in this creative city for unique and worthwhile theater.

→ **Actors Studio Teatro** (Map p254; ☑4983-9883; www.actors-studio.org; Av Díaz Vélez 3842) Offers new interpretations of old classics, along with cutting-edge productions in its 120-seat theater. Also has occasional acting classes.

→ **El Camarín de las Musas** (Map p254; ☑4862-0655; www.elcamarindelasmusas.com.ar; Mario Bravo 960) Offers contemporary dance, plays and theater. There are also workshops and classes available, and a trendy restaurant-cafe provides affordable snacks.

→ **El Cubo** (Map p254; ☑4963-2568; www.cuboabasto.com.ar; Pasaje Zelaya 3053) A hip small Abasto space, it hosts gutsy theater pieces and offbeat performances such as queer musicals.

→ **Espacio Callejón** (Map p254; ☑4862-1167; www.espaciocallejon.blogspot.com; Humahuaca 3759) A small independent venue that showcases edgy new theater, music and dance, and offers a few classes (including 'clown' acting).

LA CATEDRAL   DANCE HALL

Map p254 (☑15-5325-1630; www.lacatedralclub.com; Sarmiento 4006) If tango can be youthful, trendy and hip, this is where you'll find it. The grungy warehouse space is very casual, with funky art on the walls, thrift-store furniture and dim atmospheric lighting. It's more like a young bohemian nightclub than anything else, and there's no implied dress code – you'll see plenty of jeans on the dancers. Great for cheap alcohol; the best-known *milongas* (tango dances) occur regularly on a Tuesday night.

CLUB GRICEL   DANCE HALL

Map p254 (☑4957-7157; www.clubgriceltango.com.ar; La Rioja 1180) This old classic (far from the center; take a taxi) often has big crowds, especially on Monday. It attracts an older, well-dressed clientele – along with plenty of tourists. There's a wonderful springy dance floor and occasionally live orchestras.

AMERIKA   CLUB

Map p254 (☑4865-4416; www.ameri-k.com.ar; Gascón 1040; ☺Fri-Sun) BA's largest and feistiest gay nightclub, long-running Amerika attracts all kinds of folks – but Saturdays are especially popular with gay guys. There are two music floors, one electronica and one Latina, plus *canilla libre* (all-you-can-drink) on Fridays and Saturdays. Large video screens, stripper shows, four bars and a wild dark room keep things interesting.

☆ ENTERTAINMENT

CIUDAD CULTURAL KONEX   CULTURAL CENTER

Map p254 (☑4864-3200; www.ciudadcultural konex.org; Av Sarmiento 3131; ☺erratic hours, call ahead) Cutting-edge cultural center offering multidisciplinary performances that often fuse art, culture and technology. Famous for its amazing Monday night percussion shows that attract young party-goers.

ESQUINA CARLOS GARDEL   TANGO SHOW

Map p254 (☑4867-6363; www.esquinacarlos-gardel.com.ar; Carlos Gardel 3200; show from US$96, dinner & show from US$140) One of the fanciest tango shows in town plays at this impressive 430-seat theater, an old cantina right next to the Mercado de Abasto (p148). The Abasto neighborhood was once Carlos Gardel's old stomping ground, and he even hung out at this locale. The memorable show starts with a good film about the area, then goes on to highlight top-notch musicians and performers.

COMPLEJO TANGO   TANGO SHOW

Map p254 (☑4941-1119; www.complejotango.com.ar; Av Belgrano 2608; show from US$85, dinner & show from US$120) For those who wish to not only watch tango but also experience it, there's this classy venue in Balvanera. Should you choose to accept it, your first hour here is a free beginning tango lesson. Follow it up with a tasty dinner, then an excellent tango show – beware, however, as the performers go around towards the end, picking out audience members to dance with them (usually badly).

ESQUINA HOMERO MANZI   TANGO SHOW

Map p254 (☎4957-8488; www.esquinahomero-manzi.com.ar; Av San Juan 3601; show AR$330, show & dinner from AR$550) This tango venue, in a remodeled old-time cafe, is located right on the historic intersection of San Juan and Boedo and was named after one of Argentina's most famous tango lyricists. It has the capacity for 300 spectators and offers a decent show that's a mix of glitzy high-kicks and more traditional *milonga*-type dancing. Be warned: at some tables the waiters keep passing in front of you, interrupting views.

🏃 SPORTS & ACTIVITIES

ACATRAZ   BOWLING

(☎4982-4818; www.acatrazclub.com.ar; Av Rivadavia 3636; ☯4pm-4am Sun-Mon, to 6am Fri & Sat) Unusual restaurant-bar-bowling alley-billiards hall sorta destination. You can do it all here; a great place to come with a group of friends. There are two bowling alleys, various pool tables, sports on TVs, plenty of tables to eat at and bars to drink at. Spread out over several floors, this place is huge and takes entertainment to a new level.

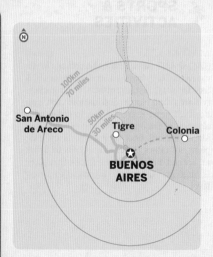

Day Trips from Buenos Aires

Tigre & the Delta p153

Take laid-back boat rides along the peaceful backwaters of the Río de la Plata. A nearby outdoor market and interesting museums are pluses.

San Antonio de Areco p155

Explore this serene village and its historic buildings, and perhaps visit a nearby *estancia* (cattle ranch). If you're lucky, you might spot a gaucho or two.

Colonia p157

Located across the Río de la Plata in Uruguay, this pleasant little colonial gem is lined with cobbled streets and charming old buildings.

Tigre & the Delta

Explore

Only an hour's drive from BA, tranquil Tigre and its huge river delta make a popular weekend getaway for cement-weary *porteños*. And while Tigre itself is a pleasant enough riverside town, it's really the swampy waterways that everyone is after. Latte-colored waters – rich with iron from the jungle streams flowing from inland Argentina – alongside reedy shores are far from any stereotypical paradise, but there are a few surprises here. Boat rides into the delta offer peeks at local houses and colonial mansions, or you can just get off and explore some nature trails. All along the shores are signs of water-related activity, from sailing, kayaking and canoeing to sculling and even wakeboarding.

The Best...
➡**Sight** Puerto de Frutos (p153)
➡**Place to Eat** Boulevard Saenz Peña (p154)
➡**Place to Drink** Maria Luján (p155)

Top Tip

Kayak or canoe tours (try www.eldorado kayak.com and www.selknamcanoas.com. ar) are a good way to explore the peaceful back waterways of the delta.

Getting There & Away
➡**Train** From Estación Retiro you can take a train straight to Tigre (one hour). The best way to reach Tigre, however, is via the **Tren de la Costa** (tickets AR$40) – a pleasant light-rail train with attractive stations and views. This train line starts in the suburb of Olivos; to get there, take a train from Retiro station and get off at the Mitre station, then cross the bridge to the Tren de la Costa. Buses 59, 60 and 152 also go to the Tren de la Costa.
➡**Bus** 60 (most 60 buses go to Tigre, but double check with the driver). The trip takes 1½ hours.
➡**Car** Take the Panamericana Hwy north to *ramal* (branch) Tigre.

➡**Boat Sturla Viajes** (☑ in BA 4314-8555, in Tigre 4731-1300; www.sturlaviajes.com.ar; Estación Fluvial, local 10 in Tigre, Grierson 400 in BA) has a commuter boat (AR$35) to Tigre that leaves from Grierson 400 in Puerto Madero, but it's only at 6.10pm from Monday to Friday. However, you can take its Tigre tour directly from Puerto Madero, which includes boat transport and a trip around the Delta (AR$260 round-trip).

Need to Know
➡**Area Code** 011
➡**Location** 35km northwest of Buenos Aires
➡**Tourist Office** (☑4512-4497; www.vivitigre. gov.ar; Mitre 305; ☺8am-6pm) Located behind McDonald's; will help you sort out the complex delta region

◉ SIGHTS

The waterways of the delta offer a glimpse into how the locals live here, along peaceful canals with boats as their only means of transportation. Frequent **commuter launches** (AR$45 to AR$68) depart from Estación Fluvial (situated behind the tourist office) for various destinations in the delta. A popular destination is the neighborhood of **Tres Bocas**, a half-hour boat ride from Tigre, where you can take residential walks on slender paths connected by bridges over narrow channels. There are several restaurants and accommodation options here. The **Rama Negra** area has a quieter and more natural setting with fewer services but is located an hour's boat ride away.

Several companies offer inexpensive **boat tours** (AR$60 to AR$120, one to two hours), but commuter launches give you flexibility if you want to go for a stroll or stop for lunch at one of the delta's restaurants.

PUERTO DE FRUTOS   MARKET
(Sarmiento 160; ☺10am-6pm) At this popular waterside market you'll find furniture, housewares, wicker baskets, dried flowers, plants and a whole lot of kitsch. Friday to Sunday is best, when a large crafts fair sets up; there are several restaurants too. There's a tourist office at the entrance to the port.

DAY TRIPS FROM BUENOS AIRES TIGRE & THE DELTA

VISITING IGUAZÚ FALLS

Many visitors to Buenos Aires tour the city and then take a side trip to one of the most spectacular sites in South America: Iguazú Falls. If you have an extra couple of days it's definitely worth the time and money. Just remember that it's much warmer and more tropical there than in BA, and that in January and February the heat and humidity can be overwhelming.

Iguazú Falls straddles the Argentina–Brazil border and some of the most stunning views are from the Brazilian side. As for Brazilian visas, if you are from the US, Canada or Australia, you officially need a visa to enter Brazil. Western Europeans do not. Brazilian visas aren't cheap, and getting one may take some time, so plan ahead. Some travelers without a visa have day-tripped across the border by taking the public bus to the Brazilian city of Foz do Iguaçu, but this may not always be possible.

Flying is the best way to go if you're short on time, but many travelers go by bus (one-way ticket AR$765, 18 hours). Bus and air packages – often including round-trip fare, transfers, guided tours and accommodations (but not visa or park admission) – are popular and easily available in BA at agencies like Tangol (p207) or Say Hueque (p207).

During July, on holiday weekends and during Semana Santa (Easter week) you should plan way ahead or be prepared to pay premium prices.

For general information on Iguazú, see the **Casa de Misiones tourist office** (Map p248; ☑4317-3722; www.misiones.gov.ar; Av Santa Fe 989).

MUSEO DE ARTE TIGRE   MUSEUM

(☑4512-4093; Paseo Victorica 972; admission AR$15; ☉9am-7pm Wed-Fri, noon-7pm Sat & Sun) Located in an old social club that dates from 1912, this beautiful art museum showcases famous Argentine artists from the 19th and 20th centuries, plus rotating exhibits. The building itself is beautiful enough to warrant a visit.

MUSEO NAVAL   MUSEUM

(Naval Museum; ☑4749-0608; Paseo Victorica 602; admission AR$10; ☉8:30am-5:30pm Mon-Fri, 10:30am-6:30pm Sat & Sun) This worthwhile museum traces the history of the Argentine navy with an eclectic mix of historical photos, model boats and airplanes, artillery displays and pickled sea critters.

MUSEO DEL MATE   MUSEUM

(☑4506-9594; www.elmuseodelmate.com; Lavalle 289; admission AR$15; ☉11am-6pm Wed-Sun) Celebrating everything connected to Argentina's national drink, this museum boasts over 2000 pieces; check out the *mates* for blind people. You can also watch a short video and – in the pleasant garden out back – sample the concoction itself.

PARQUE DE LA COSTA   AMUSEMENT PARK

(☑4002-6000; www.parquedelacosta.com.ar; General B Mitre 2; admission Tue & Wed from AR$52, Thu-Sun from AR$97) Tigre's amusement park offers roller coasters, games and everything else that makes a theme park enjoyable. Opening hours vary widely throughout the year, so check the website.

✖ EATING

Tigre's cuisine is not cutting edge, but it can be atmospheric – stroll Paseo Victorica, the city's pleasant riverside avenue, for the nicest options. Ask the tourist office about the various restaurants in the delta.

BOULEVARD SAENZ PEÑA   INTERNATIONAL $

(☑5197-4776; Blvd Saenz Peña 1400; breakfast mains AR$35-75, dinner mains AR$60-70; ☉10:30am-6pm Wed-Sat, 8:30pm to close Thu-Sat) This creative eatery offers delicious dishes (granola and yogurt for breakfast, gourmet sandwiches and salads for lunch, luscious pastries for teatime) and there's a cute patio for warm days. Dinner is by reservation only.

UN LUGAR   PARRILLA $

(☑4749-0698; Lavalle 369; mains AR$50-85; ☉noon-3pm & 8:30-11pm Tue-Sun) This *parrilla* (steak house) has comfortable indoor seating, but on warm days head to the sidewalk patio out front. Homemade pastas also available.

MARIA LUJÁN ARGENTINE **$$**

(☑4731-9613; Paseo Victorica 611; mains AR$80-150; ☺8:30am-midnight) A good choice for an upscale meal of typical Argentine fare, this beautiful, large restaurant also has a great patio boasting full river views.

🛏 SLEEPING

Tigre's huge delta region is dotted with dozens of accommodation possibilities, including camping, B&Bs, cabanas and beach resorts. Since places are relatively hard to reach (guests generally arrive by boat), the majority provide meal services, which are not always included in the price – ask beforehand. The Tigre tourist office (p153) has photos and information on all these places, and many are listed on its website.

The following places are in the city of Tigre itself. Book ahead on weekends and holidays, when prices can rise significantly.

POSADA DE 1860 HOSTEL **$**

(Tigre Hostel; ☑4749-4034; www.tigrehostel.com.ar; Av Libertador 190; dm US$12, r from US$70; ❉@☎) This odd hostel is in two buildings. One is the original mansion with en-suite private rooms and large garden, while the second is a mazelike building with little atmosphere, and with dorms and private rooms that share bathrooms.

HOTEL VILLA VICTORIA GUESTHOUSE **$$**

(☑4731-2281; www.hotelvillavictoria.com; Liniers 566; r Sun-Fri from AR$557, Sat from AR$702; ❉@☎⛱) Run by an Argentine-Swedish family, this boutique hotel is more like a fancy guesthouse. Only six (simple yet elegant) rooms are available, and there's a clay tennis court and a pool in the large grassy garden. Swedish, French and English are spoken.

CASONA LA RUCHI GUESTHOUSE **$$**

(☑4749-2499; www.casonalaruchi.com.ar; Lavalle 557; r AR$550; @☎⛱) This family-run guesthouse is in an old 1893 mansion. Most of the four romantic bedrooms have balconies; all have shared bathrooms with original tiled floors. There's a pool and large garden out back.

San Antonio de Areco

Explore

Nestled in lush farmlands, Areco is a pretty town that attracts day-tripping *porteños* who come for peaceful atmosphere and picturesque colonial streets. The town dates from the early 18th century and preserves a great deal of *criollo* (creole) and gaucho traditions, especially among its artisans, who produce very fine silverwork and saddlery. Areco's compact center and quiet streets are very walkable; around the Plaza Ruiz de Arellano are several historic buildings.

The Best...

➡**Sight** Museo Gauchesco Ricardo Güiraldes (p156)

➡**Place to Eat** Almacén Ramos Generales (p157)

➡**Place to Drink** Boliche de Bessonart (p157)

Top Tip

If you're here in early to mid-November, don't miss Día de la Tradición, when the town puts on the country's biggest gaucho celebration. Call the tourist office for exact dates.

Getting There & Away

➡**Bus** Frequent buses from Retiro bus station drop you five blocks from the center of town; travel time is two hours.

➡**Car** Take RN8 west to *ramal* (branch) Pilar.

Need to Know

➡**Area Code** 02326

➡**Location** 115km northwest of Buenos Aires

➡**Tourist Office** (☑453165; www.sanantoniodeareco.tur.ar; cnr E Zerboni & Ruiz de Arellano; ☺10am-7pm Mon-Fri, 8am-8pm Sat & Sun) Located in a white, stand-alone building in the park.

San Antonio de Areco

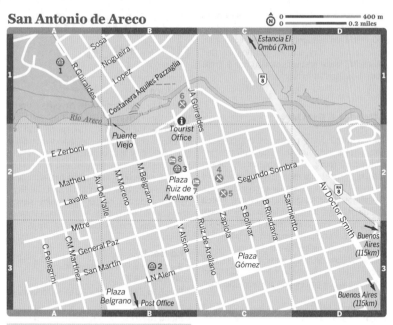

San Antonio de Areco

SIGHTS

Note that early in the week some museums are closed.

MUSEO GAUCHESCO RICARDO GÜIRALDES   MUSEUM

(cnr R Güiraldes & Sosa; ⊙11am-6pm Wed-Mon) **FREE** This sprawling museum in Parque Criollo dates to 1938 and includes an old flour mill, a re-created *pulpería* (tavern), a colonial-style chapel and a 20th-century reproduction of an 18th-century *casco* (ranch house). Displays include horse gear, gauchesco artwork and rooms dedicated to Ricardo Güiraldes, author of the novel *Don Segundo Sombra*.

MUSEO Y TALLER DRAGHI   MUSEUM

(www.draghiplaterosorfebres.com; Lavalle 387; admission AR$25; ⊙9am-1pm & 4-7pm Mon-Sat, 10am-1pm Sun) This small museum, attached to the silversmith workshop of the locally renowned Draghi family, highlights an exceptional collection of silver *facones* (gaucho knives), beautiful horse gear and intricate *mate* paraphernalia.

MUSEO LAS LILAS   MUSEUM

(www.museolaslilas.org; Moreno 279; admission AR$50; ⊙10am-8pm Thu-Sun mid-Sep-mid-Mar, to 6pm rest of year) Florencio Molina Campos is to Argentines what Norman Rockwell is to Americans – a folk artist whose themes are based on comical caricatures. This pretty courtyard museum displays his famous works.

EATING

PUESTO LA LECHUZA   PARRILLA $

(☑470136; Victorino Althaparro 423; mains AR$45-75; ⊙noon-3pm & 8pm-midnight Sat, noon-3pm Sun) Best on a warm day, when you can enjoy a lunch of *empanadas* or barbecued beef under the trees near the river. Live guitar music on Saturday night; open weekends only.

BOLICHE DE BESSONART PICADAS $

(cnr Zapiola & Segundo Sombra; picadas AR$10-65; ☺11am-late Tue-Sun) Its shelves filled with dusty bottles and and old gaucho photos, this weatherbeaten corner bar draws in locals for *picadas* (snack plates of meat, cheese and olives).

ALMACÉN RAMOS GENERALES ARGENTINE $$

(www.ramosgeneralesareco.com.ar; Zapiola 143; mains AR$65-140; ☺noon-3pm & 8pm-midnight) Come to this traditional, local mainstay if you want an old-time atmosphere in which to enjoy good fish, meat or pasta dishes.

 SLEEPING

ARECO HOSTEL HOSTEL $

(☑453120; www.arecohostel.com.ar; Arellano 121; dm AR$120, d AR$280, tr AR$420) In an atmospheric old building facing the central square, this hostel offers one spacious four-bed dorm with working fireplace, a pair of larger dorms and a lone private room up front. The clean, tiled guest kitchen, narrow but grassy backyard and friendly management add to the hostel's appeal.

★ PARADORES DRAGHI GUESTHOUSE $$

(☑455583; www.paradoresdraghi.com.ar; Matheu 380; s Sun-Thu only AR$450, d AR$580; ✳@☎☀) Large, comfortable rooms (two with kitchenette) are available at this tranquil place. There's a grassy garden with a beautiful pool, a greenhouse breakfast room and two patios in which to take a relaxing break.

Colonia

Explore

Colonia (officially Colonia del Sacramento) is a picturesque Uruguayan town whose Barrio Histórico neighborhood is a Unesco World Heritage Site. Pretty rows of sycamores offer protection from the summer heat, and the Río de la Plata provides a venue for spectacular sunsets.

Picturesque spots for wandering in Barrio Histórico include the narrow, roughly cobbled **Calle de los Suspiros** (Street of Sighs), lined with tile-and-stucco colonial houses, the **Paseo de San Gabriel**, which follows the western riverfront, the **Puerto Viejo** (Old Port) and the historic center's two main squares: vast **Plaza Mayor 25 de Mayo** and shady **Plaza de Armas** (the latter also known as Plaza Manuel Lobo).

The Best...

➡ **Sight** Faro (p159)
➡ **Place to Eat** Buen Suspiro (p160)
➡ **Place to Drink** Barbot (p161)

Top Tips

To avoid the crowds and more expensive accommodations prices, consider visiting Colonia midweek. If you want US dollars, use ATMs in Uruguay – those in Argentina do not give them out.

Getting There & Away

➡ **Ferry** Buquebus (www.buquebus.com), Colonia Express (www.coloniaexpress.com) and Seacat (www.seacatcolonia.com) have many daily ferries between Buenos Aires and Colonia. Fast ferries take an hour; slow ferries take three hours. Immigration for both countries is handled at the port before boarding.

LIFE IN THE COUNTRYSIDE

Want to get away from it all but still have some affordable fun? Check into **El Galope Hostel** (☑99-105985; www.elgalope.com.uy; Km 114.5, Ruta 1; dm US$25, d with shared/private bathroom US$70/90), a farm about 50 minutes by bus outside Colonia. You can take nature walks, go horseback riding and sweat in the sauna – all in the peaceful Uruguayan countryside. Its owners, Mónica and Miguel, are friendly and helpful, and are experienced international travelers who speak English, Spanish, French and German.

Colonia

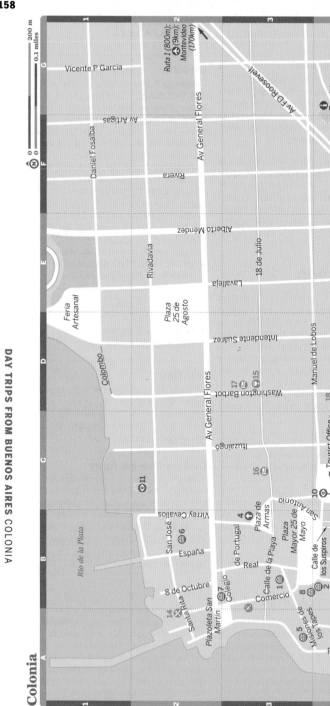

Río de la Plata

Ruta 1 (800m);
Montevideo
(170km)

Av FD Roosevelt

Vicente P Garcia

Av Artigas

Daniel Fosalba

Rivera

Alberto Méndez

18 de Julio

Lavalleja

Calle Odriozola

**BIT
Welcome
Center**

Tourist
Office - Bus
Terminal

Feria
Artesanal

Colombo

Rivadavia

Plaza
25 de
Agosto

Intendente Suárez

Manuel de Lobos

Av General Flores

Washington Barbot

Ituzaingó

17 **15**

18

Tourist Office -
Barrio Histórico

San José

Virrey Cevallos

Plaza de
Armas

4

San Antonio

16

11

10

España

de Portugal

Real

Calle de la Playa

Plaza
Mayor 25 de
Mayo

Calle de
los Suspiros

de Solís

San Francisco

12

9

Bastión de
San Miguel

8 de Octubre

Santa Rita

Plazoleta San
Martín

Colegio

Comercio

Misiones de
los Tapes

1

8

2

3

San Pedro

San Gabriel

P de San Gabriel

14

7

6

5

Colonia

Need to Know

➡ **Area Code** 4522

➡ **Location** 50km east of Buenos Aires by ferry

➡ **Tourist Offices** The **BIT Welcome Center** (☑4522-1072; www.bitcolonia.com; Odriozola 434; ☺10am-7pm Dec-Apr, 9am-6pm May-Nov) is across from the port. There's a tourist office in **Barrio Histórico** (☑4522-8506; www.coloniaturismo.com; Manuel de Lobos 224; ☺9am-6pm) and at the **bus terminal** (☑4522-8506; www.coloniaturismo.com; Av Roosevelt; ☺9am-8pm).

 **SIGHTS**

A single UR$50 ticket covers admission to Colonia's eight historical museums. All keep the same hours, but opening days vary.

PORTÓN DE CAMPO GATE
(Manuel de Lobos) The most dramatic way to enter Barrio Histórico is via the reconstructed 1745 city gate. From here, a thick fortified wall runs south along the Paseo de San Miguel to the river, its grassy slopes popular with sunbathers.

IGLESIA MATRIZ CHURCH
(Plaza de Armas) Uruguay's oldest church – begun by the Portuguese in 1680, then completely rebuilt twice under Spanish rule – is the centerpiece of pretty Plaza de Armas. The plaza also holds the foundations of a house dating from Portuguese times.

FARO LIGHTHOUSE
(admission UR$20; ☺11am-sunset) One of the town's most prominent landmarks, Colonia's 19th-century lighthouse provides an excellent view of the old town and the Río de la Plata. It stands within the ruins of the 17th-century **Convento de San Francisco**, just off the southwestern corner of Plaza Mayor 25 de Mayo.

TEATRO BASTIÓN DEL CARMEN THEATER, GALLERY
(Rivadavia 223; ☺10am-10pm) FREE Incorporating part of the city's ancient fortifications, this theater and gallery complex hosts rotating art exhibits and periodic concerts.

MUSEO PORTUGUÉS MUSEUM
(Plaza Mayor 25 de Mayo 180; ☺closed Wed & Fri) In this beautiful old house you'll find Portuguese relics including porcelain, furniture, maps, Manuel Lobo's family tree and the old stone shield that once adorned the Portón de Campo.

MUSEO MUNICIPAL MUSEUM
(Plaza Mayor 25 de Mayo 77; ☺closed Tue & Thu) Houses an eclectic collection of treasures including a whale skeleton, an enormous rudder from a shipwreck, historical timelines and a scale model of Colonia (c 1762).

ARCHIVO REGIONAL MUSEUM
(Misiones de los Tapes 115; ☺closed Sat & Sun) On the northwest edge of the plaza, Archivo Regional contains historical documents along with pottery and glass excavated from the 18th-century Casa de los Gobernadores nearby.

CASA NACARELLO MUSEUM
(Plaza Mayor 25 de Mayo 67; ☺closed Tue & Fri) One of the prettiest colonial homes in town, with period furniture, thick whitewashed walls, wavy glass and original lintels (duck if you're tall!).

MUSEO DEL AZULEJO   MUSEUM

(cnr Misiones de los Tapes & Paseo de San Gabriel; ☺closed Thu & Fri) This dinky 17th-century stone house has a sampling of French, Catalan and Neapolitan tilework.

MUSEO INDÍGENA   MUSEUM

(Comercio s/n; ☺closed Mon & Thu) Houses Roberto Banchero's personal collection of Charrúa stone tools, exhibits on indigenous history, and an amusing map upstairs showing how many European countries could fit inside Uruguay's borders (it's at least six!).

MUSEO ESPAÑOL   MUSEUM

(San José 164; ☺closed Tue & Wed) This recently reopened museum has a varied collection of Spanish artifacts, including colonial pottery, engravings, clothing and maps.

✕ EATING & DRINKING

BUEN SUSPIRO   PICADAS **$$**

(☎4522-6160; www.buensuspiro.com; Calle de los Suspiros 90; picadas from UR$205; ☺11am-midnight) Duck under the wooden beams into this cozy spot specializing in *picadas*. Sample local wines by the bottle or glass, accompanied by spinach and leek tarts, ricotta-and-sesame balls, local cheese and sausage, and more. Reserve ahead for a fireside table in winter, or while away a summer afternoon on the intimate back patio.

LENTAS MARAVILLAS   INTERNATIONAL **$$**

(Santa Rita 61; sandwiches & salads UR$280-300; ☺2-8:30pm Thu-Tue) Cozy as a friend's home, this is a dreamy spot to kick back with tea and cookies or a glass of wine and a sandwich between meals. Flip through

---

HISTORIC ESTANCIAS

One of the best ways to enjoy the wide-open spaces of Argentina is to visit an *estancia* (cattle ranch). The late-19th-century belle époque saw wealthy landowning families build up their country ranches with lavish, often fanciful homes, which they used as country retreats.

Today these establishments cater to tourists with *días de campo* – day tours that include large *asado* (barbecue) lunches, horseback rides, folk shows and, often, swimming facilities. Most also have overnight stays, which offer a longer glimpse into Argentina's history on the pampas.

El Ombú (☎in BA 4737-0436; www.estanciaelombu.com) Just outside San Antonio de Areco, this working *estancia* offers nine rooms and the opportunity to watch gauchos do their stuff.

Juan Gerónimo (☎02221-481414; www.juangeronimo.com.ar) There's excellent horseback riding and bird-watching at this working cattle farm, located within a Unesco world biosphere reserve about two hours from Buenos Aires.

La Candelaria (☎02227-494132; www.estanciacandelaria.com) Located about 1½ hours from BA. Special for its castle and manicured grounds designed by Charles Thays, who did many of BA's public parks. Polo matches often held here.

Los dos Hermanos (☎in BA 4723-2880; www.estancialosdoshermanos.com) Just about an hour outside BA, this is a good place to learn how to horseback ride. Friendly, with good food.

La Margarita (☎in BA 4951-0638; www.estancialamargarita.com) ⌀ Located at an old *estancia* about 100 miles southwest of BA. Offers a self-catering option, which makes your stay more self-sufficient and affordable.

La Oriental (☎02364-15-640866; www.estancia-laoriental.com) More authentic than luxurious is this lovely *estancia* three hours from Buenos Aires. Activities include fishing or windsurfing in a nearby lagoon.

Puesto Viejo (☎in BA 5279-6893; www.puestoviejoestancia.com.ar) Not far from Ezeiza airport is this boutique *estancia* where you can learn to play polo, ride a bicycle in the coutryside or just hang by the luxurious pool.

San Antonio's tourist office has more information on *estancias*, as does Buenos Aires' **Secretaría de Turismo de la Nación** (Map p248; ☎4312-2232; www.turismo.gov.ar; Av Santa Fe 883; ☺9am-7pm Mon-Fri).

DAY TRIPS FROM BUENOS AIRES COLONIA

an art book from owner Maggie Molnar's personal library and enjoy the river views, either from the upstairs fireplace room or the chairs on the grassy lawn below.

LA BODEGUITA — PIZZA $$

(www.labodeguita.net; Comercio 167; mini pizzas UR$115, dishes UR$220-390; ⊙8:30pm-midnight year-round, plus 12:30-3:30pm Sat & Sun Apr-Nov) Nab a table out back on the sunny two-level deck and soak up the sweeping river views while drinking sangria (UR$200 per liter) or munching on La Bodeguita's trademark mini pizzas, served on a cutting board.

BARBOT — BREWPUB

(✐4522-7268; www.facebook.com/barbot cerveceria; Washington Barbot 160; ⊙7pm-late Wed-Sun) A welcome addition to Colonia's drinking scene, this upscale brewpub (Colonia's first) opened in 2013, serving a wide selection of homebrews, accompanied by pizza, *picadas* and Mexican fare.

 SLEEPING

★EL VIAJERO HOSTEL — HOSTEL $

(✐4522-2683; www.elviajerocolonia.com; Washington Barbot 164; dm US$18-20, d US$64-74; ✸@⊛) With bike rental, horseback excursions, a bar for guests and air-con in all rooms, this hostel is brighter, fancier and somewhat cozier than the competition, and the location two blocks east of Plaza de Armas couldn't be better.

POSADA DEL ÁNGEL — HOTEL $$

(✐4522-4602; www.posadadelangel.net; Washington Barbot 59; d US$80-120; ✸@⊛⊛) Cheerfully painted in yellow and periwinkle blue, this little hotel has amenities such as down comforters and a sauna for chilly nights, and a swimming pool for the summer heat. Standard interior-facing rooms are dark; it's worth splurging on one with a view.

EL CAPULLO — B&B $$

(✐4523-0135; www.elcapullo.com; 18 de Julio 219; d US$120-165; ✸⊛⊛) Friendly and well-traveled English-speaking owners, a prime Barrio Histórico location, a grassy yard and a swimming pool are the big attractions at this remodeled colonial *posada* (inn). It's worth paying extra for one of the rooms upstairs or adjoining the back patio.

Sleeping

Buenos Aires may be the city that never sleeps – but really, who doesn't need a bit of rest once in a while? You'll find a wide range of places to rest your head here, from hostels to boutique hotels, guesthouses, rental apartments and international five-star hotels. Just remember to book ahead – or pay in cash – for the best deals.

Rates, Discounts & Payments

Buenos Aires is decent value compared with the USA or Europe. However, inflation has been running at 25% to 30% annually. To avoid sticker shock, double check the prices we list before reserving.

The prices we list – particularly for the four- or five-star hotels – are generally the rack or high-season rates from November through January. Rates for top-end hotels can vary widely on any particular day, as many are dependent on how empty or full the hotel is that day. Rates can also skyrocket during holidays such as Easter, Christmas or New Year. Some places lower their rates during slow periods, while others don't. But whatever the season, you don't always have to pay the official posted price.

Your best bet for getting a cheaper rate is to book in advance. You can do this via most hotels' websites. Calling ahead and talking to a salesperson with the power to negotiate prices can also be fruitful, especially if you plan on staying more than a few days. Offering to pay in cash can also bring about a discount.

The most expensive hotels will take credit cards, but budget or midrange places may not – or they may levy a surcharge (about 10%).

Hostels

Buenos Aires' hostels range from basic no-frills deals to beautiful, buildings more luxurious than your standard cheap hotel. Most fall in between, but all have common kitchens, living areas, shared bathrooms and dorm rooms (bring earplugs). Most have a few private rooms (with or without bathroom) and provide some traveler services. BA has a few **Hostelling International** (HI; www.hihostels.com) hostels, where members can get a small discount. Other hostel networks include **Minihostels** (www.minihostels.com) and **HoLa** (www.holahostels.com).

Hotels

As in many countries, Buenos Aires' hotels vary from utilitarian holes-in-the-wall to luxurious five-star hotels with all the usual top-tier services. In general, hotels provide a room with private bathroom, cable TV and sometimes a phone. Cheap hotels might also have cheaper rooms with shared bathroom. Higher-end hotels may have safe boxes, a refrigerator and a desk. Some hotels have a cafe or restaurant. Staff members at tourist-oriented hotels will usually speak some English.

Boutique Hotels & B&Bs

In recent years these types of accommodations have popped up like mushrooms in BA. The neighborhood of Palermo especially has become home to dozens of boutique hotels; most are pricey but beautiful, with just a handful of hip, elegant rooms and usually decent service. In BA, B&Bs are sometimes (but not always) run by the owners, and usually have fewer rooms than boutique hotels – but often offer a better breakfast.

Lonely Planet's Top Choices

Poetry Building (p171)
Lovely apartments decorated with vintage-reproduction furniture.

Cabrera Garden (p171)
Peaceful B&B boasting just three gorgeous rooms and a grassy garden.

Miravida Soho (p172)
Upscale guesthouse with friendly owners and wine-tasting opportunities.

5th Floor (p171) Modern and elegant B&B offering one of Buenos Aires' best breakfasts.

Magnolia Hotel (p172) Fine boutique hotel with a very relaxing rooftop terrace.

Casa Calma (p169) Ecologically minded luxury hotel providing a paradise in BA's busy downtown.

Best by Budget

$

America del Sur (p168)
Five-star boutique hostel, with awesome rooms and services.

Reina Madre Hostel (p170)
Very comfortable, well-run and intimate hostel.

Yira Yira Guesthouse
(p170) Friendly and intimate guesthouse with only four rooms.

$$

Abode (p172) Homey guesthouse with nice terrace and exceptional breakfast.

Racó de Buenos Aires
(p174) Beautiful boutique hotel in a nontouristy neighborhood.

Casa y Mundo Bolivar
(p169) Lovely apartments in a remodeled mansion, with patios.

$$$

Palacio Duhau – Park Hyatt (p171) Gorgeous remodeled mansion with a stunning courtyard.

Alvear Palace Hotel (p171)
Buenos Aires' most traditional and luxurious five-star hotel.

Faena Hotel + Universe
(p166) Supremely elegant and over the top – this is where celebrities stay.

Best Boutique Hotels

Magnolia Hotel (p172)
Splendid boutique hotel with a very relaxing rooftop terrace.

Mine Hotel (p173) Best for its grassy backyard with contemporary pool.

Mansión Vitraux (p169)
San Telmo's slickest spot to lay your head.

Duque Hotel (p173) Elegant and beautiful, and there's a luxurious spa too.

Best for Families

Poetry Building (p171)
Upscale apartments, all with kitchen, plus a soaking pool.

Novotel Hotel (p168) Especially family-friendly services – including two kiddie pools.

Hotel Lyon (p167) Simple budget lodgings with tons of space for large families.

NEED TO KNOW

Price Ranges
Prices are for a room with private bathroom for two people in high season.

$ under AR$500/US$80

$$ AR$500-1100/US$80-175

$$$ over AR$1100/US$175

Many high-end hotels add a 21% tax to their quoted rates. Most budget and midrange hotels already have this tax included in their quoted rates. To avoid a surprise at checkout time, ask if this tax is included in any price you're quoted. We've included this tax in the prices shown here.

Reservations
It's a good idea to make a reservation during any holidays or the busy summer months of November through February.

Breakfast
Some kind of breakfast, whether it be continental or buffet, is usually included at most accommodations. Unless you're staying somewhere fancy, however, don't expect too much – a typical breakfast will often consist of toast or *medialunas* (croissants), with some jam or butter if you're lucky, plus coffee or tea.

Where to Stay

Neighborhood	For	Against
The Center	Great transportation options; fairly close to all neighborhoods except Palermo; offers many services	Limited eating, shopping and nightlife options; noisy and crowded during the day and impersonal after dark
Puerto Madero	Very safe, calm, quiet and upscale; great strolling opportunities, both in a natural reserve and along the pleasant restaurant-lined dikes	Expensive: many restaurants are overpriced; very limited public transportation, accommodation, shopping and service options and not much interesting nightlife
Congreso & Tribunales	Reasonably central, with plenty of traditional theater and other cultural options; interesting local flavor, tending towards classic architecture and governmental vibe	Certain sections are desolate and less safe at night; limited shopping and eating possibilities
San Telmo	Endearing traditional atmosphere, reasonable shopping and nightlife, a good range of restaurants and many decent hostels	Far from Palermo; some areas can be edgy at night; public transportation is somewhat limited
La Boca		Not recommended and practically no accommodation options
Retiro	Beautiful upscale neighborhood within walking distance of Recoleta and the Center; convenient for public transportation	Very expensive; limited accommodations options; not many affordable restaurants or shops
Recoleta & Barrio Norte	Buenos Aires' most upscale neighborhood; gorgeous architecture, good transportation options and fairly safe	Most accommodations, restaurants and shopping are very expensive
Palermo	Many boutique hotels to choose from; the city's widest range of interesting restaurants, by both cuisine and budget; great shopping and nightlife	A bit of a trek to the Center and San Telmo; might be too touristy for some
South of Palermo	Up-and-coming neighborhoods with local atmosphere and some decent accommodations, restaurants and shops; quick access via Subte to the Center	Fewer traveler services; some neighborhoods are not central

🛏 The Center

Buenos Aires' Center, being right in the middle of things, has the most business-type accommodations in the city. Several pedestrian streets make it more walkable, and it's close to the upscale neighborhoods of Puerto Madero, Retiro and Recoleta. The Plaza de Mayo area contains the bustling banking district and many historic buildings, and is within walking distance of San Telmo. During the day the whole area is very busy, but at night the streets become deserted and even a bit sketchy. Your eating and nightlife options are also very limited – for this you'll have to head to Palermo.

GRAN HOTEL HISPANO   HOTEL $

Map p236 (☑4345-2020; www.hhispano.com.ar; Av de Mayo 861; s/d AR$360/490; ❄@🛜; 🅂Línea A Piedras) The tiny stairway lobby here isn't an impressive start, but upstairs there's a sweet atrium area with covered patio. Most rooms are modern and carpeted; those in front are biggest, and those on the top floor are brightest. There's also a pleasant outside sun terrace. It's a popular, central and well-tended place, so reserve ahead. Pay in cash for a 10% discount.

HOTEL AVENIDA   HOTEL $

Map p236 (☑4331-4341; www.hotelav.com.ar; Av de Mayo 623; s/d US$60/75; ❄@🛜; 🅂Línea A Peru) Just 34 plain but efficient rooms greet you at this friendly place. There's a pleasant breakfast area and the location is great, right near Plaza de Mayo. Get a back room for more peace and quiet; the front ones have nice balconies (except for the 4th floor) but are noisy. Pay in cash for a 10% discount.

V & S HOSTEL CLUB   HOSTEL $

Map p236 (☑4322-0994; www.hostelclub.com; Viamonte 887; dm US$15, r from US$60; ❄@🛜; 🅂Línea C Lavalle) 🍃 One of the best in town, this attractive, central and eco-friendly hostel is located in a pleasant older building. The common space, which is also the dining and lobby area, is good for socializing. The spacious dorms are carpeted and the private rooms are excellent; all have their own bathroom. A nice touch is the tiny outdoor patio in back.

PORTAL DEL SUR   HOSTEL $

Map p236 (☑4342-8788; www.portaldelsurba.com.ar; Hipólito Yrigoyen 855; dm US$14-17, s/d US$50/70; ❄@🛜; 🅂Línea A Piedras) Located in a charming old building, this is one of the city's best hostels. Beautiful dorms and sumptuous, hotel-quality private rooms surround a central common area, which is rather dark but open. The highlight is the lovely rooftop deck with views and attached bar and lounge. Offers free tango and Spanish lessons and a walking tour; plenty of other activities available.

HOTEL MAIPÚ   HOTEL $

Map p236 (☑4322-5142; www.nuevohotelmaipu.com.ar; Maipú 735; s/d AR$200/280, without bathroom AR$160/240; 🛜; 🅂Línea C Lavalle) Head on up the marble staircase into a dim, tiled hallway. This classic old building was once owned by the Anchorenas, a wealthy and aristocratic Argentine family. Original tiles and high ceilings add charm to these simple lodgings. The 10 rooms are unmemorable but at least have cable TV. There's no breakfast, but it's a good budget deal.

CLARIDGE HOTEL   HOTEL $$

Map p236 (☑4314-2020; www.claridge.com.ar; Tucumán 535; d US$160; ❄@🛜❄; 🅂Línea B Florida) One of downtown BA's finest hotels, the Claridge features a relatively grand entrance for the area, where space is scarce. Standard rooms, with their tiny baths, aren't as fancy as you'd think, so go for a suite (some with balcony and Jacuzzi) if you want something special. The spa and pool are highlights. Prices vary widely, so check beforehand.

HOTEL FACÓN GRANDE   HOTEL $$$

Map p236 (☑4312-6360; www.hotelfacongrande.com; Reconquista 645; r AR$1270; ❄@🛜; 🅂Línea B Florida) For those seeking a touch of the country in Buenos Aires, there's this (slightly) gaucho-themed hotel. The lobby is decorated in rustic furniture and cowhide-covered pillows, and rooms are modern and comfortable. The location on pedestrian Reconquista is good and there's an intimate vibe that's rare in hotels of this size. Get a top-floor room for views. Overall, a good deal for the price.

HOTEL LAFAYETTE   HOTEL $$$

Map p236 (☑4393-9081; www.lafayettehotel.com.ar; Reconquista 546; d AR$1330; ❄@🛜; 🅂Línea B Florida) Spacious, elegant rooms are on offer at this fine downtown hotel on a pedestrian street. The bathrooms are small but efficient, while double-glazed windows guarantee peace and quiet. Hotel amenities include a sauna and gym, a nice restaurant, and a fancy lobby with plant atrium, fireplace and sofas. Buffet breakfast; book ahead for the best rates.

🛏 Puerto Madero

There are hardly any hotels in Puerto Madero, a relatively new, upscale neighborhood that lies just east of the Center. Most buildings here are old warehouses that have been converted into fancy restaurants, offices and lofts, or they're brand-new apartment high-rises. The Reserva Ecológica Costanera Sur provides a welcome chunk of wild nature – almost nonexistent in Buenos Aires.

Public transport doesn't reach Puerto Madero, but the nearest Subte line is only three blocks away, and many buses run along Av Leandro N Alem/Paseo Colón.

FAENA HOTEL + UNIVERSE   HOTEL $$$
Map p238 (☑4010-9000; www.faenahoteland-universe.com; Martha Salotti 445; r US$760-1090; ✳@🛜🏊) Located in a renovated storage mill, this Philippe Starcke–designed fantasy hotel is more than just a place to stay. Traipse through the plush main hallway, lined with two top-notch restaurants, a sultry bar-lounge, a basement cabaret and – outside – a slick swimming pool. On arrival guests are given a personal valet and cell phone, then taken to luxurious rooms that feature claw-foot beds, etched-mirror entertainment centers and glass-walled bathrooms. Also on the premises are a Turkish bath and spa.

🛏 Congreso & Tribunales

The Congreso and Tribunales area contains many of the city's older theaters, cinemas and cultural centers. Lively Av Corrientes has many modest shops, services and bookstores, and was BA's original theater district. The Plaza de Congreso area is always moving,

---

WEBSITES

Many travelers visiting Buenos Aires love the city so much that they want to stay longer and find an apartment. But snagging a pad isn't as easy as it could be; renters often need to commit to two years and nearly always need a local's bond to guarantee monthly payments – almost impossible for most foreigners.

To cater to this demand, dozens of apartment websites have popped up in recent years. These sites charge significantly more than locals would pay, but they don't have those pesky requirements, either. You can view pictures of rental properties, along with prices and amenities. Usually the photos match what you will get, but not always; if you'd like someone to check out an apartment before you rent it, Madi Lang (p210) can make sure the place isn't on a busy street, in an outlying neighborhood or near a construction site.

➡ www.bytargentina.com
➡ www.apartmentsba.com
➡ www.buenosaireshabitat.com
➡ www.oasisba.com
➡ www.santelmoloft.com
➡ www.stayinbuenosaires.com
➡ www.jaimejensen.com

If you're just looking for a room, check www.spareroomsba.com. Or look for longer-term guesthouses (where rooms usually share bathrooms) at www.casalosangelitos.com and www.lacasademarina.com.ar. And there's always the Buenos Aires branch of Craigslist.

Another good option for short- or long-term stays is dealing directly with owners via sites like www.airbnb.com, www.homeaway.com or www.flipkey.com.

Also check hotels.lonelyplanet.com.

sometimes with mostly peaceful public demonstrations. Generally, this area is not quite as packed as in the Center and has a less business-and-touristy flavor, but still bustles day and night.

MILHOUSE YOUTH HOSTEL
HOSTEL $

Map p236 (☑4345-9604; www.milhouse hostel.com; Hipólito Yrigoyen 959; dm AR$90-95, d AR$330-350; ✷@🛜; ⑤Línea A Avenida de Mayo) BA's premiere party hostel, this popular HI spot offers a plethora of activities and services. Dorms are good and private rooms can be very pleasant; most surround an appealing open patio. Common spaces include a bar-cafe (with pool table) on the ground floor, a TV lounge on the mezzanine and a rooftop terrace above. A gorgeous annex building nearby offers similar services.

HOTEL MARBELLA
HOTEL $

Map p240 (☑4383-8566; www.hotelmarbella. com.ar; Av de Mayo 1261; s/d AR$300/400; ✷@🛜; ⑤Línea A Lima) The rooms at this hotel are basic but clean – if you can stand a bit of traffic noise, try to secure one with a balcony. More spacious (and more expensive) rooms are available, and there's a good, modern bar-restaurant where breakfast is served. From here it's an easy tramp to either Plaza del Congreso or Plaza de Mayo. Pay in cash and save 10%.

GRAN HOTEL ORIENTAL
HOTEL $

Map p240 (☑4951-6427; ghoriental@hotmail. com; Bartolomé Mitre 1840; s/d AR$210/300; ✷🛜; ⑤Línea A Congreso) Despite its name this hotel is not grand, but it is good – and a good deal. Downstairs rooms are a bit dark (get one upstairs) and showers in general are small, but the simple, high-ceilinged rooms are comfortable enough for nonfussy travelers – just don't expect many services. The tiled lobby and hallways are long and narrow, and there are a few old touches that add some personality.

SABATICO HOSTEL
HOTEL $

Map p240 (☑4381-1138; www.sabaticohostel. com.ar; México 1410; dm AR$100, r AR$400-500; ✷@🛜; ⑤Línea E Independencia) This well-maintained hostel is located off the tourist path in an atmospheric neighborhood. Rooms are small but pleasant and the good common areas include a nice kitchen, dining and living room, airy patio hallways and a pleasant rooftop terrace with *asado* (barbecue) grill and hammocks in summer.

There's occasional live music on weekends, plus a ping-pong table, foosball and bike rentals.

LA CAYETANA
HOTEL $$

Map p240 (☑4383-2230; www.lacayetanahotel. com.ar; México 1330; r US$130-180; ✷@🛜; ⑤Línea E Independencia) Located south of Congreso in Montserrat, this is a beautiful 1850s guesthouse offering 11 simple, colorful rooms, all decorated differently with rustic yet upscale furniture. They all surround three lovely outdoor patios, which are accented with original tiles and leafy plants – the last one has a grassy garden. Breakfast includes fresh fruit, yogurt, and eggs to order. It's a quiet little paradise in a nontouristy neighborhood. Reserve ahead.

LIVIN' RESIDENCE
APARTMENTS $$

Map p240 (☑5258-0300; www.livinresidence. com; Viamonte 1815; studios US$100, 1-bedroom apt US$110, 2-bedroom apt US$160; ✷🛜; ⑤Línea D Callao) One of the better deals in town, especially if you're traveling in a group, are these studio and one- or two-bedroom apartments. All have a simple, contemporary feel, with tasteful furniture, flat TVs, small kitchens and balconies. There's a tiny rooftop terrace with Jacuzzi, *asado* and nearby gym room. Security is good; reserve ahead.

HOTEL BONITO
BOUTIQUE HOTEL $$

Map p240 (☑4381-2162; www.bonitobuenos aires.com; Chile 1507, 3rd fl; r US$90-105; ✷@🛜; ⑤Línea E Independencia) Lovely boutique hotel with just five artsy, gorgeous rooms mixing the traditional and contemporary. Some have a loft, cupola sitting area or Jacuzzi; floors can be wooden or acid-finished concrete. There's a warm atmosphere, with a small bar area and a good, sizeable breakfast. It's in a nontouristy, very local neighborhood within walking distance of Congreso and San Telmo.

HOTEL LYON
APARTMENTS $$

Map p240 (☑4372-0100; www.hotel-lyon.com.ar; Riobamba 251; d/tr/q AR$530/650/770; ✷@🛜; ⑤Línea B Callao) If you're a traveling family or group and on a budget, this place is for you. The two- and three-bedroom apartments available here are basic and no-frills but very spacious, and all include entry halls, large bathrooms and separate dining areas with fridges (but no kitchens). Up to five people can be accommodated in each apartment. Reserve ahead.

NOVOTEL HOTEL
HOTEL $$$

Map p240 (☑4370-9500; www.novotel.com; Av Corrientes 1334; r from US$205; ☀@🅢🖥; ⓈLínea B Uruguay) This large, contemporary French chain hotel is tastefully designed. The comfortable rooms have unique showers with glass on two opposite sides, plus a fun colored-light system (leave it to the French). But the highlight is out back, where a beautiful deck surrounds pools – one for adults and two for the kids – along with a living wall of vegetation and a bar.

This Novotel is family friendly, offering kid discounts, a playroom and Xbox rental; it's located smack in the middle of Corrientes' entertainment district.

🛏 San Telmo

South of the center, San Telmo has some of the most traditional atmosphere in the city. Buildings are more charming and historical, and less modern, than in the Center, and they tend to be only a few stories high. Many restaurants and fancy boutiques have opened here in recent years, and there are some good bars, tango venues and other nightspots for entertainment. Many accommodation options here are hostels, guesthouses or boutique hotels.

If you're looking to house up to eight people for a week or more, check out www.playinbuenosaires.com – and reserve well in advance.

AMERICA DEL SUR
HOSTEL $

Map p242 (☑4300-5525; www.america hostel.com.ar; Chacabuco 718; dm AR$120-130, d AR$450-480; ☀@🅢; ⓈLínea C Independencia) This gorgeous boutiquelike hostel is the fanciest of its kind in Buenos Aires, and built especially to be a hostel. Beyond reception is a fine bar-bistro area with large, elegant wooden patio. Clean dorms with four beds all have amazingly well-designed bathrooms, while private rooms are tastefully decorated and better than those at many midrange hotels. A multitude of services are also on offer.

BOHEMIA BUENOS AIRES
HOTEL $

Map p242 (☑4115-2561; www.bohemiabuenos aires.com.ar; Perú 845; r from AR$420; ☀@🅢; ⓈLínea C Independencia) With its slight upscale-motel feel, this good-value San Telmo hotel offers 22 simple and neat rooms, most good-sized, if a bit antiseptic with their white-tiled floors. None of the rooms has bathtub, so instead of taking a soak enjoy the peaceful grassy backyard and small interior patios. The breakfast buffet is a plus, and there's a restaurant.

SAN TELMO COLONIAL
GUESTHOUSE $

Map p242 (☑4300-0097; www.bairescolonial. com.ar; Carlos Calvo 767; r US$65-90; ☀@🅢; ⓈLínea C Independencia) Best for the independent traveler who requires minimal service is this very informal guesthouse. Ten very spacious rooms (four with lofts) line flower-pot-strewn patio-hallways on two floors. All but one comes with small kitchenette for very simple cooking, and the furniture is hardly fancy. Minimum stay is three nights; breakfast is offered at a nearby historic cafe. No sign outside.

CIRCUS HOSTEL & HOTEL
HOSTEL $

Map p242 (☑4300-4983; www.hostelcircus. com; Chacabuco 1020; dm US$24, r from US$80; ☀@🅢; ⓈLínea C Independencia) From the trendy lounge in front to the wooden-deck-surrounded wading pool in back, this hostel-hostel exudes hipness. Both dorms and private rooms, all small and simple, have basic furniture and their own bathrooms. There's a pool table and slick TV area too, but no kitchen.

BRISAS DEL MAR
HOTEL $

Map p242 (☑4300-0040; www.hotelbrisasdel mar.com.ar; Humberto Primo 826; r with/without bathroom AR$120/100; 🅢; ⓈLínea C San Juan) Long-running old cheapie hotel with no luxuries – except for cable TV. Has basic but decent budget rooms, the cheapest ones with shared bathrooms – try for an upstairs one, as they're brighter. All face tiled hallways lined with plants, and there's a very rustic, unstocked kitchen. No breakfast.

TERRANOVA HOSTEL
HOSTEL $

Map p242 (☑4300-1957; www.terranovasan telmo.com.ar; Humberto Primo 670; dm AR$70, r AR$200-220; @🅢; ⓈLínea C San Juan) This laid-back hostel boasts a casual bar area in front and puts on weekend 'cultural' events like live music – thankfully, away from the sleeping areas. A long covered patio-hallway provides nice outdoor spaces, and rooms have high ceilings (it's an old colonial building). There are also colorful murals and free tango classes.

HOSTEL VIEJO TELMO   HOSTEL $

Map p242 (✆4331-5469; www.viejotelmo.com; México 974; d/tr/q US$45/70/100; ✴@🛜; ⓈLínea C Independencia) The highlight of this hostel is the rooftop terrace, with *parrilla* grill and nearby kitchen–dining room. It's in a 1912 building with a variety of decent rooms, nearly all with bathroom; each has cable TV and there's also a living room near reception. Conveniently located near the Center and many transportation lines; no sign outside.

★ MANSIÓN VITRAUX   BOUTIQUE HOTEL $$

Map p242 (✆4878-4292; www.mansionvitraux. com; Carlos Calvo 369; r US$135-160; ✴@🛜🏊; Ⓢ Línea C Independencia) Almost too slick for San Telmo, this glass-fronted boutique hotel offers 12 beautiful rooms, all in different colors. All have either flat-screen or projection TV, and bathrooms boast very contemporary design. The breakfast buffet happens in the basement wine bar, and a tasting is included in your stay. There are also a large Jacuzzi, a dry sauna and a fancy rooftop terrace with small lap pool.

BONITO SAN TELMO   GUESTHOUSE $$

Map p242 (✆4362-8451; www.bonitobuenos aires.com; Juan de Garay 458; r US$90-105; ✴🛜; 🚌29) The busy avenue outside seems unlikely to offer such a paradise, but after you climb the stairs you'll be surrounded by contemporary touches, from the grand piano in the living room to the elegant dining nook in back. Six lovely rooms are available (including one with kitchenette), but the best features are the lush rooftop terraces, complete with San Telmo views. Reserve ahead.

CASA Y MUNDO BOLIVAR   BOUTIQUE HOTEL $$

Map p242 (✆4300-3619; www.casabolivar.com; Bolívar 1701; US$70-90; ✴🛜) Fourteen spacious studios and loft apartments with kitchenettes have been renovated into attractive modern spaces – some with original details such as carved doorways or painted ceilings – at this amazing mansion. Separate entrances join with hallways connecting through the complex, and there are

lovely garden patios in which to relax. No breakfast, but there's a cafe-restaurant.

Línea C, Constitución, is the closest Subte stop, but consider taking a taxi here instead. Three-day minimum stay; long-term guests preferred.

SCALA HOTEL   HOTEL $$$

Map p242 (✆4343-0606; www.scalahotelbuenos aires.com; Bernardo de Irigoyen 740; r AR$1270-2060; ✴@🛜; Ⓢ Línea C Independencia) A grand lobby awaits you at this business-oriented, four-star hotel. All rooms are lovely and spacious; standard ones have wooden floors, while higher categories come with carpeting and sitting rooms. Some boast 9 de Julio views. There's a pleasant, large patio in back, along with spa, gym, restaurant and two business salons; plans are for a swimming pool by 2015.

🛏 Retiro

Retiro is a great, central place to be, *if* **you can afford it – many of BA's most expensive hotels, along with some of its richest inhabitants, are settled in here. Close by are leafy Plaza San Martín, the Retiro train and bus stations, and many upscale stores and business services. Ritzy Recoleta is to the northwest and the busy Microcentro is to the south – both just a short and pleasant stroll away.**

HOTEL TRES SARGENTOS   HOTEL $

Map p248 (✆4312-6082; www.hotel3sargentos. com.ar; Tres Sargentos 345; s/d AR$300/380; ✴🛜; Ⓢ Línea C San Martín) A great deal for the location, this simple budget hotel has a nice enough lobby and is located on a pedestrian street. The carpets in the halls need changing, but the ones in the simple, comfortable rooms are clean enough. Some rooms even offer a bit of a view – ask for a floor up high.

★ CASA CALMA   BOUTIQUE HOTEL $$$

Map p248 (✆4312-5000; www.casacalma.com. ar; Suipacha 1015; r US$220-240; ✴@🛜; Ⓢ Línea C San Martín) 🌿 Those with stuffed wallets and of an eco-conscious mind now have their perfect hideaway in BA: this central, environmentally friendly and luxurious hotel. Rooms are beautifully pristine and relaxing (some even have sauna or Jacuzzi), with Zen-like baths and serene atmosphere.

It's a world away from outside the front door, where BA noisily buzzes by.

Casa Calma does its part by using eco-certified wood in its building and outside greenery to adjust the hotel's temperatures. It recycles what it can and offers guests organic towels, bulk toiletries and even two bamboo bicycles to rent. It's so gorgeous, however, you won't even notice.

FOUR SEASONS
HOTEL $$$

Map p246 (☑4321-1200; www.fourseasons.com/buenosaires; Posadas 1086; d from US$665; ❄@🎱🏊; Ⓢ Línea C San Martín) No surprise here – the Four Seasons offers all the perks that define a five-star hotel, such as great service and white terry-cloth robes. Rooms are large and beautiful, with contemporary furnishings and decorations, and the finest suites are located in an old, luxurious mansion next door (go for the presidential – it's US$10,000 per night).

There are also a gorgeous spa, an outdoor heated swimming pool and a top-notch restaurant.

HOTEL PULITZER
BOUTIQUE HOTEL $$$

Map p248 (☑4316-0800; www.hotelpulitzer.com.ar; Maipú 907; r from US$175; ❄@🎱🏊; Ⓢ Línea C San Martín) Very well located, this large, new boutique hotel has a black-and-white lobby and minimalist decor. Rooms are spacious and stylish, boasting flat-screen TVs and elegant bathrooms; some have a balcony. The highlight, however, is the beautiful rooftop terrace with attached bar, offering great views over the city. There are also a restaurant, a cocktail bar and even a swimming pool.

🛏 Recoleta & Barrio Norte

Most of the accommodations in Recoleta and Barrio Norte (whose borders can be blurred) are expensive, and what cheap hotels there are tend to be full much of the time. Buildings here are grand and beautiful, befitting the city's richest barrio, and you'll be close to Recoleta's famous cemetery, along with its lovely parks, museums and boutiques.

YIRA YIRA GUESTHOUSE
GUESTHOUSE $

Map p240 (☑4812-4077; www.yirayiraba.com; Uruguay 911 1B; s/d US$45/65; ❄@🎱; Ⓢ Línea D Callao) This casual, intimate apartment-home is run by the helpful Paz, who lives

on-site. The floors are wooden and the ceilings high, and there are just four large rooms (all with shared bathrooms) facing the central living area with tiny patio. It's a good place to meet other travelers and centrally located near downtown. Reserve ahead.

REINA MADRE HOSTEL
HOSTEL $

Map p250 (☑4962-5553; www.rmhostelbuenosaires.com; Anchorena 1118; dm AR$95-105, s/d AR$215/235; ❄@🎱; Ⓢ Línea D Pueyrredón) This wonderful hostel is clean, safe and well run. It's in an old building that has plenty of personality, with high ceilings and original tiles, and all rooms are comfortable and modern (and share bathrooms). There's a cozy living room with balcony and small kitchen plus lots of dining tables, but the highlight is the wooden-deck rooftop with *asado*. Pet cat on premises.

HOTEL LION D'OR
HOTEL $

Map p246 (☑4803-8992; www.hotel-liondor.com.ar; Pacheco de Melo 2019; s AR$300-320, d AR$360-420, tr AR$400-560; ❄🎱; Ⓢ Línea D Pueyrredón) These digs have their charm (it's an old embassy), but rooms vary widely – some are small, basic and dark, while others are grand. Despite some rough edges, all are good value and most have been modernized for comfort. The old marble staircase and elevator are fabulous, and there's a nice rooftop area. Cheap breakfast option; some rooms share bathrooms.

PETIT RECOLETA HOSTEL
HOSTEL $

Map p246 (☑4823-3848; www.petitrecoleta.com; Uriburu 1183; dm US$14-16, s US$35-50, d US$45-65; ❄@🎱; Ⓢ Línea D Facultad de Medicina) It's hardly a stunner as far as hostels go, but you can't beat this cheapie's location. There's an interior patio, small TV room, larger dining-bar room and pool-table area. Most rooms are private; there are two dorms, one for men and one for women. Only two rooms have air-con. Long-term tenants have their own section (one-month minimum).

ART SUITES
APARTMENTS $$

Map p246 (☑4821-6800; www.artsuites.com.ar; Azcuénaga 1465; d AR$850-1450; ❄🎱; Ⓢ Línea D Pueyrredón) The 15 luxurious, modern and spacious apartments here are all bright and boast minimalist decor, full kitchens or kitchenettes, sunny balconies and slick, hip furniture. Windows are double-paned for quiet, staff speak English and security is excellent. Continental breakfast included. Long-term discounts are available; reserve ahead. An annex offers more apartments.

★ POETRY BUILDING APARTMENTS $$$

Map p246 (☑4827-2772; www.poetrybuilding. com; Junín 1280; apt US$175-235; ❋ 🛜 🆒; Ⓢ Línea D Pueyrredón) These gorgeous studios and one- or two-bedroom apartments are perfect for families or small groups. Each one is different, eclectically decorated with reproduction antique furniture, and all come with fully stocked kitchens. Some boast an outdoor balcony or patio, but there's also a beautiful common terrace with soaking pool. Amenities include flat-screen TVs, plus iPod and cell-phone rentals.

★ PALACIO DUHAU – PARK HYATT HOTEL $$$

Map p246 (☑5171-1234; www.buenosaires. park.hyatt.com; Av Alvear 1661; d from US$655; ❋ @ 🛜 🆒; 🚌130) If it's good enough for presidents, diplomats and Tom Cruise, it's good enough for you. The luxurious Park Hyatt takes up a city block and consists of two wings, including the Palacio Duhau, a renovated mansion. There's a gorgeously terraced garden with fountains and patios, plus a fine spa, indoor pool, wine and cheese bar and art gallery. Excellent service.

ALVEAR PALACE HOTEL HOTEL $$$

Map p246 (☑4808-2100; www.alvearpalace.com; Av Alvear 1891; r from US$640; ❋ @ 🛜 🆒; 🚌130) The classiest, most traditional hotel in BA. Old-world sophistication and superior service will help erase the trials of your long flight into town, while the bathtub Jacuzzi, Hermès toiletries and Egyptian-cotton bed sheets aid your trip into dreamland. There's also an excellent restaurant, elegant tea room, cigar bar, fine spa, indoor swimming pool and butler service.

AYRES DE RECOLETA APARTMENTS $$$

Map p246 (☑4801-0505; www.ayresderecoleta. com; Uriburu 1756; studios US$175; ❋ @ 🛜 🆒; 🚌59) The 37 studio apartments here (plus two penthouses) all come with king-size beds or two twins, brown-and-white color scheme and classy decoration. There are also simple kitchenettes great for heating up leftover takeout, plus a small indoor pool with Jacuzzi. And the location can't be beat – you're a block from Recoleta cemetery. Reserve ahead.

🛏 Palermo

Despite being a slight trek from the center, Palermo is the top choice for many travelers. Not only is it full of extensive parklands – which are great for weekend jaunts and sporting activities – but you'll have heaps of cutting-edge restaurants, designer boutiques and hip dance clubs at your door. Many of these places are located in the extensive sub-neighborhoods of Palermo Soho and Palermo Hollywood. Las Cañitas is another sub-neighborhood, just to the northwest, with a three-block strip of door-to-door restaurants and bars. All are connected to the center by bus or Subte.

ECO PAMPA HOSTEL HOSTEL $

Map p250 (☑4831-2435; www.hostelpampa.com. ar; Guatemala 4778; dm US$20, s/d US$70/85; @ 🛜; Ⓢ Línea D Plaza Italia) 🍃 Buenos Aires' first 'green' hostel is this casual spot sporting vintage furniture, low-energy light bulbs and a recycling system. The rooftop is home to a small veggie garden, compost pile and solar panels. Dorms are a good size and each of the eight private rooms comes with bathroom and flat-screen TV (most have air-con).

There's another branch further north in **Belgrano** (www.hostelpampa.com; Iberá 2858).

★ 5TH FLOOR B&B $$

Map p250 (☑4827-0366; www.the5thfloorba. com; r US$90-170; ❋ @ 🛜; Ⓢ Línea D Scalabrini Ortíz) This upscale B&B offers seven elegant rooms, three with private balcony. All are tastefully decorated with art deco furniture and modern amenities. The common living room is great for chatting with the English owner, a polo enthusiast, and there's also a pleasant back patio with lovely tile details. Occasional closed-door dining events happen here. Excellent breakfast; address given upon reservation.

★ CABRERA GARDEN B&B $$

Map p250 (☑4777-7668; www.cabreragarden. com; José Antonio Cabrera 5855; US$145-250; ❋ @ 🛜 🆒) One of BA's loveliest stays is this three-room B&B run by a Polish-German gay couple. The remodeled 1920s building boasts a beautiful grassy garden with small patio and pool, and there's a wonderful living room in which to hang out. Rooms are very comfortable and all different, with modern conveniences like flat-screen TVs and iPod docks.

English, German and Polish spoken; reserve ahead. The nearest Subte stop – Línea D, Ministro Carranza – is 10 blocks away.

ABODE
GUESTHOUSE $$

Map p250 (☑4774-3331; www.abodebuenos aires.com; r US$90-150; ✳@☎; ⑤Línea D Palermo) Run by an expat couple, who live on the premises, is this very intimate and homey guesthouse. Each of the four simple yet comfortable rooms comes with its own bathroom, and the largest has a balcony. The highlight: a wonderful rooftop terrace, where you can enjoy your full English breakfast. By reservation only; no walk-ins. Friendly dog on premises.

PALERMO VIEJO B&B
GUESTHOUSE $$

Map p250 (☑4773-6012; www.palermoviejobb. com; Niceto Vega 4629; s/d US$75/85; ✳@☎) This small and intimate B&B is located in a remodeled *casa chorizo* – a long, narrow house. The six rooms all front a leafy outdoor patio hallway and are simple but quite comfortable; two have lofts. All come with fridge and a good breakfast. Call them ahead of time – they often leave on errands in the afternoon.

The nearest Subte stop – Línea B, Malabia – is nine blocks away.

LIVIAN GUESTHOUSE
GUESTHOUSE $$

Map p250 (☑4862-8841; www.livianguesthouse. com; Palestina 1184; r US$90-150; @☎; ☐106, 160) Located in a lovely old building in an untouristy section of Palermo is this chill guesthouse. There are 10 colorful yet tasteful rooms on offer, one with its own terrace and most with private bathroom (a few share bathrooms or have a private bathroom down the hall). There are pleasant living-room spaces and a pretty back garden too.

INFINITO HOTEL
BOUTIQUE HOTEL $$

Map p250 (☑2070-2626; www.infinitohotel.com; Arenales 3689; r US$160; ✳@☎; ⑤Línea D Scalabrini Ortíz) Starting at its small lobby cafe-reception, this hotel exudes a certain trendiness. Rooms are small but good, boasting flat-screen TVs, fridges, wooden floors and a purple color scheme. They try to be ecologically conscious (mostly by recycling); however, there's also a sauna and Jacuzzi. Located near some parks but still

within walking distance of Palermo's nightlife. Buffet breakfast included.

CASERÓN PORTEÑO
GUESTHOUSE $$

Map p250 (☑4554-6336; www.caseronporteno. com; Ciudad de la Paz 344; s AR$550-680, d AR$680-850; ✳@☎; ⑤Línea D Olleros) Catering especially to tango dancers is this fine guesthouse with 10 simple but tastefully furnished rooms. All have private bathrooms, but four have them located outside the actual rooms. Behind the lush garden there's a small dance studio where classes take place, while other common spaces include a relaxing rooftop terrace and a kitchen for guest use.

The location is in a nontouristy residential neighborhood; four-night minimum stay in high season. Unsurprisingly, plenty of tango information is available.

RUGANTINO HOTEL
HOTEL $$

Map p250 (☑4773-2891; www.rugantinohotel. com; Uriarte 1844; r US$115; ✳@☎; ⑤Línea D Palermo) This small and intimate hotel is located in a 1920s building and run by an Italian family. Various tiny terraces and catwalks connect the seven simple but beautiful rooms, all decked out in hardwood floors and modern styling – combined with a few antiques. The climbing vine-greenery in the small central courtyard well is soothing, and you can expect espresso for breakfast.

★ MIRAVIDA SOHO
GUESTHOUSE $$$

Map p250 (☑4774-6433; www.miravidasoho. com; Darregueyra 2050; r US$205-280; ✳@☎; ⑤Línea D Plaza Italia) Run by a friendly and helpful German couple, this gorgeous guesthouse comes with six beautiful and elegant rooms. All are very comfortable and one has a private terrace. There's a wine cellar, bar-lounge area for evening wine tastings, a small and relaxing patio, and even an elevator. It serves good, full breakfasts; reserve ahead (10% discount if you pay cash).

★ MAGNOLIA HOTEL
BOUTIQUE HOTEL $$$

Map p250 (☑4867-4900; www.magnoliahotel. com.ar; J Àlvarez 1746; r US$255-350; ✳@☎; ⑤Línea D Scalabrini Ortíz) This classy boutique hotel is in a gorgeously restored old house. Its eight impeccably groomed rooms are bathed in muted colors and fitted with elegant furniture; some have a patio or balcony. Common spaces are beautiful, and the gorgeous rooftop terrace is strewn with cushy lounges. Other pluses include a welcome drink and a little patio for the breakfast.

MINE HOTEL
BOUTIQUE HOTEL $$$

Map p250 (✆4832-1100; www.minehotel.com; Gorriti 4770; d US$205-270; ❄ @ 🎘 🌊; 🚇55) 🖋
This hip boutique hotel offers 20 good-size rooms; some come with Jacuzzi and balcony and all have a desk and natural decor touches. Get one overlooking the highlight of the hotel: the peaceful backyard, which comes complete with small wading pool. There's a small bistro for the buffet breakfast, and Mine even attempts to be eco-friendly (reusing towels, low-energy bulbs, recycling).

DUQUE HOTEL
BOUTIQUE HOTEL $$$

Map p250 (✆4832-0312; www.duquehotel.com; Guatemala 4364; d US$160-205; ❄ @ 🎘 🌊; 🚇Línea D Scalabrini Ortíz) More upscale than most boutique hotels is this elegant charmer. All 14 rooms are lovely and well designed, though some can be a bit small – go for a superior or deluxe if you need more space. Pluses include a large Jacuzzi, sauna, basement spa, buffet breakfast, afternoon tea with pastries and great little backyard garden with a tiny pool.

VAIN BOUTIQUE HOTEL
BOUTIQUE HOTEL $$$

Map p250 (✆4776-8246; www.vainuniverse.com; Thames 2226; r US$190-300; ❄ @ 🎘; 🚇Línea D Plaza Italia) Fifteen elegant rooms, all with high ceilings and wooden floors, live at this nicely renovated building. All are modern in that white, minimalist way, and boast sofas and small desks. The highlight, however, is the wonderfully airy, multilevel living room with attached wooden-decked terrace – a great place to enjoy breakfast. Small bar-restaurant in the lobby; reserve ahead for discounts.

PALERMITANO
BOUTIQUE HOTEL $$$

Map p250 (✆4897-2100; www.palermitano.biz; Uriarte 1648; d US$160-265; ❄ 🎘 🌊; 🚇39, 55) Located in the middle of Palermo's nightlife, this boutique hotel has 16 tastefully decorated and contemporary rooms. The breakfast buffet is served all day, and they'll even bring it to your door. And pretty unusual for Buenos Aires is the small rooftop terrace with wading pool. A branch of the excellent Peruvian restaurant Sipan is on the ground floor.

BA SOHOTEL
BOUTIQUE HOTEL $$$

Map p250 (✆4831-1844; www.basohotel.com; Paraguay 4485; r US$170-210; ❄ @ 🎘 🌊; 🚇Línea D Plaza Italia) This 33-room boutique hotel is a good bet, with good service and an attached corner restaurant. The gorgeous rooms are spacious and come with wooden floors, desk, balcony, double-paned windows, Jacuzzi tubs and bathroom mirrors that don't fog (it's important!). There's also a tiny pool and Jacuzzi on the communal terrace. Breakfast buffet included; reserve ahead for discounts.

248 FINISTERRA
BOUTIQUE HOTEL $$$

Map p250 (✆4773-0901; www.248finisterra. com; Av Báez 248; r US$170-240; ❄ @ 🎘; 🚇Línea D Ministro Carranza) Smack in the middle of Las Cañitas' nightlife strip lies this elegant, Zen-like boutique hotel. There are 11 minimalist rooms, all beautifully contemporary, though the smallest are a bit tight. There's a dining area for breakfast and a small grassy garden in back, but the highlight has to be the rooftop terrace, with wooden lounges and a Jacuzzi. Reserve ahead.

RENDEZVOUS HOTEL
HOTEL $$$

Map p250 (✆3964-5222; www.rendezvoushotel. com.ar; Bonpland 1484; d US$165-215; ❄ @ 🎘) This boutique hotel is located in a beautiful four-story French-style building. Each of the 11 rooms is unique, styled with either antique or modern furnishings and bright colors; one has its own private balcony and outdoor Jacuzzi. There's a small bar-lounge at reception, tiny rooftop deck and cute patio at the entrance.

The nearest Subte stop – Línea B, Dorrego – is nine blocks away.

🛏 South of Palermo

With the popularity of Palermo raising property values and rents, some places to stay have popped up in the more blue-collar, historical, artsy or even 'bohemian' neighborhoods to the south. This large area is a good choice if you want to 'go local' and don't mind being a bit further from the main sights (but not *too* far away). Public transport is good – and there probably won't be another tourist in sight.

CHILL HOUSE HOSTEL
HOSTEL $

Map p254 (☑4861-6175; www.chillhouse.com.ar; Agüero 781; dm AR$85, d AR$250-360; @�\); ⓈLínea B Carlos Gardel) One of the coolest-vibe hostels in BA is at this remodeled old house, boasting high ceilings and a rustic artsy style. There are two dorms, eight private rooms with bath (No 6 is especially nice) and an awesome rooftop terrace where weekly *asados* take place. Run by a French and Argentine team; free bike rentals too.

RACÓ DE BUENOS AIRES
BOUTIQUE HOTEL $$

Map p254 (☑3530-6075; www.racodebuenosaires.com.ar; Yapeyú 271; r from US$90; ✳ @�\); ⓈLínea A Castro Barros) This Italian-designed building in a nontouristy neighborhood offers 12 lovely rooms with different styling, from virgin white classic to subdued masculine to animal print. All are spacious and have wooden floors, high ceilings and modern amenities. There's a small plant-strewn patio for breakfast and a basement wine bar for evening tastings. It's a good-value deal and just three blocks from the Subte.

QUERIDO B&B
B&B $$

Map p254 (☑4854-6297; www.queridobuenosaires.com; Juan Ramírez de Velasco 934; r US$80-130; ✳ @�\); ⓈLínea B Malabia) Run by a friendly and helpful Brazilian-English couple is this homey yet modern B&B. It's located in a nontouristy neighborhood, but within easy walking distance of Palermo. The eight clean rooms are small but comfortable, and all have private bathrooms; ask for an inside 'courtyard' room for more quiet. There's a living room in which to meet fellow travelers, plus a little gravel patio in back. Reserve ahead.

POP HOTEL
HOTEL $$

Map p254 (☑4776-6900; www.pophotelsbuenosaires.com; Juan Ramírez de Velasco 793; r from US$95; ✳�\); ⓈLínea B Malabia) Located near Villa Crespo's outlet stores is this colorful and bright hotel. Halls are carpeted (this helps with noise) and rooms are modern and comfy, all with fridge, sink and flat-screen TV; the ones on the 4th floor are larger and boast balconies. Breakfast not included. Rates vary widely; prepay for a significant discount as rack rates can be double the prepaid rate.

Understand Buenos Aires

Buenos Aires Today

Buenos Aires has two faces: it's a city that harbors both decline and prosperity. You'll see dirty, neglected buildings everywhere – yet the rebirth following the economic crash of 2001 keeps on going. Puerto Madero continues to grow, Palermo's best restaurants still attract queues, and malls are full of shoppers. Public transportation is improving and the city's restaurants keep evolving – and though president Cristina Kirchner's popularity goes up and down, you should never count her out.

Best in Print

Kiss of the Spider Woman (Manuel Puig; 1976) Two prisoners and their developing relationship in a Buenos Aires prison; made into the Oscar-winning 1985 film.

And the Money Kept Rolling In (and Out) (Paul Blustein; 2005) How the IMF helped bankrupt Argentina.

On Heroes and Tombs (Ernesto Sábato; 1961) A complex plunge into Buenos Aires' society, aristocracy and family dynamics in the 1950s.

The Tango Singer (Tomás Eloy Martínez; 2006) An American graduate student travels to Buenos Aires and tracks down a legendary tango singer.

Best on Film

La historia oficial (The Official Story; 1985) Oscar-winning film on the Dirty War.

Nueve reinas (Nine Queens; 2000) Two con men chasing the big score.

El secreto de sus ojos (The Secret in Their Eyes; 2009) Thriller that won the 2010 Oscar for best foreign-language film.

Pizza, birra, faso (Pizza, Beer, Cigarettes; 1998) Four BA gangster youths try to survive on the city streets.

Economic Roller Coaster

Argentina's currency devaluation in 2002 caused surging demand for its suddenly-cheap agricultural products. Helped along by skyrocketing government spending and strong growth in Brazil and China, this economic boom lasted through 2007 and revved up again in 2010. But high inflation (unofficially hovering at around 25%), a stronger peso and lower commodity prices have reined in the economy.

In October 2011, in an effort to curb capital from heading overseas, the government started requiring Argentines to substantiate their purchases of US dollars. This created a *mercado azul* (literally, 'blue market') for US dollars, which are highly sought after as a stable currency. The real-estate market stalled, since purchases were pretty much always transacted in US dollars. Calle Florida is now even more full of *arbolitos* (or 'little trees', since they stand around), who target tourists with dollars to change – at nearly double the official rate.

Many economists believe that the government needs to reduce spending and stop borrowing from its central bank and public pension system; control inflation; and maintain foreign-exchange reserves. Moreover, government policies need to become more transparent to encourage both domestic and foreign investment. These are tall orders and go against the traditional Argentine economic flow, but recession and even devaluation are increasing risks. Who knows – maybe another crash is just what Argentina needs to get on top again.

Cristina's Reign

In 2011 Cristina Kirchner was re-elected president by a landslide majority of 54%. She ran on a platform that appealed to the populist vote, promising to raise incomes, restore industry and maintain Argentina's economic boom. Her approach worked like a charm.

Since then, however, things haven't been so rosy. Her popularity plunged as the economy hit the brakes, inflation skyrocketed and crime kept rising. *The Economist* and international agencies such as the IMF have accused her government of cooking the books (especially inflation figures). Her health has been on the rocks: she had to have surgery to remove her thyroid in 2012, and she underwent a procedure to remove a blood clot on her brain in 2013. She lost even more political support in the October 2013 midterm elections, making a Chavez-like third term – currently not allowed in the constitution, but something that many thought Cristina was after – very unlikely.

But nobody can write *la presidenta* off yet – she still maintains majorities in both chambers, her term won't be up until 2015 and she's been known to make comebacks. And despite her many detractors, Cristina has made admirable social strides. She's addressed the abuses of the military dictatorship, championed same-sex marriage laws and, above all, supported the blue-collar classes. And her people love her for it, just as they did Evita.

Cultural Evolutions

Despite a discouraging economy and a downturn in tourism in the last few years, Buenos Aires' culinary culture continues to evolve. Intrepid young chefs are providing creative twists to the restaurant scene with relatively new-to-BA concepts like molecular gastronomy and pop-up meal nights. Meanwhile, the closed door–restaurant sphere keeps thriving, with a few places now making Argentina's *asado* – traditionally a barbecue party at a friend or family's home on a Sunday – available to tourists in town for only a few days. Add to that a few new exciting food fairs and BA is well on its way to becoming a foodie destination.

Another evolving sector of Buenos Aires is its public transportation. The final implementation of the SUBE card meant that obtaining enough coins for the bus was no longer a source of friction and stress in *porteños'* daily lives (really – it was *that* bad). And new bus-only Metrobus lanes down big avenues like 9 de Julio and Juan B Justo have eased traffic somewhat, though people continue to purchase private cars as an investment against inflation (nobody trusts banks with their savings any more). Bicycle use has also increased, as the bike-lane system keeps expanding, and the city's free bike-share program has been deemed a success.

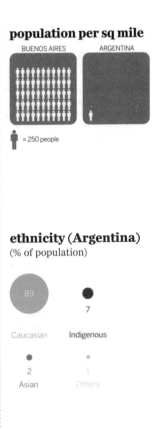

population per sq mile

BUENOS AIRES   ARGENTINA

≈ 250 people

ethnicity (Argentina)
(% of population)

89 — Caucasian
7 — Indigenous
2 — Asian
1 — Others

if Buenos Aires were 100 people

92 would be Roman Catholics
2 would be Jewish
2 would be Protestant
4 would be other

History

Like all Latin American countries, Argentina has a tumultuous history, one tainted by periods of despotic rule, corruption and hard times. But its history is also illustrious, the story of a country that fought off Spanish colonial rule and was once among the world's economic powerhouses. It's a country that gave birth to international icons such as the gaucho, Evita Perón and Che Guevara. Understanding Argentina's past is paramount to understanding its present and, most importantly, to understanding Argentines themselves.

The Spanish Arrive

Although the banks of the Río de la Plata had been populated for tens of thousands of years by nomadic hunter-gatherers, the first attempt at establishing a permanent settlement was made by Spanish aristocrat Pedro de Mendoza in 1536. His verbose name for the outpost, Puerto Nuestra Señora Santa María del Buen Aire (Port Our Lady Saint Mary of the Good Wind) was matched only by his extravagant expedition of 16 ships and nearly 1600 men – almost three times the size of Hernán Cortés' forces that conquered the Aztecs. In spite of his resources and planning, Mendoza unfortunately arrived too late in the season to plant adequate crops. The Spanish soon found themselves short on food and in typical colonialist fashion tried to bully the local Querandí indigenous groups into feeding them. A bitter fight and four years of struggle ensued, which led to such an acute shortage of supplies that some of the Spanish resorted to cannibalism. Mendoza himself fled back to Spain, while a detachment of troops who were left behind retreated upriver to Asunción (now the capital of Paraguay).

With Francisco Pizarro's conquest of the Inca empire in present-day Peru as the focus of the Spanish crown, Buenos Aires was largely ignored for the next four decades. In 1580 Juan de Garay returned with an expedition from Asunción and attempted to rebuild Buenos Aires. The Spanish had not only improved their colonizing skills since Mendoza's ill-fated endeavor but also had some backup from the cities of Asunción and Santa Fe.

TIMELINE	1536	1580	1660
	Spanish aristocrat Pedro de Mendoza reaches the Río de la Plata and attempts to set up a permanent settlement, only to return to Spain within four years.	Buenos Aires is reestablished by Spanish forces, but the city remains a backwater for years, in comparison to growing strongholds in central and northwestern Argentina.	Buenos Aires' population is around 4000; it will take another century for it to double.

Still, Buenos Aires remained a backwater in comparison to Andean settlements such as Tucumán, Córdoba, Salta, La Rioja and Jujuy. With the development of mines in the Andes and the incessant warfare in the Spanish empire swelling the demand for both cattle and horses, ranching became the core of the city's early economy. Spain maintained harsh restrictions on trade out of Buenos Aires and the increasingly frustrated locals turned to smuggling contraband.

The city continued to flourish and the crown was eventually forced to relax its restrictions and co-opt the growing international trade in the region. In 1776 Madrid made Buenos Aires the capital of the new Viceroyalty of the Río de la Plata, which included the world's largest silver mine in Potosí (in present-day Bolivia). For many of its residents, the new status was recognition that the adolescent city was outgrowing Spain's parental authority.

Although the new viceroyalty had internal squabbles over trade and control issues, when the British raided the city twice – in 1806 and 1807 – the response was unified. Locals rallied against the invaders without Spanish help and chased them out of town. These two battles gave the city's inhabitants confidence and an understanding of their self-reliance. It was just a matter of time until they broke with Spain.

Independence

When Napoleon conquered Spain and put his brother on the throne in 1808, Buenos Aires became further estranged from Madrid and finally declared its independence on May 25, 1810.

Six years later, on July 9, 1816, outlying areas of the viceroyalty also broke with Spain and founded the United Provinces of the River Plate. Almost immediately a power struggle arose between Buenos Aires and the provincial strongmen: the Federalist landowners of the interior provinces were concerned with preserving their autonomy, while the Unitarist businessmen of Buenos Aires tried to consolidate power in the city with an outward orientation toward overseas commerce and European ideas. Some of the interior provinces decided to go their own way, forming Paraguay in 1814, Bolivia in 1825 and Uruguay in 1828.

After more than a decade of violence and uncertainty, Juan Manuel de Rosas become governor of Buenos Aires in 1829. Although he swore that he was a Federalist, Rosas was more of an opportunist – a Federalist when it suited him and a Unitarist once he controlled the city. He required that all international trade be funneled through Buenos Aires rather than proceeding directly to the provinces, and he set ominous political precedents, creating the *mazorca* (his ruthless political police) and institutionalizing torture.

Argentina's national beer, Quilmes, is named after the now decimated indigenous group of northwest Argentina. It's also the name of a city in the province of Buenos Aires.

1776	1806 & 1807	May 25, 1810	1829
Buenos Aires becomes capital of the new Spanish Viceroyalty of the Río de la Plata, which included what are today Bolivia, Argentina, Paraguay and Uruguay.	British troops raid the city but are beaten back by the people of Buenos Aires in two battles, now celebrated as La Reconquista (the Reconquest) and La Defensa (the Defense).	Buenos Aires declares its independence from Spain, although actual independence is still several years off. The city renames its main square Plaza de Mayo to commemorate the occasion.	Federalist *caudillo* Juan Manuel de Rosas takes control of Buenos Aires and becomes its governor; BA's influence increases dramatically during his 23-year reign.

SMUGGLING IN BUENOS AIRES

It's not a coincidence that one of the most popular whiskeys served in Buenos Aires is called Old Smuggler. The city's history of trading in contraband goes all the way back to its founding. Some argue that the culture of corruption, so pervasive in Argentina, is tolerated because the historical role of smuggling in Buenos Aires led to a 'tradition' of rule-bending.

The Spanish empire kept tight regulations on its ports and only certain cities were allowed to trade goods with other countries. Buenos Aires, originally on the periphery of the empire, was hard to monitor and therefore not allowed to buy from or sell to other Europeans. Located at the mouth of the Río de la Plata, the settlement was an ideal point of entry to the continent for traders. Buenos Aires merchants turned to smuggling everything from textiles and precious metals to weapons and slaves. Portuguese-manufactured goods flooded the city and made their way inland to present-day Bolivia, Paraguay and even Peru.

Later, the British and high-seas pirates found a ready and willing trading partner in Buenos Aires (and also introduced a taste for fine whiskeys). An increasing amount of wealth passed through the city and much of the initial growth of Buenos Aires was fueled by the trade in contraband. As smuggling was an open game, without favored imperial merchants, it offered a chance for upward social mobility and gave birth to a commercially oriented middle class.

One of the best-known contemporary accounts of postindependence Argentina is Domingo Faustino Sarmiento's *Life in the Argentine Republic in the Days of the Tyrants* (1868). Also superb is his seminal classic, *Facundo, Or Civilization and Barbarism* (1845).

The Fleeting Golden Years

Rosas' overthrow came in 1852 at the hands of Justo José de Urquiza, a rival governor who tried to transfer power to his home province of Entre Rios. In protest, Buenos Aires briefly seceded from the union, but it was reestablished as the capital when Bartolomé Mitre crushed Urquiza's forces in 1861. From there, Buenos Aires never looked back and became the undisputed power center of the country.

The economy boomed and Buenos Aires became a port town of 90,000 people in the late 1860s. Immigrants poured in from Spain, Italy and Germany, followed by waves of newcomers from Croatia, Ireland, Poland and Ukraine. Its population grew nearly seven-fold from 1869 to 1895, to over 670,000 people. The new residents worked in the port, lived tightly in crammed tenement buildings, developed tango, and jump-started the leftist labor movement. The onslaught of Europeans not only expanded Buenos Aires into a major international capital but gave the city its rich multicultural heritage, famous idiosyncrasies and sharp political differences.

1852	1862	1868	1869–95
Federalist and former Rosas ally Justo José de Urquiza defeats Rosas at the Battle of Caseros and, in 1853, draws up Argentina's first constitution.	Bartolomé Mitre, governor of Buenos Aires province, poet and founder of *La Nación* newspaper, becomes president after defeating Urquiza's federal forces.	Intellectual Domingo Faustino Sarmiento is elected president. He encourages immigration, ramps up public education and pushes to Europeanize the country.	The Argentine economy booms, immigration skyrockets and Buenos Aires' population grows from 95,000 to 670,000.

By Argentina's centennial in 1910, Buenos Aires was a veritable metropolis. The following years witnessed the construction of the subway, while British companies built modern gas, electrical and sewer systems. Buenos Aires was at the height of a golden age, its bustling streets full of New World businesses, art, architecture and fashion. Argentina grew rich during this time based on its meat production. Advances in refrigeration and the country's ability to ship beef to distant lands was key to its economic success. In fact, by the beginning of WWI, Argentina was one of the world's 10 richest countries, and ahead of France and Germany.

Conservative forces dominated the political sphere until 1916, when Radical Party leader Hipólito Yrigoyen took control of the government in a move that stressed fair and democratic elections. After a prolonged period of elite rule, this was the first time Argentina's burgeoning middle class obtained a political voice.

It was also at this time that Argentina's fortunes started to change, but unfortunately not for the better. Export prices dropped off, wages stagnated and workers became increasingly frustrated and militant. La Semana Trágica (Tragic Week), when over 100 protesters were killed during a metalworkers' strike, was the culmination of these tensions; some say this radical reaction was due to the government being pressured by moneyed interests. The Wall Street crash of 1929 dealt the final blow to the export markets and a few months later, in 1930, the military took over the country in a coup led by General José Félix Uriburu. The golden age rapidly became a distant memory.

This was the first of many military coups that blemished the rest of the century and served to shackle the progress of the nation. Scholars have argued that the events that culminated in the 2001 economic collapse can be traced back to the 1930 military takeover.

The Age of the Peróns

During WWII the rural poor migrated into Buenos Aires in search of work. The number of people living in the city nearly tripled and it soon held a third of the national population (which is in fact similar to the percentage today). The growing strength of these urban working classes swept populist Lieutenant-General Juan Domingo Perón into the presidency in 1946. Perón had been stationed for a time in Italy and developed his own brand of watered-down Mussolini-style fascism. He quickly nationalized large industry, including the railways, and created Argentina's first welfare state. Borrowing from Fascist Italy and Germany, Perón carefully cultivated his iconic image and held massive popular rallies in Plaza de Mayo.

A fascinating, fictionalized version of the life of ex-president Juan Perón, culminating in his return to Buenos Aires in 1973, is Tomás Eloy Martínez' *The Perón Novel* (1998).

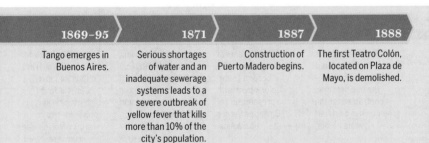

1869–95	1871	1887	1888
Tango emerges in Buenos Aires.	Serious shortages of water and an inadequate sewerage systems leads to a severe outbreak of yellow fever that kills more than 10% of the city's population.	Construction of Puerto Madero begins.	The first Teatro Colón, located on Plaza de Mayo, is demolished.

The glamorous Eva Duarte, a onetime radio soap-opera star, became the consummate celebrity first lady upon marrying Perón, and an icon who would eclipse Perón himself. Known as Evita, her powerful social-assistance foundation reached out to lower-class women through give-aways of such things as baby bottles and strollers, and the construction of schools and hospitals. The masses felt a certain empathy with Evita, who was also born into the working class. Her premature death in 1952 came just before things went sour and her husband's political power plummeted.

After Evita's death Perón financed payouts to workers by simply printing new money, bungled the economy, censored the press and cracked down on opposition. He was strikingly less popular without Evita, and was deposed by the military in 1955 after two terms in office. Perón lived in exile in Spain while a series of military coups ailed the nation. When he returned in 1973, there were escalating tensions from left and right parties; even if he'd lived to serve his term of re-election, Perón would have had too much on his plate. His successor, his hapless third wife Isabel, had even less staying power and her overthrow by a military junta in 1976 came as no surprise.

Although the effects of Perón's personal political achievements are debatable, the Peronist party, based largely on his ideals, has endured.

Nunca Más (Never Again; 1984), the official report of the National Commission on the Disappeared, systematically details military abuses from 1976 to 1983 – during Argentina's Dirty War.

The Dirty War

The new military rulers instituted the Process of National Reorganisation, known as El Proceso, and this was headed by the notorious Jorge Rafael Videla. Ostensibly an effort to remake Argentina's political culture and modernize the flagging economy, El Proceso was little more than a Cold War–era attempt to kill off or intimidate all leftist political opposition in the country.

Based in Buenos Aires, a left-wing guerrilla group known as the Montoneros bombed foreign buildings, kidnapped executives for ransom and robbed banks to finance its armed struggle against the government. The Montoneros were composed mainly of educated, middle-class youths; they were hunted down by the military government in a campaign known as La Guerra Sucia (the Dirty War). Somewhere between 10,000 and 30,000 civilians died – many of them simply 'disappeared' while walking down the street or sleeping in their beds. Many were tortured to death, or sedated and dropped from planes into the Río de la Plata. Anyone who seemed even sympathetic to the Montoneros could be whisked off the streets and detained, tortured or killed. A great number of the 'disappeared' are still unaccounted for today.

Hectór Olivera's 1983 film *Funny Dirty Little War* is an unsettling but excellent black comedy set in a fictitious town just before the 1976 military coup.

1897	1908	1916	1930
Puerto Madero is completed, but Eduardo Madero – the businessman contracted for the project – has died four years earlier.	After 20 years of construction, the second Teatro Colón opens with a presentation of Giuseppe Verdi's opera *Aida*.	Hipólito Yrigoyen, leader of the Radical Party popular with the middle classes, is elected president and introduces minimum wage to counter inflation; he's re-elected in 1928.	Hipólito Yrigoyen is overthrown in a military coup led by General José Félix Uriburu, who stays in power for two years, after which civilian rule is restored.

ESMA: ARGENTINA'S AUSCHWITZ

Along a busy road in the BA neighborhood of Nuñez is an imposing building officially called the Naval Mechanics School but better known as ESMA. During Argentina's 1976–83 military rule it served as an infamous detention center where some 5000 people were brutally tortured and killed. Truckloads of blindfolded prisoners were unloaded outside the building, taken to the basement, sedated and killed. Some were murdered by firing squads and others were drugged and dropped from planes into the Río de la Plata on twice-weekly 'death flights'. The building also served as a clandestine maternity center that housed babies taken from their mothers (many of whom were subsequently killed) to be given to police and military couples without children.

In 2004, as part of president Néstor Kirchner's effort to revisit the Dirty War crimes, the building was designated a memorial museum, handed over to a human-rights group and named the Space for Memory and Promotion and Defense of Human Rights. But reviving the memory was like opening Pandora's box. A public debate ensued on how to tackle the museum: whether to make it educational, poignant, moralizing or realistic. This debate – together with the human-rights group's insistence that all campus buildings, some of which were still occupied by the Navy, be vacated – delayed the museum's launch. (In the end, the Navy did move to another locale.)

Eventually, it was agreed that it was best to leave the space bare, with few explanatory signs, and so commemorate the victims. On the public tours (see www.espaciomemoria.ar) through the bleak rooms, guides tell the stories of detainees' tragic lives. According to photographer Marcelo Brodsky, whose brother disappeared in ESMA, 'The site is charged with torture sessions, muffled screams, odors and sounds'. This reminder of Argentina's state terror allows visitors to ponder the frailty of democracy and contemplate the evil of military dictatorships not only in Argentina but around the world.

The military leaders let numerous aspects of the country's well-being slip into decay, along with the entire national economy. When Ronald Reagan took power in the USA in 1981, he reversed Jimmy Carter's condemnation of the junta's human-rights abuses and even invited the generals to visit Washington, DC. Backed by this relationship with the USA, the military was able to solicit development loans from international lenders, but endemic corruption quickly drained the funds into their Swiss bank accounts.

The Return to Democracy

The military dictatorship that ruled the country with an iron fist lasted from 1976 to 1983. General Leopoldo Galtieri took the reins of the draconian military junta in 1981, but its power was unraveling: the economy

1946	1952	1955	1976–83
Populist Lieutenant-General Juan Domingo Perón is elected president; Perón and his young wife Eva Perón ('Evita') make sweeping changes to the political structure.	Evita dies of cancer on July 26 at age 33, one year into Juan Perón's second term as president. Her death severely weakes the political might of her husband.	After the economy slides into recession, Perón loses further political clout; he is thrown from the presidency and exiled to Spain after a military coup.	Under the military leadership of General Jorge Videla, Argentina is launched into the Dirty War. In eight years, up to 30,000 people 'disappear'.

was in recession, interest rates skyrocketed and protesters took to the streets of Buenos Aires. A year later, Galtieri tried to divert national attention by goading the UK into a war over control of the Falkland Islands (known in Argentina as Las Islas Malvinas). The British had more resolve than the junta had imagined and Argentina was easily defeated. The greatest blow came when the British nuclear submarine *Conqueror* torpedoed the Argentine heavy cruiser *General Belgrano,* killing 323 men. Argentina still holds that the ship was returning to harbor.

Embarrassed and proven ineffectual, the military regime fell apart and a new civilian government under Raúl Alfonsín took control in 1983. Alfonsín enjoyed a small amount of success and was able to negotiate a few international loans, but he could not limit inflation or constrain public spending. By 1989 inflation was out of control and Alfonsín left office five months early, when Carlos Menem took power.

Menem & the Boom Years

Under the guidance of his shrewd economic minister, Domingo Cavallo, the skillfully slick Carlos Menem introduced free-market reforms to stall Argentina's economic slide. Many of the state-run industries were privatized and, most importantly, the peso was fixed by law at an equal rate to the American dollar. Foreign investment poured into the country. Buenos Aires began to thrive again: buildings were restored and new businesses boomed. The capital's Puerto Madero docks were redeveloped into an upscale leisure district, tourism increased and optimism was in the air. People in Buenos Aires bought new cars, talked on cell phones and took international vacations.

Although the Argentine economy seemed robust to the casual observer, by Menem's second term (1995–99) some things were already amiss. The inflexibility imposed by the economic reforms made it difficult for the country to respond to foreign competition, and Mexico's 1995 currency collapse jolted a number of banks in Buenos Aires. Not only did Menem fail to reform public spending but corruption was so widespread that it dominated daily newspaper headlines.

The Economic Crisis

As an economic slowdown deepened into a recession, voters turned to the mayor of Buenos Aires, Fernando de la Rúa, and elected him president in 1999. He was faced with the need to cut public spending and hike taxes during the recession.

The economy stagnated further, investors panicked, the bond market teetered on the brink of oblivion and the country seemed unable to service its increasingly heavy international debt. Cavallo was brought

The Falklands War is still a somewhat touchy subject in Argentina. If the subject comes up, try to call the islands the Malvinas instead of the Falklands, as many Argentines have been taught from a young age that they have always belonged to Argentina.

Carlos Menem's Syrian ancestry earned him the nickname 'El Turco' (The Turk). In 2001 he married Cecilia Bolocco, a former Miss Universe 35 years his junior; they're now separated.

1982	1983	1989	1992
General Leopoldo Galtieri provokes the UK into a war over control of the Falkland Islands (Las Islas Malvinas), but Argentina is easily defeated by the British.	The military regime collapses, ending the Dirty War; civilian government is restored under Radical leader Raúl Alfonsín, but he leaves office early due to growing inflation problems.	Peronist Carlos Menem succeeds Alfonsín as president and overcomes the hyperinflation that reached nearly 200% per month by instituting free-market reforms.	A bomb attack at the Israeli embassy kills 29 and injures over 200.

back in as the economic minister and in January 2001, rather than declaring a debt default, he sought over US$20 million more in loans from the IMF.

Argentina had been living on credit and it could no longer sustain its lifestyle. The facade of a successful economy had been ripped away, and the indebted, weak inner workings were exposed. As the storm clouds gathered, there was a run on the banks. Between July and November, Argentines withdrew around US$20 billion, hiding it under their mattresses or sending it abroad. In a last-ditch effort to keep money in the country, the government imposed a limit of US$1000 a month on bank withdrawals. Called the *corralito* (little corral), the strategy crushed many informal sectors of the economy that function on cash (taxis, food markets), and rioters and looters inevitably took to the streets. As the government tried to hoard the remaining hard currency, all bank savings were converted to pesos and any remaining trust in the government was broken. Middle-class protesters joined the fray in a series of pot-and-pan-banging protests, and both Cavallo and de la Rúa bowed to the inevitable and resigned.

Two new presidents came and went in the same week and the world's greatest default on public debt was declared. The third presidential successor, former Buenos Aires province governor Eduardo Duhalde, was able to hold onto power. In order to have more flexibility, he dismantled the currency-board system that had pegged the peso to the American dollar for a decade. The peso devalued rapidly and people's savings were reduced to a fraction of their earlier value. In January 2002 the banks were only open for a total of six days and confidence in the government was virtually nonexistent. The economy ceased to function: cash became scarce, imports stopped and demand for nonessential items flat-lined. More than half of the fiercely proud Argentine people found themselves below the national poverty line: the once comfortable middle class woke up in the lower classes and the former lower classes were plunged into destitution. Businesspeople ate at soup kitchens and homelessness became rampant.

At least two terms came about due to Argentina's economic crisis: *el corralito* (a little corral) refers to the cap placed on cash withdrawals from bank accounts during 'La Crisis', while *cacerolazo* (from the word *cacerola*, meaning pan) is the street protest where angry people bang pots and saucepans.

Enter Néstor Kirchner

Duhalde, to his credit, was able to use his deep political-party roots to keep the country together through to elections in April 2003. Numerous candidates entered the contest; the top two finishers were Menem (making a foray out of retirement for the campaign) and Néstor Kirchner, little-known governor of the thinly populated Patagonian province of Santa Cruz. Menem bowed out of the runoff election and Kirchner became president.

1994	1999	2001–02	2003
Eighty-five people are killed and over 100 are wounded when a Jewish community center is bombed.	The mayor of Buenos Aires, Fernando de la Rúa, is voted president of Argentina as a result of dissatisfaction with the corrupt Menem administration; he inherits $114 billion in public debt.	Argentina commits the largest debt default in world history; Argentina's economy is ruined, which sparks massive riots and looting around the country.	Néstor Kirchner – a governor from Patagonia's province of Santa Cruz – is sworn in as Argentina's president, with 22% of the vote.

Kirchner was the antidote to the slick and dishonest Buenos Aires establishment politicians. He was an outsider, with his entire career in the provinces and a personal air of sincerity and austerity. The people were looking for a fresh start and someone to believe in – and they found that in Kirchner.

During his term Kirchner defined himself as a hard-nosed fighter. In 2003 he managed to negotiate a debt-refinancing deal with the IMF under which Argentina would only pay interest on its loans. In 2006 Argentina repaid its $9.5 billion debt, not a small feat, which drove his approval rating up to 80%. Annual economic growth was averaging an impressive 8%, the poverty rate dropped to about 25% and unemployment nose-dived. A side effect of the 2001 collapse was a boom in international tourism, as foreigners enjoyed cosmopolitan Buenos Aires at bargain prices, injecting tourist money into the economy.

But not everything was bread and roses. The fact that Argentina had repaid its debt was fantastic news indeed, but economic stability didn't necessarily follow. In fact, a series of problems ensued during Kirchner's presidency: high inflation rates caused by a growing energy shortage, unequal distribution of wealth, and a rising breach between rich and poor that was slowly obliterating the middle class.

On the foreign-policy front, Kirchner's belligerence became aimed at outside forces. In November 2005, when George Bush flew in for the 34-nation Summit of the Americas, his presence sparked massive demonstrations around the country. Although anti-US sentiment unites most Argentines, some feared that Kirchner's schmoozing with Venezuelan president Hugo Chávez alienated potential investors in the United States and Europe.

Kirchner made admirable strides toward addressing the human-rights abuses of the military dictatorship. In 2005 the Supreme Court lifted an amnesty law that protected former military officers suspected of Dirty War crimes, and this led to a succession of trials that put several of them away for life.

The Trials & Tribulations of Cristina

When Néstor Kirchner stepped aside in July 2007 in favor of his wife's candidacy for the presidential race, many started wondering: would 'Queen Cristina' (as she's often called due to her regal comportment) be just a puppet for her husband, who intended to rule behind the scenes?

In the October 2007 presidential election, Cristina Fernández de Kirchner succeeded in her ambition to move from first lady to president. Weak opposition and her husband's enduring clout were some of the reasons for Cristina's clear-cut victory, despite the lack of straight-

Unlike your typical politician, Amado Boudou – Cristina Kirchner's vice president – drives a Harley-Davidson and jams with his band on a Fender guitar. But like your typical politician, he's been accused of embezzlement and money laundering.

2005	2007	May 2010	Oct 27, 2010
An amnesty law that protected Dirty War military officers suspected of human-rights abuses is abolished	Lawyer, senator and former first lady Cristina Fernández de Kirchner becomes Argentina's first woman president elected by popular vote.	Argentina celebrates its bicentennial with a bang; BA's Av 9 de Julio shuts down for many colorful festivities, and the Teatro Colón reopens after four years of restoration.	Néstor Kirchner dies of heart failure.

forward policies during her campaign. While this was not the first time Argentina had had a female head of state (Isabel Perón held a brief presidency by inheriting her husband's term), Cristina was the first woman to be elected president by popular vote in Argentina. As a lawyer and senator she has often been compared to Hillary Clinton; as a fashion-conscious political figure with a penchant for chic dresses and designer bags, she also evokes memories of Evita.

Cristina's tumultuous presidency has been laced with scandals, unpopular decisions and roller-coaster approval ratings. In March 2008 she significantly raised the export tax on soybeans, infuriating farmers, who soon went on strike and blockaded highways. In June 2009 Kirchner's power base was shattered during the mid-term elections, when her ruling party lost its majority in both houses of Congress. Soon after, she enacted an unpopular law set to break apart Clarín, a media conglomerate that often reflected unfavorably on her presidency. All the while, Argentina has been hounded by inflation that has been unofficially estimated at up to 25%.

Her presidency has seen some positive sides, however. The economy grew strongly during the first part of her tenure, bolstered by high consumer spending and strong demand for the country's agricultural exports and manufactured goods. In a true Peronist vein, Cristina implemented a wide range of social programs to beef up the pension system, benefit impoverished children and help fight cases related to crimes against humanity. And in July 2010 she signed a bill that legalized same-sex marriage in Argentina, making it Latin America's first country to do so.

On October 27, 2010, Cristina's presidency was dealt a serious blow when Néstor Kirchner died suddenly of a heart attack. As Néstor was expected to run for the presidency in 2011, this was widely seen as a disaster for the Kirchner dynasty. But the country rallied around Cristina's sorrow, and her popularity in early 2011 remained high enough that she ran for office again and was easily re-elected. She had run on a platform that appealed to the populist vote, promising to raise incomes, restore industry and maintain Argentina's economic boom. Her approach worked like a charm, but her popularity wasn't to last. For more, see p176.

2011	2012	2013	2014
Her husband's untimely death late the previous year leaves Cristina Kirchner in the lurch, but she easily wins re-election in October.	Inflation is running at about 25% (though government figures say it's less than 10%). Kirchner passes a law restricting the sale of US dollars, creating huge black-market demand.	Kirchner loses major support during October's mid-term elections. Her dreams of changing the constitution to allow her to run for a third presidential term quickly evaporate.	Argentina experiences its largest currency devaluation since 2002.

Music

A variety of music genres are well represented in Buenos Aires, especially when it comes to the city's most famous export, the tango. But BA's music scene is also about hybrids of overlapping sounds and styles. Traditional kinds of folklore, tango and *cumbia* (Colombian music) are melded with digital technology to create global tunes that are gaining recognition in living rooms and music festivals all around the world.

Tango Music

Small musical ensembles that accompanied early tango dances were influenced by polka, habanera, Spanish and Italian melodies, plus African *candombe* drums. The *bandoneón,* a type of small accordion, was brought into these sessions and has since become tango's signature instrument. The tango song was permeated with nostalgia for a disappearing way of life; it summarized the new urban experience for the immigrants. Themes ranged from profound feelings about changing neighborhoods to the figure of the mother, male friendship and betrayal by women. The lyrics, sometimes raunchy and sometimes sad, were sung in the street argot known as *lunfardo*.

No other musician has influenced tango like Carlos Gardel, the legendary singer who epitomized the soul of the genre

No other musician has influenced tango like Carlos Gardel, the legendary singer who epitomized the soul of the genre. He achieved stardom during tango's golden age, then became a cultural icon when his life was cut short by a plane crash at the height of his popularity. Over the years, other figures like Osvaldo Pugliese, Susana Rinaldi and Eladia Blásquez have also given life to the tango song. It was Àstor Piazzolla, however, who completely revolutionized the music with his *nuevo tango,* which introduced jazz and classical-music currents into traditional songs – and ruffled some feathers along the way.

Today, a clutch of new arrivals is keeping tango music alive and well, and in the spotlight. The most popular is the 12-musician cooperative **Orquesta Típica Fernández Fierro** (www.fernandezfierro.com), with its charismatic singer Walter Chino Laborde and several fantastic albums boasting new arrangements of traditional tangos. An award-winning documentary was made about them by Argentine-born, Brooklyn-based director Nicolas Entel.

Two other young orchestras to watch out for are **Orquesta Típica Imperial** (www.orquestaimperial.com.ar), which sometimes plays at *milongas* around town, and **El Afronte** (www.elafronte.com.ar), which plays on Monday and Wednesday at Bendito and Maldita Milongas in San Telmo (both at Perú 571).

Neo Tango

Like the rest of the music scene in Buenos Aires, a newer tango has evolved that's a hybrid of sounds and styles – making tango cool again with a younger audience. Musicians have been sampling and remixing classic tango songs, adding dance beats, breaks, scratches and synth lines, and committing other delightful heresies. This edgy genre has been called by many names: fusion tango, electrotango, tango electronica or neo-tango. Paris-based Gotan Project (a Franco-Suizo-Argentine trio) was the first to popularize this style, with its debut album *La Revancha del Tango,* which throws into the mix samples from speeches by Che Guevara and Eva Perón and remixes by the likes of Austrian beatmeister Peter Kruder. Its follow-up albums don't break the mold like the first but are still great if you like the Gotan sound.

THE STARS OF TANGO

Gardel

In June 1935 a Cuban woman committed suicide in Havana, and a woman in New York and another in Puerto Rico tried to poison themselves, all over the same man – whom none of them had ever met. The man was tango singer Carlos Gardel, known as El Zorzal Criollo (the King of Tango) or the songbird of Buenos Aires, who had just died in a plane crash in Colombia.

Born in France, Gardel was the epitome of the immigrant porteño whose destitute single mother brought him to Buenos Aires at the age of three. In his youth he worked at a variety of menial jobs and entertained his neighbors with his rapturous singing. A performing career began after he befriended Uruguayan-born José Razzano, and the two of them sang together in a popular duo until Razzano lost his voice. From 1917 onward Gardel performed solo.

Carlos Gardel played an enormous role in creating the tango *canción* (song). Almost single-handedly, he took the style out of Buenos Aires' tenements and brought it to Paris and New York. His crooning voice, suaveness and overall charisma made him an immediate success in Latin American countries. The timing couldn't have been better, as he rose to fame in tango's golden years of the 1920s and 1930s. Gardel became a recording and film star, but his later career was tragically cut short by that fatal plane crash. Every day a steady procession of pilgrims visits Carlos Gardel's sarcophagus in the Cementerio de la Chacarita in Buenos Aires, where a lit cigarette often smolders between the metal fingers of his life-size statue. The large, devoted community of his followers, known as *gardelianos,* cannot pass a day without listening to his songs or watching his films. Another measure of his ongoing influence is the common saying 'Gardel sings better every day'. Elvis should be so lucky.

Piazzolla

Gardel may have brought tango to the world, but it was El Gran Ástor (the Great Ástor), as Argentines like to call Ástor Piazzolla (1921–92), who pushed its limits. The great Argentine composer and *bandoneón* (small accordian) virtuoso, who played in the leading Aníbal Troilo orchestra in the late 1930s and early 1940s, was the greatest innovator of tango. He revolutionized traditional tango by infusing it with elements of jazz and classical music such as counterpoints, fugues and various harmonies.

This new style, known as *nuevo tango*, became an international hit in Europe (Piazzolla lived on and off in Italy and France) and North America (he spent his early years and a couple of later stints in New York). In his native land, however, it encountered considerable resistance; a saying even stated 'in Argentina everything may change – except the tango'. It took years for Piazzolla's controversial new style to be accepted, and he even received death threats for his break with tradition.

Piazzolla was an incredibly prolific composer; it's estimated that his output includes some 1000 pieces. These include soundtracks for about 40 films; an opera that he wrote with poet Horacio Ferrer, *María de Buenos Aires*; and compositions based on texts and poems by Jorge Luis Borges.

Piazzolla's legacy lives on. Some of the greatest contemporary musicians, such as Yo-Yo Ma, have recorded albums dedicated to El Gran Ástor (such as the 1999 *Soul of the Tango – The Music of Ástor Piazzolla*). The new wave of electronic tango often samples his music and the 2003 album *Astor Piazzolla Remixed* features his songs remixed with dance beats and added vocals, all done by an international cast of DJs and producers.

TANGO MUSIC HALL OF FAME

→ Carlos Di Sarli (1903–60) – Pianist, composer and orchestra leader.

→ Juan D'Arienzo (1900–76) – Violinist and orchestra leader.

→ Carlos Gardel (1890–1935) – Singer and actor.

→ Ástor Piazzolla (1921–92) – *Bandoneón* (accordionlike instrument) player and composer.

→ Roberto Goyeneche (1926–94) – Singer.

→ Aníbal Troilo (1914–75) – *Bandoneón* player, composer and orchestra leader.

→ Osvaldo Pugliese (1905–95) – Pianist, composer and orchestra leader.

→ Enrique Santos Discépolo (1901–51) – Composer and poet.

→ Homero Manzi (1907–51) – Lyricist and poet.

→ Horacio Salgán (b 1916) – Pianist, composer and orchestra leader.

→ Julio Sosa (1926–64) – Singer.

→ Eladia Blázquez (1931–2005) – Singer, pianist and composer.

→ Susana Rinaldi (b 1935) – Singer.

→ Adriana Varela (b 1952) – Singer.

The best of the genre's albums so far is likely *Bajofondo Tango Club,* by the Grammy-winning collective Bajofondo. It's spearheaded by Argentine producer Gustavo Santaolalla, who won two best-original-score Oscars for *Brokeback Mountain* and *Babel;* he also scored the films *Amores Perros* and *21 Grams,* and produced albums by such prominent artists as Café Tacuba and Kronos Quartet. Praised as more Argentine than Gotan Project (whose trio is composed of only one Argentine), its first album has subtle performances by a variety of *bandoneonistas* within a hypnotic framework of lounge, house and trip-hop. Its third album, *Mar Dulce,* is a catchy creation that throws more folk and rock into the mix and has a strong international cast of singers, such as Spanish hip-hop star Mala Rodríguez and the Canadian-Portuguese Nelly Furtado.

Another neo-tango collective to make an international name for itself is Tanghetto, with two Latin Grammy nominations. This six-member group mixes elements of rock, jazz, flamenco and *candombe* (a drum-based musical style of Uruguay).

Rock & Pop

Argentine rock started in the late 1960s with a trio of groups – Almendra (great melodies and poetic lyrics), Manal (urban blues) and Los Gatos (pop) – leading the pack. Evolution was slow, however; the 1966 and 1976 military regimes didn't take a shine to the liberalism and freedom that rock represented. It didn't help that anarchy-loving, beat-music rocker Billy Bond induced destructive mayhem at a 1972 Luna Park concert, re-enforcing the theme of rock music as a social threat.

Underground groups and occasional concerts managed to keep the genre alive, and after the Falklands War in 1982 (when English lyrics were not actually allowed on the air) radio stations founded *rock nacional* and helped the movement's momentum gain ground. Argentine rock produced national icons like Charly Garciá (formerly a member of the pioneering group Sui Generis) and Fito Páez (a socially conscious pop-hippie). Sensitive poet-songwriter Alberto Luis Spinetta of Almendra fame also had an early influence on the Argentine rock movement, later incorporating jazz into his LPs. Another mythical figure is Andrés

Charly García's version of the Argentine national anthem does what Jimi Hendrix did for 'The Star-Spangled Banner', but it earned García a court appearance for 'lacking respect for national symbols'.

Calamaro, frontman of the popular 1970s band Los Abuelos de la Nada. He later emigrated to Spain, where he formed the acclaimed Los Rodríguez; he's been performing solo since the late 1990s.

More recent Argentine groups that have played *rock nacional* include Soda Stereo (ex-member Gustavo Cerati's *Fuerza Natural* won the 2010 Latin Grammy for best rock album); cultlike Patricio Rey y sus Redonditos de Ricota (its legendary leader Indio Solari now has a solo career); versatile Los Piojos (mixing rock, blues, ska and the Uruguayan music styles *murga* and *candombe*); and Los Ratones Paranóicos, who in 1995 opened for the Rolling Stones' spectacularly successful five-night stand in Buenos Aires.

Los Fabulosos Cadillacs (who were the winners of a Grammy award in 1998 for best alternative Latin rock group) have popularized ska and reggae, along with groups such as Los Auténticos Decadentes, Los Pericos and Los Cafres. Almafuerte, descended from the earlier Hermética, is Buenos Aires' leading heavy-metal band. The bands Dos Minutos and Expulsados seek to emulate punk-rock legends the Ramones, who are popular in Argentina. Other classic bands include hippyish Los Divididos (descendants of the famous group Sumo), Mendozan trio Los Enanitos Verdes and the wildly unconventional Babasónicos.

The band Les Luthiers satirizes the middle class or the military using irreverent songs played with unusual instruments, many of which have been built by the band members themselves. Another quirky character is the late Sandro – known as the Argentine Elvis – whose death in January 2010 saw tens of thousands of *porteños* gather in the streets of Buenos Aires to mourn his demise.

Argentine women also rock. Singer Patricia Sosa has a captivating voice and performs a mix of rock, soul and blues; her closest counterpart in the English-speaking world is Janis Joplin. The most recent singer-songwriter who has gained fame abroad is Juana Molina, whose ambient music with electronic flair has been compared to Bjork's. Juana Chang and the Wookies combined indie-rock, garage and punk (she now sings with the Kumbia Queers). Keep an eye out for Denise Murz, a Lady Gaga–style electro-pop diva, and the multitalented, folksy Sol Pereyra.

Today some of Argentina's most cutting-edge bands include catchy Miranda! (electro-pop), wacky Bersuit Vergarabat (utilizing multigenre tunes with political, offensive and wave-making lyrics), free-willed La Renga (blue collar, no nonsense and political), La Portuaria, who collaborated with David Byrne (rock fusion influenced by jazz and R&B), and Valentin y Los Volcanos (indie-pop with great guitar music). And don't miss the multicultural, alternative and eclectic Kevin Johansen.

CUARTETO

Born in Córdoba in the early 1940s, *cuarteto* is Argentina's original pop music. Despised by the middle and upper classes for its arresting rhythm and offbeat musical pattern (called the '*tunga-tunga*'), as well as for its working-class lyrics, it's definitely music from the margins. Although definitively *cordobés* (from Córdoba), it's played in working-class bars, dance halls and stadiums throughout the country.

Blues & Jazz

The high degree of crossover between Buenos Aires' blues and rock scenes is illustrated by the path of the late guitar wizard Pappo (1950–2005). An elder statesman, Pappo was in the groundbreaking rock group Los Abuelos de la Nada and became involved with the seminal blues-rock band Pappo's Blues, as well as Los Gatos and others. He played hard-driving, full-tilt rockin' blues and was especially great when covering such American masters as Howlin' Wolf, BB King and Muddy Waters.

Guitarist-singer Miguel 'Botafogo' Vilanova is an alumnus of Pappo's blues and an imposing figure in his own right. Also worth checking out is La Mississippi, a seven-member group that has been performing rock-blues since the late 1980s. Memphis La Blusera was around BA's blues scene for a long time until it broke up in 2008; it once worked with North American legend Taj Mahal.

Lalo Schifrin is an Argentine pianist, composer and conductor with a jazz background; he's most famous for writing the *Mission: Impossible* theme. He's also won four Grammy awards and has been nominated for six Oscars. In the late 1950s, Schifrin performed with Gato Barbieri, another notable composer and jazz saxophonist. Carlos Alberto Franzetti is a big-band composer who wrote *The Mambo Kings* (1992) and won a Latin Grammy in 2001 for his *Tango Fatal* album.

Guitarist Luis Salinas is known for his mellow and melodic tunes that run along George Benson lines but are a bit less poppy; be sure to check out his jazz takes on such traditional Argentine forms as the *chacarera, chamamé* and tango. Dino Saluzzi, a *bandoneón* player originally from Salta who began recording in the '70s, was one of the first Argentine musicians to mix folklore, tango and jazz. Dino's son José is a renowned guitarist in his own right.

Another musician and son of an Argentine jazz legend is Javier Malosetti, son of pianist Walter Malosetti. Javier's group Electrohope blends jazz, blues, rock and swing with Latin rhythms and funk. Meanwhile, jazz guitarist Tomás Becú's debut album, *Bushwick* (2007), is stellar. For wildly experimental jazz check out the Gordöloco Trío, which fuses ambient, funk and jazz in its 20-minute-long songs.

Drummer Sebastián Peyceré, who favors a funk-tinged fusion, has played with the likes of Paquito D'Rivera, BB King and Stanley Jordan. Finally, BA's own version of the Sultans of Swing is the Caoba Jazz Band, who for years has been playing 1920s and '30s New Orleans–style jazz for the love of it.

Latin & Electronica

DIGITAL CUMBIA

In 2007 electronic musicians from Zizek Records, a homegrown BA label, created 'digital *cumbia*' by fusing various forms of *cumbia* and Argentine traditional music with reggaeton, dance-hall, hip-hop and electronic beats.

Buenos Aires' young clubbers have embraced the *música tropical* trend that's swept Latin America in recent years. Many a BA booty is shaken to the lively, Afro-Latin sounds of salsa, merengue and especially *cumbia*. Originating in Colombia, *cumbia* combines an infectious dance rhythm with lively melodies, often carried by brass. An offshoot is *cumbia experimental* or *cumbia villera,* a fusion of *cumbia* and gangsta posturing with a punk edge and reggae overtones. Born of Buenos Aires' shantytowns, its aggressive lyrics deal with marginalization, poverty, drugs, sex and the Argentine economic crisis.

A forerunner of the movement is Axel Krygier, the king of psychedelic Latin, whose latest album *Pesebre* (2010) is a brilliant fusion of jazz, rock, *cumbia*, electronica, Argentine folklore and experimental sounds. Kumbia Queers is a female band from Argentina and Mexico whose version of *cumbia* is known as tropipunk.

Dance music is big in BA, with DJs working the clubs well into the morning. A few major electronic names to look out for are Bad Boy Orange (big on drums and bass); Aldo Haydar (a true veteran of progressive house); local boy made international star Hernán Cattaneo (you loved him at Burning Man, remember?); Gustavo Lamas (a blend of ambient pop and electro house) and Diego Ro-K (also known as the Maradona of Argentine DJs).

One of BA's most `interesting music spectacles is La Bomba del Tiempo, a collective of drummers that features some of Argentina's leading percussionists. Its explosive performances are conducted by Santiago Vázquez, who communicates with the musicians through a language of mysterious signs – the result is an incredible improvisational union that simulates electronic dance music and sounds different every time. During the summer it plays open-air at Ciudad Cultural Konex (p150) every Monday evening; it's also featured at various happenings and parties in BA's clubs.

Folk Music

The folk music of Argentina is inspired by generations of immigrants and spans a variety of styles, including *chacarera, chamamé* and *zamba*. The late Atahualpa Yupanqui was a giant of Argentine folk music, which takes much of its inspiration from the northwestern Andean region and countries to the north, especially Bolivia and Peru. Los Chalchaleros, a northern Argentine folk institution, was around from 1948 to 2003. Probably the best-known Argentine folk artist outside of South America, however, is the late Mercedes Sosa of Tucumán, whose progressive, politicized lyrics earned her the title 'the voice of the voiceless ones'.

Current contemporary performers include El Chaqueño Palavecino of Salta; Suna Rocha (also an actress) of Córdoba; Antonio Tarragó Ross; Víctor Heredia; León Gieco (aka 'The Argentine Bob Dylan') and the Conjunto Pro Música de Rosario. Singer-songwriter-guitarist Horacio Guarany's 2004 album *Cantor De Cantores* was nominated for a Latin Grammy in the Best Folk Album category.

Of the younger generation, the artists to watch out for are Chango Spasiuk (an accordion player who popularized *chamamé* music abroad), Mariana Baraj (a singer and percussionist who experiments with Latin America's traditional folk music as well as elements of jazz, classical music and improvisation) and Soledad Pastorutti (whose first two albums have been Sony's top sellers in Argentina – ever!).

Every genre of Argentine music is experiencing the same hybrid phenomenon of blending electronic music with more traditional sounds. Digital folklore, much like digital *cumbia* and neo-tango, is exploding. Tonolec, a duo (singer and synth player), combine traditional folk songs of the Toba indigenous community from Argentina's north (some of which have been passed down orally) with an electronic sound. The singer also uses traditional instruments in live gigs, creating a warm, world-music-style fusion. Two other digital-folklore groups to look out for are Onda Vaga, an acoustic band with smooth harmonies that add a jazzy feel to traditional folklore sounds, and Tremor, who mixes Andean flutes, the Argentine *bombo legüero* (drum), electric guitars and a synthesizer into a blend of ancient and digital sounds. Finally, there's Chancha via Circuito, whose 2010 album *Río Arriba* mixes melodic flutes and slow tempos, making it more meditative than dance oriented.

MUSIC LATIN & ELECTRONICA

Murga is a form of athletic musical theater composed of actors and percussionists. Primarily performed in Uruguay, *murga* in Argentina is more heavily focused on dancing than singing. You're most likely to see this exciting musical art form at Carnaval celebrations.

Literature & Cinema

Perhaps because of its history of authoritarian rule, Argentina has developed a strong literary heritage, with many contemporary writers using the country's darkest moments as inspiration for their complex and sometimes disturbing novels. Leading the classic writers' pack are Jorge Luis Borges, Julio Cortázar and Ernesto Sábato. Buenos Aires is also home to Argentina's vibrant, evolving film industry. The country has won two Oscars for best foreign-language film (in 1985 and 2009) – the only Latin American country ever to have won the award – and continues to produce excellent directors and movies.

Literature

One of Argentina's most influential pieces of classic literature is the epic poem by José Hernández, *Martín Fierro* (1872). Not only did this story about a gaucho outlaw lay the foundations of the Argentine *gauchesco* literary tradition but also it inspired the name of the short-lived but important literary magazine of the 1920s that published avant-garde works based on the 'art for art's sake' principle.

Julio Cortázar (1914–84) is an author well known to readers outside Argentina. He was born in Belgium to Argentine parents, moved to Buenos Aires at age four and died in self-imposed exile in Paris at the age of 70. His stories frequently plunge their characters out of everyday life into surrealistic situations. One such story was adapted into the film *Blow-Up* by Italian director Michelangelo Antonioni. Cortázar's novel *Hopscotch* takes place simultaneously in Buenos Aires and Paris and requires the reader to first read the book straight through, then read it a second time, 'hopscotching' through the chapters in a prescribed but nonlinear pattern for a completely different take on the story.

Another member of Borges' literary generation is Ernesto Sábato (1911–2011), whose complex and uncompromising novels have been extremely influential on later Argentine literature. *The Tunnel* (1948) is Sábato's engrossing existentialist novella of a porteño painter so obsessed with his art that it distorts his relationship with everything and everyone else.

Adolfo Bioy Casares (1914–99) and Borges were close friends and occasional collaborators. Bioy's sci-fi novella *The Invention of Morel* (1940) gave Alain Resnais the plot for his classic film *Last Year at Marienbad* and also introduced the idea of the holodeck decades before *Star Trek* existed.

The contemporary, postboom generation of Argentine writers is more reality-based, often reflecting the influence of popular culture and directly confronting the political angles of 1970s authoritarian Argentina. One of the most famous postboom Argentine writers is Manuel Puig (1932–90), whose first love was cinema. Much of his writing consists solely of dialogue, used to marvelous effect. Puig's novel *The Buenos Aires Affair* (1973) is a page-turner delving into the relationship between murderer and victim (and artist and critic), presented as a deconstructed crime thriller. His most famous work is *Kiss of the Spider Woman* (1976), a captivating story of a relationship that develops between two men inside an Argentine prison; it was made into the 1985 Oscar-winning film starring William Hurt.

Argentines are pretty well read – their literacy rate is over 97%. And in 2011 Buenos Aires was voted Unesco World Book Capital.

Being openly gay and critical of Perón did not help his job prospects in Argentina, so Puig spent many years in exile.

Another prolific writer is Tomás Eloy Martínez (1934–2010). His *The Perón Novel* (1988), a fictionalized biography of the controversial populist leader, and its sequel, *Santa Evita* (1996), which traces the worldwide travels of Evita's embalmed corpse, were both huge hits.

Award-winning Ricardo Piglia (b 1941) is one of Argentina's most well-known contemporary writers. He pens hard-boiled fiction and is best known for his socially minded crime novels with a noir touch, such as *The Absent City* (1992), *Money to Burn* (1997) and *Nocturnal Target* (2010).

Osvaldo Soriano (1943–97), perhaps Argentina's most popular contemporary novelist, wrote *Funny Dirty Little War* (1986) and *Winter Quarters* (1989). Juan José Saer (1937–2005) penned short stories and complex crime novels, while Rodrigo Fresán (b 1963), the youngster of the postboom generation, wrote the international bestseller *Argentine History* (1991).

The first novel of Federico Andahazi (b 1963), *The Anatomist,* caused a stir when it was published in 1997. Its ticklish theme revolves around the 'discovery' of the clitoris by a 16th-century Venetian who is subsequently accused of heresy. Andahazi based his well-written book on historical fact, and manages to have some fun while still broaching serious subjects. His prize-wining *El Conquistador* (2006) is a historical novel about an Aztec youth who 'discovers' Europe before Columbus reaches America, while his latest book *Pecar como Dios manda* (To Sin Like You Mean It; 2008), hypothesizes that to understand the essence of a society you have to understand the web of sexual relations on which it's built.

JORGE LUIS BORGES

Many of the greatest lights of Argentine literature called Buenos Aires home and all but one had been extinguished by the end of the 20th century. The light that burned brightest was without doubt Jorge Luis Borges (1899–1986), one of the foremost writers of the 20th century. A prolific author and an insatiable reader, Borges possessed an intellect that seized on difficult questions and squeezed answers out of them. Though super-erudite in his writing, he was also such a jokester that it's a challenge to tell when he's being serious and when he's pulling your leg (though often it's a case of both at once). From early on one of his favorite forms was the scholarly analysis of nonexistent texts, and more than once he found himself in trouble for perpetrating literary hoaxes and forgeries. A few of these are contained in his *Universal History of Iniquity* (1935), a book that some point to as the origin of magic realism in Latin American literature.

Borges' dry, ironic wit is paired (in his later work) with a succinct, precise style that is a delight to read. His paradoxical *Ficciones* (1944) – part parable, part fantasy – blurs the line between myth and truth, underscoring the concept that reality is only a matter of perception and the number of possible realities is infinite. Other themes that fascinated Borges were the nature of memory and dreams, labyrinths, and the relationship between the reader, the writer and the written piece. *Collected Fictions* (1999) is a complete set of his stories.

Though he received numerous honors in his lifetime – including the Cervantes Prize, the Legion of Honor and an OBE – Borges was never conferred the Nobel. He joked of this in typical fashion: 'Not granting me the Nobel Prize has become a Scandinavian tradition. Since I was born they have not been granting it to me.'

Pilgrims can head to his last residence in BA: a private apartment building near the corner of Florida and Santa Fe in Retiro. Look for a plaque on the wall.

Two of the younger generation of Argentine writers are Washington Cucurto and Gabriela Bejerman. Cucurto runs Eloísa Cartonera, a small publishing house that releases books by young authors made of recycled cardboard collected by the city's *cartoneros*. Bejerman, a multimedia artist who launched a music career as Gaby Bex, released an album in 2007 that incorporates some of her poetry with electro music. Other names to watch out for are Andrés Newman, Oliverio Coelho and Pedro Mairal.

Cinema

Buenos Aires is at the center of the Argentine film industry, which generated a wave of directors and films of the New Argentine Cinema. While this movement can't be pinned down as a school of cinema, as it includes a hodgepodge of themes and techniques, it is certainly a new movement of film-making that has been attracting international attention, earning awards and screenings at festivals in New York, Berlin, Rotterdam and Cannes.

Sadly, much of the homegrown production is more acclaimed abroad than in Argentina, where people are generally more drawn to multiplexes that show Hollywood flicks and romantic comedies. Perhaps it's because these art-house films deal with themes that are too close to home – such as survival, alienation, the search for identity and suppressed sexuality.

The film that's considered to have spearheaded the New Argentine Cinema is *Rapado* by Martín Rejtman, a minimalist 1992 feature that for the first time pushed the boundaries in a country where films were generally heavy with bad dialogue. In the late 1990s the government withdrew subsidies pledged to film schools and the movie industry. Despite this, two films ignited 'the new wave' – the low-budget *Pizza, birra, faso* (Pizza, Beer, Cigarettes; 1998) by Adrián Caetano and Bruno Stagnaro, and Pablo Trapero's award-winning *Mundo grúa* (Crane World; 1999), a black-and-white portrait of Argentina's working-class struggles.

Trapero went on to become one of Argentina's foremost filmmakers, whose credits include *El bonaerense* (2000); the ensemble road movie *Familia rodante* (Rolling Family; 2004); *Nacido y criado* (Born and Bred; 2006) a stark story about a Patagonian man's fall from grace; and the 2010 noir film *Carancho,* a love story whose protagonist is a sleazy opportunist who frequents emergency rooms and accident scenes to find new clients for his legal firm. Trapero's most recent film is *Elefante blanco* (White Elephant; 2012), which screened at Cannes.

Metegol (Foosball; 2013) is a 3D film directed by Juan José Campanella; it cost US$22 million, making it the most expensive Argentine movie ever produced.

One of the brightest stars of the New Argentine Cinema is Daniel Burman, Argentina's answer to Woody Allen, who deals with the theme of identity in the character of a young Jew in modern-day Buenos Aires. His films include *Esperando al mesíah* (Waiting for the Messiah; 2000), *El abrazo partido* (Lost Embrace; 2004) and *Derecho de familia* (Family Law; 2006). Burman's other claim to fame is his co-production of Walter Salles' Che Guevara–inspired *The Motorcycle Diaries*. His most recent film, *Dos hermanos* (Brother and Sister; 2010), the story of aging siblings who've recently lost their mother, is based on the Argentine novel *Villa Laura.*

Another director to have made a mark on Argentina cinema is the late Fabián Bielinsky. He left behind a small but powerful body of work that includes his award-winning feature *Nueve reinas* (Nine Queens; 2000), which inspired a 2004 Hollywood remake, *Criminal.* His last film, the 2005 neo-noir flick *El Aura,* screened at Sundance and was the official Argentine entry for the 2006 Oscars.

VICTORIA & SILVINA OCAMPO

In 1931 Victoria Ocampo (1890–1979) – a writer, publisher and intellectual – founded *Sur*, a renowned cultural magazine that introduced Virginia Woolf, Albert Camus and TS Eliot to Argentine readers. *Sur* also featured writers like Jorge Luis Borges, Adolfo Bioy Casares, Ernesto Sábato and Julio Cortázar.

Ocampo was an inexhaustible traveler and a pioneering feminist, and was loathed by some for her lack of convention. A ferocious opponent of Peronism, chiefly because of Perón's interference with intellectual freedom, Ocampo was arrested at her summer chalet, Villa Victoria, at the age of 63. She entertained her fellow inmates by reading aloud and acting out scenes from novels and cinema.

Ocampo never went to university, but her voracious appetite for knowledge and her love of literature led her to become Argentina's leading lady of letters. She hosted intellectuals from around the globe at Villa Victoria, in Mar del Plata, creating a formidable literary and artistic salon. (The villa is now a cultural center.)

Today you can also visit Victoria Ocampo's restored mansion in San Isidro, Villa Ocampo (www.villaocampo.org), for a reminder of a bygone era.

If Victoria is remembered as a lively essayist and a great patroness of writers, her younger sister, Silvina, was the literary talent, writing both short stories and poetry. Silvina won several literary prizes for her work, and in 1940 she married Adolfo Bioy Casares, a famous Argentine writer and friend of Jorge Luis Borges.

Lucrecia Martel has left an indelible trace on Argentina's contemporary cinema. Her 2001 debut, *La ciénaga* (The Swamp), and the 2004 follow-up, *La niña santa* (The Holy Girl), both set in Martel's native Salta province, deal with the themes of social decay, Argentine bourgeois and sexuality in the face of Catholic guilt. Another acclaimed director, Carlos Sorin, takes us to the deep south of Argentina in two of his neorealist flicks, the 2002 *Historias mínimas* (Minimal Stories) and the 2004 *Bombón el perro* (Bombón the Dog).

Juan José Campanella's *El hijo de la novia* (Son of the Bride) received an Oscar nomination for best foreign-language film in 2001. His 2004 award-winning film *Luna de avellaneda* (Moon of Avellaneda) is a masterful story about a social club and those who try to save it. And in 2010 Campanella won the Oscar for best foreign-language film with his *El secreto de sus ojos* (The Secret in Their Eyes).

Other noteworthy films include Luis Puenzo's Oscar-winning *La historia oficial* (The Official Story; 1985), Sandra Gugliotta's bust-out directorial debut *Un día de suerte* (A Lucky Day; 2002), *Un oso rojo* (A Red Bear; 2002) by Israel Adrián Caetano, *Roma* (2004) by Adolfo Aristarain, *Iluminados por el fuego* (Enlightened by Fire; 2006) by Tristan Bauer and *El hombre de al lado* (The Man Next Door; 2009) by Mariano Cohn and Gastón Duprat.

And up-and-coming director is Lucía Puenzo (daughter of Luis Puenzo). Her *XXY* (2007) won multiple awards at Cannes that year; it follows the travails of a 15-year-old hermaphrodite. In 2013 Puenzo directed *Wakolda* (The German Doctor), a true story about the family who unknowingly lived with Josef Mengele during his exile in South America.

Argentina's biggest film event is the Buenos Aires International Festival of Independent Film, held in April. Check out www.bafici.gov.ar for more information.

Art & Architecture

Over the years, Argentina has been able to boast various notable artists such as Antonio Berni, Benito Quinquela Martín and Marta Minujín, each with their own style and trigger for helping to break the mold of what was and is acceptable in their country's art world. As for architecture, Buenos Aires still has examples of the many styles in vogue at one time or another throughout the city's life. You'll find old and new juxtaposed in sometimes jarring and often enchanting ways, though the new has been asserting itself more and more in recent years.

Art

Eduardo Sívori (1847–1918) was one of Argentina's first notable artists and well-known realist painters. He created landscapes and portraits and helped found one of Argentina's first artist guilds. Other early artists included Cándido López (1840–1902) – a soldier who learned to paint with his left hand after losing his right arm in war – and Ernesto de la Cárcova, who depicted social issues such as poverty.

Lino Enea Spilimbergo (1896–1964) was a diverse painter and engraver whose subjects ranged from classical to postimpressionism to stark and surreal human figures. His contemporary, Antonio Berni (1905–81), would sometimes visit shantytowns and collect materials to use in his works. Various versions of his theme *Juanito Laguna bañándose* (Juanito Laguna Bathing) – a protest against social and economic inequality – have commanded wallet-busting prices at auctions. You can see both artists' work in the restored ceiling murals of the Galerías Pacífico shopping center (p61).

Some of the best times to be in Buenos Aires if you want to discover the art world is during the Arte BA festival (www.arteba. com) and the annual La Noche de los Museos (Night of the Museums; www. lanochedelos museos.gob.ar).

Other famous Argentine artists of this era are Juan Carlos Castagnino, a realist and figurative painter; Jorge de la Vega, who dabbled not only in various styles of visual art but also became a popular singer and songwriter; and Emilio Pettoruti, who affronted Buenos Aires with his 1924 cubist exhibition. Roberto Aizenberg was well known as one of Argentina's top surrealists.

One of the more interesting contemporary artists is Roberto Jacoby (b 1944), who has been active in diverse fields since the 1960s, from organizing socially flavored multimedia shows to setting up audiovisual installations. His most famous work, *Darkroom*, is a video performance piece with infrared technology meant for a single spectator.

Guillermo Kuitca (b 1961) is known for his imaginative techniques that include the use of digital technology to alter photographs, maps and other images and integrate them into larger-themed works. His work is on display at major international collections and he's had solo and group shows at key art expos around the world.

Other internationally recognized artists who experiment with various media are Buenos Aires–born, New York–based Liliana Porter, who imaginatively plays with video, paintings, 3D prints, photos and an eclectic collection of knickknacks; Graciela Sacco, whose politically and socially engaging installations often use public space as their setting; and the pho-

---

BEST ART MUSEUMS

➡ Museo Nacional de Bellas Artes (p118)
➡ Museo de Arte Latinoamericano de Buenos Aires (p128)
➡ Museo Nacional de Arte Decorativo (p130)
➡ Colección de Arte Amalia Lacroze de Fortabat (p74)
➡ Fundación Proa (p101)

---

tographer Arturo Aguiar, known for playing with light and shadow in his mysterious works. Also watch out for highly eclectic Argentine pop artist Marta Minujín, who has added fire to the Marshall McLuhan quote 'Art is anything you can get away with'.

Buenos Aires has also seen a rise in urban art interventions, a movement of diverse activist artists whose work calls attention to social and urban issues in the city's public spaces. The most prominent figure is Marino Santa María (www.marinosantamaria.com), whose award-winning *Proyecto Calle Lanín* is a series of colorful murals along the narrow Calle Lanín in the up-and-coming artist neighborhood of Barracas.

The late Benito Quinquela Martín, who put the working-class barrio of La Boca on the artistic map, painted brightly colored oils of life in the factories and on the waterfront. Xul Solar, a multitalented phenomenon who was a good friend of Jorge Luis Borges, painted busy, Klee-inspired dreamscapes. The former homes of both Quinquela (p101) and Solar (p131) are now museums showcasing their work.

Architecture

Little trace remains of the modest one-story adobe houses that sprang up along the mouth of the Riachuelo following the second founding of Buenos Aires in 1580. Many of them were occupied by traffickers of contraband, as the Spanish crown forbade any direct export or import of goods from the settlement. The restrictions made the price of imported building materials prohibitively high, which kept things simple, architecturally speaking. For an idea of how BA's first settlements used to be, visit El Zanjón de Granados (p89) in San Telmo.

Buenos Aires' Cabildo (p60) is a fair example of colonial architecture, although its once plaza-spanning colonnades were severely clipped by the construction of Av de Mayo and the diagonals feeding into it. The last of the Cabildo's multiple remodels was a 1940s restoration to its original look, minus the colonnades. Most of the other survivors from the colonial era are churches. Sharing Plaza de Mayo with the Cabildo, the Catedral Metropolitana (p60) was begun in 1752 but not finished until 1852, by which time it had acquired its rather secular-looking neoclassicist facade.

Many examples of postindependence architecture (built after 1810) can be found in the barrios of San Telmo, one of the city's best walking areas, and Montserrat. San Telmo also holds a wide variety of vernacular architecture such as *casas chorizos* (sausage houses) – so called for their long, narrow shape (some have a 2m frontage on the street). The perfect example is Casa Mínima (at San Lorenzo 380).

In the latter half of the 19th century, as Argentina's agricultural exports soared, a lot of money accumulated in Buenos Aires, in both private and government hands. All parties were interested in showing off their wealth by constructing elaborate mansions, public buildings and wide Parisian-style boulevards. Buildings in the city in the first few decades of the boom were constructed mostly in Italianate style, but

ROGELIO YRURTIA

Rogelio Yrurtia (1879–1950) was one of Argentina's best-known sculptors. Many of Yrurtia's pieces are displayed at his own museum (p134) in the BA neighborhood of Belgrano, or you can see his masterpiece *Canto al Trabajo* on the Plazoleta Olazábal in San Telmo.

toward the end of the 19th century a French influence began to exert itself. Mansard roofs and other elements gave a Parisian look to parts of the city, and by the beginning of the 20th century art nouveau was all the rage.

Among the highlights of the building boom's first five decades is the presidential palace, known as the Casa Rosada (p59), created in 1882 by joining a new wing to the existing post office. Others include the showpiece Teatro Colón (p78) and the imposing Palacio del Congreso.

The 1920s saw the arrival of the skyscraper, in the form of the 100m-high, 18-story Palacio Barolo (p79). This rocket-styled building was the tallest in Argentina (and one of the tallest in South America) from its opening in 1923 until the completion of the 30-story art deco Edificio Kavanagh (p109) in 1936. The Kavanagh in turn, when finished, was the largest concrete building in the world and remains an impressive piece of architecture.

In the 1930s, in Palermo and Recoleta, fancy apartment buildings started popping up. This trend would continue intermittently into the 1940s, by which time the city would also have a subway system with multiple lines.

Buenos Aires continued to grow upward and outward during Juan Perón's spell in power (1946 to 1955). Though the economy flagged, anonymous apartment and office blocks rose in ever greater numbers. Bucking the trend were such oddball buildings as the Banco de Londres on Reconquista, designed in 1959 by Clorindo Testa, whose long architectural career in BA began in the late 1940s. The bank was finished by 1966, but Testa's Biblioteca Nacional (p131) – which must've looked pretty groovy to him on the drawing board in 1962 – was hideously dated by the time it opened (following many delays) in 1992. Its style is somewhere between late Offshore Oil Platform and early Death Star.

A heartening trend of 'architectural recycling' took off in Buenos Aires in the latter 20th century and continues today, helping to preserve the city's glorious old structures. Grand old buildings have been remodeled (and sometimes augmented) to become luxury hotels, museums and cultural centers; notable examples include the Centro Cultural del Bicentenario (p61), which used to be the city's main post office, and the Usina del Arte (p103), a concert hall that used to be an old electricity factory. Old markets have also been restored to their original glory to live again as popular shopping malls, such as the Mercado de Abasto (p148) and Galerías Pacífico (p61).

At the same time, the first decade of the 21st century has seen an increasingly modern skyline develop in Buenos Aires. Soaring structures of glass and steel tower above earlier efforts, many innovative and quite striking, such as the Edificio República in Buenos Aires' downtown. It was designed by César Pelli, who also did Kuala Lumpur's Petronas Towers.

The renovation of Puerto Madero turned dilapidated brick warehouses into offices, upscale restaurants and exclusive lofts. Contrasting with these charming low, long buildings is one of the city's tallest structures, the 558ft-high Torres El Faro, standing at the eastern section of Puerto Madero. It's a pair of joined towers that now house fancy apartments. Other architectural gems here include Calatrava's Puente de la Mujer (p74) and the glass-domed Museo Fortabat (p74) by Uruguayan-born architect Rafael Viñoli.

Street art – which is not illegal in Buenos Aires – has become more and more prominent in neighborhoods like Barracas, San Telmo, La Boca and Palermo. Colorful murals, political stencils and graffiti-inspired creations cover public and private walls, sometimes commissioned by the city and property owners.

Survival Guide

Transportation

ARRIVING IN BUENOS AIRES

BA is Argentina's international gateway and easily accessible from North America, Europe and Australasia, as well as most other capital cities in South America. Aerolíneas Argentinas is the country's main airline, but smaller Argentine airlines are in constant flux and come and go very frequently. Even airline offices will often move. Always check current travel information during your tenure here.

Flights, cars and tours can be booked online at lonely planet.com.

Ezeiza Airport

Almost all international flights arrive at Buenos Aires' Ezeiza airport (EZE; officially Aeropuerto Internacional Ministro Pistarini), about 35km south of the center. Ezeiza is a modern airport with decent services like ATMs, restaurants, bookstore, pharmacy, duty-free shops and a small **post office** (Ezeiza Airport; ☺9am-5pm Mon-Fri, to noon Sat, mailbox 24hr). There's also a Telecentro *locutorio* (long distance telephone office; open 24 hours) with telephone cabins and internet access, near Farmacity and McDonald's. Wi-fi is available at La Pausa Restaurant, past gate 9 upstairs and in Terminal C.

EZEIZA ARRIVAL & DEPARTURE TIPS

» Citizens from some countries have to pay a **reciprocity fee** (*tasa de reciprocidad*) before arriving in Argentina; ideally you'll be reminded of this when you buy your airplane ticket. This fee is equal to what Argentines are charged for visas to visit those countries. You'll need to pay this fee online via credit card; see www.migraciones.gov. ar/accesibleingles and click on 'Pay your Reciprocity Rate' on the left column.These fees are US$100 for Australians (good for one year), US$160 for Americans (good for 10 years) and US$75 for Canadians (per entry – sucks, eh? Or go for the US$150, good-for-five-years option). You'll need to prepay this fee before entering Argentina via other airports, borders or ports (that means you, cruise ship passengers) too, or you might be turned around.

» To **change money** at Ezeiza, don't use a *cambio* (exchange house) there – their rates are generally bad. Better rates are found at the local bank branch; after exiting customs, pass the rows of transport booths, go outside the doors into the reception hall and make a U-turn to the right to find Banco de la Nación's small office. Its rates are identical to downtown offices, there's an ATM and it's open 24 hours, though long lines are common. There are other ATMs at Ezeiza.

» There's a **tourist information booth** (☺24hr) just beyond the city's Taxi Ezeiza stand.

» When leaving Buenos Aires, **get to Ezeiza at least two to three hours before your international flight out**; security and immigration lines can be long (and be aware that traffic is often bad *getting* to Ezeiza; it can take an hour or more). Also, even when you get past main security there may be bag checks at the gate, and neither food nor liquids may be allowed onto airplanes. Eat and drink up before boarding.

Flight information

(☎5480-6111; www.aa2000.com.ar.) is available in English and Spanish.

Bus

If you're alone, the best way to and from Ezeiza is taking a shuttle with transfer companies such as **Manuel Tienda León** (MTL; Map p248; ☎4315-5115; www.tiendaleon.com; Av Madero 1299, Ezeiza airport). You'll see its stand immediately as you exit customs, in the transport 'lobby' area. Frequent shuttles cost AR$80 to AR$95 per person to the city center, run all day and night and take 40 to 60 minutes, depending on traffic. They'll deposit you either at the MTL office (from where you can take a taxi) or at some limited central addresses.

Another shuttle service, directed at independent travelers, is **Hostel Shuttle** (☎4511-8723; www.hostelshuttle.com.ar). Check the website for prices, schedules and drop-off destinations (only at certain hostels), and try to book ahead. You can also try www.minibusezeiza.com.ar.

If you're really on a penny-pinching budget, take public bus 8, which costs AR$6 and can take up to two hours to reach the Plaza de Mayo area. Catch it outside the Aerolíneas Argentinas terminal (Terminal B), a 200m walk from the international terminal. You'll need coins; there's a Banco de la Nación just outside customs.

Taxi

If taking a taxi, avoid MTL's overpriced taxi service. Instead, go past the transport 'lobby' area outside customs, walk past the taxi touts, and you'll see the freestanding city taxi stand (with a blue sign saying **Taxi Ezeiza** (☎5480-0066; www.taxiezeiza.com.ar)). In late 2013 it charged AR$270 to the center. Note that if you pre-arrange your taxi back to

Ezeiza after your stay in BA, the rate can be 20% cheaper (this is due to airport and taxi regulations); your taxi driver might remind you about this fact.

Chauffeur-Driven Car

For a special treat, reserve a luxury car from **Silver Star Car** (☎in Argentina 15-6826-8876, in the USA 214-502-1605; www.silverstarcar.com); you'll be driven by native English speakers to the destination of your choice (US$150). There are car-rental booths at Ezeiza, but we do not recommend renting a car for your stay in Buenos Aires.

Aeroparque Airport

Most domestic flights use **Aeroparque airport** (Aeroparque Jorge Newbery; ☎5480-6111; www.aa2000.com.ar), a short distance from downtown Buenos Aires.

Bus

Manuel Tienda León (MTL; Map p248; ☎4315-5115; www.tiendaleon.com; Av Madero 1299, Ezeiza airport) does hourly transfers from Ezeiza to Aeroparque for AR$95. To get from Aeroparque to the center, take public bus 33 or 45 (don't cross the street; take them going south). MTL also has shuttles to the center for AR$30.

Taxi

A taxi to the center costs around AR$80.

Boat

There's a regular ferry service to and from Colonia and Montevideo, both in Uruguay. Most ferries leave from the Buquebus terminal at the corner of Avs Antártida Argentina and Córdoba in Puerto Madero; there are other Buquebus offices at Av Córdoba 879 and at Pueyrredón 1786. **Colonia Express** (Map p244; ☎4317-4100; www.coloniaexpress.com; Córdoba 753) is cheaper than Buquebus but has fewer departures; its central office is at Av Córdoba 753, but its terminal is in an ugly, industrial neighborhood near La Boca.

Both companies have many more launches in the busy summer season; book online in advance for discounts.

GETTING AROUND BUENOS AIRES

Bicycle

Buenos Aires is generally not the best city to cycle around: traffic is dangerous, with scant respect for cyclists, and the biggest vehicle wins

---

WATCH THAT POCKET!

When traveling on BA's crowded bus or Subte lines, watch for pickpockets. They can be well dressed, men or women, often with a coat slung over their arm to hide nefarious activities going on near your bag or pocket. Occasionally there are several of them, working as a team, and they'll try to shove or distract you. The best thing to do is not look like a tourist, keep your wallet well ensconced in your front pocket, wedge your purse under your arm and wear your backpack in front – like the locals do. Don't make yourself an easy target and they'll move on – and you might not even notice they exist.

CRITICAL MASS

Started in San Francisco in 1992, Critical Mass is an international bicycling event dedicated to improving bicycle awareness and reaffirming cyclists' rights. It's held in over 300 cities throughout the world, and though its goal is different in each city, it's not meant to be a race, a protest, a demonstration or a means to cause trouble by maliciously blocking vehicular traffic. In Buenos Aires, Masa Crítica has no set leaders or destinations. People just show up at the Obelisco with their bikes at 4pm on the first Sunday of each month – and start riding somewhere. Expect several hundred people to participate – up to a thousand on nice, warm days. And you'll see all sorts of folks: activists, families, hipsters, foreigners, on tall bikes, low bikes and everything in between. There's even the odd skateboarder, rollerblader or cyclist in costume. You'll be riding in the streets, but you're more protected than you think – there's safety in numbers. Lots of yelling, cheering and horn-blowing is required; expect to have a blast.

There's also a Masa Nocturna every full moon, starting at the Obelisco at 9pm. It's the same concept, but the end point is at the planetarium in Palermo's Parque 3 de Febrero – and that's where the full-moon party starts.

the right of way, so bikes are low on the transport totem pole.

However, things are getting better. New bike lanes were installed in 2010 and are expanding; a **bike-share program** (www.mejoren bici.gob.ar) also exists, but it's more geared towards residents (one-hour rental limits). Every day there seem to be more cyclists on the streets – but even so, BA has a long way to go to be seen as a bike-friendly city.

The city's best places for two-wheeled exploration are Palermo's parks and the Reserva Ecológica Costanera Sur; on sunny weekends you can rent bikes at these places. You can also join city bike tours, which include bicycle and guide (p207).

Bus

Buenos Aires has a huge and complex bus system. If you want to get to know it better you'll have to buy a *Guia T* – it's sold at any newsstand, but get the pocket version (about AR$10). It details hundreds of the city's bus routes. Just look at the grids to find out where you are and where you're going, and find a matching bus number. You can also check www.xcolectivo.com.ar for an online version. For information (in English) on how to get to your destination on city buses, check out www.omnilineas.com/argentina/buenos-aires/city-bus/.

Bus ticket machines on board will give you small change from your coins. Rides around town are cheap; just mention your destination to the driver and he'll cue the machine. If you're staying in BA awhile, consider getting a **SUBE card** (www.sube.gob.ar) for cheaper fares and to make paying easier.

Most bus routes (but not all) run 24 hours; there are fewer buses at night. Seats up front are offered to the

HANDY BUS ROUTES

ROUTE	BUS
Microcentro to Palermo Viejo	111
Microcentro to Plaza Italia (in Palermo)	29, 59, 64
Once to Plaza de Mayo to La Boca	64
Plaza de Mayo to Ezeiza airport (placard says 'Ezeiza')	8
Plaza Italia to Microcentro to San Telmo	29
Plaza Italia to La Boca via Retiro & Plaza de Mayo	152, 29
Plaza Italia to Recoleta to Microcentro to Constitución	59
Plaza San Martín to Aeroparque airport	33, 45
Recoleta to Congreso to San Telmo to La Boca	39
Retiro to Plaza de Mayo to San Telmo	22

EASY BUS TICKETS

You can buy nearly any long-distance bus ticket without taking a special trip to Retiro bus station. Use the practical booking services of **Omnilíneas** (☎4326-3924; www.omnilineas.com; Maipú 459, 9B). Just reserve and buy your ticket over the website, and either print it out at home or pick it up at the office. Prices are the same as at Retiro bus station, and English is spoken.

elderly, pregnant women and those with young children.

If you're arriving in Buenos Aires at Retiro bus terminal for the first time, it'll be difficult to sort out the local bus system – there are a lot of bus lines outside. It's worth spending a few pesos to take a *remise* (radio taxi) directly to your destination. There are two small *remise* booths near bus slots 8 and 9 that are open 24 hours. And remember to keep an eye on your bags at this station!

Car & Motorcycle

Anyone considering driving in Buenos Aires should know that most local drivers are reckless, aggressive and

even willfully dangerous. They'll ignore speed limits, road signs, road lines and often traffic signals. They'll tailgate you mercilessly and honk even before signals turn green. Buses are a nightmare to reckon with, potholes are everywhere, traffic is worse every day and parking can be nonexistent in places (and cost a bundle). To top it off, pedestrians haphazardly cross the road, seeming to beg to be run over at times.

Reconsider your need to have a car in this city: public transportation will often get you anywhere faster, cheaper and with much less stress. And you won't have to worry about the police, who have been known to stop cars to

check for violations, while subtly asking for *coimas* (bribes). If this happens to you when you weren't doing anything illegal, insist on contacting your embassy – too much trouble for some officers.

Driving

Driving outside BA is another story. Drivers are still crazy, but there are fewer of them, and you'll have more flexibility in your travels. If you drive in Argentina – especially in your own car – it may be worth joining the Automóvil Club Argentino (ACA), which has many nationwide offices. ACA recognizes members of overseas affiliates, such as the American Automobile Association (AAA), and often grants them similar privileges, including discounts on maps, accommodations, camping, tours and other services. For more information contact the **ACA head office** (☎4802-6061; www.aca.org.ar; Av del Libertador 1850).

Rental

If you want to rent a car, expect to pay US$30 or US$50 or more per day. International chains can be more expensive than local rental agencies; call around. You'll need to be at least 21 years of age and have a valid driver's license; having an international driver's license wouldn't be a bad idea, though you don't necessarily need one. A credit card and passport are also necessary.

Avis (☎4326-5542; www.avis.com.ar; Cerrito 1535)

Hertz (☎4816-8001; www.hertz.com.ar; Paraguay 1138)

New Way (☎4515-0331; www.new-wayrentacar.com; Marcelo T de Alvear 773)

If you have experience driving scooters and are up to the challenge of getting around BA on an electric version, check out **Green Scooter** (☎6091-9060;

RETIRO BUS TERMINAL

Buenos Aires' modern Retiro bus terminal is 400m long, three floors high and has slots for 75 buses. The bottom floor is for cargo shipments and luggage storage, the top for purchasing tickets, and the middle for everything else.

There's an **information booth** (☎4310-0700; ◎6am-midnight) that provides general bus information and schedules, plus a **tourist office** (Map p248; Retiro bus station, across from bus slot 35; ◎7:30am-2:30pm Mon-Fri, to 4:30pm Sat & Sun) near Puente 3 on the main floor, on the same level as bus slot 35. Other services include ATMs, lockers, telephone offices (some with internet access), restaurants, cafes and dozens of small stores. Various *remise* (call-taxi) booths are also available, some open 24 hours. You can also purchase a **SUBE card** (www.sube.gob.ar) and get it charged at a booth near the southern entrance.

You can buy a ticket to practically anywhere in Argentina and departures are fairly frequent to the most popular destinations. Reservations are not necessary except during peak summer and winter holiday seasons.

www.thegreenscooter.net; Soler 4717; ⊙10:30am-6:30pm). You'll need to pay an AR$2500 deposit (cash or credit card) and bring your passport. The cost is AR$190 per day, helmet and lock included.

For motorcycle rentals, be at least 25 years of age and head to **Motocare** (☑4761-2696; www.motocare.com.ar/rental; Echeverria 738, Vicente Lopez). Bring your own helmet and riding gear. Crossing into Chile, Uruguay, Paraguay and Brazil is possible.

Taxi & Remise

Buenos Aires' very numerous (about 40,000) and relatively inexpensive taxis are conspicuous by their black-and-yellow paint jobs. They click every 200m (or every minute of waiting time) and cost 20% more after 6pm. Make sure that the meter's set to the current price when you start your ride. Drivers do not expect a big tip, but it's customary to let them keep small change. Taxis looking for passengers will have a red light lit on the upper right corner of their windshield.

Most cab drivers are honest workers making a living, but there are a few bad apples in the bunch. Try not to give them a 100 peso note

for a small fare; sometimes they're short on change, but there have been cases where the driver quickly and deftly replaces a larger bill with a smaller (or fake) one. One solution is to state how much you are giving them and ask if they have change for it ('¿Tiene usted cambio de un cien?' – 'Do you have any change for a hundred?').

Be wary of receiving counterfeit bills; drivers have been known to switch your valid bill for a fake one. If you're suspicious this might happen, note aloud the last three numbers/letters on a bill as you're paying him (it's pretty much always a 'him').

At night the driver will turn on the light (or luz) so you can carefully check your change (look for a watermark on bills). They'll do the same with your bills. And make sure you get the right change.

Try to have an idea of where you're going or you might be taking the 'scenic' route (though also be aware there are many one-way streets in BA, and your route to one place may be quite different on the way back). A good way to give the impression that you know where you're going is to give the taxi driver an intersection rather than a specific address. Also, if you are obviously a tourist going to or from a touristy spot, it's not

a good idea to ask how much the fare is; this makes quoting an upped price tempting, rather than using the meter. And try not to take a taxi right outside a tourist spot or after you've withdrawn money from an ATM – walk a block or two and flag one down instead.

Finally, make an attempt to snag an 'official' taxi. These are usually marked by a roof light and license number printed on the doors; the words radio taxi are usually a good sign. Official drivers must display their license on the back of their seat or dashboard; you can write down the taxi's number and agency telephone in case you have problems with the ride or forgot something.

Most porteños will recommend you call a remise instead of hailing cabs off the street. A remise looks like a regular car and doesn't have a meter. It costs a bit more than a street taxi but is considered more secure, since an established company sends them out. Most hotels and restaurants will call a remise for you; expect a short wait for them to show up.

Train

Trains connect Buenos Aires' center to its suburbs and nearby provinces. They're

---

HELPFUL TRAIN INFORMATION

DESTINATION(S)	STATION	CONTACT
Belgrano, San Isidro, Tigre, Rosario	Retiro	**Línea Mitre** (☑0800-222-8736; www.mitresarmiento.com.ar)
Southern suburbs & La Plata	Constitución	**Línea Roca** (☑0800-362-7622; www.ugofe.com.ar/general_roca)
Bahía Blanca, Tandil & Mar del Plata	Constitución	**Ferrobaires** (☑0810-666-8736; www.ferrobaires.gba.gov.ar)
Southwestern suburbs & Luján	Once	**Línea Sarmiento** (☑0800-222-8736; www.mitresarmiento.com.ar)

best for commuters and only occasionally useful for tourists. Several private companies run different train lines; train stations are all served by Subte.

Tram

A light-rail system in Puerto Madero is called the Tranvía del Este. It's currently 2km long and has only four stops, with plans to extend the line from Retiro to Constitución. It's cheap to ride, but consider skipping it – stroll Puerto Madero's lovely cobbled lanes instead.

Subte (Underground)

BA's **Subte** (www.subte.com. ar) opened in 1913 and is the quickest way to get around the city, though it can get mighty hot and crowded during rush hour. It consists of *líneas* (lines) A, B, C, D, E and H. Four parallel lines run from downtown to the capital's western outskirts, while *Línea* C runs north–south and connects the two major train stations of Retiro and Constitución. *Línea* H runs from Once south to Av Caseros, with plans to expand it.

One-ride magnetic cards for the Subte cost AR$3.50. To save time and hassle, buy several rides, since queues can get backed up (espe-

cially during rush hour). If you're planning on staying in BA for a while, **SUBE** (www. sube.gob.ar) is a convenient, rechargeable card that negates the need for coins.

Trains operate from 5am to around 10:30pm Monday to Saturday and 8am to around 10pm Sunday and holidays, so don't rely on the Subte to get you home after dinner. Service is frequent on weekdays; on weekends you'll wait longer. At some stations platforms are on opposite sides, so be sure of your direction *before* passing through the turnstiles.

TOURS

Buenos Aires has tours for every style and stripe, from the large tourist-bus variety to guided bike rides to straight-up walks. The city of Buenos Aires organizes free monthly tours from April to December, with themes ranging from art to historic bars to particular neighborhoods. Stop by any government tourist information office (p216) for more information.

Most companies listed here offer tours in English and possibly other languages; some companies also do private tours.

Say Hueque (Map p250; ☑5258-8740; www.sayhueque. com; Thames 2062) This independent travel agency special-

izes in customized adventure trips all around Argentina, and will also make air, bus and hotel reservations. It offers various BA tours as well. Also downtown at Viamonte 749, 6th fl, and in San Telmo at Chile 557.

Tangol (Map p248;☑4363-6000; www.tangol.com; Av Florida 971, Suite 31) Do-all agency that offers city tours, tango shows, guides to *fútbol* games, hotel reservations, Spanish classes, air tickets and country-wide packages. Also offers unusual activities including helicopter tours and skydiving. Another branch in San Telmo at Defensa 831.

Anda Responsible Travel (Map p250; ☑3221-0833; www. andatravel.com.ar; Agüero 1050, 4A) Most notable for its La Boca tour, which introduces travelers to local organizations working towards improving the lives of its citizens. Also does many tours around Argentina that benefit local citizens, which are sometimes indigenous groups.

BA Cultural Concierge (☑15-3876-5937; www. baculturalconcierge.com) Customized single-day tours of Buenos Aires, Tigre and the Mataderos fair. Also tango and *milonga* tours.

BA Walking Tours (☑15-5773-1001; www.ba-walking-tours.com) Day tours, night tours, historic tours and tango tours.

Biking Buenos Aires (☑4040-8989; www.biking buenosaires.com) Friendly American and Argentine guides take you on various tours of Buenos Aires; theme tours include a graffiti and architecture tour.

Buenos Aires Bus (☑5239-5160; www.buenosairesbus. com; locals/foreigners AR$90/120) Hop-on, hop-off topless bus that runs

---

SUBE CARD

If you're planning on staying in BA for a while, the **SUBE card** (www.sube.gob.ar) is a very handy and inexpensive rechargeable card that you can use for the Subte, local buses and some trains. It saves you money and you don't have keep a stash of coins on hand. Get it at some kioskos and Correo Argentino or OCA post offices around the city (check the website for locations or look for the SUBE logo at businesses). Ezeiza airport and Retiro bus station also have Sube booths where you can get and recharge this card. You'll need your passport or a copy. Charging the card itself is easy, and can be done at many kiosks or Subte stations.

frequently over two dozen stops (see website).

Buenos Tours (☑5984-2444; www.buenostours.com) Well-run private tours guided by friendly, knowledgeable and responsible local expats. Great website too.

Cultour (☑15-6365-6892; www.cultour.com.ar) Good tours run by teachers and students from UBA (University of Buenos Aires). Prepare to learn the historical and cultural facets of Buenos Aires.

Graffitimundo (☑15-3683-3219; www.graffitimundo.com) Excellent tours of some of BA's best graffiti, by those in the know. Learn artists' history and the local graffiti culture. Several tours available, including a La Boca 'Hidden Walls' tour. Stencil workshops too.

Seriema Nature Tours (☑5410-3235; www.serie-matours.com) It does nature tours to all South America, but around BA the most popular outings are to Costanera Sur.

Urban Biking (☑4314-2325; www.urbanbiking.com) One-day cycling tours – including an alternative 'nightlife' bike trip – and bike and kayak excursions to Tigre.

Directory A–Z

Customs Regulations

Argentine officials are generally courteous and reasonable toward tourists. Electronic items, including laptops, cameras and cell phones, can be brought into the country duty free, provided they are not intended for resale. If you have a lot of electronic equipment, however, it may be useful to have a typed list of the items you are carrying (including serial numbers) or a pile of purchase receipts.

Depending on where you have been, officials focus on different things. Travelers south-bound from the central Andean countries may be searched for drugs, and those from bordering countries will have fruit and vegetables confiscated.

Discount Cards

Travelers of any age can obtain a Hostelling International card at any **HI hostel** (www.hostels.org.ar) or at the tiny HI office in **Retiro** (☑4511-8723; www.hostels.org.ar; Av Florida 835). With this card you can obtain discounts at any HI hostel in Argentina, usually 10% to 15% off regular prices. International Student Identity Cards are also sold here; you'll need current student ID.

For non-HI hostels, check out **minihostels** (www.minihos tels.com), a network of quality,

'good-vibe' hostels throughout Argentina and expanding to other places in Central and South America. The **HoLa** (www.holahostels.com) card works in a similar way for a different network of hostels.

Travelers over the age of 60 can sometimes obtain discounts on museum admissions and the like. Usually a passport with date of birth is sufficient evidence of age.

Electricity

Argentina's electric current operates on 220V, 50 Hertz. There are two types of electric plugs: either two rounded prongs (as in Europe) or

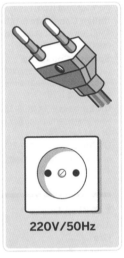

220V/50Hz

220V/50Hz

three angled flat prongs (as in Australia). See www.kropla. com/electric2.htm for details. Adapters are readily available from almost any *ferretería* (hardware store), or visit a travel store.

Most electronic equipment (such as cameras, PDAs, telephones, computers and laptops) are dual/multivoltage, but if you're bringing in something that's not, use a voltage converter or you might short out your device.

Embassies & Consulates

Some countries have both an embassy and a consulate in

Buenos Aires, but only the most central location is listed here.

Australian Embassy
(☑4779-3500; www.argentina.embassy.gov.au; Villanueva 1400)

Canadian Embassy
(☑4808-1000; www.canadainternational.gc.ca; Tagle 2828)

French Embassy (☑4515-7030; www.embafrancia-argentina.org; Cerrito 1399, Retiro)

German Embassy (☑4778-2500; www.buenosaires.diplo.de; Villanueva 1055)

Italian Consulate (☑4114-4800; www.consbuenosaires.esteri.it; Reconquista 572)

Spanish Consulate
(☑4814-9100; www.spanish-embassy.com/buenos-aires.html; Guido 1770)

UK Embassy (☑4808-2200; www.ukinargentina.fco.gov.uk; Dr Luis Agote 2412)

US Embassy (☑5777-4533; http://argentina.usembassy.gov; Colombia 4300)

Emergency

Ambulance (☑107)
Fire (☑100)
Police (☑911, 101)
Tourist Police (Comisaría

CONCIERGE SERVICE

BA Cultural Concierge (☑15-3876-5937; www.baculturalconcierge.com) Madi Lang's concierge service helps you plan itineraries, arrange airport transportation, run errands, get a cell phone, reserve theater tickets, scout out a potential apartment and do a thousand other things that'll help your trip to run smoothly.

del Turista; ☑0800-999-5000, 4346-5748; Av Corrientes 436; ⏰24hr) Provides interpreters for travel insurance reports.

Gay & Lesbian Travelers

Argentina is a strongly Catholic country with heavy elements of machismo. In Buenos Aires, however, there is a palpable acceptance of homosexuality. In 2002 BA became the first Latin American city to legalize same-sex civil unions, and in July 2010 Argentina became the first Latin American country to legalize same-sex marriage. In fact, gay tourism has become so popular that BA is now South America's top gay destination.

Argentine men are more physically demonstrative than their North American and European counterparts, so behaviors such as kissing on the cheek in greeting or a vigorous embrace are considered innocuous even to those who express unease with homosexuals. Lesbians walking hand-in-hand should generally attract little attention, since heterosexual Argentine women sometimes do so, but this would be very conspicuous behavior for males. If you are in any doubt, it's better to be discreet.

Health

Buenos Aires is a modern city with good health and dental services. Sanitation and hygiene at restaurants is relatively high, and tap water is generally safe to drink. If you want a glass of tap water, ask '¿Me podés traer un vaso de agua de la canilla?' (Can you bring me a glass of tap water?).

Public health care in Buenos Aires is reasonably good and free, even if you're a foreigner. Waits can be long, however, and quality spotty.

Those who can afford it usually opt for the superior private care system, and here most doctors and hospitals will expect payment in cash. Many medical personnel speak English.

If you develop a life-threatening medical problem you may want to be evacuated to your home country. Since this may cost thousands of dollars, be sure to have the appropriate insurance before you depart. Your embassy can also recommend medical services.

A signed and dated note from your doctor, describing your medical conditions and medications (with their generic or scientific names) is a good idea. It's also a good idea to bring medications in their clearly labeled, original containers. Most pharmacies in Argentina are well supplied.

For more specific information on vaccinations to get before traveling to Argentina, see wwwnc.cdc.gov/travel/destinations/argentina.htm.

Insurance

A travel-insurance policy to cover theft, loss and medical problems is a good idea. Some policies offer a range of lower and higher medical-expense options; the higher ones are chiefly for countries, such as the USA, that have extremely high medical costs. There is a wide variety of policies available, so read the small print.

Some policies specifically exclude 'dangerous activities', which can include scuba diving, motorcycling and even trekking. Check that the policy you're considering covers ambulances and an emergency flight home.

Internet Access

Buenos Aires is definitely online. Internet cafés and *locutorios* (telephone offices) with internet access are common everywhere in the center; you can often find one by just walking a few blocks in any direction. Rates are cheap and connections are quick. To find the @ (*arroba*) symbol, try holding down the Alt key and typing 64. Or ask the attendant *'¿Cómo se hace la arroba?'* ('How do you make the @ sign?').

Nearly all hotels have wi-fi or in-room internet connections for guests traveling with their own laptops, and the fancier ones also feature 'business centers' with one or more computers. Many hostels provide free internet to guests. Also, many cafes and restaurants (even McDonald's) offer free wi-fi.

Language Courses

BA has become a major destination for students of Spanish. Good institutes are opening up all the time and private teachers are a dime a dozen. Cultural centers also offer language classes; the **Centro Cultural Ricardo Rojas** (Map p240; ☑4954-5523; www.rojas.uba.ar; Av Corrientes 2038) has an especially good range of offerings, from Korean to Russian to Yiddish.

Most private language institutes organize social activities, private classes and (usually) volunteer opportunities. Homestay programs are also available but often cost more than finding a place yourself. Check websites for fees and schedules.

University of Buenos Aires (www.idiomas.filo.uba. ar) Offers intensive, long-term classes (one to four months) in Spanish, Italian, German, French, Portuguese and Japanese. It's cheap, and great for serious students, but classrooms can be run-down.

Spanglish (www.spanglishexchange.com) Set up like speed dating; you'll speak five

minutes in English and five in Spanish, then switch partners (and it's a bit of a pick-up scene too).

Academia Buenos Aires (Map p236; ☑4345-5954; www. academiabuenosaires.com; Hipólito Yrigoyen 571, 4th fl)

DWS (Map p254; ☑4777-6515; www.dwsba.com.ar; Av Córdoba 4382)

Expanish (Map p236; ☑5252-3040; www.expanish.com; Juan Perón 698)

Rayuela (Map p242; ☑4300-2010; www.spanish-argentina. com.ar; Chacabuco 852, 1st fl, No 11)

VOS (Map p246; ☑4812-1140; www.vosbuenosaires.com; Marcelo T de Alvear 1459)

Vamos (Map p250; ☑5352-0001; www.vamospanish.com; Coronel Díaz 1736)

Legal Matters

You're hardly likely to get involved with the local police if you follow the law. If you drive a car, however, officers are not above petty harassment. So-called safety campaigns often result in motorists receiving citations for minor equipment violations (such as a malfunctioning turn signal) that carry fines. In most cases, corrupt officers will settle for less

expensive *coimas* (bribes), but this requires considerable caution and tact. A discreet hint that you intend to contact your consulate may minimize or eliminate such problems – often the police count on foreigners' ignorance of Argentine law. Another tactic, whether you know Spanish or not, is to pretend you don't understand what an officer is saying.

Medical Services

Highly regarded hospitals include **Hospital Italiano** (☑4959-0200; www. hospitalitaliano.org.ar; Juan D Perón 4190), **Hospital Alemán** (☑4827-7000; www.hospitalaleman.org.ar; Pueyrredón 1640) and **Hospital Británico** (☑4309-6400; www.hospitalbritanico.org.ar; Perdriel 74). Another popular medical facility is **Swiss Medical** (☑0810-333-8876; www.swissmedical.com.ar; cnr Santa Fe & Scalabrini Ortiz), with various branches around town.

Dental Argentina (☑4828-0821; www.dental-argentina.com.ar; Laprida 1621, 2B) provides modern facilities and good dental services with English-speaking professionals.

NEED AN OFFICE FOR AN HOUR OR A DAY?

The brainchild of one of BA's many expat entrepreneurs, **Areatres** (☑5353-0333; www.areatresworkplace.com; Malabia 1720; ☺8:30am-8pm Mon-Fri) is a secure working office where you can rent a desk, cubicle, office or meeting room. There are fax and copy services, complete internet and wi-fi connections, networking social events, a business lounge, a large presentation room and even a Zen-like patio at the back for the stress-prone. Facilities are cutting-edge – it's like you never left Silicon Valley. It's even eco-conscious. It's also at **Humboldt 2036** (☑5258-7600; www.areatresworkplace.com; Humboldt 2036).

Pharmacies

Pharmacies are common in Buenos Aires. The biggest chain is **Farmacity** (www.farmacity.com), with dozens of branches throughout the city; they're modern, bright and well stocked with sundries. They have a prescription counter and some are open 24 hours. It's hard to miss their blue-and-orange color theme.

Money

Argentina's unit of currency is the peso (AR$).

Banks and *cambios* (foreign-exchange offices) are common in the city center; banks have longer lines and more limited opening hours but may offer better rates.

For international transfers, **Western Union** (www.westernunion.com) has several agents in BA.

Carrying cash and using ATM and credit cards is the way to go in Argentina.

ATMs

ATMs (*cajeros automáticos*) are everywhere in BA and the handiest way to get money. ATMs dispense *only* Argentine pesos (not US dollars, despite what the screen says) and can be used for cash advances on major credit cards. There's often an English-translation option if you don't read Spanish.

There may be limits per withdrawal, but you may be able to withdraw several times per day – just beware of per-transaction fees. To avoid having a fistful of large-denomination bills, withdraw odd amounts like 990 pesos.

Also, a small fee is charged on ATM transactions by the *local* bank (not including charges by your home bank, which are extra). Note that this is a *per transaction* fee, so consider taking out your maximum allowed limit – if you feel safe doing so.

Cash

Notes come in denominations of two, five, 10, 20, 50 and 100 pesos. One peso equals 100 centavos; coins come in denominations of five, 10, 25 and 50 centavos, as well as one and two pesos. The $ sign in front of a price is usually used to signify pesos.

Don't be dismayed if you receive dirty and hopelessly tattered banknotes; they will still be accepted everywhere. Some banks refuse worn or defaced US dollars, however, so make sure you arrive in Buenos Aires with pristine bills.

Counterfeiting of both local and US bills has become something of a problem in recent years, and merchants are very careful when accepting large denominations. You should be, too; look for a

clear watermark or running thread on the largest bills, and be especially careful when receiving change in dark nightclubs or taxis. For photos, check www.landingpadba.com/ba-basics-counterfeit-money.

Getting change from large denominations can be a problem for small purchases. Large supermarkets and restaurants are your best bet. Always keep a stash of change with you, in both small bills and coins.

US dollars are accepted by many tourist-oriented businesses.

Credit Cards

Many tourist services, larger stores, hotels and restaurants take credit cards such as Visa and MasterCard, especially for big purchases. Be aware, however, that some businesses add a *recargo* (surcharge) of up to 10% to credit-card purchases; ask ahead of time. Some lower-end hotels and private businesses will not accept credit cards, and tips can't usually be added to credit-card bills at restaurants. Many places will give you a small discount if you pay in cash, rather than use a credit card.

The following local representatives can help you replace lost or stolen cards:

American Express (☑4310-3000)

MasterCard (☑0800-444-5220)

Visa (☑4379-3400)

Tipping

In restaurants and cafes it's customary to tip about 10% of the bill for decent service. An interesting note: when your server is taking your bill with payment away, saying '*gracias*' usually implies that the server should keep the change as a tip. If you want change back, don't say '*gracias*' – say '*cambio, por favor*' instead.

Note that tips can't be added to credit-card bills, so

carry cash for this purpose. Also note that the *cubierto* that some restaurants charge is not a tip; it's a sort of 'cover charge' for the use of utensils and bread. Yes, it's silly, but that's the custom.

Bartenders Usually no tip, but it's OK to give a small bill for a drink or good cocktail.

Delivery persons A small bill.

Hotel cleaning staff A few pesos per day (only at fine, upscale hotels).

Hotel porters A small bill.

Restaurant servers Tip 10%; 15% for fine restaurants with great service.

Spas Tip 15%.

Taxi drivers No tip unless they help with luggage; many people round up to nearest peso.

Tour guides Tip 10% to 15%.

Traveler's Checks

Traveler's checks are very impractical in Argentina, and even in BA it's very hard to change them. Only the fancier hotels and a few banks and *cambios* will take them, and they'll charge a very hefty commission. Stores will *not* change them.

Outside BA it's almost impossible to change traveler's checks. If you do decide to bring some, get them in US dollars.

Post

The more-or-less reliable **Correo Argentino** (www. correoargentino.com.ar) is the government postal service, with numerous branches scattered throughout BA. Essential overseas mail should be sent *certificado* (registered). For international parcels weighing over 2kg, take a copy of your passport

and go to the Correo Internacional near the Retiro bus station. Check the website for all prices.

If a package is being sent to you, expect to wait awhile for it to turn up within the system (or to receive notice of its arrival). Unless you have a permanent address, your parcel will likely end up at the Correo Internacional. To collect the package you'll have to wait – first to get it and then to have it checked by customs. There might also be a small holding fee, charged per day. Don't expect any valuables to make it through.

Privately run international and national services are available. Federal Express has its central branch at Maipú 753. Other choices are **DHL International** (Map p248; ☑0810-122-3345; www.dhl. com.ar; Av Córdoba 783). **OCA** (Map p236; www.oca.com.ar) and **Andreani** (www.andreani. com.ar) are good for domestic

---

BUENOS AIRES' BLUE (IE BLACK) MARKET

Because many Argentines are desperate for hard currency to combat their country's high inflation, mistrust the peso's stability *and* are not allowed to easily buy them – Argentina has a robust black market for US dollars, especially in Buenos Aires. This market is also called the *mercado azul* (blue market, or 'cambio blue'). The blue market rate can be nearly twice the official exchange rate, though rates fluctuate daily. Many people think this parallel market can't last forever, and the government is constantly tinkering with laws to combat it.

In BA, some people use this market on Calle Florida, where *arbolitos* (touts; literally, 'little trees') constantly call out *'cambio, cambio, cambio'*. The *arbolito* leads the interested party to a *cueva* (unofficial exchange office) for the transaction. Unobtrusive storefront *cuevas* also exist in some tourist neighborhoods in BA; many locals use them and know where they are located. Be aware that this shady activity – although commonplace (newspapers even publish the going blue rate) – is technically illegal. Scams and fake bills do exist, and unwary travelers make very good targets.

Instead of using *arbolitos*, some people change money (or pay for services) at certain stores, travel agents, restaurants and accommodations for rates close to the blue market's. Outside BA, some *cambios* might give you the unofficial rate. Hundred-dollar bills get the highest rates.

Note that ATMs in Argentina don't give out US currency, no matter what their screen says. Some ATMs in Uruguay will, however – though there are daily limits for withdrawals.

Another way travelers bypass the official exchange rate is by using international money-transfer services such as www.xoom.com (for those with US bank accounts) or Azimo (for those with UK bank accounts).

Do your research very carefully before coming to Argentina. And no matter how you end up getting your pesos, use them all up before your flight home. It's unlikely you'll be able to change them back to a hard currency at a decent rate – if at all.

OPENING HOURS

There are always exceptions, but the following are general opening hours:

Banks 8am to 3pm or 4pm Monday to Friday; some open till 1am Saturday.

Bars 8pm or 9pm to between 4am and 6am nightly (downtown, some open and close earlier).

Cafes 6am to midnight or much later; open daily.

Clubs 1am to 2am to between 6am and 8am Friday and Saturday.

Office business hours 8am to 5pm.

Post offices 8am to 6pm Monday to Friday, 9am to 1pm Saturday.

Restaurants Noon to 3:30pm, 8pm-midnight or 1am (later on weekends).

Shops 9am or 10am to 8pm or 9pm Monday to Saturday.

packages; both have many locations around town.

Public Holidays

Government offices and businesses are closed on the numerous national holidays. If a holiday falls midweek or on a weekend day, it's often bumped to the nearest Monday; if it falls on a Tuesday or Thursday, then the in-between Monday or Friday are taken as holidays.

Public-transportation options are more limited on holidays, when you should reserve tickets far in advance. Hotel booking should also be done ahead of time.

January 1 Año Nuevo; New Year's Day

February or March Carnaval – dates vary; a Monday and Tuesday become holidays

March 24 Día de la Memoria; anniversary of the day that started the 1976 dictatorship and subsequent Dirty War

March/April Semana Santa (Easter week) – dates vary; most businesses close on Good 'Thursday' and Good Friday; major travel week

April 2 Día de las Malvinas; honors the fallen Argentine soldiers from the Islas Malvinas (Falkland Islands) war in 1829

May 1 Día del Trabajor; Labor Day

May 25 Día de la Revolución de Mayo; commemorates the 1810 revolution against Spain

June 20 Día de la Bandera (Flag Day); anniversary of death of Manuel Belgrano, creator of Argentina's flag and military leader

July 9 Día de la Independencia; Independence Day

August (third Monday) Día del Libertador San Martín; marks the anniversary of José de San Martín's death (1778–1850)

October (second Monday) Día del Respeto a la Diversidad Cultural; a day to respect cultural diversity

November (fourth Monday) Día de la Soberanía Nacional; day of national sovereignty

December 8 Día de la Concepción Inmaculada; celebrates the immaculate conception of the Virgin Mary

December 25 Navidad; Christmas Day

Note that Christmas Eve and New Year's Day are treated as semi-holidays, and you will find some businesses closed for the latter half of those days.

Safe Travel

Buenos Aires is generally pretty safe. You can comfortably walk around at all hours of the night in many places, even as a lone woman. People stay out very late, and there's almost always somebody else walking on any one street at any hour of the night. (Some areas where you should be careful at night, however, are around Constitución's train station, the eastern border of San Telmo, and some parts of Once and La Boca – where, outside tourist streets, you should be careful even during the day).

Like all big cities, BA has its share of problems. The economic crisis of 1999–2001 plunged a lot of people into poverty, and street crime has subsequently risen. As a tourist you're much more likely to be a target of petty crimes like pickpocketing and bag-snatching than armed robbery or kidnapping. Be careful on crowded buses, on the Subte and at busy *ferias* (street markets). Don't put your bag down without your foot through the strap (especially at sidewalk cafes), and even then keep a close eye on it. Be especially careful at Retiro bus station.

Minor nuisances include lack of respect shown by cars toward pedestrians, lax pollution controls and high noise levels. Many Argentines are heavy smokers, and you can't help but be exposed to it on the street (smoking is banned in most restaurants, bars and public transport). The **tourist police** (Comisaría del Turista; ☎0800-999-5000, 4346-5748; Av Corrientes 436; ◷24hr) may be of some help.

Using your head is good advice anywhere: don't flash

any wealth (including expensive jewelry), don't stagger around drunk, always be aware of your surroundings and look like you know exactly where you're going (even if you don't). Be careful showing off expensive electronics like laptops, smart phones, iPods or iPads. But realize that if you're reasonably careful, the closest thing to annoyance you'll experience is being shortchanged, tripping on loose sidewalk tiles, stepping on the ubiquitous dog pile or getting flattened by a crazy bus driver. Watch your step.

Taxes & Refunds

One of Argentina's primary state revenue-earners is the 21% value-added tax known as the Impuesto de Valor Agregado (IVA). Under limited circumstances, foreign visitors may obtain IVA refunds on purchases of Argentine products upon departing the country. A 'Tax Free' window decal (in English) identifies participants in this program, but always check that the shop is part of the tax-free program before making your purchase.

You can obtain tax refunds on purchases of AR$70 or more made at one of these participating stores. To do so, present your passport to the merchant, who will make out an invoice for you. On leaving the country keep the purchased items in your carry-on baggage. A customs official will check them and stamp your paperwork, then tell you where to obtain your refund. Be sure to leave yourself a bit of extra time at the airport to get this done.

Telephone

Two companies, Telecom and Telefónica, split the city's telephone services.

Street phones require coins or tarjetas telefónicas (magnetic phone cards available at many kioskos, or small markets). You'll only be able to speak for a limited time before you get cut off, so carry enough credit.

Toll-free numbers in BA have '0800' before a seven-digit number.

Cell Phones

It's best to bring your own factory unlocked tri- or quad-band GSM cell phone to Argentina, then buy an inexpensive SIM chip (you'll get a local number) and credits as needed. Both SIM chips and credits can be bought at many kioskos or locutorios (small telephone offices); look for the 'recarga facil' signs. Many Argentines use this system with their cell phones. Phone-unlocking services are available; ask around.

You can also buy cell phones that use SIM chips; these usually include some credits for your first batch of calls. Be careful renting phones as they're not usually a better deal than outright buying a cell phone.

If you plan to travel with an iPhone or other 3G smart phone, prepare yourself – you may need to purchase an international plan to avoid being hit by a huge bill for roaming costs. On the other hand, it's possible to call internationally for free or very cheaply using a VoIP (Voice over Internet Protocol) system such as Skype. This is a constantly changing field, so do some research before you travel.

Cell-phone numbers in Argentina are always preceded by '15'. If you're calling a cellular phone number from a landline, you'll have to dial 15 first. But if you're calling a cell phone from another cell phone, you don't need to dial 15 (at least within the same area code).

When calling cell phones from outside Argentina, dial your country's international access code, then 54

9 11 and then the eight-digit number, leaving out the 15.

Locutorios & Internet Cafes

One way to make a local or international phone call is to find a locutorio, a small telephone office (sometimes marked telecentro) with private booths from which you make your calls and then pay at the register. There's a locutorio on practically every other block in the center. They cost a bit more than street phones, but you can sit down, you won't run out of coins and it's much quieter.

When making international calls from locutorios ask about off-peak discount hours, which generally apply after 10pm and on weekends. Making international calls over the internet using Skype is a cheap option; many internet cafes have this system in place.

Faxes are cheap and widely available at most locutorios and internet cafes.

Phone Codes

The Buenos Aires area code is 011. You will need to dial this when calling BA from outside the city, but you

ELECTRONICS WARNING

Note that buying a smart phone, especially an iPhone, is extremely expensive in Argentina due to import restrictions – and they are not widely available. If you do bring your smart phone, don't flash it around unnecessarily or leave it unprotected somewhere. This goes for iPads, iPods and laptop computers too.

don't need to dial it when calling from within BA.

Phonecards

Telephone calling cards are sold at nearly all *kioskos* and make domestic and international calls far cheaper than calling direct. However, they must be used from a fixed line such as a home or hotel telephone (provided you can dial outside the hotel). They cannot be used at most pay phones. Some *locutorios* allow you to use them, and although they levy a surcharge, the call is still cheaper than dialing direct. When purchasing one, tell the clerk the country you will call so that they give you the right card.

Time

Argentina is three hours behind GMT and generally does not observe daylight-saving time (though this situation can easily change). Many *porteños* use the 24-hour clock to differentiate between am and pm.

Toilets

Public toilets in BA are generally decent and usually stocked with toilet paper (carry some anyway), but soap and towels are rarer. If you're looking for a bathroom while walking around, note that the largest shopping malls (such as Galerías Pacífico) always have public bathrooms available, but in a pinch you can always walk into a McDonald's or large cafe. Changing facilities for babies are not always available.

Some may find bidets a novelty; they are those strange shallow, ceramic bowls with knobs and a drain, often accompanying toilets in hotel bathrooms. They are meant for between-shower cleanings of nether regions. Turn knobs slowly,

or you may end up spraying yourself or the ceiling.

Tourist Information

The **Secretaría de Turismo de la Nación** (Map p248; ☑4312-2232; www.turismo.gov. ar; Av Santa Fe 883; ⊗9am-7pm Mon-Fri) dispenses information on Buenos Aires but focuses on Argentina as a whole.

The **tourist police** (Comisaría del Turista; ☑0800-999-5000, 4346-5748; Av Corrientes 436; ⊗24hr) can provide interpreters and helps victims of robberies and rip-offs.

There's a tourist kiosk at **Ezeiza airport** (Ezeiza airport; ⊗24hr) and another one at **Retiro bus station** (Retiro bus station; ⊗7:30am-2pm Mon-Fri) near Puente 3 on the main floor, across from bus slot 36.

There are several tourist offices and kiosks in Buenos Aires. Note that hours vary depending on the season and number of volunteers. The official tourism site of Buenos Aires is www.bue.gov.ar and the government site is www.buenosaires.gov.ar.

Plaza San Martín (Map p248; cnr Av Florida & MT de Alvear)

Florida (Map p236; cnr Av Florida & Diagonal Roque Sáenz Peña)

Puerto Madero (Map p238; Dique 4)

Recoleta (Map p246; Av Quintana 596)

Esmeralda (Map p236; cnr Av Rivadavia & Esmeralda)

Travelers with Disabilities

Negotiating Buenos Aires as a disabled traveler is not the easiest of tasks. City sidewalks are narrow, busy and dotted with many broken

tiles. Not every corner has a ramp, and traffic is ruthless when it comes to pedestrians (and wheelchair-users). A few buses do have *piso bajo* (they 'kneel' and have extra-large spaces), but the Subte (subway) does not cater to the mobility-impaired.

International hotel chains often have wheelchair-accessible rooms, as do other less fancy hotels – accessibility laws have changed for the better over the last few years. Some restaurants and many important tourist sights have ramps, but BA is sorely lacking in wheelchair-accessible bathrooms – although the city's shopping malls usually have at least one, restaurants don't often have the appropriate installations.

In Buenos Aires, **QRV Transportes Especiales** (☑15-6863-9555, 011-4306-6635; www.qrvtransportes. com.ar) offers private transport and city tours in vans fully equipped for wheelchair users. **BA Cultural Concierge** (☑15-3876-5937; www. baculturalconcierge.com) offers service for low-mobility travelers, by helping with errands. Or you could head to BA with a company like **Accessible Journeys** (www. disabilitytravel.com), which has tours and cruises in South America – including one that includes Buenos Aires.

Other than the use of brail on ATMs little effort has been dedicated to bettering accessibility for the vision impaired. Stoplights are rarely equipped with sound alerts. The **Biblioteca Argentina Para Ciegos** (BAC, Argentine Library for the Blind; ☑4981-0137; www.bac.org.ar; Lezica 3909) maintains a brail collection of over 3000 books, as well as other resources.

Visas

Nationals of the USA, Canada, most Western European countries, Australia and New Zealand do not need visas to visit Argentina, but check current regulations. Most foreigners receive a 90-day visa upon arrival.

To get yourself a 90-day extension (AR$300), visit the **Dirección Nacional de Migraciones** (☎4317-0234; www.migraciones.gov.ar/accesibleingles/?categorias; Antártida Argentina 1355; ⏰8am-2pm Mon-Fri). Set aside some time, as there are lines and this process can take an hour or two. Get your extension the same week your visa expires. Overstaying your visa (AR$300) costs as much as an extension, but it's also much more stressful – and the rules can change quickly.

Another option if you're staying more than three months is to cross into Colonia or Montevideo (both in Uruguay; Colonia can be an easy day trip) and return with a new three-month visa. This strategy is most sensible if you are from a country that does not require a visa to enter Uruguay.

Americans, Australians and Canadians need to pay a reciprocity fee (*tasa de reciprocidad*) when arriving in Argentina, see p202.

Women Travelers

Buenos Aires is a modern, sophisticated city, and women travelers – even those traveling alone – should not encounter many difficulties. Men do pay more overt attention to women in Argentina, however, and a little open-mindedness might be in order. Argentina's machismo culture is, after all, alive and well.

A few men feel the need to comment on a woman's attractiveness. This often happens when you're walking alone and pass by a man; it will never occur when you're with another man. Comments usually include whistles or *piropos,* which many Argentine males consider the art of complimenting a woman. *Piropos* are often vulgar, although a few can be poetic. Much as you may want to kick them where it counts, the best thing to do is completely ignore the comments. After all, many *porteñas* are used to getting these 'compliments', and most men don't necessarily mean to be insulting; they're just doing what is socially acceptable in Argentina.

On the plus side of machismo, men will hold a door open for you and let you enter first, including getting on buses.

CULTURAL CENTERS

Buenos Aires has good cultural centers offering all sorts of art exhibitions, classes and events. They're listed in the neighborhood chapters.

There are also several foreign cultural centers in the Microcentro, such as the **Instituto Cultural Argentino-Norteamericano** (Map p236; ☎5382-1500; www.icana.org.ar; Maipú 672), which has Spanish classes and workshops; the **Alianza Francesa** (Map p236; ☎4322-0068; www.alianzafrancesa.org.ar; Av Córdoba 946), which concentrates on French-themed instruction and arts; and the **Instituto Goethe** (Map p236; ☎4318-5600; www.goethe.de/hs/bue; Av Corrientes 319), which offers German-language instruction, lectures, films and even concerts. All have good libraries in their respective languages.

The **British Arts Centre** (Map p248; ☎4393-6941; www.britishartscentre.org.ar; Suipacha 1333) has well-priced theater, films, music and workshops (among other things) in English and Spanish.

Language

Latin American Spanish pronunciation is easy, as most sounds have equivalents in English. Read our coloured pronunciation guides as if they were English, and you'll be understood. Note that kh is a throaty sound (like the 'ch' in the Scottish *loch*), v and b are like a soft English 'v' (between a 'v' and a 'b'), and r is strongly rolled. Also note that the letters *ll* (pronounced ly or simplified to y in most parts of Latin America) and *y* are pronounced like the 's' in 'measure' or the 'sh' in 'shut' in Buenos Aires, which gives the language its very own local flavor. In this chapter, we've used the symbol sh to represent this sound. You'll get used to this idiosyncracy very quickly listening to and taking your cues from the locals.

The stressed syllables are indicated with an acute accent in written Spanish (eg *días*) and with italics in our pronunciation guides.

The polite form is used in this chapter; where both polite and informal options are given, they are indicated by the abbreviations 'pol' and 'inf'. Where necessary, both masculine and feminine forms of words are included, separated by a slash and with the masculine form first, eg *perdido/a* (m/f).

BASICS

Hello.	*Hola.*	o·la
Goodbye.	*Adiós./Chau.*	a·dyos/chow
How are you?	*¿Qué tal?*	ke tal
Fine, thanks.	*Bien, gracias.*	byen gra·syas
Excuse me.	*Perdón.*	per·don

WANT MORE?

For in-depth language information and handy phrases, check out Lonely Planet's *Latin American Spanish phrasebook*. You'll find it at **shop.lonelyplanet.com**, or you can buy Lonely Planet's iPhone phrasebooks at the Apple App Store.

Sorry.	*Lo siento.*	lo syen·to
Please.	*Por favor.*	por fa·vor
Thank you.	*Gracias.*	gra·syas
You're welcome.	*De nada.*	de na·da
Yes./No.	*Sí./No.*	see/no

My name is ...
Me llamo ...   me sha·mo ...

What's your name?
¿Cómo se llama Usted?   ko·mo se sha·ma oo·ste (pol)
¿Cómo te llamas?   ko·mo te sha·mas (inf)

Do you speak English?
¿Habla inglés?   a·bla een·gles (pol)
¿Hablas inglés?   a·blas een·gles (inf)

I don't understand.
Yo no entiendo.   yo no en·tyen·do

ACCOMMODATIONS

I'd like a ... room.	*Quisiera una habitación ...*	kee·sye·ra oo·na a·bee·ta·syon ...
single	*individual*	een·dee·vee·dwal
double	*doble*	do·ble

How much is it per night/person?
¿Cuánto cuesta por noche/persona?   kwan·to kwes·ta por no·che/per·so·na

Does it include breakfast?
¿Incluye el desayuno?   een·kloo·she el de·sa·shoo·no

air-con	*aire acondicionado*	ai·re a·kon·dee·syo·na·do
bathroom	*baño*	ba·nyo
campsite	*terreno de cámping*	te·re·no de kam·peeng
guesthouse	*hostería*	os·te·ree·a
hotel	*hotel*	o·tel
youth hostel	*albergue juvenil*	al·ber·ge khoo·ve·neel
window	*ventana*	ven·ta·na

Signs

Abierto	Open
Cerrado	Closed
Entrada	Entrance
Hombres/Varones	Men
Mujeres/Damas	Women
Prohibido	Prohibited
Salida	Exit
Servicios/Baños	Toilets

DIRECTIONS

Where's ...?
¿Dónde está ...?   don·de es·ta ...

What's the address?
¿Cuál es la dirección?   kwal es la dee·rek·syon

Could you please write it down?
¿Puede escribirlo,   pwe·de es·kree·beer·lo
por favor?   por fa·vor

Can you show me (on the map)?
¿Me lo puede indicar   me lo pwe·de een·dee·kar
(en el mapa)?   (en el ma·pa)

at the corner	en la esquina	en la es·kee·na
at the traffic lights	en el semáforo	en el se·ma·fo·ro
behind ...	detrás de ...	de·tras de ...
far	lejos	le·khos
in front of ...	enfrente de ...	en·fren·te de ...
left	izquierda	ees·kyer·da
near	cerca	ser·ka
next to ...	al lado de ...	al la·do de ...
opposite ...	frente a ...	fren·te a ...
right	derecha	de·re·cha
straight ahead	todo recto	to·do rek·to

EATING & DRINKING

Can I see the menu, please?
¿Puedo ver el menú,   pwe·do ver el me·noo
por favor?   por fa·vor

What would you recommend?
¿Qué me recomienda?   ke me re·ko·myen·da

Do you have vegetarian food?
¿Tienen comida   tye·nen ko·mee·da
vegetariana?   ve·khe·ta·rya·na

I don't eat (red meat).
No como (carne roja).   no ko·mo (kar·ne ro·kha)

That was delicious!
¡Estaba buenísimo!   es·ta·ba bwe·nee·see·mo

Cheers!
¡Salud!   sa·loo

The bill, please.
La cuenta, por favor.   la kwen·ta por fa·vor

I'd like a table for ...	Quisiera una mesa para ...	kee·sye·ra oo·na me·sa pa·ra ...
(eight) o'clock	las (ocho)	las (o·cho)
(two) people	(dos) personas	(dos) per·so·nas

Key Words

appetisers	aperitivos	a·pe·ree·tee·vos
bottle	botella	bo·te·sha
bowl	bol	bol
breakfast	desayuno	de·sa·shoo·no
children's menu	menú infantil	me·noo een·fan·teel
(too) cold	(muy) frío	(mooy) free·o
dinner	cena	se·na
food	comida	ko·mee·da
fork	tenedor	te·ne·dor
glass	vaso	va·so
hot (warm)	caliente	ka·lyen·te
knife	cuchillo	koo·chee·yo
lunch	almuerzo	al·mwer·so
main course	plato principal	pla·to preen·see·pal
plate	plato	pla·to
restaurant	restaurante	res·tow·ran·te
spoon	cuchara	koo·cha·ra
with	con	kon
without	sin	seen

Meat & Fish

beef	carne de vaca	kar·ne de va·ka
chicken	pollo	po·sho
duck	pato	pa·to
fish	pescado	pes·ka·do
lamb	cordero	kor·de·ro
pork	cerdo	ser·do
turkey	pavo	pa·vo
veal	ternera	ter·ne·ra

Question Words

How?	¿Cómo?	ko·mo
What?	¿Qué?	ke
When?	¿Cuándo?	kwan·do
Where?	¿Dónde?	don·de
Who?	¿Quién?	kyen
Why?	¿Por qué?	por ke

Fruit & Vegetables

apple	manzana	man·sa·na
apricot	damasco	da·mas·ko
artichoke	alcaucil	al·kow·seel
asparagus	espárragos	es·pa·ra·gos
banana	banana	ba·na·na
beans	chauchas	chow·chas
beetroot	remolacha	re·mo·la·cha
cabbage	repollo	re·po·sho
carrot	zanahoria	sa·na·o·rya
celery	apio	a·pyo
cherry	cereza	se·re·sa
corn	choclo	cho·klo
cucumber	pepino	pe·pee·no
fruit	fruta	froo·ta
grape	uvas	oo·vas
lemon	limón	lee·mon
lentils	lentejas	len·te·khas
lettuce	lechuga	le·choo·ga
mushroom	champiñón	cham·pee·nyon
nuts	nueces	nwe·ses
onion	cebolla	se·bo·sha
orange	naranja	na·ran·kha
peach	durazno	doo·ras·no
peas	arvejas	ar·ve·khas
(red/green) pepper	pimiento (rojo/verde)	pee·myen·to (ro·kho/ver·de)
pineapple	ananá	a·na·na
plum	ciruela	seer·we·la
potato	papa	pa·pa
pumpkin	zapallo	sa·pa·sho
spinach	espinacas	es·pee·na·kas
strawberry	frutilla	froo·tee·sha
tomato	tomate	to·ma·te
vegetable	verdura	ver·doo·ra
watermelon	sandía	san·dee·a

Other

bread	pan	pan
butter	manteca	man·te·ka
cheese	queso	ke·so
egg	huevo	we·vo
honey	miel	myel
jam	mermelada	mer·me·la·da
oil	aceite	a·sey·te
pasta	pasta	pas·ta
pepper	pimienta	pee·myen·ta
rice	arroz	a·ros
salt	sal	sal
sugar	azúcar	a·soo·kar
vinegar	vinagre	vee·na·gre

LUNFARDO

Below are are some of the spicier *lunfardo* (slang) terms you may hear on your travels in Argentina.

boliche – disco or nightclub

boludo – jerk, asshole, idiot; often used in a friendly fashion, but a deep insult to a stranger

bondi – bus

buena onda – good vibes

carajo – asshole, prick; bloody hell

chabón/chabona – kid, guy/girl (term of endearment)

che – hey

diez puntos – OK, cool, fine (literally '10 points')

fiaca – laziness

guita – money

laburo – job

macanudo – great, fabulous

mango – one peso

masa – a great, cool thing

mina – woman

morfar – eat

pendejo – idiot

piba/pibe – cool young guy/girl

piola – cool, clever

pucho – cigarette

re – very, eg *re interestante* (very interesting)

trucho – fake , imitation , bad quality

¡Ponete las pilas! – Get on with it! (literally 'Put in the batteries!')

Me mataste. – I don't know; I have no idea. (literally 'You've killed me')

Le faltan un par de jugadores. – He's not playing with a full deck. (literally 'He's a couple of players short')

che boludo – The most *porteño* phrase on earth. Ask a friendly local youth to explain.

Drinks

beer	cerveza	ser·ve·sa
coffee	café	ka·fe

(orange) juice	jugo (de naranja)	khoo·go (de na·ran·kha)
milk	leche	le·che
tea	té	te
(mineral) water	agua (mineral)	a·gwa (mee·ne·ral)
(red/white) wine	vino (tinto/ blanco)	vee·no (teen·to/ blan·ko)

EMERGENCIES

| Help! | ¡Socorro! | so·ko·ro |
| Go away! | ¡Vete! | ve·te |

Call ...!	¡Llame a ...!	sha·me a ...
a doctor	un médico	oon me·dee·ko
the police	la policía	la po·lee·see·a

I'm lost.
Estoy perdido/a.   es·toy per·dee·do/a (m/f)

I'm ill.
Estoy enfermo/a.   es·toy en·fer·mo/a (m/f)

I'm allergic to (antibiotics).
Soy alérgico/a a   soy a·ler·khee·ko/a a
(los antibióticos).   (los an·tee·byo·tee·kos) (m/f)

Where are the toilets?
¿Dónde están los   don·de es·tan los
baños?   ba·nyos

SHOPPING & SERVICES

I'd like to buy ...
Quisiera comprar ...   kee·sye·ra kom·prar ...

I'm just looking.
Sólo estoy mirando.   so·lo es·toy mee·ran·do

Can I look at it?
¿Puedo verlo?   pwe·do ver·lo

I don't like it.
No me gusta.   no me goos·ta

How much is it?
¿Cuánto cuesta?   kwan·to kwes·ta

That's too expensive.
Es muy caro.   es mooy ka·ro

Can you lower the price?
¿Podría bajar un   po·dree·a ba·khar oon
poco el precio?   po·ko el pre·syo

There's a mistake in the bill.
Hay un error   ai oon e·ror
en la cuenta.   en la kwen·ta

ATM	cajero automático	ka·khe·ro ow·to·ma·tee·ko
credit card	tarjeta de crédito	tar·khe·ta de kre·dee·to
internet cafe	cibercafé	see·ber·ka·fe
market	mercado	mer·ka·do
post office	correos	ko·re·os
tourist office	oficina de turismo	o·fee·see·na de too·rees·mo

TIME & DATES

What time is it?	¿Qué hora es?	ke o·ra es
It's (10) o'clock.	Son (las diez).	son (las dyes)
It's half past (one).	Es (la una) y media.	es (la oo·na) ee me·dya
morning	mañana	ma·nya·na
afternoon	tarde	tar·de
evening	noche	no·che
yesterday	ayer	a·sher
today	hoy	oy
tomorrow	mañana	ma·nya·na

EL VOSEO

Spanish in the Río de la Plata region differs from that of Spain and the rest of the Americas, most notably in the use of the informal form of 'you'. Instead of *tuteo* (the use of *tú*), Argentines commonly speak with *voseo* (the use of *vos*), a relic from 16th-century Spanish requiring slightly different grammar. All verbs change in spelling, stress and pronunciation. Examples of verbs ending in *-ar*, *-er* and *-ir* are given below; the *tú* forms are included to illustrate the contrast. Imperative forms (commands) also differ, but negative imperatives are identical in *tuteo* and *voseo*.

The Spanish phrases in this chapter use the *vos* form. An Argentine inviting a foreigner to address him or her informally will say *Me podés tutear* (literally 'You can address me with *tú*'), even though they'll use the *vos* forms in subsequent conversation.

Verb	Tuteo	Voseo
hablar (speak): You speak./Speak!	Tú hablas./¡Habla!	Vos hablás./¡Hablá!
comer (eat): You eat./Eat!	Tú comes./¡Come!	Vos comés./¡Comé!
venir (come): You come./Come!	Tú vienes./¡Ven!	Vos venís./¡Vení!

Monday	lunes	loo·nes
Tuesday	martes	mar·tes
Wednesday	miércoles	myer·ko·les
Thursday	jueves	khwe·ves
Friday	viernes	vyer·nes
Saturday	sábado	sa·ba·do
Sunday	domingo	do·meen·go

TRANSPORTATION

boat	barco	bar·ko
bus	colectivo/ micro	ko·lek·tee·vo/ mee·kro
plane	avión	a·vyon
train	tren	tren
first	primero	pree·me·ro
last	último	ool·tee·mo
next	próximo	prok·see·mo

A ... ticket, please.	Un boleto de ..., por favor.	oon bo·lee·to de ... por fa·vor
1st-class	primera clase	pree·me·ra kla·se
2nd-class	segunda clase	se·goon·da kla·se
one-way	ida	ee·da
return	ida y vuelta	ee·da ee vwel·ta

I want to go to ...
Quisiera ir a ...   kee·sye·ra eer a ...

Does it stop at ...?
¿Para en ...?   pa·ra en ...

What stop is this?
¿Cuál es esta parada?   kwal es es·ta pa·ra·da

What time does it arrive/leave?
¿A qué hora llega/sale?   a ke o·ra she·ga/sa·le

Please tell me when we get to ...
¿Puede avisarme   pwe·de a·vee·sar·me
cuando lleguemos   kwan·do she·ge·mos
a ...?   a ...

I want to get off here.
Quiero bajarme aquí.   kye·ro ba·khar·me a·kee

airport	aeropuerto	a·e·ro·pwer·to
bus stop	parada de colectivo	pa·ra·da de ko·lek·tee·vo
platform	plataforma	pla·ta·for·ma
ticket office	taquilla	ta·kee·sha
timetable	horario	o·ra·ryo
train station	estación de trenes	es·ta·syon de tre·nes

Numbers		
1	uno	oo·no
2	dos	dos
3	tres	tres
4	cuatro	kwa·tro
5	cinco	seen·ko
6	seis	seys
7	siete	sye·te
8	ocho	o·cho
9	nueve	nwe·ve
10	diez	dyes
20	veinte	veyn·te
30	treinta	treyn·ta
40	cuarenta	kwa·ren·ta
50	cincuenta	seen·kwen·ta
60	sesenta	se·sen·ta
70	setenta	se·ten·ta
80	ochenta	o·chen·ta
90	noventa	no·ven·ta
100	cien	syen
1000	mil	meel

I'd like to hire a ...	Quisiera alquilar ...	kee·sye·ra al·kee·lar ...
bicycle	una bicicleta	oo·na bee·see·kle·ta
car	un coche/ auto	oon ko·che/ aw·to
motorcycle	una moto	oo·na mo·to

helmet	casco	kas·ko
hitchhike	hacer dedo	a·ser de·do
mechanic	mecánico	me·ka·nee·ko
petrol/gas	nafta	naf·ta
service station	estación de servicio	es·ta·syon de ser·vee·syo
truck	camion	ka·myon

Is this the road to ...?
¿Se va a ... por   se va a ... por
esta carretera?   es·ta ka·re·te·ra

Can I park here?
¿Puedo estacionar acá?   pwe·do es·ta·syo·nar a·ka

The car has broken down.
El coche se ha averiado.   el ko·che se a a·ve·rya·do

I've run out of petrol.
Me he quedado sin nafta.   me e ke·da·do seen naf·ta

I have a flat tyre.
Tengo una goma   ten·go oo·na ·go·ma
pinchada.   peen·cha·da

GLOSSARY

arbolito – literally 'little tree'; a street money-changer and to be avoided

arroyo – creek, stream

autopista – freeway or motorway

bandoneón – an accordion-like instrument used in tango music

barrio – neighborhood or borough of the city

cabildo – colonial town council; also, the building that housed the council

cambio – money-exchange office; also casa de cambio

campo – the countryside; alternately, a field or paddock

cartelera – an office selling discount tickets

cartoneros – people who pick through garbage looking for recyclables

coima – a bribe; one who solicits a bribe is a coimero

correo – post office

costanera – seaside, riverside or lakeside road or walkway

dique – a dam; the resultant reservoir is often used for recreational purposes; can also refer to a drydock

edificio – a building

ejecutivo – executive class

esquina – street corner

estancia – extensive ranch for cattle or sheep; some are now open to tourists

feria – a street fair or street market

fútbol – soccer

locutorio – private long-distance telephone office, often with fax and internet

manzana – literally 'apple'; also used to define one square block of a city

paseo – an outing, such as a walk in the park or downtown

FOOD GLOSSARY

a punto – cooked medium well (referring to steak)

agua de canilla – tap water (drinkable in BA)

agua mineral – mineral water, usually available con/sin gas (still or sparkling)

ajo – garlic

alfajor – two flat, soft cookies filled with dulce de leche and covered in chocolate or meringue

almuerzo – lunch

amargo – bitter

asado – Argentine barbecue (both the food and the event), often a family event on Sunday

bien cocido – well done (referring to steak)

bife (de chorizo/costilla/lomo) – (sirloin strip/T-bone/tenderloin) steak

bombilla – metal straw with filter for drinking mate

bondiola – cured pork shoulder

budín de pan – bread pudding

café – coffee

casero – homemade

carne – meat

cerdo – pork

cena – dinner

cerveza – beer

chimichurri – a spicy marinade for meat, usually made of parsley, garlic, spices and olive oil

chinchulines – intestines

choclo – corn

chopp – draft beer

choripán – a spicy sausage served in a bread roll

chorizo – sausage (note the difference from bife de chorizo)

comedor – basic cafeteria

confitería – a shop that serves quick meals

cortado – espresso with steamed milk added

costillas – short ribs

crudo – raw

cubierto – in restaurants, the cover charge you pay for utensil use and bread

desayuno – breakfast

dulce – sweet

dulce de leche – Argentina's national sweet, found in many desserts and snacks; a type of thick, milky caramel

empanada – a meat or vegetable hand pie; a popular Argentine snack

entrada – appetizer

entraña – skirt steak

facturas – pastries; also receipts

frito/a – fried

fruta – fruit

frutos secos – nuts (nuts are also called nueces)

helado – ice cream

heladería – an ice-cream shop

hielo – ice

hígado – liver

hongo – mushroom (also called champignon)

huevos – eggs

jamón – ham

jarra – pitcher

jengibre – ginger

jugo (exprimido) – juice (freshly squeezed)

jugoso – medium rare (referring to steak); also general term for juicy

lengua – tongue

lenguado – flounder (fish)

licuado – fruit shake

locro – a traditional meat and corn stew from northern Argentina

lomito – a steak sandwich

lomo – tenderloin

manteca – butter

mariscos – seafood

matambre – a thin cut of beef, sometimes made into a stuffed roll (matambre relleno)

mate – a gourd used for drinking yerba mate or the tea itself

medialuna (de manteca/de grasa) – croissant (sweet/savory)

merienda – afternoon tea

merluza – hake (fish)

mermelada – jam or jelly

miel – honey

milanesa – breaded cutlet (usually beef)

minuta – in a restaurant or confitería, a short order such as spaghetti or milanesa

mollejas – sweetbreads

morcilla – blood sausage

ñoquis – gnocchi

ojo de bife – rib-eye steak

pancho – hot dog

papas frita – french fries

parrillada – a mixed grill of steak and other beef cuts

parrilla – a restaurant specializing in steak dishes

pescado – fish

picada – a cheese and cured meat sample plate

pollo – chicken

postre – dessert

propina – tip (gratuity)

puchero – soup combining vegetables and meats, served with rice

recargo – an additional charge (such as for use of a credit card, usually about 10%)

sandwiches de miga – thin sandwiches made from crustless white bread

sorrentino – a stuffed pasta, like ravioli but large and round

submarino – hot milk served with a bar of dark chocolate

tallarines – noodles

tenedor libre – literally 'free fork'; an all-you-can-eat restaurant

tira de asada – grilled beef ribs

vacio – flank steak

verduras – vegetables

vegetariano/a – vegetarian

vinoteca – wine bar

vino (blanco/tinto) – (red/white) wine

yerba mate – 'Paraguayan tea' (Ilex paraguariensis), which Argentines and Uruguayans consume in very large amounts

Behind the Scenes

SEND US YOUR FEEDBACK

We love to hear from travelers – your comments keep us on our toes and help make our books better. Our well-traveled team reads every word on what you loved or loathed about this book. Although we cannot reply individually to postal submissions, we always guarantee that your feedback goes straight to the appropriate authors, in time for the next edition. Each person who sends us information is thanked in the next edition – the most useful submissions are rewarded with a selection of digital PDF chapters.

Visit **lonelyplanet.com/contact** to submit your updates and suggestions or to ask for help. Our award-winning website also features inspirational travel stories, news and discussions.

Note: We may edit, reproduce and incorporate your comments in Lonely Planet products such as guidebooks, websites and digital products, so let us know if you don't want your comments reproduced or your name acknowledged. For a copy of our privacy policy visit lonelyplanet.com/privacy.

OUR READERS

Many thanks to the travelers who used the last edition and wrote to us with helpful hints, useful advice and interesting anecdotes:
Bettina Becker, Arturo Costa, Loli Delger, Alexandra Goller, Cathy McCloy, Eben Pullman.

AUTHOR THANKS

Sandra Bao

I'm grateful for the support of my excellent (and now ex) commissioning editor Kathleen Munnelly – best of luck in your future adventures, Kathleen; I'll miss you. Also many thanks to Graciela and Silvia Guzmán, who kept me entertained with their raucous company. This book wouldn't be the fine thing that it is without the help of Lucas M, Sylvia Z, Alan S, Madi L, Jed R and Dan P – you all know who you are. A big gracias to Gustavo and Miriam for their companionship and opinions, and also to Sally Blake, Jimena Moses, Andy Symington and Marina Charles for their contributions. *Un beso grande* to my godmother, Elsa, and her son Jorge for their hospitality. Love to Fung and David Bao, and to Daniel for their support over the years. Finally, lots of love to my husband, Ben Greensfelder, for keeping our home in good order while I was away.

ACKNOWLEDGMENTS

Climate map data adapted from Peel MC, Finlayson BL & McMahon TA (2007) 'Updated World Map of the Köppen-Geiger Climate Classification', *Hydrology and Earth System Sciences*, 11, 1633¬44.

Cover photograph: Tango dancers' feet, Hervé Hughes/Alamy©

THIS BOOK

This 7th edition of Lonely Planet's *Buenos Aires* guidebook was researched and written by Sandra Bao. The 6th edition was written by Sandra Bao and Bridget Gleeson, and the 5th edition by Sandra Bao. This guidebook was commissioned in Lonely Planet's Oakland office, and produced by the following:

Commissioning Editor Kathleen Munnelly

Coordinating Editors Sarah Bailey, Tracy Whitmey

Senior Cartographer Mark Griffiths

Book Designer Clara Monitto, Virginia Moreno, Wendy Wright

Associate Product Directors Sasha Baskett, Angela Tinson

Senior Editor Catherine Naghten, Karyn Noble

Assisting Editors Michelle Bennett, Kate Evans, Carly Hall

Assisting Cartographer Julie Dodkins

Cover Research Naomi Parker

Language Content Branislava Vladisavljevic

Thanks to Anita Banh, Elin Berglund, Ljubomir Ceranic, Ryan Evans, Larissa Frost, Anna Harris, Genesys India, Jouve India, Anne Mason, Martine Power, Amanda Williamson

See also separate subindexes for:

🍴 **EATING P230**

🍷 **DRINKING & NIGHTLIFE P230**

⭐ **ENTERTAINMENT P231**

🛍 **SHOPPING P231**

🏃 **SPORTS & ACTIVITIES P232**

🛏 **SLEEPING P232**

Index

✕ EATING

Buenos Aires Maps

Map Legend

Sights
- Beach
- Buddhist
- Castle
- Christian
- Hindu
- Islamic
- Jewish
- Monument
- Museum/Gallery
- Ruin
- Winery/Vineyard
- Zoo
- Other Sight

Eating
- Eating

Drinking & Nightlife
- Drinking & Nightlife
- Cafe

Entertainment
- Entertainment

Shopping
- Shopping

Sleeping
- Sleeping
- Camping

Sports & Activities
- Diving/Snorkelling
- Canoeing/Kayaking
- Skiing
- Surfing
- Swimming/Pool
- Walking
- Windsurfing
- Other Sports & Activities

Information
- Post Office
- Tourist Information

Transport
- Airport
- Border Crossing
- Bus
- Cable Car/Funicular
- Cycling
- Ferry
- Monorail
- Parking
- S-Bahn
- Taxi
- Train/Railway
- Tram
- Tube Station
- U-Bahn
- Underground Train Station
- Other Transport

Routes
- Tollway
- Freeway
- Primary
- Secondary
- Tertiary
- Lane
- Unsealed Road
- Plaza/Mall
- Steps
- Tunnel
- Pedestrian Overpass
- Walking Tour
- Walking Tour Detour
- Path

Boundaries
- International
- State/Province
- Disputed
- Regional/Suburb
- Marine Park
- Cliff
- Wall

Geographic
- Hut/Shelter
- Lighthouse
- Lookout
- Mountain/Volcano
- Oasis
- Park
- Pass
- Picnic Area
- Waterfall

Hydrography
- River/Creek
- Intermittent River
- Swamp/Mangrove
- Reef
- Canal
- Water
- Dry/Salt/Intermittent Lake
- Glacier

Areas
- Beach/Desert
- Cemetery (Christian)
- Cemetery (Other)
- Park/Forest
- Sportsground
- Sight (Building)
- Top Sight (Building)

MAP INDEX

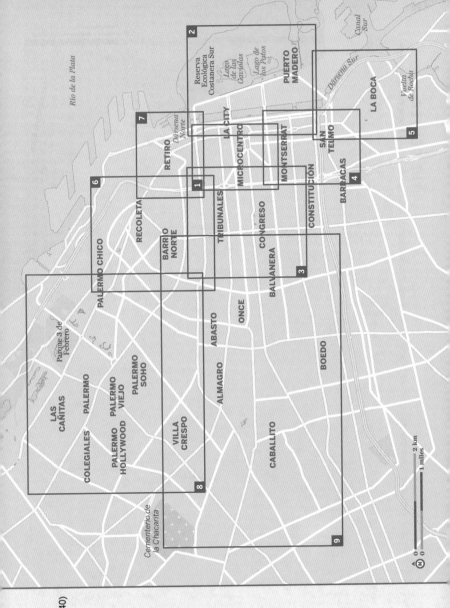

Río de la Plata

Reserva
Ecológica
Costanera Sur

Lago
de las
Garciolas

Lago de
los Patos

Canal
Sur

PUERTO
MADERO

Dársena Sur

Dársena Norte

LA CITY

MICROCENTRO

MONTSERRAT

SAN
TELMO

LA BOCA

Vuelta
de Rocha

RETIRO

CONSTITUCIÓN

BARRACAS

RECOLETA

PALERMO CHICO

BARRIO
NORTE

TRIBUNALES

CONGRESO

BALVANERA

ABASTO

ONCE

Parque 3 de
Febrero

Cementerio de
la Chacarita

LAS
CAÑITAS

COLEGIALES

PALERMO

PALERMO
VIEJO

PALERMO
HOLLYWOOD

PALERMO
SOHO

VILLA
CRESPO

ALMAGRO

CABALLITO

BOEDO

2 km

1 miles

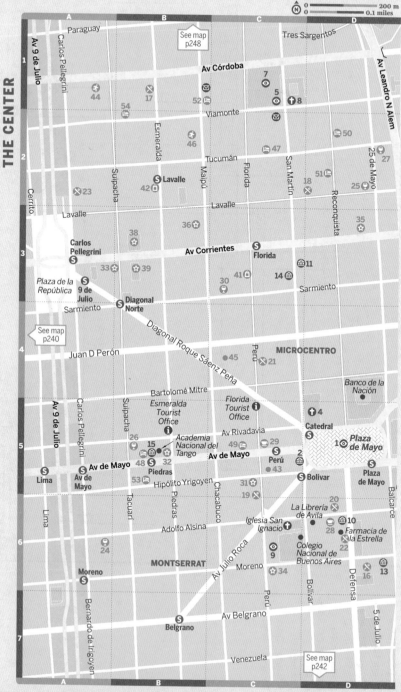

THE CENTER

THE CENTER

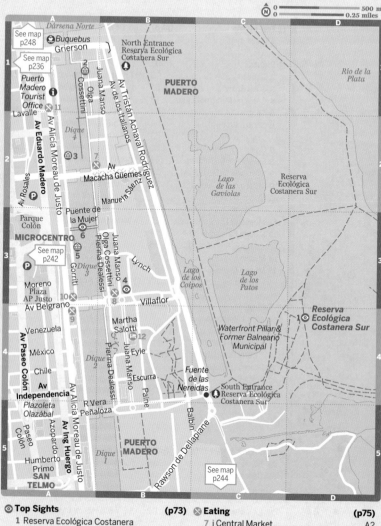

CONGRESO & TRIBUNALES *Map on p240*

CONGRESO & TRIBUNALES

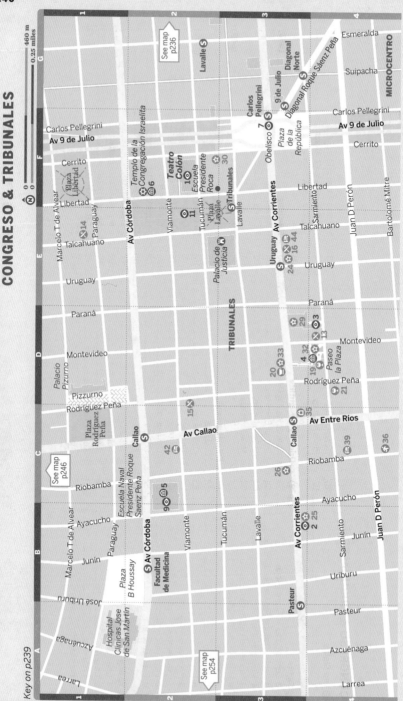

See map p236

See map p246

See map p254

Key on p239

460 m
0.25 miles

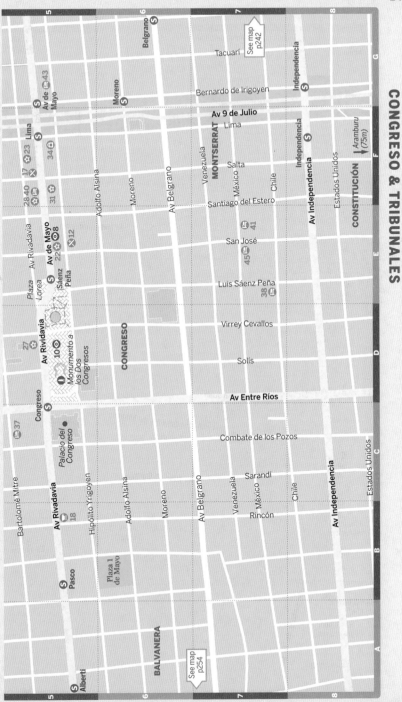

CONGRESO & TRIBUNALES

Tacuarí

See map p242

Independencia Ⓢ

Av de Mayo 🚇43 Ⓢ

Moreno Ⓢ

Belgrano Ⓢ

Bernardo de Irigoyen

Av 9 de Julio

Lima Ⓢ

Lima

MONTSERRAT

Venezuela

Salta

17 ✗ 23 🚇

34 🛍

México

Chile

Independencia Ⓢ

28 40 🚇🛍 31 ✪

Adolfo Alsina

Moreno

Av Belgrano

Santiago del Estero

Estados Unidos

Av Independencia

CONSTITUCIÓN

🛍 41

San José 🛍 45

Arámburu (75m)

Plaza Lorea

Av Rivadavia

Av de Mayo 22 ✪ 🌀8 ✗12

Sáenz Peña Ⓢ

Luis Sáenz Peña 🛍 38

27 🌀10 🌀

Virrey Cevallos

Solís

Monumento a los Dos Congresos

CONGRESO

Av Entre Ríos

Congreso Ⓢ

🚇37

Combate de los Pozos

Palacio del Congreso ●

Estados Unidos

Av Rivadavia 🛍18

Hipólito Yrigoyen

Bartolomé Mitre

Adolfo Alsina

Moreno

Av Belgrano

Venezuela

Sarandí

México

Av Independencia

Chile

Rincón

Plaza 1 de Mayo

Pasco Ⓢ

BALVANERA

See map p254

Alberti Ⓢ

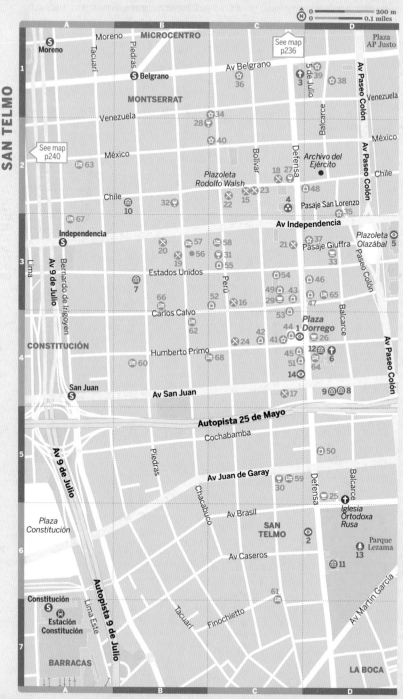

SAN TELMO

N
0 ____ 200 m
0 ____ 0.1 miles

MICROCENTRO

Moreno

Moreno

Tacuarí

Piedras

Av Belgrano

See map
p236

Belgrano

36

5 de Julio

39

3

38

Plaza
AP Justo

Venezuela

MONTSERRAT

Venezuela

28

34

40

See map
p240

63

México

Bolívar

Defensa

18 27

Archivo del
Ejército

48

México

Chile

Chile

10

32

Plazoleta
Rodolfo Walsh

22

15

23

4

Pasaje San Lorenzo

35

Av Independencia

67

Independencia

Lima

Bernardo de Irigoyen

Av 9 de Julio

20

19

57

56

58

31

55

Estados Unidos

Perú

21

37

Pasaje Giuffra

33

Plazoleta
Olazábal 5

Paseo Colón

7

66

Carlos Calvo

52

16

54

49

29

43

53

46

65

47

Balcarce

62

42

24

41

44 1

Plaza
Dorrego

26

CONSTITUCIÓN

Humberto Primo

68

45

51

14

12 6

64

San Juan

60

Av San Juan

17

9

8

Autopista 25 de Mayo

Cochabamba

Av 9 de Julio

Piedras

Av Juan de Garay

50

30

59

Defensa

25

Balcarce

Chacabuco

Av Brasil

**SAN
TELMO**

Iglesia
Ortodoxa
Rusa

Plaza
Constitución

2

Parque
Lezama

13

Av Caseros

11

Constitución

Estación
Constitución

Autopista 9 de Julio

Lima Este

Tacuarí

Finochietto

61

Av Martín García

Av Paseo Colón

BARRACAS

LA BOCA

A B C D

1
2
3
4
5
6
7

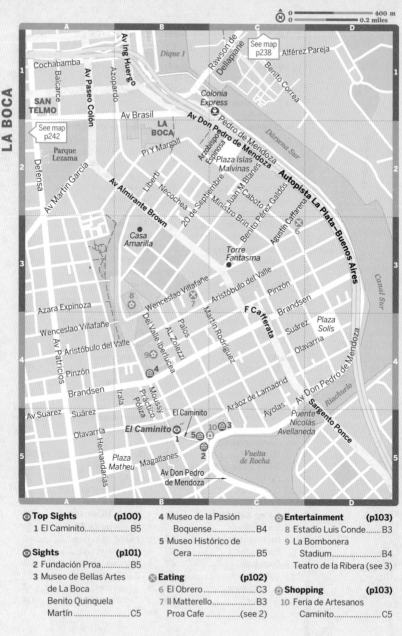

RECOLETA & BARRIO NORTE

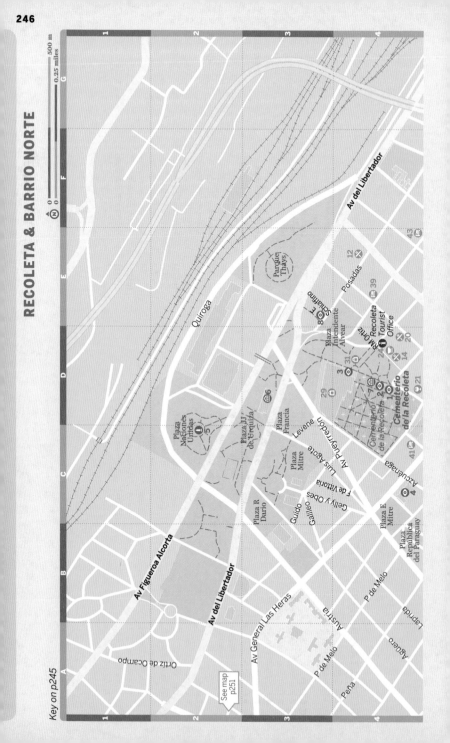

Key on p245

See map p251

500 m
0.25 miles

Av Figueroa Alcorta

Av del Libertador

Ortiz de Ocampo

Av General Las Heras

Austria

P de Melo

Peña

Agüero

Laprida

P de Melo

Plaza Naciones Unidas

Quiroga

Plaza JJ de Urquiza

Plaza Francia

Plaza Mitre

Plaza R Darío

Guido

Galileo

Gelly y Obes

F de Vittoria

Luis Agote

Av Pueyrredón

Levene

Plaza E Mitre

Plaza República del Paraguay

Parque Thays

Plaza Intendente Alvear

Av del Libertador

Posadas

RM Ortiz

Recoleta Tourist Office

Cementerio de la Recoleta

Cementerio de la Recoleta

Azcuénaga

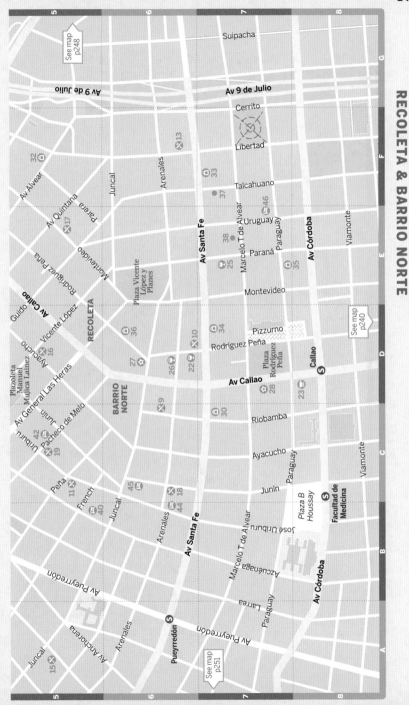

RETIRO

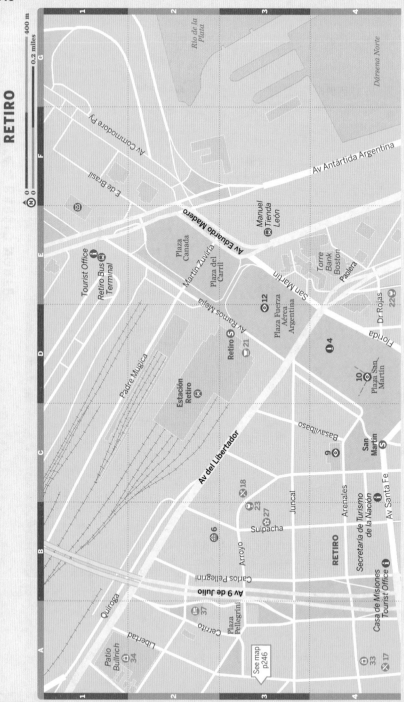

400 m
0.2 miles

Río de la Plata

Dársena Norte

Av Commodore Py

E de Brasil

Av Antártida Argentina

Tourist Office

Retiro Bus Terminal

Av Eduardo Madero

Manuel Tienda León

Plaza Canada

Martín Zuviría

Plaza del Carril

Torre Bank Boston

Padera

San Martín

Av Ramos Mejía

12

Plaza Fuerza Aérea Argentina

Retiro S

21

Dr Rojas

22

Florida

4

Padre Mugica

Estación Retiro

10

Plaza San Martín

Av del Libertador

Basavilbaso

9

San Martín S

18

23

Juncal

27

Suipacha

6

Arenales

RETIRO

Secretaría de Turismo de la Nación

Av Santa Fe

Arroyo

Carlos Pellegrini

Quiroga

Av 9 de Julio

37

Cerrito

Plaza Pellegrini

See map p246

Casa de Misiones Tourist Office

Patio Bullrich

34

Libertad

33

17

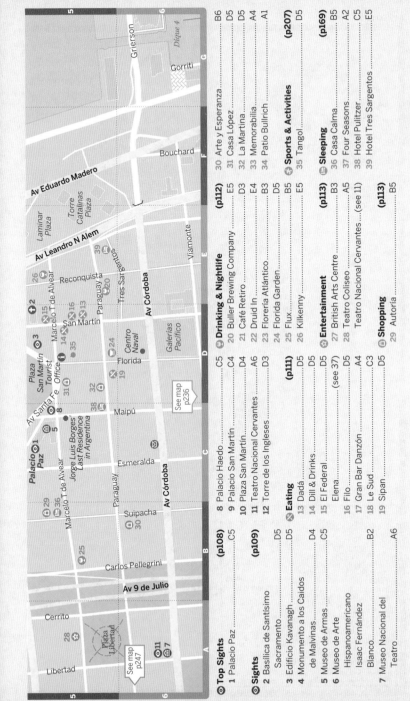

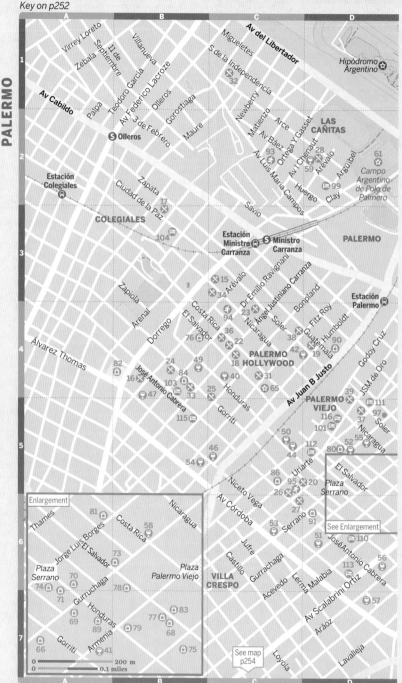

Key on p252

PALERMO

Av del Libertador

Virrey Loreto
Zabala
11 de Septiembre
Villanueva
Miguletes
S de la Independencia

Av Cabildo

Palpa
Taodoro García
Av Federico Lacroze
Olleros
Gorostiaga
Maure

32

Av 3 de Febrero

Newberry
Matienzo
Arce
Av Báez
Ortega y Gasset
LAS CAÑITAS

Olleros

93
Av I Chenaut
28
Arévalo
61

Av Luis María Campos
59
Argüibel
Campo Argentino de Polo de Palermo

Estación Colegiales

Zapata
Ciudad de la Paz
17

Huergo
Clay
99

COLEGIALES

Savio

104

Estación Ministro Carranza
Ministro Carranza

PALERMO

Zapiola

15
Arévalo
Dr Emilio Ravignani

Estación Palermo

Arenal

34
94
23
Angel Justiniano Carranza
Bonpland
Fitz Roy

Dorrego

Costa Rica
El Salvador
36
76
22
Nicaragua
Soler
38
Guatemala
Humboldt
90

Álvarez Thomas

82
16
José Antonio Cabrera
103
84
33
24
49
25
40
18
PALERMO HOLLYWOOD
42
19
31
65

Godoy Cruz

47
115
Honduras
Gorriti

Av Juan B Justo

39
JSM de Oro
111
97
Soler
PALERMO VIEJO
116
37
101
Nicaragua

50
112
52
55
80

46
54
44

Uriarte
86
95
20
26
El Salvador
Plaza Serrano

Niceto Vega
Av Córdoba
27
Serrano
91
See Enlargement

53
51
José Antonio Cabrera
110

Jufre
Castillo
Gurruchaga
Acevedo
Lerma
Malabia
56
113
Av Scalabrini Ortiz
57
Aráoz
Loyola
Lavalleja

Enlargement

Thames
81
Costa Rica
58
Nicaragua

Jorge Luis Borges
El Salvador
73

Plaza Serrano
70
74
71
Gurruchaga
78
Plaza Palermo Viejo
VILLA CRESPO

69
Honduras
89
Armenia
77
79
83
68

66
Gorriti
41
75

0 ___ 200 m
0 ___ 0.1 miles

See map p254

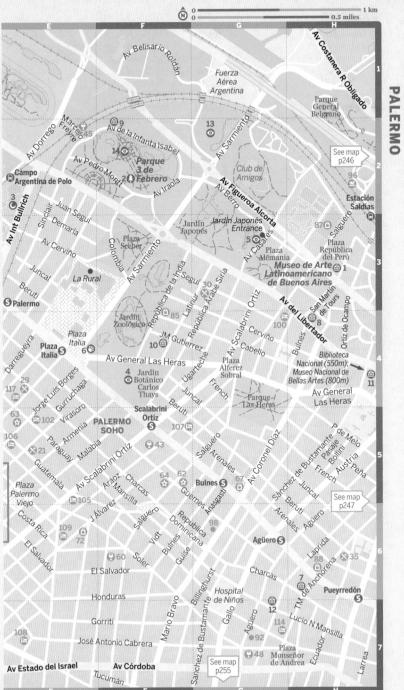

PALERMO *Map on p250*

See map p250

SOUTH OF PALERMO

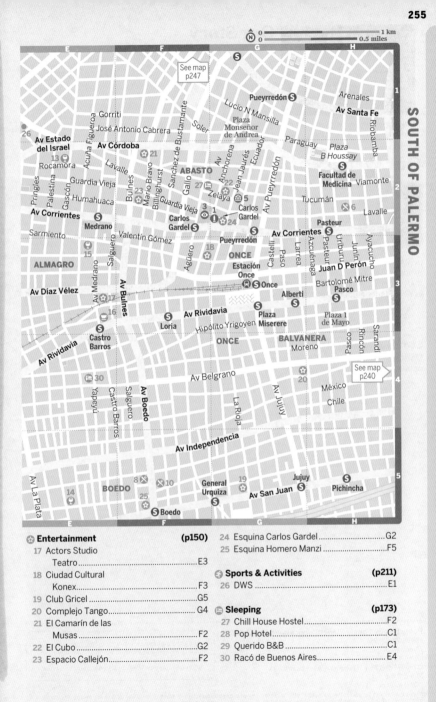

Our Story

A beat-up old car, a few dollars in the pocket and a sense of adventure. In 1972 that's all Tony and Maureen Wheeler needed for the trip of a lifetime – across Europe and Asia overland to Australia. It took several months, and at the end – broke but inspired – they sat at their kitchen table writing and stapling together their first travel guide, *Across Asia on the Cheap*. Within a week they'd sold 1500 copies. Lonely Planet was born.

Today, Lonely Planet has offices in Melbourne, London and Oakland, with more than 600 staff and writers. We share Tony's belief that 'a great guidebook should do three things: inform, educate and amuse'.

Our Writers

Sandra Bao

Coordinating Author Sandra's mom and her family escaped China's communist regime in the years following WWII, eventually boarding a freighter bound for Argentina in 1952. After months at sea they arrived in Buenos Aires – just two days after the death of Evita Perón. Sandra's parents married in Montevideo, Uruguay, then raised Sandra and her brother, Daniel, in BA. They lived the carefree *porteño* life (with *asados* every Sunday) until 1974, when things got politically dicey. Once again the Baos emigrated to greener pastures, this time the USA. Sandra is proud to be a *porteña* and has regularly returned to her homeland as an adult, watching the peso fluctuate wildly through the decades. Over the last 14 years Sandra has contributed to dozens of Lonely Planet guidebooks.

Read more about Sandra at:
lonelyplanet.com/members/sandrabao

Contributing Author

Marina Charles wrote the Street Art essay. She is a British expat and Buenos Aires resident who cofounded Graffitimundo in 2009.

Published by Lonely Planet Publications Pty Ltd
ABN 36 005 607 983
7th edition – Aug 2014
ISBN 978 1 74220 218 1
© Lonely Planet 2014   Photographs © as indicated 2014
10 9 8 7 6 5 4 3 2 1
Printed in China

Although the authors and Lonely Planet have taken all reasonable care in preparing this book, we make no warranty about the accuracy or completeness of its content and, to the maximum extent permitted, disclaim all liability arising from its use.